D1623856

THINK FOR A MINUTE
ABOUT WHAT YOU WANT FOR YOUR CHILDREN

You want them to be fair and honest and trustworthy.

You want them to respect the rights of others. You want them to respect legitimate authority, rules and laws.

You want them to be responsible for their own behavior. You want them to feel a decent measure of concern for their fellow human beings.

You want them to be able to stand on their own feet and resist pressure to go with the crowd.

You want them to be capable of generosity and love.

Of all the tasks of parenting, none is as important, or as difficult, as raising good children.
—Dr. Thomas Lickona
in RAISING GOOD CHILDREN

RAISING
GOOD
CHILDREN

THOMAS LICKONA, PH.D.

BANTAM BOOKS
NEW YORK · TORONTO · LONDON · SYDNEY · AUCKLAND

RAISING GOOD CHILDREN

Bantam Hardcover edition / September 1983
Bantam paperback edition / February 1985

Grateful acknowledgment is made to the following for
permission to quote from copyrighted work:

Abbey Press: Excerpt from When A Story Would Help by Lucie W. Barber,
copyright © 1981, St. Meinrad Archabbey, and reprinted with permission of
Abbey Press, St. Meinrad, Indiana.

Abbey Press: One line from an Abbey Press catalogue, "A child is the only known
substance...," reprinted with permission of Abbey Press, St. Meinrad, Indiana.

Field Newspaper Syndicate: One Ann Landers letter, reprinted with permission
of Ann Landers, Field Newspaper Syndicate.

Guidance Associates Publishers: "Sharon's Dilemma," excerpted from Teacher
Training: A Workshop in Relationships and Values, by Dr. Edwin Fenton,
copyright © 1976. Reprinted with permission of Guidance Associates.

The New Yorker: Drawing by Dana Fradon; copyright © 1975
The New Yorker Magazine, Inc. Reprinted with permission of The New Yorker.

Universal Press Syndicate: Taken from the Dear Abbey column.
Copyright © 1983, Universal Press Syndicate. Reprinted with permission.

Library of Congress Cataloging-in-Publication Data

Lickona, Thomas.
Raising good children.

Bibliography: p. 431. Includes index.
1. Child rearing.   2. Child development.
3. Moral education.   4. Moral development.   I. Title.
HQ769L474   1983   649'.1   83-7081
ISBN 0-553-27443-0

Published simultaneously in the United States and Canada

Bantam Books are published by Bantam Books, a division of Bantam Doubleday
Dell Publishing Group, Inc. Its trademark, consisting of the words "Bantam
Books" and the portrayal of a rooster, is Registered in U.S. Patent and
Trademark Office and in other countries. Marca Registrada. Bantam Books,
666 Fifth Avenue, New York, New York 10103.

PRINTED IN THE UNITED STATES OF AMERICA

O   13 12 11 10 9 8 7

To my family—
Judith, Mark, and Matthew—
and to parents and children
everywhere

ACKNOWLEDGMENTS

ACKNOWLEDGMENTS

I owe many thanks:

To Lawrence Kohlberg, who has been a warm and generous colleague, and whose nearly thirty years of dedicated study of moral development has helped to inspire my own work and that of psychologists and educators around the globe.

To the many other psychologists whose research has helped to illuminate the process by which children come to moral maturity.

To countless parents, for sharing memories of their childhood and stories of their own efforts to raise good children.

To my father and mother, Edward and Winifred Lickona, and my "second parents," Tom and Mary Barker, for their love and encouragement.

To my wife Judith, who read every word of the half-dozen drafts of the manuscript, for serving as my first editor, for careful critiques as well as encouragement, for countless discussions that helped to clarify and form my thinking, and for helping me balance family life and writing when that wasn't easy.

To my sons, Mark and Matthew, for all they've taught me about children and parenting, and for the joy and meaning they've brought to my life.

To my high school English teacher, Jean Walker, for invaluable lessons on how to write clearly.

To two esteemed professors, Morris Eson and James Mancuso, who encouraged my interest as a graduate student in the study of moral development.

To Mary Belenky, a respected colleague, for her thoughtful and helpful comments on the manuscript.

To Natalie Chapman, for her supportive counsel in the very early stages of the book.

To Bruce Mermelstein, for his kindness in sending me to Milly Marmur at Random House; and to Milly Marmur, who gave me useful feedback on an earlier draft and found me a wonderful agent.

To Robin Straus, my agent, for appreciative readings and helpful suggestions on the shape and substance of the book, for finding me such a good publisher, and, most of all, for believing in the book and giving me such warm and unflagging moral support over these last four years.

To Toni Burbank, my present editor at Bantam, for her strong support of the book from start to finish, for stimulating conversations and insightful guidance, and for all the caring and committed work she has done to make this book a reality.

To Michael Hayes, Bantam's copy editor, for her thoughtful and meticulous attention to the manuscript.

And, finally, to Alan Rinzler, my first editor at Bantam—whose contribution to the book has been enormous and to whom I felt a fresh debt of gratitude every time I sat down to revise a chapter—for wise and detailed direction on organization, content, and style, and for cheering me on at every step of the way. A more sensitive, skilled, and supportive editor I cannot imagine.

I am deeply and humbly grateful to all of these people for the part they have played in this book.

Tom Lickona
Cortland, New York
March 1983

CONTENTS

"Miss Dugan, will you send someone in here who can distinguish right from wrong?"

A child is the only
known substance from which
a responsible adult can
be made.

RAISING GOOD CHILDREN

PART I

THE MORAL DEVELOPMENT APPROACH TO RAISING GOOD CHILDREN

CHAPTER 1

RAISING GOOD CHILDREN

Of all the tasks of parenting, none is as important as raising good children.

As parents, we may also want our children to be smart. We may want them to be good at sports, artistically talented, or physically attractive. But they are no less persons, no less human, if they do not possess these qualities.

It's a different matter, however, if our children are not good and decent people. In that case, they do stand tall as persons. Their humanity is diminished.

But what does it mean to "be good"? Is a good child one who obeys without question? Or does being good include a certain amount of independence, an ability to think for yourself and follow what your conscience tells you is right?

Think for a minute about what you want for your children when you want them to be good.

You want them to be fair and honest and trustworthy.

You want them to respect the rights of others. You want them to respect legitimate authority, rules, and laws.

You want them to be responsible for their own behavior. You want them to feel a decent measure of concern for their fellow human beings.

You want them to be able to stand on their own feet and resist pressure to go with the crowd.

You want them to be capable of generosity and love.

All of these things are part of being a good person. And I think all parents who are concerned about raising good children want their children to have these qualities.

WHAT CAN PARENTS DO?

What does it take to raise a good child?

There's no doubt in my mind that it takes more from parents than it ever did before. In the old days, Mom and Dad were part of a bigger team. Home, school, and church all taught the same basic values and pulled together to keep kids on the straight and narrow. That's certainly far less true today. In the old days, kids had many "parents." If your own mother or father didn't catch you when you were up to no good, your grandmother did, or your Uncle Nick, or the lady next door. As one mother says, "In those days, everybody supervised everybody's kids. Now a lot of people don't even supervise their own." It wasn't long ago when a mother and a father had at least each other to share the task of caring for kids and guiding their development. Now, with the rapid rise in single-parent families, the whole job often falls on one parent's shoulders.

Parents not only have less help than they used to, but they're also up against a lot more. They face a social environment that is actively hostile to many of the values they would like to teach their children. TV and movies present violence, law-breaking, and casual sex as standard human behavior. The peer group is an ever more powerful shaper of kids' thinking and behavior, and it often teaches values that go directly against what we want our children to learn. A study by Cornell University's Dr. Urie Bronfenbrenner found that American children were *more* likely to break a rule or law if they thought their peers would know about it. Says a father,

"I find a black and white contrast between my values and the values kids get from their peer group. I was brought up on self-discipline and self-denial. Be a good student, and you'll get a good job. Be a good person, and you'll go to heaven. To today's peer group, whatever feels good is cool. Getting in trouble is great. Their ethic is immediate satisfaction. Pleasure now."

Says a mother of two teenage girls,

> "The kids are forever saying, 'Everybody's doing it.' 'Everybody goes to parties where there's drinking.' 'Everybody goes to R movies.' They keep it up. After a while, it starts to wear you down."

Researchers confirm what parents fear: kids at every grade level are more dependent on peers than they used to be.[1]

Other parents are part of the problem. Not everybody makes raising good kids a high priority. Not everybody wants to invest the time and effort it takes to monitor what kids are doing and guide their thinking and actions. Says one father, "I hate to admit it, but frankly, it's too much of a hassle to keep after the kids. I don't have the energy for it." Not everybody takes the trouble to discipline their kids or say no to them when they want to go to unsupervised parties or drink before they're of age. Not everybody sets a good example for their children. Said a high school principal to the mother of a failing student, a boy who was known to be a heavy marijuana user: "Your son is smoking a lot more dope than is good for him." Replied the mother: "He gets better stuff than we do."

THE NEW MORALITY

The "new morality" obviously isn't limited to our children's peer group. It runs through much of the adult culture as well. It says "Look out for number one" and "Do as you damn well please." It came partly out of the sixties, which advanced individual human rights but also fostered disrespect for law and authority and ballyhooed the idea that people should "do their own thing." It came partly out of the seventies, which exposed corruption in all walks of life and left people with the feeling that everybody else is out for himself, so why not me? The old morality, with roots in religion, speaks of respect, service to others, sacrifice, resistance to temptation, and moderation in the pursuit of pleasure. The new morality celebrates self-centeredness and self-indulgence. Grab what you can get, because you only go around once.

In view of all this, it's not surprising that so many kids are in trouble. True, there are a lot of good kids who *aren't* in trouble, and we can be thankful for that. But there are alarming signs of a widespread decline of morality among young people. Consider the following:

• *Juvenile crime.* More than *half* of all serious crimes in the United States are now committed by youths 10 to 17 years of age. Juvenile delinquency is increasing so fast that one of every nine kids will appear in court by age 18. And studies by the National Council on Crime and Delinquency show that criminal acts are as common among middle-class kids as they are among those from low-income homes.

• *Disrespect for authority.* Teachers everywhere agree that students of all ages have far less respect for authority than they once had. Children and teenagers defy their teachers, even swear at them. Says one substitute teacher who has worked for 10 years in an affluent suburb: "Every obscene word you can possibly think of has come out of the mouths of elementary-school students. And these aren't 'bad' schools."

• *Violence and vandalism in the schools.* In 1975 a U.S. Senate subcommittee determined that the annual cost of vandalism and theft in American schools was $600 million. That's equivalent to the annual national expenditure on school textbooks. And violence continues to mount: each year more than 100,000 teachers and hundreds of thousands of students are assaulted in school.

• *Children's cruelty to each other.* Says a veteran elementary-school principal: "We're seeing more just plain meanness. On the playground kids don't seem to play like they used to; they rove around in gangs. They're quick to identify the weak ones, kids on the fringe, kids who don't wear the right sneakers or jeans. They go after them, taunt them; there's a vicious edge to it. Some kids are literally devastated. We've tried to stop it, but we haven't been very successful."

• *Cheating.* Says a 15-year-old girl: "All my friends are cheating on tests and getting good grades as a result." In one high school survey 95 percent of juniors and seniors admitted cheating.[2] At the college level, according to a survey of research by psychologist Roger Burton, 50 percent to 80 percent of students, given the chance, will cheat on a test.[3] Many colleges and universities have had to abandon honor codes because of the frequency of violations. In some cases, students have been found bribing custodians to get copies of an exam and then selling them to their fellow students. Explains one student at a major university: "Cheating is a way of life here."

• *Self-centeredness.* A 1981 Carnegie Commission report on American colleges and universities found a rising "meism" (a combination of individualism, cynicism, and materialism) among today's college students.[4] "The students I teach," says a college ethics professor, "seem to be concerned about one thing: their career. It's hard to find signs of social conscience." Says a Princeton University student quoted in the Carnegie report: "College students today have no collective orientation. We are out for ourselves."

• *Drugs and drinking.* Drug abuse and excessive drinking may not seem at first glance like *moral* problems, but they are. Kids who are into drugs risk ruining their own bodies, and that's a violation of respect for themselves. They're also usually breaking the law, either by possessing the drug or stealing to support their habit. Likewise, kids who drink to excess risk making a mess of their own lives, and when they get behind a wheel, they endanger the lives of others. There's hardly a community that doesn't face the problems of teenage drug abuse and drinking. The number of teenage alcoholics is estimated to be 2½ million. During the 1970s, the number of 12- to 17-year-olds experimenting with marijuana and cocaine doubled. Often it starts even younger. Says a mother of two boys in a white-collar town: "The elementary schools in this community are full of drugs. Our kids were into it before we knew what was happening."

• *Teenage sex.* The age at which teenagers begin to have sexual relations gets younger all the time. One in five has had intercourse by 15. Teenagers account for 25 percent of the 1 million reported cases of gonorrhea each year. Half of all illegitimate babies in this country are now born to teenage mothers.[5]

"WE'RE NOT DOING ANYTHING WRONG"

Even more disturbing than the irresponsible behavior of many young people is the kind of thinking that underlies it. *Kids don't think they're doing anything wrong.*

In one high-school survey, 90 percent of the students said they didn't see anything wrong with cheating.[6]

Said the director of a university bookstore to investigator Michael Drosnin: "The thing that gets me is that they (student shoplifters) don't seem to care when they get caught. They don't seem to think they've done anything wrong."

A 9th-grade teacher asked her class: "How many of you have ever shoplifted?" Almost all raised their hands. "Don't you think it's wrong to shoplift?" she asked. Their answer: "We have a right to the material things in life."

Says a college student: "There's a terrific amount of stealing in the dorms and other buildings. And people think nothing of breaking something or bashing it in. They say, 'What do I care? It's not mine.'" College library directors across the country report mounting theft of books (the University of California at Berkeley lost 18,000 volumes over a three-year period) and increasing mutilation of books and periodicals (students razor out assigned articles).[7]

These are depressing things to read about. It's clear that the need has never been greater for parents to act as deliberate moral educators of their children.

THE MORAL DEVELOPMENT APPROACH TO RAISING GOOD CHILDREN

This book shows a way to go about the complex and challenging job of raising good children. I call it the "moral development" approach.

This approach views a child's moral growth as a developmental process, beginning at birth and continuing all the way through adulthood. It makes use of important discoveries psychologists have made about the moral development of children and teenagers. It also makes use of the wisdom of the ages about how to raise good children. As you read along, I think you'll find many ideas that are familiar to you, things you're already doing to foster your child's moral development.

Ten "big ideas" make up the moral development approach. These are the recurring themes of the book, the points I consider most important in trying to help our kids grow morally. I'd like to introduce these 10 big ideas here.

1. MORALITY IS RESPECT

Before talking about how morality develops, we need to define what it is. The first big idea is that the core of morality is *respect*: respect for ourself, respect for other people, respect for all forms of life and the environment that sustains them.

Respect for ourself requires us to treat our own life and person as having value. That's why it's wrong to engage in self-destructive behavior. Respect for others requires us to treat all other human beings as having worth, dignity, and rights equal to our own. That's the heart of the Golden Rule ("Do unto others as you would have them do unto you"), a moral principle that can be found in religions and cultures all over the world. Respect for the whole complex web of life prohibits cruelty to animals and calls us to act with care toward the natural environment, the fragile ecosystem on which all life depends.

By saying that morality is respect, I don't mean to say that's all it is. As you try to raise your children to be good people, you may want to teach them much more than a morality of respect. In our own family, for example, religion is an important part of our lives, so we try to teach our kids values like love of God, faith, worship, and prayer. As I'll illustrate later in the book, you can teach values like these in the same way that you try to teach a morality of respect.

But even though respect isn't all there is to morality, it's central—and it's something that all people, whatever their other beliefs, can agree on. Developing a morality of respect is a big part of bringing our children to moral maturity.

2. KIDS DEVELOP MORALITY SLOWLY, AND IN STAGES

The second big idea is that a morality of respect doesn't burst forth, fully formed, at a particular age. Instead, it *develops*, slowly.

The story of that development is one of the great dramas of human growth, and one of the major contributions of developmental psychology to our understanding of children.

This book tells the story of moral development in two parts. The first part begins with babies and shows how the foundation of moral development is laid during the developmental periods from birth through 3. The second part describes the stages of moral reasoning and shows how they develop, with the help of parents and others, between the preschool years and adulthood.

The Developmental Periods From Birth Through Three

You can think of the first four years of your child's life as consisting of four developmental periods: infancy (year 1), toddlerhood (year 2), "the twos" (year 3), and "the threes" (year 4).

It may seem strange to think of kids as growing morally while they're still in diapers or not even able to talk. But much happens during the first four years of life that's important for moral development.

Given a loving environment, kids make huge strides in their relationships with other people. Babies get attached to those who cuddle and care for them, and that's their first vital link to the human community. One-year-olds learn to walk, investigate the world, understand language, and make their first tentative assertions of independence. Two-year-olds assert that independence more definitely, often with a vengeance. That assertion represents a "breaking away" from other people, a pattern we'll see repeated later on in the stages of moral reasoning. Around age 3, if parents have been trying to socialize their child, the pendulum typically swings toward cooperation. Threes, to a greater extent than twos, try to go along, fit in—another developmental pattern we'll see repeated later on.

At all of these ages, given the opportunity, kids can do a lot of moral learning. They can learn about rules and limits. It's okay to play with the measuring spoons, but it's not okay to put them down the toilet. It's okay to play with your little sister, but it's not okay to bite her or sit on her. Young children can learn to obey their parents and respond to such directions as "Come here," "Give it to me," and "Pick up your toys." They can learn to be responsive to the needs of others as well as their own. They can take their first important steps down the long road to moral maturity.

The Stages of Moral Reasoning:
Preschool to Adulthood

The second part of the story of moral development raises the curtain on the six stages of moral reasoning.

These stages of moral reasoning begin in the preschool years and may still be developing during adulthood. The chart on the next page gives a thumbnail sketch of these stages; later I'll devote a chapter to each of them. Think of these stages as *theories of right and wrong* that we carry around in our heads as children, teenagers, or adults. Each stage or theory has a different idea of *what's right* and a different idea of *the reason why a person should be good*. Each new stage of moral reasoning brings a person a step closer to a fully developed morality of respect.

For each stage, the chart also indicates what I think are reasonable developmental goals: that is, the approximate age period when I think kids of normal intelligence, growing up in a supportive and stimulating moral environment, have a good chance of attaining a particular stage. Take a minute to look at this chart.

You are a big part of your child's moral environment, but you're not the only influence on your child's progress through these stages of moral reasoning. Your child's general intelligence and amount and variety of social interaction (friendships, participation in groups) are also important. As kids get older, social and intellectual experiences beyond the family are especially important in developing the society-wide "big picture" that's part of Stages 4 and 5.

What do these stages of moral reasoning tell us? They tell us, first of all, that *kids are not short adults*. They think differently from us. They don't see the world the way we do.

THE STAGES OF MORAL REASONING*

(Ages indicate reasonable developmental
expectations for a child of normal intelligence growing up
in a supportive moral environment.)

STAGE 0: **EGOCENTRIC REASONING** (preschool years— around age 4)	WHAT'S RIGHT:	I should get my own way.
	REASON TO BE GOOD:	To get rewards and avoid punishments.
STAGE 1: **UNQUESTIONING OBEDIENCE** (around kindergarten age)	WHAT'S RIGHT:	I should do what I'm told.
	REASON TO BE GOOD:	To stay out of trouble.
STAGE 2: **WHAT'S-IN-IT-FOR-ME FAIRNESS** (early elementary grades)	WHAT'S RIGHT:	I should look out for myself but be fair to those who are fair to me.
	REASON TO BE GOOD:	Self-interest: What's in it for me?
STAGE 3: **INTERPERSONAL CONFORMITY** (middle-to-upper elementary grades and early-to-mid teens)	WHAT'S RIGHT:	I should be a nice person and live up to the expectations of people I know and care about.
	REASON TO BE GOOD:	So others will think well of me (social approval) and I can think well of myself (self-esteem).
STAGE 4: **RESPONSIBILITY TO "THE SYSTEM"** (high-school years or late teens)	WHAT'S RIGHT:	I should fulfill my responsibilities to the social or value system I feel part of.
	REASON TO BE GOOD:	To keep the system from falling apart and to maintain self-respect as somebody who meets my obligations.
STAGE 5: **PRINCIPLED CONSCIENCE** (young adulthood)	WHAT'S RIGHT:	I should show the greatest possible respect for the rights and dignity of every individual person and should support a system that protects human rights.
	REASON TO BE GOOD:	The obligation of conscience to act in accordance with the principle of respect for all human beings.

*Stages 1 through 5 are adapted from Lawrence Kohlberg's stages of moral reasoning as described in Kohlberg (1975, 1978, 1981); Stage 0 is adapted from William Damon (1977) and Robert Selman (1980). (See Appendix A for full references.)

Parents are often surprised to learn that kids' moral reasoning is so different from their own and goes through such swings as they move through the stages. At Stage 0 (Egocentric Reasoning), which usually rules the roost at age 4 (but may start to show up even sooner), kids' moral logic is almost laughably self-centered. "Not fair! Not fair!" they say, meaning, "I'm not getting what I want!" Their moral indignation comes from a real belief that whatever they want is fair, just because they want it!

At Stage 1 (Unquestioning Obedience), often dominant at around age 5, kids do an about-face and reason, "Grown-ups have a right to be boss, and I should do what they say!" At Stage 2 (What's-in-It-for-Me Fairness), which usually breaks through between 5½ and 7, kids do another flip-flop and think, "We kids have got our rights! Parents shouldn't order us around!" Stage 2 thinkers also develop a fierce but narrow sense of fairness and look at being good as kind of a tit-for-tat deal ("I'll help with the dishes, but what'll you do for me?").

I want to stress that even in the early stages of moral reasoning development, you can't be sure of a child's moral stage just from knowing his or her chronological age. One 5-year-old may be mainly Stage 0, another Stage 1. One 7-year-old may be predominantly Stage 1, another Stage 2. And the higher the moral stage, the more variation there is in when kids reach it. Many teenagers, for example, are still stuck in Stage 2 and are responsible for a lot of the me-centered behavior that we looked at earlier in the chapter. Other kids, especially if their social environment has demanded more than a what's-in-it-for-me morality, may begin to develop Stage 3 (Interpersonal Conformity) as early as the middle-to-upper elementary grades and continue to develop it through their early teens.

At Stage 3, kids are very much concerned about what people think of them. They figure, "If I want people to like me, I'd better be a nice person." By living up to other people's expectations, Stage 3 kids can also feel good about themselves. This kind of thinking can be the source of a lot of cooperative and caring behavior.

But Stage 3 has an obvious weakness: it confuses what's right with what other people want you to do. That's okay as long as the other people are presenting positive moral values (be kind, honest, respectful of others). The challenge for parents of

Stage 3 teenagers is to keep them tuned into positive values and strong enough to resist the peer-group seduction to get into things like sex, drugs, and drinking because "everybody's doing it."

Many teenagers, some during high school, some later, come to realize the shortcomings of Stage 3 reasoning and go on to develop the more independent, society-wide perspective of Stage 4 (Responsibility to the System). They keep the best of Stage 3—they still care about people they know personally—but they look farther and see more. Stage 4 reasons: "There's more to being a good person than pleasing my family and friends. There's a bigger society out there, and I'm part of it. I've got certain responsibilities and obligations to think of."

The particular social system that a Stage 4 thinker feels obligated to may not be the one that most people support. A Stage 4 socialist living in a capitalistic society, for example, would be opposed to the values of the prevailing system. But regardless of their particular beliefs or values, Stage 4 thinkers share a sense of commitment and duty to some kind of a larger system beyond themselves. Most of the time, that system includes familiar social institutions: church, school, family, and country.

When Stage 4 considers irresponsible behavior, it thinks, "What if everybody did it? What if everybody shoplifted? What if everybody did as they pleased? The whole system would collapse." The great majority of Stage 4 thinkers believe that people should obey the law, pay their taxes, vote in elections, take care of their children, help their community, and serve their country. They believe in being a good and conscientious citizen. They're the backbone of any society. Teenagers and young adults who don't develop Stage 4 moral reasoning—and, sadly, a great many do not—lack the understanding of civic responsibilities required for good citizenship.

The major drawback of Stage 4 is that it sometimes gets carried away with the system it believes in and rides roughshod over the rights of individual people. A Stage 4 reasoner might say, for example, that people shouldn't be allowed to assemble to protest government policy if it's going to "stir up trouble" or cause problems for the government. Some societies and some individuals use Stage 4 reasoning to suppress individual freedom in the name of "law and order" or for the sake of a "cause."

When Stage 4 sees a conflict between the system and individual rights, it comes down on the side of the system.

Stage 5, the stage of principled conscience, reorders the moral priorities. It says, "Look, any social system exists to benefit its individual members, not the other way around. No system should ever violate the rights of the people it was founded to protect." The founding fathers were thinking Stage 5 when they told us that if the government doesn't protect our inalienable individual rights, we should throw it out and get a new one! And yet Stage 5 has the highest respect for law, because it knows that law is the chief instrument for securing human rights. But it also knows that there's something even more basic than law which is the reason for law in the first place. And that's morality. Respect for persons.

Stage 5 also has a strong social conscience, based on the moral principle of respect for individual persons. That principle enables Stage 5 thinkers to mentally "stand outside" their social system and ask, "Are things as good as they ought to be? Is justice being served? Are individual human rights being fully protected? Is there the greatest good for the greatest number? And as I go about my personal life, do I show respect for the rights and dignity of all the individuals I deal with?"

At present, the research shows, only a minority of adults attain Stage 5. How many would attain it if homes and schools made a systematic effort to foster moral reasoning, starting in the earliest years, nobody knows.

Why Horizontal Development Is Important, Too

Moving up through the moral stages, from one level to the next, is called *vertical development*. But there's another kind of stage development that I want to introduce, and that's *horizontal development*.

Suppose Kathy starts to show Stage 3 as early as 8. She'll probably take until 11 or 12 to develop Stage 3 as her *dominant* stage, the one she uses most of the time. (In the meantime, she'll use a lot of Stage 2 reasoning.) Horizontal development is this process by which a brand-new stage slowly becomes a well-established way of dealing with the world. Developing horizontally means spreading or stretching out a new stage over a wider and wider range of life experiences. It means *applying* a stage of reasoning with increasing consistency to all different kinds of situations you come in contact with.

Horizontal development is what makes a stage part of a person's moral *behavior*. Some kids advance to a higher stage of moral *reasoning* but don't apply it in their day-to-day *actions*. One 6th-grade boy, for example, was capable of Stage 3 reasoning ("Two wrongs don't make a right") in an interview, but retaliated in a primitive, eye-for-an-eye way whenever a younger schoolmate called him a name. His horizontal development was very much lacking.

You can see that horizontal development is a very real and important kind of development, *just as important as vertical development*. What good does it do for a person to develop better moral reasoning if he or she never uses it? We all know plenty of people like that.

So when kids are in a particular moral stage, like Stage 2, for a period of several years, it's important to keep both kinds of development in mind. You can help kids develop vertically toward the next stage, but there's also a lot of developing they can do within their present stage. At Stage 2, a parent can foster horizontal development by helping kids apply their tit-for-tat reasoning to issues like why they should do their chores ("Parents do a lot for kids"), be nice to brothers and sisters, obey, play nicely with friends, and so on. The more they use their best available reasoning to deal with real-life problems, the better they'll get at it. Eventually, they'll be ready to move on to the next stage.

Later, in the chapters on each of the stages, I'll show how to help kids develop horizontally as well as vertically. For now, I don't want you to think of moral development as some sort of high-pressure scramble up the ladder of the stages. Appreciate each stage for the achievement it is. You may even find yourself taking delight in recognizing the signs of a stage, such as a Stage 2 six-year-old's saying to a friend, "You know, sometimes it really pays to be good!"

One final and very important point: even *after* a new stage of moral reasoning gets "horizontally established" as a well-practiced way of dealing with the world, *lower stages still get used*. We don't always put our best moral foot forward. Just about all people, big people as well as kids, show *stage mix*, using different stages in different situations. In some cities, for example, otherwise mature people seem to regress to a Stage 2, every-man-for-himself morality whenever they step into a car! Sometimes a large part of society will put its higher-stage reasoning on the shelf and start acting like Stage 2 children. You could interpret today's "new morality" of looking out for number one as a lot of people backsliding into the self-centered spirit of Stage 2.

The moral stages as I've just described them are based on the nearly three decades of research by Harvard University psychologist Lawrence Kohlberg. Kohlberg is widely recognized as the leading figure in the psychology of moral development, and his work has stimulated research and applications to education in many different countries. Other psychologists, doing separate studies, have come up with stages or "levels" which are at least broadly similar to Kohlberg's and which have further refined our understanding of moral development. Appendix A provides more information about both Kohlberg's work and that of other investigators.

In Part 3 of the book, drawing on my own work, I flesh out the moral development research into a fuller account of how the stages show up in kids' interactions with parents, peers, and the wider world. But I'd encourage you not to take these moral stages (or any other psychological theory or research, for that matter) on faith. Test them against your own experience—your own moral development, for example, and your observations of your children's development. Seeing the stages develop in my own children, perhaps more than anything else, has helped to convince me that they are indeed real.

How Can Understanding Moral Stages Help You as a Parent?

I believe that understanding the stages of moral reasoning can help you in the work of raising good children. How?

For one thing, the stages take you *inside* a child's mind for a child's-eye view of morality. They help you appreciate your child as a *thinker*, somebody who's got his own ideas about what's right and what's wrong. They help you understand why kids say and do the things they do.

Once you understand kids from the inside, you can "plug into" where they are in the development of their moral understanding. Says one mother: "The stages keep me from expecting my kids to be where they're not ready to be." You can go with the flow of kids' present stages and help them develop horizontally. You can challenge their present way of reasoning and help them develop vertically. When you understand the stages, you have an idea of where kids are coming from, and where you want to help them head (toward the next stage of development).

So that's the second big idea of the moral development approach: morality develops slowly. It starts during the developmental periods from birth through 3. It continues to develop, through the stages of moral reasoning, clear into adulthood. Research indicates that these stages of reasoning are like a natural staircase, which kids go up one step at a time. The higher the stage, the broader the child's respect for others. Kids, just like adults, often slip down the staircase and use lower stages. Some kids move faster through the stages. But moral development isn't a race; it's a process. The important thing is to keep the process going.

How can parents keep kids moving through the stages of moral reasoning? And how can they help them learn to *act* on their best moral reasoning, so kids actually do what they know is right?

These questions lead to the other big ideas in the moral development approach.

3. RESPECT KIDS AND REQUIRE RESPECT IN RETURN

One of the most basic ways to develop kids' respect for themselves and others is to *respect them, and require respect in return*.

"The first step in raising a moral child," says Dr. Kohlberg, "is to treat a child morally."

Treating kids with respect means treating them like persons. As one mother said, "I have to remind myself that my children are human beings with rights, not puppets waiting to be manipulated by me."

Treating kids like persons means trying to be fair with them. Being fair means relating to kids at their level and making some allowances for the immaturity of their developmental stage. For example: it means understanding that Stage 2 kids, who have decided that they've got rights, will accuse you of being unfair whenever you thwart their will. It means being willing to explain your reasons, or to sometimes work out what's fair with them, instead of just saying, "Do it because I said so!"

In the area of discipline, as the mother of a 5-year-old and a 7-year-old says, being fair means "asking for and at least considering my kids' opinions when setting up rules and consequences." It means giving kids the feeling that you're trying to consider their point of view. Remembers another mother: "I always felt that my parents respected our ideas and feelings. Although it was clear who had the final say—they did, they still made us feel that our opinions were worthwhile."

It's a mistake, however, to think that just because we respect kids, they'll respect us. I'm sure you can think of lots of adults who don't automatically return the respect you give them. So it shouldn't surprise us when kids, who are at immature stages of moral development, often fail to return the respect we give them. So, to develop respect, we need to give it to our children *but also require it in return.*

Bruno Bettleheim, the renowned psychoanalyst, gives a good explanation of why it's so important to require respect from children. In the old days, he reminds us, morality began in fear. Fear of hell, fear of the woodshed, fear of not being loved, fear of something. Today we know the risk of relying heavily on this kind of fear to teach children. It can stunt personality, inhibit growth. But if we don't want to base our child's conscience on fear, we need to make sure we are doubly respected. If respect does not take the place of fear, Bettleheim argues, kids will not take morality seriously, now or later.

Unfortunately, all too many children are not learning to respect their parents. Consider this scene between a mother and her 11-year-old son, Tommy:

Tommy came into the kitchen as his mother was visiting with a friend and went to get himself a piece of cake. His mother said he couldn't have it; it was too near dinner. Tommy became insulting and abusive. The mother tried to reason but got nowhere. Finally, Tommy shouted, "You go to hell!", grabbed a piece of cake, and ran from the room. The mother turned to her friend and sighed, "He's going through a phase, and it requires an enormous amount of maturity on my part not to show anger when he gets like that. It's a real challenge to raise a child these days when the kids are so smart. Don't you agree?"[8]

I agree with this mother that it's a challenge to raise kids today, but I definitely *don't* agree that the way to do it is to let them walk all over us. We aren't being mature when we let them do that, and we certainly aren't helping *them* become more mature. Parents should never let a child get away with disrespectful, abusive talk—not to them, not to anyone. We must insist on courtesy. Expect consideration. Require, in firm and unmistakable ways, the special respect that's due us as mothers and fathers and the simple respect that's due every human being. We should remind kids of the respect we're trying to show them and ask them if they prefer that to being treated disrespectfully.

By giving kids respect and requiring it in return, we teach them a moral lesson that lies at the very heart of moral development. Morality is a two-way street. Give and take. Do unto others as you would have them do unto you. It's *mutual* respect that we should strive for in our relationship with our children.

That's the third big idea.

4. TEACH BY EXAMPLE

One of the surest ways to help our children turn their moral reasoning into positive moral behavior is to teach by example.

Teaching kids respect by respecting them is certainly one way to teach by example. When we respect our children, we're letting our actions say what we think is the right way to treat other people. We're practicing what we preach.

But teaching by example goes beyond how we treat our children. It has to do with how we treat each other as adults. It has to do with how we treat and talk about others outside the family— relatives, friends, strangers. It has to do with how we lead our lives.

Over the years, in workshops I've done for parents, I've asked them "How did your own parents influence your moral development?" Time and again, they remember the example their parents set. One man speaks of his father:

> "I remember my Dad. Long before the protection of unions, he worked long hours five days a week at his regular job and took on extra jobs on Saturday and worked long hours then. I can remember waking while it was still dark and hearing my father get up and quietly go to work while the rest of the family slept. I can't remember his ever getting sick or even taking a day off from work.
>
> "The one day he did have off, Sunday, was always spent with us doing something together—visiting relatives, going for a drive, etc. His family was his life. His work ethic and his total devotion to his family left a deep impression on me and affect me to this day."

Many people remember how their parents extended a helping hand beyond their own family. Says one mother:

> "The thing that sticks out in my mind is an atmosphere of very genuine concern for others outside the home. My father was a volunteer fireman and rescue worker and still is, in his sixties. My mother was always a volunteer of some sort and was always helping out others in the community. They were generous to others in need, even when they had little for themselves. Many people would praise my parents to my sister and me because of their kindness."

Unfortunately, the world doesn't always praise us for doing the right thing. Acting morally, as people come to understand at the highest stages of moral reasoning, sometimes requires going against what those around us want us to do. A young woman shares this memory:

> "We moved to a new neighborhood when I was 7. A year later a house was being sold on the street, and an Indian (Asian) family wanted to buy it. It was a white-collar neighborhood, and there was protest from the neighbors. They even circulated a petition against it. I remember my mother refused to sign it. When the Indian family moved in, she baked a cake for them and was the only neighbor to welcome them."

We teach respect for all persons by the example we set. Nothing else is more indelibly etched in our children's minds.

5. TEACH BY TELLING

Even though it's extremely important to teach by example, it's not enough. Kids are surrounded by *bad* examples. They need our words as well as our actions. They need to see us leading good lives, but they also need to know why we do it. For our example to have maximum impact, they need to know the values and beliefs that lie behind it.

That's the fifth big idea in the moral development approach. We teach, *directly,* by telling. We need to practice what we preach, but we also need to preach what we practice.

Parents don't have to be perfect to teach by telling. They can say to their children, "I do the best I can. I don't know everything. I've made my share of mistakes. You'll make some, too. But I want to tell you what I've learned."

Parents used to try to give all the answers. Kids resented and rejected that. Now a lot of parents don't give any answers. Kids suffer from a lack of guidance and grow up without values to live by. There's a middle ground. Parents can tell kids what they believe without playing God. They can guide and instruct, listen and advise.

Says a mother: "I believe in telling kids what you think is important, what you think can help them in their lives. You have to catch them at the right time, and you can never be sure when that is. You may have to say it a lot before they start taking it in. But they'll remember it. They'll say, 'My mother always used to say. . . .'"

Here's how three people remember what their parents taught them:

> "My mother always said, 'Dare to be different. If people are painting themselves yellow and jumping in the pond, feel perfectly free to paint yourself green and walk backwards. Never mind what the rest of the world is doing; you are your own person.' She also taught us that we were sacraments and our lives were a prayer."

"When I was 15, I fell in a hole in the street and broke my foot. We had a good case and could have taken the town to the cleaners. My mother only wanted medical expenses covered, even though the lawyer thought she was nuts. Her philosophy was, 'You only take what you earn.' In my own life, I've done as my mother did. Now I try to pass this same value on to my daughter."

"My father always emphasized that to help a friend in need was one of the best things you could do in life. This had always been a rewarding experience for him. It has been an equally rewarding experience for me when I've helped friends in need."

How does this kind of direct moral teaching relate to the stages of moral reasoning?

Within the same stage of moral reasoning, a person can do good or bad. One big influence on which we choose are the values we've been taught.

For example: One Stage 2 child, growing up in a home that stresses mutual helping, might reason, "I should be good to others so others will be good to me!" Another Stage 2 child, growing up around selfishness, might reason, "Other people just look out for themselves, so why shouldn't I?" Both kids are thinking of themselves, both using Stage 2 moral logic. But in the first case, the child thinks being helpful is important, and in the second case he doesn't. And the difference is that in the first home, the parents are making an effort to *teach the value* of helpfulness.

As kids develop higher stages of moral reasoning, it does get easier to get certain values to "take." At Stage 3, when kids aren't so me-centered and when they're more concerned about social approval, it's easier to get them to be helpful and kind than it is at Stage 2. But even at Stage 3, their moral behavior is greatly affected by the values they've learned at home. One Stage 3 child, whose parents teach the importance of being kind, might reason, "It's not nice to be mean" and so be friendly to a lonely child at school that other kids shun. Another Stage 3 child, whose parents don't stress kindness, might focus on her peer group's reaction and reason, "My friends wouldn't like me if I talked with a kid like that."

We can't "change the stripes" of a stage—even the best Stage 2 kid will be selfish some of the time, and even the best

Stage 3 kid will do some things he shouldn't because of peer pressure. But by directly teaching our children positive moral values such as helpfulness, courtesy, honesty, being a good friend, responsibility for their actions, and love, we increase the chances that they'll use their moral reasoning to choose good actions rather than bad ones.

Teach by telling.

6. HELP KIDS LEARN TO THINK

It's not enough to set a good example and tell kids what we think, important as those things are. We also have to teach them to think for themselves.

The sixth big idea of the moral development approach is that we help our kids become moral persons by helping them learn to think.

A father describes how his parents did that:

> "Whenever I did something wrong, my parents didn't just demand that I stop my behavior. Instead, they almost always asked, 'How would you feel if someone did that to you?' That gave me a chance to reflect on whatever I did and how I'd like to have it done to me.
>
> "I feel this has helped me throughout my life. Now I always try to stop and ask myself that question before I do something rather than after the fact."

This man's parents taught him two very important moral lessons. First, take the *time* to think. Second, put yourself in the other guy's shoes. Neither of those things comes naturally to kids. We can help their moral development by giving them constant encouragement to stop and think and to take the viewpoint of others. Getting better at taking the perspective of others is, in fact, a critical part of what's involved in developing through the moral stages.

There are lots of ways we can help kids exercise and sharpen their powers of moral reasoning. One mother, now a teacher, recalls the homespun moral dilemmas her father used to pose:

> "When I was young, it was a common practice in our home, usually after dinner, to have my Dad ask in his casual way, 'Do

you think you should put a nickel in the subway turnstile or wait until no one is looking and duck under?' A nickel, we knew, could buy candy.

"This was generally the beginning of a long discussion. An hour or so later, Dad was asleep in the chair, the dishes were washed, dried, and put away. How? I can't remember, because my brother, sister, and I had been concentrating on subway labor problems, litter, and how far you could go for a nickel. Looking back on those kitchen discussions, I'm glad my father taught us how to think."

Kids who think about and discuss moral issues like these, several studies show, make better headway through the stages of moral reasoning than kids who don't.[9]

7. HELP KIDS TAKE ON REAL RESPONSIBILITIES

We can help kids learn to act morally as well as reason morally by helping them take on real responsibilities. That's the seventh big idea.

All of us want our children to become responsible people. But to develop responsibility, kids have to *have* responsibility. That includes responsibility for themselves—taking care of their person and possessions, doing their homework, keeping their commitments, earning their spending money when they're old enough to do that (through baby-sitting, a paper route, summer jobs, and the like). But even more importantly, developing responsibility means having opportunities to care for others, to make some tangible contribution to the welfare of other human beings.

There was a time in our history when the survival of the family required contributions from all members, even young children. Since that's far less true today, many parents limit their kids' responsibilities to doing their schoolwork and taking care of their room. But those responsibilities aren't enough, because they are self-oriented rather than other-oriented. They don't help kids see themselves as needed, contributing members of their families.

Kids very much need other-oriented responsibilities, like supervising, playing with, or reading to a younger brother or sister; sharing the housecleaning; helping in the kitchen (with the cooking as well as the clean-up); caring for a pet; or pitching in on the gardening, yardwork, or house repair. They can also learn about being a responsible member of the neighborhood by shoveling snow or cutting the grass for an elderly neighbor. As teenagers, they can develop the feeling of contributing to their community by doing volunteer work at a hospital, nursing home, or day care center. Even during the elementary school years, kids can contribute to the wider human community by collecting money for UNICEF, participating in a walkathon for multiple sclerosis, or setting aside a portion of their allowance for a worthy charity.

Responsibility training should start early. Even 2-year-olds can help with setting the table, putting away the silverware, or folding the dishtowels. The more kids help, the more they'll be accustomed to helping. As their moral reasoning develops (giving them a better understanding of *why* they should help others), they'll have the force of good habit going for them.

A mother remembers her training in helpfulness:

"I come from a Quaker background. Somehow I always knew that whatever I did when I grew up, it would have to be, in some way, a service to others.

"Both my mother and my father were always involved in one or another kind of community work. And I can remember coming home after school when I was just a little girl and my mother saying, 'Susan, Mrs. Flannigan'—an old lady who lived down the street—'has been alone all day, and I'm sure she would like to talk with you for a while.' I remember asking now and then why *I* had to do this and other kids didn't. She told me that what other kids did didn't matter—that I should do all that I was capable of doing."

Kids learn to care by performing caring actions. It's not always easy, however, when our lives are hectic and harried, to take the time to involve kids in responsible, caring roles. Sometimes it's more work to get kids to help than to do the job ourselves. But we need to remember that work that serves others is critical for their moral development. If more kids learned early in life that they have responsibilities as well as rights, there'd be fewer teenagers, and fewer adults, who are always demanding their rights but have no sense of their obligations.

8. BALANCE INDEPENDENCE AND CONTROL

Says a popular book on parenting: "Children, like adults, fight fiercely when their freedom is threatened."

Says a mother of three grown children, asked what advice she would give parents of teenagers: "I'd tell them you must not be afraid to say no."

Says a current book on surviving the teens: "Allow your teenager the right to make his own decisions." And another: "Letting go is the key to peaceful coexistence between parent and teenager."

Say several studies of children growing up in high-crime areas: those kids who did *not* get into trouble with the law had *strict supervision* from their parents.

How does a parent put all of this together? Should you let go or hold on? Give kids independence or exercise control?

The answer, of course, is that kids need *both*. They need both independence and control throughout their development, from toddlerhood right through the teens. That's a key principle of parenting and the eighth big idea in the moral development approach.

Why isn't independence enough? Because a child isn't an adult. Neither are teenagers, even though they may stand taller than you. They're still at immature stages in their development. In both childhood and adolescence, kids need your guidance. Sometimes they need your very clear limits and control. If you gave kids just independence and no limits, you wouldn't be doing them any favors. You'd be giving them more than they can handle, overloading their circuits. You'd actually be hindering their development.

Why isn't control enough? Because kids are persons with rights and a point of view that we must respect. Because they learn to make choices by having choices. Because they don't become problem-solvers unless they have a chance to rely on their own resources and solve their own problems. Because the ultimate goal of all our parenting is not to control our children but to help them become mature adults who can make their own decisions and lead their own lives.

We know that kids want independence. Two-year-olds tell us

that. Sixteen-year-olds tell us that. But it's easy to forget what they don't tell us: they also want control. Small children need it to feel secure. Big teenagers still need it. Many don't get nearly enough. If you read the "Dear Abby" or "Ann Landers" columns, every so often you'll come across a letter that goes like this:

> Dear _____,
>
>   I'm 20, and I've made a mess of my life. When I was a teenager, my parents let me do anything I wanted. I could go anywhere, stay out as late as I pleased. I never got grounded. My friends all thought I was lucky. Now I realize they were the lucky ones. I wish my parents had cared enough to say no.
>
> Wise Too Late

Independence and control. A tricky balancing act. But absolutely essential for raising good kids.

9. LOVE KIDS AND HELP THEM DEVELOP A POSITIVE SELF-CONCEPT

The ninth big idea is that we raise good children by giving them love. The kind of love that helps them develop a positive self-concept. A sense of their worth. An inner strength.

Why is love so important? Listen to a young woman's bittersweet memory of her childhood:

> "My parents were opposing forces in my moral development. My mother had nothing but leisure time, yet she was always late for anything that involved me. The thing that is indelible in my mind is that school let out at *exactly* the same time every day. Everyone else's mother was always there early. My mother was always at least 15 minutes late. I remember standing there in the doorway, alone. This gave me a really rotten feeling about myself in terms of how my mother felt about me.
>
> "My father, on the other hand, never had any time for himself. He is a doctor and was just getting his practice together when I was young. But he always set aside one afternoon a week to spend with me. We went bowling or played golf, went to a museum, went shopping, and so on. I knew that this was my time that he put aside for me. Nothing else was more important (and there were

always other things that demanded his time). He always showed up on time, or called to let me know if he was going to be late.

"I revered my father. He made me feel that I was important to him. And that made me feel that I was worth spending time with."

Love is important for many reasons. It binds us to each other. It makes us part of the human family.

But most important for our self-concept, being loved helps us to love ourselves.

The Biblical command to "Love your neighbor as yourself" recognizes that in order to be a good person, we have to first feel good about ourselves. We have to have a sense of our own value as persons. That was the gift the father gave to his daughter when he gave her his time and love.

Loving our children is the most basic way we can help them develop a positive self-concept. But there are other ways, too. We can help them develop their skills and talents and pride in what they can do. That's an important source of self-esteem. We can encourage them to find friends who accept them for the person they are. We can point out their good qualities to them, strengths they might not be able to see themselves. We can praise and appreciate more than we criticize and complain.

People who don't feel loved, who don't have their own needs met, have trouble being open to the needs of others, no matter how high their capacity for moral reasoning. Their cup runneth short.

So give your children your attention, your support, your time. Help them develop a sense of themselves as good and competent and independent persons who can stand on their own feet and who don't need the group's approval at any price.

Help them feel loved.

10. FOSTER MORAL DEVELOPMENT AND A HAPPIER FAMILY AT THE SAME TIME

The last big idea in the moral development approach is this: You can foster moral development and create a happier family life at the same time.

You don't have to do one set of things to foster kids' moral growth and a completely different set of things to survive the week. Helping kids grow morally and making good families are really opposite sides of the same coin. When you're doing one, you'll be doing the other.

Let me give an example.

James, 7, and Elizabeth, 5, fought constantly. When they did, their mother often lost her temper and yelled. Tension increased. Happiness in the home did not.

The mother decided to get James and Elizabeth together for a "fairness discussion." A fairness discussion (which I describe at greater length in Chapter 13) is designed to help a child's moral development in two ways:

1. By developing the ability to understand somebody else's point of view

2. By developing the ability to reach a fair agreement that takes everybody's viewpoint into account.

But in addition to fostering moral development, a fairness discussion is also a very practical tool. It can help to solve all kinds of problems between parents and kids, between kids and each other, and even between husbands and wives.

At their fairness discussion, James and Elizabeth's mother explained: "Kids, I get so irritated when I see the two of you fighting with each other or hitting one another. When I get irritated, I start to yell at you, and everything becomes upset. I would like to see the two of you try a little harder to get along."

James said: "Elizabeth always wants to do *everything* I do! She wants to sit in the same seat that I do, and she wants to play with the same toys. Sometimes she hits me, too."

Elizabeth said: "James punches me. He makes me cry. He won't play with me either."

In the "fair plan" worked out by James, Elizabeth, and their mother, James agreed to teach Elizabeth some of his games, Elizabeth agreed to try to find things to do by herself sometimes, both agreed not to hit, and their mother agreed to try not to yell if the kids forgot their agreements. They also decided to keep a list on the refrigerator of "nice things said and done by all family members over the next two days."

Two days later they had a follow-up discussion. Says the mother: "We decided that everyone had indeed tried to be kinder." She reports this exchange:

Mom: James, I'm so pleased that you've been trying to include Elizabeth in your playing. Do you realize I've had to speak to you only twice in two days? I think that's quite an improvement. And Elizabeth, you certainly are trying to be nicer to everyone.

James: I'm glad you're not yelling, Mommy. And I don't think Elizabeth has hit me at all.

Elizabeth: James played with me, and he let me sit in the bean bag yesterday.

A week later the mother commented:

"Our household is now a much happier one. We continue to add to the list of nice things said to or done for others. Dad has also gotten involved. I can foresee using this method with other problems that come up with my children, and even with my husband. The fairness discussion seems to be a good way to get things out in the open. Often we don't think about how the other person views a situation. It helps to hear the other side of the story."

Of course, fairness discussions and other methods I'll describe later won't eliminate conflict from family life. Conflict in families is inevitable, and a certain amount is even healthy for kids' development, since it can prepare them to handle the inevitable conflict they'll encounter outside the home. The issue isn't how to prevent conflicts from ever occurring in your family, but how to deal with them when they do occur. The idea I want to stress here is that the same approaches that help kids grow morally also help families manage their conflicts constructively and enjoy a greater measure of happiness.

The reverse is also true. Just as fostering moral development makes for a good family life, a good family life fosters moral development. A close family gives kids people to identify with, examples to learn from, values and traditions to uphold, and a support system to turn to in times of need. When kids feel connected to the family, part of it, they've got a rudder that helps them hold to a course of responsible conduct in the face of pressure from peers.

A recent study by Nick Stinnett, chairman of the Department of Human Development and Family at the University of Nebraska-Lincoln, identified characteristics common to "strong families." Among those that stood out were:

(1) **Time together.** In all areas of their lives—meals, work, recreation—strong families structured their schedules to spend time together; and

(2) **Mutual commitment.** Strong families promoted each member's happiness and welfare and made the family their top priority.

The breakdown of morality among young people, many analysts believe, can be laid at the doorstep of a destructive combination: rising peer influence and weakening family ties. It's clear that family ties—and the time it takes to keep them strong—have never been more important in raising good children.

So that's the tenth big idea: raising good kids and making good families go hand in hand.

THE TEN BIG IDEAS OF THE MORAL DEVELOPMENT APPROACH

1. Morality Is Respect
2. Kids Develop Morality Slowly, and in Stages
3. Respect Kids and Require Respect in Return
4. Teach by Example
5. Teach by Telling
6. Help Kids Learn to Think
7. Help Kids Take on Real Responsibilities
8. Balance Independence and Control
9. Love Kids and Help Them Develop a Positive Self-Concept
10. Foster Moral Development and a Happier Family at the Same Time

HOW THIS BOOK WORKS

The ten big ideas of the moral development approach are woven throughout the book, rather than treated in separate chapters. That's because they're valid all through a child's development. Respecting kids and requiring it in return, setting a good example, teaching by telling, helping kids think, giving them responsibilities, loving them, balancing independence and control—these are principles that are important whether you're dealing with a 4-year-old or a 14-year-old.

During my discussion of each period or stage of development, I'll emphasize the big ideas that I think are especially relevant to kids' needs at that time. Love, for example, is center stage during infancy—when it's obviously too soon to give kids responsibilities. Giving them responsibilities becomes increasingly important as they develop language and the ability to follow directions and do a job. Once kids are into the stages of moral reasoning, it's important to keep the wheels turning and stretch their ability to think. Teaching values by telling what you think is right and wrong is important even with preschoolers and becomes crucial during Stage 3 of moral reasoning, when kids lean so heavily on others for their ideas about what's right. Balancing independence and control, always important, becomes a critical issue in the teens.

The big ideas, of course, are general principles. Specific ways to apply them is what the rest of the book is about. Part 2 describes the developmental periods from birth through 3 and ways to help moral development during those periods. Part 3 describes the stages of moral reasoning from preschool to adulthood and ways during each stage that you can challenge kids' stage of reasoning (and help them develop toward the next stage), or talk the language (go with the flow) of their present way of reasoning.

Part 4 of the book elaborates on practical methods (the fairness discussion, for example) which are briefly introduced in Parts 2 and 3 and which I believe are helpful over a wide range of ages and stages. Part 4 illustrates these methods with real-life examples drawn from families I've worked with over the years.

It also provides guidelines for dealing with influences or activities that can undermine kids' moral development: television (Chapter 16), sex (Chapter 17), and drugs and drinking (Chapter 18).

Different readers will have different ways of reading this book; some parents, for example, may wish to begin with a chapter in Part 4 that deals with an issue they're particularly concerned about. But let me offer my own view of how to get the most out of the book. You'll have the most complete understanding of your child's moral development, and how the various parenting methods contribute to that development, if you read all the chapters in Parts 2 and 3, even those which describe kids who are developmentally younger or older than your own. Each of these chapters builds on the ones before, and you'll find them more meaningful and more helpful if you haven't skipped any. For example, Chapter 2, on babies, develops the idea that love is vital for moral development, an idea of which there are only brief reminders in later chapters. Chapter 4, on 2-year-olds, deals with issues such as giving kids choices and spanking, and makes points that are relevant to other ages as well. Chapter 6, on Stage 0 of moral reasoning, introduces ideas that are important for understanding all the later stages of moral reasoning. And so on. So I encourage you to read Parts 2 and 3 straight through.

WHO IS THIS BOOK FOR?

Families, as everyone knows, are changing. You might wonder, "Is this book for me, in my kind of family situation?"

The 10 big ideas—both the understandings of kids' development and the ways of acting on those understandings—are clearly important no matter what your situation. They apply to:

- Traditional nuclear families, where the father works outside the home and the mother works as homemaker;
- Families where both parents work outside the home;
- Second-marriage families where stepmothers, stepfathers, and stepchildren are trying to blend into one unit;
- Single-parent families;

- Families with adopted or foster children;
- Alienated or conflict-torn families who are trying to pick up the pieces and put them back together.

Wherever there's parenting going on, there's a need to relate to kids in a way that helps them become good people. Raising good children is a concern whether you're just starting out as a parent, whether you're halfway through the process, whether you feel you've "blown it," or whether you're at your rope's end trying to cope with teenagers who reject your reasoning and guidance and seem determined to learn the hard way.

I want to say a special word to divorced parents. Immediately after you and your spouse break up, your kids have three basic needs: (1) to know that it wasn't their fault; (2) to know that you aren't divorcing *them*; and (3) to have a reasonable amount of continuity and consistency in their lives. As time goes on, the toll that divorce takes on kids depends on how much positive parenting they're getting. That's why it's important, if at all possible, for them to have ongoing nurturing contact with both parents.

But frequent contact with the out-of-home parent can actually *hurt* a child if the divorced parents are embroiled in continuing conflict. Here are the findings of a major, long-range study by University of Virginia psychologist Mavis Hetherington on the impact of divorce in 72 middle-class families where custody was awarded to the mother:

- When the divorced parents agreed about child rearing, had positive attitudes toward each other and low conflict, and when the father was emotionally mature, frequent father-child contact was associated with a *positive* mother-child relationship and a positive overall adjustment on the part of the child.
- But when there was disagreement about child rearing and conflict and ill will between the divorced parents, frequent father-child contact was associated with *poor* mother-child interactions and disruptions in the child's behavior (such as loss of self-control and increases in antisocial behavior).

There are always exceptions to such general patterns, of course; an unusual mother can handle high conflict with her ex-husband and still manage to keep a good relationship going with her child. But for the most part, if a father fights with his ex-wife, he creates stress that interferes with her ability to be a good mother, and that hurts a child's adjustment. If, however, he respects and supports his ex-wife, that helps her be a good mother, and the child is the beneficiary.

So whether kids live primarily with their mother, primarily with their father, or equally with both, their general welfare and moral development require that the divorced parents put old conflicts behind them as best they can. Honest differences that still exist or conflicting needs that arise should, wherever possible, be settled in a spirit of fairness. If you're a divorced parent, I'd encourage you to try a fairness approach (Chapter 13) to working out agreements with your ex-spouse regarding issues like visitations (can they be spontaneous as well as scheduled?), holidays (who gets the kids for how long?), and, hardest of all, values and discipline (what rules and expectations should hold in both households?). I realize that in some cases old wounds and bitterness make communication extremely difficult. But it may be easier to bury the hatchet if you focus on the needs of your child.

"AM I A GOOD ENOUGH PARENT?"

A father of three teenage boys said to me recently:

> "There's so much guilt that goes with being a parent. You're always second-guessing yourself. Was I too tough? Should I have given them another chance? Was I tough enough? You can never be sure you made the right decision."

All of us are vulnerable to the feeling, "Am I a good enough parent?" All of us have done things we regret or failed to do things we wish we had. None of us is the "perfect parent" who always does all the "right things" described in books like this. I certainly am not. Fortunately, our children can grow up to be fine people with less-than-perfect parents.

I think we need to be comfortable doing the best we can, under often difficult circumstances and operating on the basis of what we know at any point in time. When we know more, we can do a little better. But we shouldn't put ourselves down for past mistakes. Kids aren't the only ones who need to feel good about themselves; parents need to just as much.

As parents, I think we also need to be very careful not to want our children to be perfect, not to be furious or feel like failures when they turn out to be human, with faults and foibles like the rest of us. We also need to remind ourselves that they are *developing,* and that many of the foolish or irresponsible things they do are the product of their developmental immaturity.

Finally, we need to recognize a point made very well by Dr. John White, associate professor of psychiatry at the University of Manitoba and author of the compassionate book, *Parents in Pain.* Our children, he says, do not belong to us. Rather, they are a temporary trust. We're obligated to watch over their development, and give them love, discipline, and moral direction. We can hope and pray that they'll be strong and lead a good life. But we need to remember that no matter what we do, our children remain their own persons, free to choose, for good or ill.

With that in mind, let's look at the very beginnings of your child's long journey toward moral maturity—and at what you can do to help.

PART 2

LAYING THE FOUNDATION OF MORAL DEVELOPMENT . . . FROM BIRTH THROUGH THREE

CHAPTER 2

BABIES:
THE BEGINNINGS OF MORAL DEVELOPMENT

Moral development, like all other forms of human development, begins in love.

In order for human beings to develop socially and morally, they have to first get attached to people. That's why it's important, from the standpoint of raising good children, to understand how this attachment or "bonding" occurs.

In the early 1970s, a team of pediatricians at Case Western Reserve School of Medicine in Cleveland did an ingenious experiment that shed new light on the process of bonding between a mother and her newborn child.

The Case Western pediatricians were motivated by this concern: Did the separation of mother and newborn baby brought about by hospital routine interfere with the beginnings of the mother-child relationship? What would happen if human mothers had the same opportunity for extended close contact with their newborn that animal mothers have?

To find out, the doctors got a hospital to change its procedure for 14 mothers. These mothers were allowed to have their naked infants with them for about an hour after delivery and for several hours each day after that. To avoid chilling, a special heat panel was provided over the mother's bed. A comparison group of 14 mothers and their infants was treated according to the usual hospital routine (a glance at the baby at birth, followed by 20- to 30-minute feedings every 4 hours).

Every one of the mothers in the extra contact group showed essentially the same pattern of behavior, as if a powerful maternal instinct had suddenly been released. To a person, these mothers touched their babies extensively, massaged their bodies gently with the palm of their hand, and spent a great deal of time looking closely at their baby's face.

One month later, both the extra-contact mothers and the normal-contact comparison group mothers brought their infants to the hospital for their first physical examination. Extra-contact mothers were more likely to stand by the examination table and to soothe their babies when they cried. They also fondled their babies more, made greater eye contact when feeding them, and were more willing to pick them up when they cried.

A full year later, mothers in the extra-contact group reported missing their babies more when they were separated from them. Once again, during the physical examination, they were more likely than normal-contact mothers to stand by the tableside and assist the doctor. They kissed their babies more, and more often soothed them when they cried.

Two years after the experiment, there were even differences in how the extra-contact mothers *talked to* their babies! They used more questions, more adjectives, more words per sentence, and fewer commands with their 2-year-olds than did the normal-contact mothers.[1]

LESSONS ABOUT LOVE

What can we learn from this remarkable study?

First of all, I *don't* think the study proves there's a "critical period" immediately after birth during which you must have close contact with your baby in order to have a good relationship later on. Millions of mothers who don't get to handle their baby very much in the hospital make up for lost time when they get home. Similarly, parents who adopt a baby and show appropriate affection are able to establish a loving relationship.

The Case Western experiment does suggest something about the origins of love. It suggests that the feeling of love springs, at least in part, from loving behavior. Extra-contact mothers appeared to fall more deeply in love with their babies because they behaved so lovingly toward them—touching them, gazing at them—for long periods of time. Love begets love.

The experiment also points to something we intuitively know to be true: physical contact is an important source of the feelings of love. If we want to feel a close, loving relationship with our child (and this goes for fathers as well as mothers), we should *be* in touch, literally.

The love that comes from early nurturing contact, the Case Western study also shows, may even set the pattern for the overall way we relate to our child. To the extent that it does, it has potential long-range effects on our child's moral development. A mother who, because she feels a loving relationship with her child, asks her youngster more questions (thereby encouraging more thinking) and uses reasoning and not just commands to get cooperation is a mother who's fostering her child's moral growth.

BABIES WHO ARE NONCUDDLERS

What if *you* want to establish a close, loving relationship with your baby that includes lots of holding and hugging, but your child won't put up with all that contact?

A study by researchers H. R. Schaffer and Peggy Emerson at the University of Strathclyde, Glasgow, found that about 25 percent of the babies in their sample did in fact resist close contact, except during feeding. They called these babies "noncuddlers." Their mothers said things like, "He's never liked cuddling—always squirms and struggles to get away."

On closer examination, however, the researchers discovered that it was *restraint* that these babies didn't like. Noncuddlers *did* enjoy being stroked, tickled, or kissed when they weren't picked up. They also responded happily to being swung, bounced, danced around, or romped with in any way that involved contact—just so long as they weren't restrained.

So babies may differ in how they like their contact, but all appear to need it. To make contact emotionally, to form their first human relationships, they need to make contact physically. With babies, just as with the mothers in the Case Western study, a love that's "only skin deep" can be very deep indeed.

WHAT HAPPENS WHEN BABIES ARE STARVED FOR LOVE?

What happens to the moral development of children who don't get enough loving contact and attention when they're babies?

In 1945 William Goldfarb, an American psychiatrist, investigated the development of 70 children who had been raised for the first three years of their lives in institutions that provided them with little social interaction or intellectual stimulation. He compared them with 70 children who had been brought up in foster homes, where they generally got more attention and affection than children in the impoverished institutional settings. Goldfarb was shocked by his findings. The institutionalized children, by comparison, seemed totally unable to control their impulses and showed "an incomprehensible cruelty to other children and animals."[2]

Such behavior can also be found in children who are brought up by their own parents in a home without love.

Paul, a 10-year-old boy, offers a pathetic case in point. From age 3, Paul was extremely aggressive. In public school he attacked several children, set the teacher on fire, and ravaged the classroom. In the reformatory home to which he was committed, he set fire to the furniture and curtains and horrified the other children by killing goldfish with pins and pulling out their intestines. From earliest childhood, Paul had been severely rejected and brutally beaten by his parents.[3]

Paul was diagnosed as a "child psychopath." Psychopathic children lie, cheat, steal, and engage in aggressive and cruel behavior. But they show not the least bit of guilt about their actions. They seem to have no conscience whatever. They also seem very detached, devoid of feelings for other people. Something very basic, something fundamentally human, seems to be missing.

When psychopaths grow up, we often hear about their exploits in the news. Since they have no feelings for other people, they are able to hurt or even kill them casually.

Charles Manson is a good example. He exhibited no guilt at all about the fiendish murders he perpetrated. "I could kill everyone without blinking an eye," he told Vincent Bugliosi, the prosecutor who sent him to prison. Like many other psychopaths, Charles Manson was rejected as a child, left with neighbors for days and weeks by a sexually promiscuous young mother who didn't even give him a name when he was born. When Manson was 12, his mother put him in a caretaking institution. He ran away, back to his mother. She didn't want him, so he ran away again. Then the crimes began.

Charles Manson suffered from severe deficiencies in socialization. He never became a member of the human community.

The time for a child to join the human community is the very first year of life. If a positive attachment to a parent figure is not formed during that first year and continued through the early years, normal human relations and moral development may never occur.

HOW RESPONSIVE LOVE CAN TEACH A BABY TO OBEY

Forming a positive attachment to a parent helps a baby learn to perform one of its first cooperative acts: obeying a parent's simple commands (such as "No, no!"; "Don't touch!"; "Come, here"; "Give it to me").

Why do some babies obey more readily than others? Heredity appears to have something to do with it. Parents report that some children are just "easy" by nature, others stubborn from the start.

But there's evidence that parenting also plays a part. In 1971 researchers Donelda Stayton, Robert Hogan, and Mary S. Ainsworth of Johns Hopkins University investigated infant obedience by observing 25 mothers and their 9- to 12-month-old babies. The babies who obeyed most readily, they found, were *not* the ones whose mothers gave the most verbal commands or most often intervened physically to stop a behavior. Instead, the most obedient babies had mothers who got high marks on three scales:

1. **Sensitivity-Insensitivity**
   • How finely attuned was the mother to her baby's signals and communications?

- Could she see things from her baby's point of view?
- Was she mainly geared toward her own wishes, moods, and activities, with her interventions coming more from her own internal signals than from her baby's?

2. Acceptance-Rejection

- To what extent did a mother accept her baby's "babiness," including those things she found distasteful?
- To what extent did she accept the responsibility of caring for her baby without strongly resenting the restriction of her activities?

3. Cooperation-Interference

- To what extent did a mother try to avoid imposing her will on her baby by arranging the environment and her schedule so as to minimize the need to interrupt and control her baby?
- Was she able to create situations where her baby happily went along with her wishes and needs?
- Did she fail to see her baby as a separate person and interrupt her baby arbitrarily, without regard for her infant's moods, wishes, or activities in progress?

Mind you, no babies obeyed all the time. But there was a definite trend. The most cooperative babies, as a rule, had the most sensitive, accepting, and cooperative mothers.

That makes a lot of sense. These sensitive mothers took pains to be responsive to their babies' signals—for food, attention, comfort, time for rest or play, and so on. In short, they tried to keep their babies happy. On the whole, a happy baby tended to be an obedient baby.

Put another way: *When a mother was willing to comply with her baby's signals, her baby was willing to comply with hers.*

What does that remind you of?

It reminds me of two of the big ideas about moral development: (1) morality is respect; and (2) kids are more likely to give respect when they receive it.

By accommodating to their mothers' signals, obedient babies were practicing "respect" on their level. And they seemed to be doing it because they loved a mother who loved and respected them. Through this unspoken "mutual accommodation pact," these mothers and babies were laying the foundation for the more conscious and generalized respect for persons that comes later in moral development.

FEEDING, LOVE, AND MORAL DEVELOPMENT

The study of infant obedience shows there's more to parenting than meets the eye.

Loving babies means a lot more than just holding them or comforting them when they cry. Responsive parents are really "tuned in" to their baby's needs. They're constantly making adjustments to try to meet their baby's needs and their own needs at the same time.

The idea I want to emphasize here is that by loving babies in this responsive way, you help them get attached to you. That first attachment, that human bond, is the indispensable basis for later moral development.

From this perspective, all the ways you interact with your baby contribute to the kind of attachment you have and therefore, eventually, to your child's moral development. No single event or facet of your relationship has a "make-or-break" influence, of course, but everything contributes.

Take feeding as a case in point. Suppose you're about to give your baby some solid foods. What will your approach be?

One parent may bring the spoon up slowly, carefully waiting for the baby's mouth to open. Another parent may stuff another spoonful into the baby's mouth even before the last one has been swallowed.

When introducing a new food, some parents take their cues from their baby's reactions. If their baby makes a face or spits out the food, they may switch to a different food and come back to the new one a little later. If that doesn't work, they may decide to save the rejected fare for another occasion. But other parents will make a battle of it, because they think their babies are being defiant and they don't want them to "get away with anything."[4]

Two psychologists, Mary Ainsworth and S. M. Bell, went so far as to identify nine different ways that mothers feed their babies. They arranged these feeding patterns along a continuum according to how responsive the different patterns were to baby's signals or emotional states.

They wondered: If they knew how a mother fed her baby during the first three months, could they predict how securely a baby would be attached to its mother at one year of age?

Sure enough, they could. Mothers who were responsive feeders were very likely to have securely attached 1-year-olds. These babies were able to use their mothers as a home base for exploring in the presence of a strange experimenter. And they showed obvious signs of missing their mother when she left the experimental room. Missing their mothers was a measure of the strength of the attachment they felt.

Mothers who were *not* responsive feeders were likely to have babies with a relatively poor attachment to them. Some of these babies showed an "avoidant attachment." They often ignored their mothers and could just as easily be comforted by a stranger. Their mothers seemed to be nothing special to them. Other babies showed a "resistant attachment." They had trouble using their mothers as a home base for exploring in the presence of a stranger, and they got mad at their mothers if they left the room.[5]

So mothers who were responsive feeders had securely attached babies. Is there any direct evidence that the security of a baby's attachment is related to its personality and moral development in later childhood?

SECURELY ATTACHED BABIES BECOME SELF-CONFIDENT 3-YEAR-OLDS

Fortunately, there's at least one study of attachment that followed the same children from the time they were babies to the time they were 3½-year-olds.[6] The researchers rated the security of babies' attachment to their mothers at 15 months of age. Then they observed the same children when they were in nursery school.

There was a world of difference between children who had been securely attached as babies and children who had not. In nursery school, securely attached children tended to be social leaders. Other kids often sought them out. They frequently initiated activities. When another child showed distress, a securely attached child was likely to respond with empathy (seeing what was the matter, offering to help, etc.). Teachers rated these children as forceful, self-directed, and eager to learn.

Children who had been insecurely attached as 15-month-olds presented a sad contrast. They tended to be hesitant and uncertain as nursery-schoolers. In social situations they were likely to withdraw, even when other kids tried to play with them. Teachers rated them as low in curiosity and ability to pursue a goal.

Is it a paradox that securely *attached* 1-year-olds become self-confident, *independent* 3-year-olds?

Not if you realize that *there's a direct relationship between security and independence*. Babies who are secure in their attachment to their parents have the confidence to explore their world. They've got a home base. As they grow up, their self-confidence will enable them to be independent. Always, love remains the ground from which self-confidence and independence spring. It's no different for us as adults. It's easier to face the world, to stand on our own feet in moral or other kinds of situations, if we know somebody loves us.

Securely attached children are not the kids who hang on their mother's apron strings. Those are overdependent children. Parents can try to avoid overdependence (which can be quite a challenge with youngsters who are naturally shy) by providing their children with lots of different kinds of experiences, giving them increasing freedom to explore, allowing them to make choices, and encouraging them to do things for themselves. You can do all of these things as babies grow up. But the very first step in developing an independent child is to make sure the bond of love is strong and secure.

HOW ATTACHMENT AFFECTS LONG-RANGE MORAL DEVELOPMENT

At 3½, securely attached children are already more morally mature than insecurely attached children. Because secure kids have their own need for love met, they're more open to the needs of others.

There's another important difference between these two groups of children that has profound implications for their long-range moral development. Securely attached children enjoy better peer relations. They actively seek out and participate in social interactions.

We know that a child's continuing moral growth is stimulated by just these opportunities for social interaction. When kids play and talk together, and even when they argue or fight, they have a chance to learn to take the viewpoint of others. They can learn the meaning and necessity of mutual respect. When kids are deprived of these opportunities, or when they shy away from them, they're missing out on something that's very important for their moral development.

So by loving children when they're babies, we help them develop positive relations with their peers later on. That in turn supplies another crucial condition for their ongoing moral growth.

HOW LOVE LEADS TO LEARNING

The study that followed babies into nursery school adds a new wrinkle to our picture of early development.

Securely attached children were not only better developed socially and morally. They were also *better learners*. That suggests that a parent's love helps kids become smart as well as good, that intellectual development and moral development go hand in hand.

I want to underscore that relationship. Developing through the moral stages is in large part a matter of learning to reason better about questions of right and wrong. It involves thinking.

Being able to think doesn't guarantee, of course, that you'll make good moral decisions. Lots of people use their brains not to help their neighbors but to do them in. In human history great genius has often been the source of great evil.

But the development of the ability to think does increase a person's *potential* for thinking and acting morally. So anything you do to raise a brighter child has the potential of raising a good child, too.

Let's go back to the finding that babies who were securely attached to their mothers turned out to be the eager learners in nursery school. How is it that love leads to learning?

Think of early infancy and one of the simplest ways that responsive mothers show their love for their babies: They pick them up.

Have you ever watched what babies do when they're picked

up and put on a shoulder? If they're crying, they very often stop. *Then they look around.* In psychological jargon, they become "visually alert" and "scan the environment."

Observation of young babies shows that this state of visual alertness occurs *by itself* only rarely in the first several weeks of life. Left to lie in their cribs, most newborns spend only a small fraction of the day really looking at their environment.

Why is that significant? It's significant because young babies handle the world with their eyes. They're pretty helpless otherwise. Vision is one of the few ways they can make contact with their environment and become interested in learning about it.

So when you pick up your baby, you're creating an "optimal learning state." You're helping your baby explore its world. And that world includes you. Babies who are picked up often take the opportunity to explore the face of this large creature that has given them a new perspective on things.

MEETING YOUR NEEDS AND YOUR BABY'S

In saying that it's important to pick up babies in order to stimulate their learning, I don't mean to say that you have to pick them up *every* time they fuss or cry. I know that's not possible. It wouldn't even be good for them if you did. Babies should learn, gradually, to amuse themselves so they're not entirely dependent on other people for stimulation.

I think it's helpful, in this context, to remember the study of infant obedience. Mothers who had the most obedient babies tried as much as they could to work out ways of meeting their babies' needs *and* their own needs at the same time. Now, I know that's not always possible either. Being a parent often means putting aside your own needs when the situation requires it in order to meet your child's. But meeting both sets of needs is a good goal to shoot for.

Let me point out a few ways to do that with babies, even if they seem obvious. If babies are fussing or crying, and you can't pick them up at the moment, you can try various forms of distraction. Change their position or view. Give them something interesting to listen to, like a record or a tape recording of their own sounds or you talking or singing. Give them something interesting to look at, like a mobile (not always the same one) or their own reflection in a mirror that's fastened to the side of their crib or dressing table. Give them safe things they can touch and explore on their own.

By providing these interesting distractions, parents are not only helping themselves. They're also providing a stimulating "inanimate environment" that helps meet their baby's need to learn. And that learning helps to develop the general intelligence that's required for moral reasoning in later years.

Because learning develops the intelligence that's an important part of moral development, I'd like to say two other things about what helps babies learn. First, *variety* is a key factor. Studies show that the babies who do the most exploring, and who score the highest on tests of mental and motor development, tend to be the ones who have lots of different kinds of toys and other objects to play with.

Second, a rich inanimate environment produces the greatest learning when it's *combined* with a rich social environment. The smartest, best developed, most socially responsive babies tend to have parents who bring the inanimate environment to life by getting involved in their babies' play. *They not only give their babies toys but they also actively play with their babies and express pleasure at their pleasure.*

So, teach babies to amuse themselves with interesting sights and sounds and opportunities to touch, explore, and experiment. That way you'll have some time for yourself. But be sure to keep a hand in your baby's play, remembering that responsive parents make for responsive babies. It's that mutual responsiveness between parent and child that fosters learning as well as love. And learning, like love, is one of the essential ingredients in moral development.

BABY STEPS TOWARD MORAL DEVELOPMENT

The early years are critical for moral development, and the first year is the most critical of all. Let's review all the reasons why that's so:

1. Your baby's infancy is the time you form your attachment to your child. The more you touch and handle and play with your baby, the stronger that attachment will be.

2. When you handle your baby, you meet a basic need for contact. That's one of the first ways your baby gets attached to you.

3. If babies don't get love and don't form an attachment in the first year of life, they may never develop the ability to love other people. Psychopaths are people who never learned to love.

4. In the first year of life, by tuning into and accommodating your baby's needs, you create the kind of relationship that helps babies learn to obey. Babies get their first experience in mutual accommodation and respect.

5. By being a responsive parent, you help your baby develop a secure attachment to you. That in turn helps your child develop self-confidence, independence, and the ability to interact with others and respond to their needs.

6. By providing babies with an interesting inanimate environment and a responsive social environment, you stimulate their exploration and their learning. That in turn develops their general intelligence, which helps them later to develop through the stages of moral reasoning.

This has been a chapter about the first year of life. We've looked at the important baby steps your child takes down the long road of moral development.

But it's also been a chapter about love.

In Chapter 1, we saw that love, by itself, is not enough for moral development. Especially as they get older, kids also need discipline, discussion, direct teaching, and good example. But even though love isn't enough, it's essential. It remains so all through development.

I've tried to show why it's best to begin a loving relationship with your child from day one. But love is always needed, and it's never too late to start.

There's a true and tragic story of a child, a little girl, who spent the first five years of her life tied to a chair.

She was the illegitimate baby of a young woman whose grandfather, out of shame, had secluded the child in a closed room.

When she was finally discovered by child welfare workers at age 5, the little girl could not walk, talk, or feed herself. She just barely responded to loud noises made near her.

Placed in an institution, she showed very little improvement. Then she was moved to a foster home. Here, finally, she was given love. She began to respond. Although she never developed normal intelligence or normal social relationships, she did, given loving attention, learn to feed herself, walk, and talk.[7]

Love lights the lamp of human development. If we wish to raise good children, we should begin by giving them our love.

CHAPTER 3

ONES:
THE FIRST STEP TOWARD
INDEPENDENCE

Attachment is the "main event" of the first year of life. By the end of that year, babies who are loved are secure in their first human relationships. Now they're ready to take a major step toward independence.

They learn to walk. They enter the age of toddlerhood.

Learning to walk has two dramatic consequences. The first is that exploration really takes off.

When you hear a mother say, "He's into *everything*!" you know she's talking about a toddler. Toddlers are simply great at getting into things. They love to open drawers, boxes, and cabinets. They love to take out—better yet, *dump* out—all the interesting stuff they find. All of this may be hard on you, but it's great for them.

The second consequence of your toddler's new ability to tool around and explore the world is a spirit of independence. Toddlers have a stronger sense of themselves than they did during infancy. They're more in charge of their own behavior. They want to do what they want to do.

Your first job during the toddler period is not to stifle your baby's exploration and independence. Exploring, remember, is how babies learn. And becoming independent is one of the important ways kids gradually grow toward maturity. Being a mature person, morally or otherwise, requires being able to think for yourself, make your own decisions. If you take this long view, it'll help you be more patient with your toddler's independence when you feel the urge to squelch it.

Your second job during toddlerhood is to set some limits on your toddler's exploration and independence. That's the job of discipline, of balancing independence with control.

Since toddlers can do a lot more than infants, you'll find yourself needing to exercise more control over their behavior. And since toddlers have a stronger sense of who they are and what they want, they won't always accept your restrictions or obey your commands as readily as they used to.

As a result, there's more potential for conflict between you and your toddler. For example:

> Barry, 16 months old, was into everything. Before, he generally obeyed his parents' noes when they told him he couldn't have or do something. But now if he couldn't get what he wanted, he'd hit or crash into things in frustration. Sometimes, if his mother or father were within range, he'd swing at them, too.

The challenge you face at a point like this is the same challenge you'll face again and again as a parent: *How do you discipline in a way that simultaneously fosters your child's long-range moral development?*

That comes down to the question: *How do you get your child to respect your rights and needs, and at the same time respect the rights and needs of your child?*

Let's look at some ways to do that with toddlers.

1. MAXIMIZE OPPORTUNITIES FOR SAFE EXPLORATION

Remember the study of obedience in 9- to 12-month infants (Chapter 2)? It showed that when mothers respected their babies' needs, babies were more likely to obey their mothers. That same principle of mutual accommodation applies with toddlers. If you give them lots of chances to satisfy their need to explore, they'll be better able to accept the limits you set.

Babyproofing your child's environment is one way to maximize the opportunities for safe exploration. The more babyproofing you do, the fewer limits you'll need to impose, and the more happy exploring your toddler can do.

2. TEACH LIMITS

Setting some limits is essential for a child's moral development. Why?

Imagine what it would be like if you grew up in a home where nobody ever said no. It would be a make-believe world. When it came time to enter the real world, you'd be in for a shock. The real world is full of rules that people have to understand and obey.

Why start so soon to teach limits?

Toddlers are doing a tremendous amount of learning. They're busy organizing their world, finding out the "laws" that govern it.

They're discovering physical laws. When you throw a ball, it bounces. When you bump your head, it hurts.

They're discovering the laws of language. Everything has a name, a sound that you make. When you make the right sound, people understand what you mean.

They're discovering moral laws, the ones that tell you what you should and shouldn't do. When you run toward the street, pick up a knife, or climb up on the table, your parents say, "No! Mustn't do that!"

In short, kids should begin to learn limits or rules at this age because it goes right along with all the other kinds of learning they're doing. It's a time of figuring out how their world works. Limits give them one more way to do that. And they need to learn them from you.

If you want limits to be effective, be *consistent*. If you're going to say no, say it *every time* you see your child doing the action you want to prohibit. If you're not consistent, you'll just confuse kids. You'll frustrate their effort to figure things out. Or you'll lead them to think it's a game, and the idea is to find out when they can get away with something and when they can't. A certain amount of "testing behavior" is normal for toddlers, but if they're acting up constantly, they may be sending you a message: "I'm not sure what the limits are, and I need to know!"

In teaching limits it's also important to be *specific*. Don't just say "No." *State the rule and the reason for it.*

For example: If your toddler pulls the cat's tail, say, "No! We don't pull kitty's tail! [the rule] It *hurts* kitty! [the reason for the rule]."

If you give kids reasons for rules even when they're toddlers, you'll be getting off on the right foot as a parent. Reasoning with kids will get to be a habit, something that's second nature. By reasoning with them, you'll help them develop *their* ability to reason about right and wrong. And by reasoning with your children, by treating them as having a mind that's capable of understanding, you're showing respect for them as persons.

In lots of situations, of course, your toddler won't listen to reason, and you'll need to use other strategies. Sometimes, especially when you're frazzled or your child is cranky, the simplest thing is to enforce a limit nonverbally (you simply take away a contested object or you pick your child up and put him in his high chair). There's a time to reason and a time not to reason, and you have to be the judge.

3. TEACH ALTERNATIVES

Another way to respect children is to teach them what they *may* do as well as what they may not. Teach acceptable alternatives. If a toddler scribbles on the wall, you can say, "No. You may not write on the wall [the rule]. It makes a mess [reason for the rule]." But don't stop there. Give your toddler some paper and say, "Here—you *may* write on paper."

If toddlers hit you or other children because they want attention or are just being exuberant, take their hand and show them how to touch or stroke *gently*. Whenever there's an opportunity, *demonstrate* the behavior you want your child to substitute for an undesirable action.

4. USE DISTRACTION

It's important for toddlers to bang up against the boundaries you set. That's how they learn what's acceptable behavior and what isn't. That's how they learn the important moral lesson that they can't do everything they want to do.

But don't turn limit-setting into a needless contest of wills. You can avoid a lot of power struggles through the tried-and-true method of distraction. After you say no to one thing, you can quickly offer another that will capture your child's attention. "No, you can't have that knife, but look at these great pots and pans!" Or open one of your child's favorite storybooks and start asking questions: "Hey, what's this guy doing?" "What's happening over here?" Even before kids can talk, questions like these capture their interest.

5. REINFORCE DESIRABLE BEHAVIOR

We all know the old saying that you can catch more flies with honey than you can with vinegar. But sometimes we forget to apply that principle with kids. We scold them when they're bad and ignore them when they're good. They quickly learn that they get more attention for misbehaving than they do for behaving.

If you think this might be true in your house, make it a point to try to catch your toddler being good. If you're trying to establish a particular behavior, like coming when called or eating a new vegetable, get your whole family to give your toddler a big round of cheers, whistles, and applause for doing as requested. Your child will love it.

Reinforcing a child's positive behavior also reinforces a positive relationship between parent and child. As we've already seen, that's important all through development.

6. WHEN POSSIBLE, IGNORE UNDESIRABLE BEHAVIOR

Some child-rearing books tell you to "ignore undesirable behavior." As blanket advice, that's unrealistic. If a toddler is reaching for a lamp, about to put a penny in her mouth, or hitting a younger child, a parent has to take action.

Some behaviors, however, can and should be ignored as a general rule. Temper tantrums, which are normal toddler behavior (another sign of growing self-assertion), are a good example. If your child throws a tantrum, a first course of action is to ignore it completely. Turn your back, busy yourself with some task, pick up a magazine and start reading, or just walk out of the room. If you do this sort of thing consistently, each time your child starts carrying on, tantrums may soon cease.

Some toddlers' temperament, however, is such that they may

continue for a period of weeks or months to have a tantrum when they get frustrated. But even if ignoring tantrums doesn't completely eliminate them, it's still an appropriate response. It teaches kids another important moral lesson: Screaming is not a way to get what they want.

The first time you try ignoring a tantrum, your child may think, "Maybe if I keep this up long enough, Mom or Dad will give in!" So be prepared to stick out the screaming. If it makes you more comfortable, put your youngster in his crib and leave him there to finish the tantrum. But don't go back before the tantrum stops.

Many toddlers will try a tantrum at bedtime, when parents are usually at their lowest ebb. When our older son, Mark, was about a year old and protested being put in for the night, we made the mistake of rocking him to sleep. After several nights of doing that, it became impossible to put him to bed awake without setting off furious crying! We got out our copy of Dr. Spock's *Baby and Child Care,* which offered this counsel to parents with our dilemma: put your child to bed, say good night, close the door, and *don't go back,* no matter how much the sobbing breaks your heart. The first night, Dr. Spock said, your child may cry for 20–30 minutes (Mark lasted a full hour!). The second night it would be down to 10 minutes or so, and the third night there probably wouldn't be any crying at all. We followed this prescription (agonizingly hard as that was to do), and sure enough, after three nights Mark was going down for the count without a whimper.

What if your child throws a tantrum in a public place, like the supermarket? The first rule is still that you *not* give in to your child's demand, since giving in teaches a child that Mom or Dad would rather capitulate than have a big scene. To stop the tantrum behavior, you can try the "hold and talk" technique developed by psychologist Kit Trapasso.

Take your child outside, off in a corner, or somewhere else where you can have relative privacy. Then restrain your child firmly from behind, either kneeling behind your child or having your child sit in your lap. Hold your child's arms in a crossed position, and, if you're sitting, cross your legs over your child's legs. If you're sitting, you can also rock gently. The idea is to restrain physical movement while you "talk your child down" in a soft, steady voice:

> "I'm not going to let you behave this way, it isn't good, it's not helping you, it's not helping me, it's not going to work, I want you to calm down, just calm down. . . ."

With repeated use, this technique has reportedly reduced or eliminated tantrums even in 2-year-old children who had a chronic pattern of such behavior, and is especially helpful with the occasional child who tries to hurt himself (by banging his head, for example) when his tantrum is ignored.

7. IF NECESSARY, IMPOSE A LOGICAL CONSEQUENCE FOR MISBEHAVIOR

There'll be times when you have to impose a negative consequence to change your child's behavior.

Consequences for misbehavior should be logical. There should, whenever possible, be a clear connection between a child's offense and the consequence it brings.

With toddlers and other young kids, three kinds of consequences are logical and therefore appropriate. One is *scolding*. Scolding is a logical consequence because it says to kids, "If you don't treat people nicely, they get mad at you." To make scolding effective, don't do it too often. If you do, it'll lose its effect. But when you do scold, be stern. Let your child know you mean it.

The parents of Barry, the 16-month-old who took to hitting when he got frustrated, used scolding to good effect. When he hit them, they reacted dramatically, with stern indignation. They made an angry face, pointed their finger at him, and said in a very loud voice, *"No!"* The hitting stopped.

A second kind of logical consequence is *deprivation*. If children hit with a toy, for example, they lose that toy for a period of time.

A third kind of logical consequence is a *"time-out."* Suppose Barry, despite scoldings, had continued to hit his parents or other children. In that case, I'd advise marching him off to his crib for 5 or 10 minutes by himself the next time he hit someone.

A time-out is a logical and fair consequence for hitting because hitting hurts. If you're going to hurt people, you can't be with them. If you want to be with them, you have to treat them with respect.

Try to Avoid Spanking

If you're like most parents, you'll be tempted to spank your toddler. And it's not such a terrible thing if, once in a while, you do. Kids aren't made of glass.

In the next chapter, I'll spell out the limited conditions under which I think spanking can be used as an occasional means of controlling the behavior of young children. During toddlerhood, however, I'd urge you to avoid, as much as possible, spanking

---

SEVEN METHODS FOR DISCIPLINING TODDLERS

1. *Maximize opportunities for safe exploration.* That respects toddlers' need to investigate their world.

2. *Teach limits.* That gives kids their introduction to rules and the reasons for them.

3. *Teach alternatives.* That shows toddlers what they may do as well as what they may not.

4. *Use distraction.* That avoids a needless contest of wills.

5. *Reinforce desirable behavior.* That improves kids' behavior and your relationship with them by "catching them being good."

6. *When possible, ignore undesirable behavior.* That teaches children that tactics like temper tantrums don't work.

7. *If necessary, impose a logical consequence for misbehavior.* That teaches kids that people react negatively when they're treated badly.

your child. It's a bad pattern to get into. If hitting gets to be a habit, it will have a negative effect on your relationship with your toddler and can even hinder your child's moral development. You'll better serve your child's long-range interests if you work on developing the other methods of discipline.

The seven methods I've suggested, taken together, should enable you to manage your toddler's behavior (which isn't to say that it'll be easy!). These methods seek to respect toddlers' emerging independence and foster their moral understanding. Using them, you'll be meeting your own day-to-day needs as well as those of your child, and doing it in a way that contributes to your child's long-range moral development. That's the essence of the moral development approach.

For an in-depth picture of the needs and behavior of toddlers and helpful advice to mothers and fathers in all different situations (working parents, single parents, parents of hyperactive children, parents of withdrawn children), I'd recommend the book Toddlers and Parents *by the noted pediatrician, Dr. T. Berry Brazelton.*

CHAPTER 4

TWOS: THE FIRST DECLARATION OF INDEPENDENCE

Two-and-a-half-year-old Heidi refused to hold her mother's or father's hand whenever it came time to cross a street. She'd protest: "You don't have to hold my hand!"

"Heidi," her parents would explain, "it's dangerous for you to cross the street without holding our hand. You could get hit by a car and hurt very bad, or even killed."

"I'll be careful!" Heidi would say.

Then her parents would insist: "Heidi, we *have* to hold your hand!" When one of them took it, Heidi would always pull away before giving in. Sometimes she'd continue to put up a fight, and the tug of war would end in tears.

Heidi is a typical 2-year-old. Sometime around the age of 2 (sometimes as early as 18 or 19 months!), the budding individuality of your toddler turns into a full-blown Declaration of Independence.

Besides wanting to do almost everything for themselves, twos are notoriously negative. "No!" becomes practically a reflex response to a wide range of parental requests, however reasonable they may be. "No dinner!" "No, I don't wanna take a bath!" "No, I don't wanna go to bed!" Everything seems to be a struggle.

Although the twos are especially trying, they're not unique. As we've already seen, the thrust toward independence begins as early as toddlerhood. At later stages in childhood and adolescence, independence will again surge to the fore. Each time it does, it puts new strains on parent-child relations. And each time it does, it challenges us to maintain a developmental perspective, the long view. We need to remind ourselves that in the long run, independence is one of the major forces that carry our children toward greater maturity.

At the same time that we're respecting our child's independence, however, we also want to stimulate the cooperative tendencies that are the other side of moral development. Cooperation isn't the strong suit of twos, but we want to keep it growing, and we obviously need a certain amount of cooperation from our child in order to get through the day. How do you do both of those things—respect independence and foster cooperative behavior—during the "terrible twos"?

The discipline methods you used with toddlers are still helpful with 2-year-olds. But because the twos are a period of rising independence and intensified conflict, new strategies are also needed. In this chapter I'll focus on ways I think you can reduce conflicts with 2-year-olds and stimulate their moral development: offering choices, reasoning by questioning, using stories to distract a child and to teach appropriate behavior, and others. You can use these methods with twos, threes, and (except for distraction) with older kids as well.

If you use these ways of avoiding conflict and dealing with it when it occurs, the twos may still be tough, but they're less likely to be terrible.

HOW TO AVOID AND HANDLE CONFLICTS BY OFFERING CHOICES

Let's go back to Heidi, the 2½-year-old who wouldn't take her parents' hand to cross the street, and see how that conflict got solved.

> One winter day, Heidi's mother went to take her mittened hand as they came to an intersection. As usual, Heidi resisted. Only this time, as she wiggled loose from her mother's grip on one hand, she offered the other one instead. "Here," she said, "take this one."

WHAT TO KEEP IN MIND ABOUT TWOS

1. Their fiercely independent spirit and ornery negativism are a part of growing up. *They're pulling away from you and becoming their own person.* That's essential for their personality development and their moral development. The principled moral courage that you admire in an adult has its first roots in the feisty independence of age 2.

2. You should respect the independence of twos, just as you did with toddlers. But once again, you have a crucial task of moral training: to help your child learn to respect your authority and to accommodate to reasonable requests and rules. You can achieve both of these—respect for your child's independence and accommodation to you—by:

   • Offering choices;
   • Asking questions that get your child to think;
   • Using developmentally appropriate distraction, like storytelling;
   • Using stories to teach appropriate behavior;
   • Time-outs;
   • Rhyming rules;
   • Spanking only as a last resort.

After that, Heidi's parents always remembered to let her choose: "Heidi, I have to hold your hand now. Which one would you like me to hold—this one or that one?"

The battle over hand-holding was no more.

From this story, it's possible to extract a simple principle for trying to avoid parent-child conflicts and for handling them when they occur: *When you anticipate or encounter a conflict, give your child a choice.*

3. Even more than toddlers, twos need you to give them wide berth. Don't overdo the limit-setting; don't feel you *always* have to assert your authority. Enjoy their emerging selfhood.

4. Don't expect twos to be more mature than they are. In many ways, they're still babies. You should certainly *encourage* more mature behavior when you think that's appropriate; the spur of rising expectations is one of the things that keeps kids developing. But don't expect twos to be good at sharing, to play "nicely" with peers, to accept younger brothers or sisters without jealousy, to have polite table manners, or to show gratitude for all the nice things you do for them.

5. Don't expect to be a saint yourself. Twos are tough. Expect to lose your temper now and then, and don't feel guilty about it. If you feel you were in the wrong, say you're sorry, then let it pass.

6. Twos thrive on things to do. They love to be read to, to roughhouse, to explore, to "mess about" with sand, dirt, water, clay, Play-Doh, and paint. They love songs, surprises, and simple games. They need lots of room, lots of stuff, and lots of attention from you. Give them all you can.

In some situations, it's most effective to offer kids a choice between cooperating and an alternative they'll want to avoid. For example:

Todd, not quite 2, took to crying when he was put in his high chair for dinner. No amount of coaxing helped.

Finally, his father said, "Todd, would you like to eat dinner with us or go to your crib? You decide."

Todd stopped crying to think about his father's question. He decided to stay and eat dinner.

Did Todd's father threaten him with punishment if he didn't eat? No, and here's the difference: When you threaten ("If you don't stop crying and eat, you're going straight to your crib!"), *you* exercise all the control. When you offer your child a choice ("Do you wish to eat dinner or go to your crib?"), you still exercise control, but *so does your child*. Though Todd's father set the choices, Todd was still able to feel in control of his fate. That's important at 2, as it will be in later years.

There are all sorts of conflict situations where it can be helpful to offer a choice. Suppose your daughter says "No milk!" when you offer her her usual glass of milk with dinner. You can say, "Would you like your milk in this glass tonight, or in a different glass?" Or, "Would you like a big glass of milk tonight, or just a little glass?"

Suppose it's bathtime, and your 2-year-old says "No bath!" You can say, "Would you like your bath right now or in a few minutes?" Or, "It's time for your bath—would you like to take it with your boats today or without them?"

Suppose your child wants to bring his Darth Vader doll to the dinner table (this used to happen to us), and you have a "No toys at the table" rule because toys at the table cause trouble. You can say, "Would you like to put Darth Vader over here on the counter during dinner, or closer to you on the radiator?" (but still out of reach).

You can also offer choices in a way that makes a direct appeal to a 2-year-old's spirit of independence. Suppose your daughter won't get dressed. You can say, "Do you need me to dress you, or can you do it yourself?" Or suppose you're visiting a friend, it's time to leave, and your 2-year-old son, engrossed in playing, says "No go home!" You pick him up and he starts shouting, "Put me down! Put me down!" You can say, "Do I need to carry you, or can you walk with me?"

How does offering choices help a child's moral development?

1. By offering choices, you're avoiding the kind of war of wills that creates tension and undermines mutual respect between parent and child.

2. By defining what the choices are, you're asserting your authority as a parent and teaching your child to respect the limits you set.

3. By giving kids a chance to choose, you're respecting their dignity as persons, their ability to think, and their right to have their wishes considered. By treating them with respect, you help them learn the meaning of respect and to give it in return.

4. You're giving kids practice in making decisions. Multiplied over the years, these decisions will give them the feeling that they really are in charge of their own behavior, *that they always have a choice*. That feeling will serve them well when somebody suggests that they cheat on a test, try some drugs, or join in a little shoplifting.

5. Growing up with choices, a child can learn the importance of respecting other people's right to choose.

As kids grow older, your method of offering choices should change to match their changing level of maturity. Older kids will want more input into the range of choices available. That can be negotiated in a spirit of fairness (see Chapter 13). Even then, you're still exercising your authority as a parent by setting the "outer limits" and by requiring that your kids consider your viewpoint at the same time that you're considering theirs. You're still balancing independence with control.

Offering choices certainly doesn't mean you should never give your child a command. There'll still be lots of times when you need to give a direct order and get compliance to it. If there are many other times when you're giving kids a chance to choose, they'll be more likely to go along when you need them simply to obey you.

Don't offer a choice when it causes more problems than it solves. Says a mother of a 2-year-old:

"I say to my daughter, 'Do you want a peanut butter sandwich for lunch or a baloney?' She says, 'Peanut butter.' When I give her peanut butter, she screams for baloney. Now I simply serve her a sandwich with no discussion of choices. It works a lot better."[1]

This mother discovered that offering a choice at lunch was a needless complication; it created a conflict instead of avoiding one. Deciding between two things, both of which are appealing, can be a very real stress for a 2-year-old. So as a general rule, it's best to keep things simple (especially meals) and not tax a 2 with unnecessary decisions. Save choices for situations where kids are resisting what you want them to do and where a choice is a way out of the conflict. And once kids do make a choice, teach them that they have to stick to it. ("I'm sorry, but you chose peanut butter. It's peanut butter or nothing.")

OTHER WAYS TO STEER CLEAR OF CONFLICTS

Offering choices is one way to respect the independence of young children and to try to avoid a war of wills. Another is to avoid making a statement that is likely to arouse resistance.

Suppose when you say "It's time for dinner," your 2-year-old son responds, "Don't want any dinner!" At that point, you could fall back on offering a choice: "Let's see . . . would you like your dessert right after you finish your dinner tonight, or later, before you go to bed?" But if saying "No!" when he's called to dinner is a pattern with your child, you could try to avoid the conflict in the first place—by not making the "trigger statement." Instead of announcing "It's time for dinner," you could simply pick up your child in a casual way, carry him out to his chair (chatting along the way), sit him down, and begin serving his food.

Another approach is to turn a potential conflict into a challenge. Counting often works like a charm at this age and even with older children. "Let's see if you can get in your chair (the car, the bed, the tub) by the time I count to 10. One, two, three, four . . ." With our kids, counting saved us many a frustrating moment when we were tired or hurried and had no patience with shenanigans.

You can also reduce conflict by giving kids plenty of chances to get the independence "out of their system." Two-year-olds who've been able to run around a playground for an hour are usually easier to deal with, once they've had a moment to settle down, than ones who have been pent up all day.

Personal space is also important to young children. Try giving 2- and 3-year-olds an "office"—a space of their very own behind a sofa or big chair (corners are great). Here they have a private retreat where they can still be close to the action. They can draw there, listen to records, look at books, play with blocks or other toys, or just lie around. They'll feel like a very important person.

USE QUESTIONS TO MAKE KIDS THINK

Two is not too young to begin to use what I call the "ask-don't-tell" method of reasoning with children. Chapter 14 goes into this method in detail and gives lots of examples of how to use it with kids of different ages. Here's an anecdote that shows how the ask-don't-tell principle can help solve conflicts with young children:

> Kevin, age 2½, wanted to go out and play. His mother said that he could, but reminded him of the rule: "You must stay in the driveway. If you go out of the driveway, you have to come in the house."
>
> Five minutes later, Kevin's mother looked out the front door to see him running up the sidewalk. As she escorted a crying Kevin back to the house, she reminded him of the rule: "Kevin, I told you if you went out of the driveway, you'd have to come back in the house!"
>
> As the screen door closed behind him, Kevin wailed through his tears, "I want to go outside!" "No," his mother said firmly, "you may *not* go outside." Whereupon Kevin banged on the door with his fists and cried all the louder, *"I want to go outside!"*

Telling Kevin he had broken the rule and couldn't go outside wasn't helping. It only caused him to protest all the more. Here's where his mother switched from telling Kevin what he had done to *asking him questions.*

> Kevin's mother walked him away from the door. She knelt down to meet him eye to eye and put her hands on his shoulders.
>
> "Kevin," she said softly, "I want to talk with you. When you went outside, where did I say you had to stay?"
>
> "In the driveway," Kevin sniffed.
>
> "And did you stay in the driveway, Kevin?"
>
> "No."

"That's right," his mother said matter-of-factly, "you went up the sidewalk. Now here's a tissue—blow your nose."

Kevin blew his nose, and went off to play indoors.

Why did asking succeed where telling had failed? I think there are three reasons why questions got Kevin to stop crying and accept his fate:

1. Kevin had to *think* about his mother's questions. Questions inhibit crying, because you can't think and cry at the same time!

2. The questions redirected his attention, away from his mother's behavior ("She's making me come in") and toward his own ("I didn't follow the rule").

3. Once he focused on his own behavior, having to stay inside seemed like the logical consequence of breaking the rule instead of an arbitrary punishment by his mother.

Even if questioning doesn't immediately work magic with a young child, it's important to do. It gets kids to think. At the same time you're managing behavior, you're developing moral reasoning. There are double dividends with the questioning method, just as there are with offering choices.

USE DISTRACTION

The sleight-of-hand forms of distraction ("Hey, look at what I've got over here!") won't work with 2-year-olds the way they did with infants and toddlers. Two-year-olds are less distractible because they know their minds better than younger children. But if twos are complaining or crying because they couldn't get what they wanted, you can still bring them out of it by involving them in something else.

You can ask them about something you think they'd like to talk about ("Say, does Daddy know what you did in the backyard today?"). Or you can simply sit down next to them with one of their favorite books and start reading. Chances are they'll stop fussing and start listening.

Storytelling

Young children love to hear homespun stories in which they are the central character, thinly disguised.

I used storytelling with our younger son, Matthew, to stem the protests or tears when the time came to leave a playground, carnival, or other favorite place. I would pick him up, hold him close to me, and begin a story about "Matthew Bebona" while walking to the car. For example:

> Once upon a time, there was a little boy named Matthew Bebona. He loved to go to the carnival and go on the rides. So one day his father and mother took him to the carnival that had come to town. He went on the Merry-Go-Round and the Boat Ride and the Airplane Ride and the Fun House Ride and other rides, too.
>
> But when Daddy Bebona said it was time to go home, Matthew Bebona didn't want to go. He said, "Daddy, can I *please* have just one more ride on the airplanes?" His father said, "I know you would like to go on the airplane ride again, Matthew. But it's time to go home now. It's late, and Mom and I are tired."
>
> Matthew Bebona felt so sad. He cried big tears that rolled down his cheeks and off his chin. His father picked him up, held him in his arms, and carried him to the car. Matthew put his head on his father's shoulder. He began to get sleepier and sleepier . . . and to dream of the time when the carnival would come to town again.

Because I wanted to respond to what Matthew was feeling at the moment, my stories were always about the very situation we were experiencing or something close to it. I found that stories like these cast a soothing spell—until Matthew was about 5. At that age he announced, "I don't want any more Matthew Bebona stories!" He'd give me a look as if to say, "I know what you're up to, Dad. Don't think you're going to fool me with that old Matthew Bebona routine!" My intent hadn't been to "fool" him, of course, but that's how he experienced it at age 5. This is an example of how a method that's a good match for one developmental stage won't necessarily be a good match for a later, more sophisticated stage of development.

If you have a preschooler, try spinning a story about a difficult situation you find yourselves in. Make your child, with a twist on his or her name, the star of the story. Give it a happy ending.

This kind of storytelling has the advantage of giving kids some distance from their own experience of the problem and at the same time acknowledging their feelings through the medium of the story.

A mother told me of how she used a creative variation of this approach. She had taken her 2½-year-old son to the playground one summer evening, and when she said it was time to go home, he insisted on staying. When she insisted on leaving, he began to cry. So she picked him up and began singing a song to him about a little boy who loved to go to the playground so much that he never wanted to leave. That did the trick.

Using stories in this manner is just one more way of trying to respect your child's feelings while simultaneously meeting your own needs.

USE STORIES TO TEACH APPROPRIATE BEHAVIOR

You can also make up stories that teach kids appropriate moral attitudes and behavior.

I recently discovered an inexpensive little book, *When a Story Would Help* ($2.45, Abbey Press), by Lucie W. Barber, that's full of examples of how parents can use homespun stories for a whole variety of purposes. One is to teach a young child cooperative behavior. Here's a story recommended for a 2-year-old who says "No!" when he's asked to pick up his toys:

> Speedy is a little puppy. He has curly golden hair. He has long, soft ears. Speedy loves his mother and father. He feels so good when Mother and Father tell him they are proud of him and that they are happy he belongs to their family.
>
> One day Speedy was having fun playing with his little cars. He had played for a long time. He heard Father say, "Speedy, would you please put your cars away now? It is time for your nap." Speedy started to say, "No, I don't want to put my cars away," when he remembered he liked to hear his father say he was proud of him.
>
> Speedy picked up all his little cars and put them on the shelf. Father said, "Oh, Speedy, you are such a good puppy!" That

made Speedy feel good. Then he heard Father say, "You make me so happy."

"Oh," thought Speedy, "I made Father feel happy, and I feel good, too."[2]

A story like this won't necessarily get a 2-year-old to run right in and pick up his toys; you may have to use other inducements to get behavioral compliance (for example, "Can you pick up your toys, or do you want me to take them away?"). But with retelling (and young children love to hear stories retold), a story can stimulate a child to think about what you want him to do, and why. And offering young kids story characters they can imitate capitalizes on their desire to show that "I can do it, too!"

TIME-OUTS

If you're like most parents, you'll sometimes get to the point where you don't think you can stand your kids' behavior another minute. Nothing seems to be working. That's a good time to use the time-out method that I introduced in the chapter on ones. For example:

Daniel: Bobby won't let me play with the blocks!

Mom: Okay, it looks like you guys need a break from each other right now. So I'm going to call a time-out for 10 minutes. Go to your rooms and find something to do. I'll let you know when the 10 minutes are up.

With kids as young as 2 and 3, you may want to have them take their time-out in a nearby chair where you can keep an eye on them. To help the time pass, you can give them a book to look at or a record to listen to.

Or you can try a "come back when you can behave" time-out:

Roxanne: (screaming at her sister) Gimmee that!

Dad: Okay, time out. Roxanne, go to your room, settle down, and come back when you can ask for something without screaming.

This "conditional" time-out has the advantage of giving kids an incentive to behave. The sooner they decide to shape up, the sooner they can get back into the action. Sometimes, though, kids will come back before they're ready, and in a minute they're at it again. When that happens, you can call for a "fixed" time-out—5, 10, 15 minutes, whatever seems necessary.

Time-outs help parents by giving them a needed break from the sometimes exhausting task of managing kids' behavior. They help kids by giving them the break they sometimes need from each other, and by giving them a chance to calm down and get control of their behavior.

Time-outs also reinforce the idea that if you want to be with other people, you have to play by the rules. And time-outs do all of this without violating the dignity of a child.

RHYMING RULES

Moral development doesn't have to be all serious business. You can introduce a little fun by capitalizing on young kids' love of rhymes. Behavior expectations can be turned into rhyming rules.

Twos don't by nature take very well to rules, but they may learn them and follow them better if they rhyme. You'll also find that it's easier for you to appeal to a rule that rhymes. Somehow, it doesn't seem like something that you made up but more like something that's "out there"—a feature of the world that simply must be accommodated.

Here are three rhyming rules that you can use with twos:

> **If you hit,**
> **You must sit.**

> **Put your dinner**
> **In your tummy**
> **And you will get**
> **A snack that's yummy.**

> **Toys left out**
> **Make parents sad**
> **Toys picked up**
> **Make parents glad.**

Post your rhyming rules where your child can easily see them. With time, a 2-year-old may even get to recognize some of the words in the rhymes. In the meantime, you can read the rule out loud for your child at the appropriate time.

The idea here is to get across the message, "Rules are part of our family," and to *begin* to develop rule-following behavior. (Don't expect too much from a 2-year-old!)

At later stages, kids will have a better understanding of the reasons for rules. When you teach rules at 2, you're laying the foundation. By the time kids do develop an understanding of the fairness and necessity of rules, they'll have some good habits of rule-following behavior going for them.

SPANKING

Should you spank your child? When parents of young children ask questions about child rearing, that's one of the ones that tops the list.

First, let me say why I think you *shouldn't* make spanking a regular means of disciplining your child.

Spanking is physical punishment. Relying on physical punishment is a poor way to foster moral development. For one thing, it provides the wrong kind of example ("This will teach you not to hit your little sister!"). If we want our children to use words instead of force to deal with conflicts, we should try to model that through our own behavior.

Physical punishment, moreover, doesn't foster mutual respect between parent and child. Kids usually resent being hit. It makes them want to get even, not better. Even small children may try to get back at their parents by repeating the very same behavior for which they've just been punished.

Finally, physical punishment doesn't engage or develop a child's mind. It doesn't teach kids *why* what they did was wrong or what they should do instead. It doesn't get them to take the viewpoint of the person they've offended. It leaves them feeling sorry for themselves instead of sorry for their offense. Better moral understanding doesn't come from the palm of the hand.

For all of these reasons, I urge you to use discipline methods, like the ones described in this chapter and the chapter on toddlers, that do set a good example, do foster mutual respect between parent and child, and do engage and develop a child's moral understanding. If you practice these methods—and practice is what it takes to make them your own—you'll have a repertoire of things you can do other than spanking to manage your child's behavior.

Does that mean you should never spank kids? Are there any arguments that can be made for *occasionally* spanking a young child? I believe there are.

1. **Spanking is an assertion of a parent's authority, which is better than no assertion at all.** Spanking is usually not the *best* way to assert your authority. I've described lots of other ways that are both more effective in the short run and better for long-range moral development. But if a child defies a parent or wallops a playmate, I'd rather see the parent apply a swat to the rear than stand there and do nothing at all. Doing nothing teaches a child that there may be rules, but nothing happens if you break them.

2. **A spank can supply the "jolt" that sometimes brings a child out of a pattern of surly or defiant behavior.** Sometimes a spank has the effect of a bucket of cold water. Once in a while with a 2-year-old, that shock effect may be needed to interrupt an undesirable behavior pattern that has gathered momentum and is not responding to other methods.

3. **Spanking may help you.** Cartoons of parents spanking kids used to be captioned, "This hurts me more than it hurts you." Now parents know that spanking usually helps them more than it helps their child. It can function as a safety valve that relieves a parent's mounting tension and clears the air. One study found that parents who *occasionally* spank their children do not nag or yell at them as much as parents who never spank. So in that indirect way, spanking does help children.

4. **Spanking may succeed in controlling a particular behavior.** Spanking may modify a child's behavior. If it's not used to often, it can give a child dramatic feedback. That feedback can act like "avoidance conditioning" to prevent kids from repeating the behavior. You're letting them know that what they've done cannot be tolerated, ever again.

Many parents, for example, spank their children for running out into the road. They have good cause for concern: Every day, six children in the United States are killed because they dart out in front of cars. Some parents also spank if a child bites, in the belief that biting, too, calls for dramatic consequences. So in cases where the repetition of your child's behavior is intolerable, spanking is the lesser of the evils.

The danger with spanking is not that an occasional whack on the bottom will harm a child's psyche, destroy mutual respect, or impede a child's moral development. *The danger is that spanking can easily get to be a habit, a first response.* Then it has diminishing returns and potentially negative effects on your child's moral development.

HOW TO KEEP SPANKING UNDER CONTROL

Parents need limits as well as kids. I urge you to put these limits on your use of spanking:

1. Except in rare cases like the running-in-the-road situation, try something else first. You can ask a question, appeal to a rule, impose an isolation, or offer a choice. If you offer a choice, a spank can be one of the alternatives. For example: "Do you need a spank to get into bed, or can you get in without one?"

2. If you spanked because you blew your stack and you know you should have tried something else first, apologize to your child. You'll feel better, and so will your child.

3. When you feel you must spank, try to make do with a single swat. That should get the message across. Even in special cases like the running-in-the-road example, 3 or 4 spanks should be the maximum. Put yourself in your child's pants.

4. Never hit with anything harder than the open hand.

5. As a general rule, don't spank kids much younger than 2 or older than 4. Use spanking less and less as your child approaches 5.

6. Make it a goal never to spank. That way you'll end up spanking no more than you should.[3]

TOILET TRAINING

Toilet training is a major task—at times it will seem like *the* task*—for both parents and children during this developmental period. For good advice about how to go about it, I refer you to Dr. Spock's *Baby and Child Care* and Dr. Fitzhugh Dodson's *How to Parent*.

The main thing is to keep from getting too uptight (*some* exasperation is unavoidable) and to keep punishment out of the picture. Punishment produces anxiety, and that won't help you get the desired results. Ask other parents about their experience with toilet training. Try to bring the same sympathetic understanding of your child's level of development to this task that you bring to the rest of your relationship. Respect your 2-year-old as a person, and try to minimize conflict. With time and patience, you'll clear this hurdle, too.

CHAPTER 5

THREES:
FROM BREAKING AWAY
TO GOING ALONG

The good news about the threes is that they're easier than the twos.

All of the developmental discipline methods you began to use with twos can still be used with threes. The only difference is, you should find everything less of a struggle.

Threes will certainly have their moments of stubborn independence, and that's a healthy sign of self-assertion, just as it was at 2. But there's a new spirit of wanting to please at 3 that begins to show up in all sorts of ways:

- Threes are more obedient, more responsive to the spoken word. Dr. Arnold Gesell writes of the 3-year-old: "Sometimes a single word spoken by his mother instantaneously reorganizes his whole stream of activity, with startling suddenness."[1]
- Threes are easier to reason with.
- Threes will sometimes ask permission before they do something ("Is it okay if I have a cookie?").
- Threes may ask, "Did I do it right?" because they want to conform to your expectations.
- Threes are generally willing to help out when asked.

What happened to your resisting and rebellious 2-year-old? How did this responsive and cooperative 3-year-old emerge on the scene?

To throw light on this mysterious metamorphosis, I'd like to bring in a bit of developmental theory which I think helps us understand human development at any age.

TWO GREAT HUMAN LONGINGS

This theory is the work of Dr. Robert Kegan, a Harvard University psychologist who has studied the development of "ego" (the sense of self). Kegan identifies two great human longings. "We see their expression everywhere," he writes, "in ourselves and in those we know, in small children and in mature adults, in cultures East and West, modern and traditional."[2]

One longing is the need to be *independent*. Part of that need is wanting to be recognized as a distinct, individual person. We don't want to be swallowed up, taken for granted, or treated as an extension of somebody else.

Another part of independence is wanting to feel in control of our lives. We don't want to feel bossed around or helplessly dependent on somebody else.

We need recognition of our individuality and a sense of being in control in order to feel good about ourselves. We want to be able to say to the world and to ourselves, "Hey, I'm my own person! I'm in charge of my life!" All of this is an expression of the need to be independent.

But it's not enough to be independent. There's another human yearning deep down in our souls. It's the need to be *included*.

All of us want to be accepted, liked, and loved. We want to belong. We want to have relationships. We want to be part of something larger than ourselves. We want to be part of the human community.

We want to be able to say to the world and to ourselves, "Other people appreciate me, care about me, need me. I matter to somebody else."

So those are two rock-bottom, terribly important needs that you'll find in little kids and in grown-ups wherever you look.

The need to be independent.

The need to be included.

These two great human needs, Kegan says, are reflected in two basic developmental processes that virtually all developmental psychologists recognize: "differentiation" and "integration."

Differentiation is the process by which we make ourselves *different from* our environment. It's the process by which we separate ourselves from others, stand apart, assert our individuality.

Integration, by contrast, is the process by which we're *integrated into* our social environment. It's the process by which we make connections with other people, form relationships, become more fully a member of the human family.

Both of these processes—differentiation and integration—go on to some degree at every stage of human development. That's because both needs are always present.

But at different stages, Kegan points out, one or the other process is dominant. In any period of growth, we're either preoccupied with developing our individuality (often through new achievements) or preoccupied with developing our relationships. You can no doubt think of periods in your own life when this has been true.

"Differentiators" Are Hard to Live With

Now, what happens when differentiation is dominant? When the developing person is mainly concerned with establishing his or her identity as an individual?

There tends to be more friction between the individual and the social environment.

Think of the adult relationships you know, between men and women, for example. People who are investing a lot of psychic energy in differentiating themselves, in asserting their individuality, tend to be harder to get along with. They're not in a "going along with" frame of mind. They're busy "breaking away."

That's exactly what happens with 2-year-olds. Through all their assertions of independence, twos are breaking away from the old relationships of an earlier period. It's as if they're saying, "I'm not your baby anymore!" They're behaving like the 15-year-old daughter who says to her father, "I'm not your little girl anymore!"

Once that task of differentiation is accomplished, however,

twos can take a deep breath and say to themselves, "Whew, I made it! I'm a new person, and Mommy and Daddy still love me. Guess I can relax a little."

FROM TWO TO THREE: JOINING THE WORLD A LITTLE MORE

From their new position of balance, with their hard-won independence secure, kids are able to venture out again. Only now the developmental task is integration.

Children are now ready to join the world a little more. Having become their own person, they're ready to become more a part of other persons. Having laid down the guns of independence, they're able to build new alliances.

So threes, by and large, exchange the role of rebels for the role of joiners. It's not an all-at-once transformation, of course. Developmental transitions always take time and lots of interactions between kids and their environment. But one day it will dawn on you that you have this civilized little person living in your house instead of your cantankerous 2-year-old.

How can you foster moral development during this relatively cooperative period?

TEACH MANNERS

You can start to teach "please" and "thank you" to children as young as 2, but 3-year-olds' desire to please makes them more receptive to learning simple courtesies (though for many years they'll need reminders to carry them out).

Manners will gradually become important to children only if they are important to their parents. For quite a while, unfortunately, manners among adults have been in a state of decline. We encounter more rudeness almost everywhere: in stores, in lines, on the job, on the road. I think this is partly because somewhere along the way, people got it in their heads that manners weren't important. So they stopped stressing good manners with their children and stopped practicing good manners themselves.

The fact is, however, that *manners are morals*.[3] They're ways of respecting other people. Saying please when we'd like something, thanking people (waitresses, for example) when they do us a service, waiting to speak instead of interrupting, holding a door instead of letting it slam in the face of the person behind us, eating with grace, cleaning up after ourselves, using language that doesn't offend—all these are small but important ways of trying to make life a little more pleasant for the people around us.

So I'd urge you to start manners training early. Explain to kids that good manners make other people feel good. Show them good manners, and give them plenty of praise when they remember their manners (don't just point out when they forget). If you can get kids learning and practicing simple good manners when they're at this eager-to-please stage, you'll have something to build on at later stages when the forces of independence are back in the saddle.

THE HABIT OF HELPING

Three is also a good age to develop the habit of helping and to get kids to begin to see themselves as contributing members of the family.

There are lots of little jobs that threes can manage or at least help out with: picking up toys, emptying wastebaskets, setting and clearing the table, making the orange juice, adding or stirring ingredients for something you're cooking, or caring for a younger brother or sister. Here's a mother who describes how she involves her 3-year-old along with her other children in sharing the work of the family:

> "I expect my children to help around the house. Ever since they've been able to walk, I've made them pick up most of their toys. When we found we were expecting another baby, I explained to them that I would be very busy with the baby and I would need their help. My 3-year-old brings the wash downstairs every day and gets diapers, etc., for me when I need them. He feels good about helping and being a part of the family. And he also understands that by helping me do things around the house, he gives me more time to do things with him."

RULES AND LABELS AT THREE

Whereas twos resisted rules, threes are much more disposed to go along with them, and may even take a certain pleasure in learning them. The rhyming rules I described in Chapter 4 can be a hit at this age. Here are a couple more:

Help keep our house Neat as a pin Hang up your coat When you come in.

When you get up From the table Please take out What you are able.

Threes also take satisfaction in learning to apply moral labels—"good," "bad," "naughty," "nice"—to their world. Read them stories in which there's mischief or villainy, and ask them who did the naughty things. They'll delight in pointing out the misdeeds of the fox in *Pinocchio* or the wolf in *Little Red Riding Hood*. One 3-year-old said solemnly that Bugs Bunny was "*very bad*" for stealing the carrots out of Elmer Fudd's garden. Another announced to his family that *King Kong* was a "very naughty movie—too much violence!"

Because kids are fascinated with moral labels during this period, they're more responsive to them when they're applied to their own behavior. It means a lot to 3-year-olds to hear that they "did something nice for Mommy" or were "a big help to Daddy." You may be able to encourage sharing or generosity in your 3-year-old by saying, "Here's a chance to be a *generous* person" (explaining what "generous" means). Or you can encourage taking turns by saying, "Here's a chance to show you know how to be a *fair* person."

Don't abuse this power of labeling, however. If you tell kids, for example, that they're a "bad boy" or a "bad girl," you run the risk of negatively affecting their self-concept. They may begin to live *down* to the bad-person role that you've assigned them. When your child misbehaves, stick to labeling *actions*:

"Hitting is naughty! It hurts!" "It's not fair to grab someone's toy!"

THREES AND PEER INTERACTION

Talking and playing with other kids is important for children at any age, but it's especially so for threes. Threes are better able to share, better able to make friends, better able to enter into truly cooperative play. They really enjoy, and need, companions.

Even though threes are more mature than twos in their social play, they still have a long way to go. They still often have trouble incorporating what somebody else wants to do into their plan of action. By playing with other kids, they're able to learn and relearn important moral lessons. They learn that they can't always have their own way. They learn that if they don't share with others, others won't share with them. They learn that if they hit people, people hit back. They learn that if they don't "play nice" with other kids, other kids won't want to play with them. These are lessons kids learn best from each other, not from us. So make sure your youngster has plenty of chances for peer interaction at this and later stages.

DON'T OVERESTIMATE THREES

Because threes are so much more sociable and cooperative than twos, it would be easy to overestimate them. Keep in mind that even though they've matured in a lot of ways, they're still very young children. Three-year-olds:

- May still have temper tantrums (though they come out of them more quickly than they did at 2);
- May react to frustration by making violent attacks against a physical object like a chair or toy;
- May react with acute insecurity and jealousy to the arrival of a baby brother or sister.

Threes are still very limited in their ability to put themselves in somebody else's shoes. You know this if you've ever played hide-and-seek with 3-year-olds. They usually "hide" by covering their eyes and leaving much or all of themselves in clear view!

I once came upon a 3-year-old in nursery school who was looking at slides in a Viewmaster. "You want to see this one?" he said to me. When I said I did, he inserted the slide disc into the viewer, held it up to *his* eyes, and said, "Look at that!"

So make allowances for the lapses and developmental limitations of threes and don't have unrealistic expectations.

We've looked at the beginnings of moral development in the bond of love that forms between you and your child in infancy.

We've looked at the first step toward independence that your child takes in toddlerhood.

We've looked at how that independence comes into full and furious bloom in the twos, and at how it gradually gives way to greater accommodation in the threes.

We've looked at how you can avoid and manage conflict, maintain a loving relationship, and foster your child's moral development during all of these periods.

All of this growth has been leading up to a new period in moral development: the stages of moral reasoning. These are the stages that describe moral growth not only in children but also in teenagers and young adults.

Let's turn now to these next crucial stages of human development and what you can do to help your children through them.

PART 3

HOW TO HELP YOUR CHILD THROUGH THE STAGES OF MORAL REASONING . . . FROM PRESCHOOL TO ADULTHOOD

CHAPTER 6

STAGE 0:
"WHATEVER I WANT IS
WHAT'S FAIR!"

When David was 4½, his parents got him a new set of blocks for Christmas. Soon after he got them, he recruited his 8-year-old brother, Peter, to build blocks with him. All was peaceful for about five minutes, and then David let out a scream. His father went to investigate.

"Peter's not being *fair*!" David cried. "He's not connecting his building with mine!"

Peter was building a structure next to David's but had not linked the two together as David desired. David's father asked him, "Why do you say Peter's not being fair?"

"He's not doing what I *want* him to!" David said. "Peter, you ruined the whole thing!"

"Gee, David," his father said, "that's not what being fair means. You can't call somebody unfair just because they don't do what you want them to all the time."

"Well," said David, unpersuaded, "he's not being fair!"

His father gave it another try. "What if Peter wanted *you* to build a different kind of a building and you didn't want to? Would you want him to say that *you* weren't being fair?"

"I wouldn't build that kind of a building," David said, and he continued to complain about Peter's being unfair.

Parents who have lived with a 4-year-old will recognize David's moral logic. He has a strong sense of fairness, all right. But to him, being "fair" means getting what *he* wants. Anything else in unfair. So firmly does he believe in this definition of fairness

A PROFILE OF STAGE 0

At Stage 0 of moral reasoning, kids:

1. Begin to express their independence in moral terms ("It's not fair!"), but think "fair" means getting their way.

2. Are highly egocentric, especially in conflict situations, seeing things only from their point of view.

3. Take an "I want it, it's mine" approach to property.

4. Do everything they can to try to make the world conform to their wishes, including manipulating parents, telling "lies," and "cheating" at games, without understanding why these behaviors are wrong.

5. Often break rules, show off, use bad language, or engage in other provocative, out-of-bounds behavior, all as part of a pattern of experimentation and self-assertion.

6. Can, like children at other moral stages, understand moral reasoning that is at a higher level than the reasoning they can produce on their own.

7. May show spontaneous helping or compassion in situations where their desires don't conflict with someone else's.

8. Show individual differences in social-moral behavior that reflect differences in kids' total moral personality.

that his father's appeals to a broader idea of fairness fall on deaf ears.

David is at "Stage 0" of moral reasoning. You can expect Stage 0 to emerge sometime between 3½ and 4. In many ways, it looks like a regression. Parents may wonder, "What happened to my cooperative 3-year-old? Is this a rerun of the terrible twos?"

Stage 0 *is* a lot like the twos. Once again, the sense of "I" is much stronger than the sense of "we." Once more, the pendulum is swinging toward differentiation, toward independence. Only now kids experience and express their independence in moral terms. Twos say "I want it." Stage 0 kids reason, "I want it, therefore it's not *fair* if I don't get it!"

That may not seem like developmental progress, but it is. Children at Stage 0 are now seeing and talking about their desires from a moral viewpoint. It's a very primitive, self-centered viewpoint, to be sure. But it's part of the long developmental process of learning to think morally, learning to reason about questions of fairness and unfairness, right and wrong.

In a way, "Stage 0" is a misnomer. It implies that there's no moral development, no sense of rules or right and wrong, before this stage. That's just not so. As we've already seen, children younger than 3½ can begin to use the categories of good and bad to organize their social world. They begin to label things right and wrong, naughty and nice. And, at least some of the time, they act accordingly.

But once kids start to be moral philosophers, once they begin to do their *own* reasoning about what's fair, they focus exclusively on what they know best: their own desires. And from the standpoint of moral reasoning, that's Stage 0.

With that introduction, let's look at the specific characteristics of Stage 0 and how to deal with them.

EGOCENTRISM

Stage 0 is called the stage of "egocentric reasoning" because kids at this developmental level recognize one point of view: their own. It's not that they deliberately ignore other people's viewpoints. Other points of view just don't penetrate their awareness.

Sometimes Stage 0 kids are so openly egocentric that you have to laugh. When our younger son, Matthew, was 4, I used to take him and one of his pals swimming at the local YMCA when my back hurt from too much time at the typewriter. It was a good way to have fun with them and loosen up my back muscles at the same time. Once when we got home, Matthew said cheerfully,

"It's a good thing you hurt your back, Dad, so we can go swimming at the Y!"

It helps to remember that Stage 0 kids aren't being egocentric out of meanness. Egocentrism is just the nature of the beast at this stage.

"WHAT'S YOURS IS MINE!"

There's no clearer evidence of the egocentrism of Stage 0 thinkers than their approach to property rights. At this stage, possession is 100 percent of the law. Once you get your hands on something you want, it's yours. That's why nursery school teachers often check pockets before kids leave at the end of the day!

As an example of Stage 0's thinking about property, consider the following conversation between 5½-year-old Billy and his father:

Dad: How'd school go today?

Billy: Jason and I got into an argument.

Dad: What about?

Billy: On the way to school I found this little wooden thing—a stick, sort of—with carvings on it. When Jason saw it, he said it was his.

Dad: Hmmm, I see. Well, how did you solve that problem?

Billy: (shrugging shoulders) I wanted the stick, so I kept it.

The father should insist, of course, that if the stick is Jason's, Billy should return it. (Finding out if the stick really is Jason's may require a call to his parents.) But the father shouldn't think he's got a confirmed thief and a potential juvenile delinquent on his hands. Billy's casual "I want it, it's mine" logic is par for the course at Stage 0.

Remembering that Stage 0 usually begins at 3½ to 4, you may wonder if it's unusual for a child to still be using Stage 0 thinking at 5½, as Billy did. It's not. First of all, a stage of moral reasoning often takes more than a year to give way to a new dominant stage (and the higher the stage, the slower the change). In the second place, as I pointed out in Chapter 1, kids can slip back to lower stages even after they have the ability to use higher ones. Billy might have developed some Stage 1, obedience-oriented reasoning, but still fall into Stage 0 reasoning in certain situations, especially those where his self-interest is strongly involved.

If Billy were using *mostly* Stage 0 at age 5½, he'd be developmentally behind most of his peers. And that brings up a point that I'd like to emphasize here. Depending on their intelligence and social experience, kids differ considerably in the rate at which they move through these stages of moral reasoning. Some kids may take as much as several years longer than the average child to reach a particular stage.

Tommy, a hyperactive and very aggressive 8-year-old from a "chaotic" family background, is an example of a child whose moral development was severely delayed. His therapist, Dr. Robert Selman, describes his behavior:

> "During our diagnostic sessions, Tommy would come into my office and insist that I buy him a present or give him one of the toys in the office. When I refused or was unable to meet his request, he became furious.
>
> "Similarly, if the teacher of Tommy's special class did not pay extra attention to him, he would sulk and claim that she hated him. When he discovered her home phone number, he began to call her up at 6:00 A.M. on weekdays and on Sundays in a pathetic effort to gain more individual attention.
>
> "In addition to suffering from powerful affective needs and tragic desperation, Tommy lagged at Stage 0 at an age when most children are in transition between Stages 1 and 2. In the moral domain, Tommy's justification for the judgment, 'I should get X,' was 'Because I want it.' Good was what he wanted; bad was what he did not want."[1]

Effective therapy for Tommy meant changing his social environment. He was enrolled in a special summer camp where the counselors continually emphasized the reasons behind rules and the motives behind the actions of counselors and other campers. Gradually Tommy came to understand the expectations of others and to comprehend social situations. By the end of the summer camp experience, he had grown out of Stage 0 thinking and had won the friendship of many of the children in his cabin.

Tommy is an extreme case, but the lessons from his experience have wider applicability. All children, even those who are not lagging in their social-moral development, benefit from having consistent rules, having the reasons for those rules clearly explained, and having the motives of others made known, all in a caring and supportive environment. These experiences are very important in helping kids move beyond the moral reasoning of Stage 0.

STAGE 0 AND MANIPULATION

Stage 0 kids tend to be manipulators. Sometimes it's subtle. A single-parent mother of an aggressive, hard-to-manage 6-year-old said to me:

> "I try to reason with Alex. I get out maybe a sentence or less, and he's going like this (looking off in a spaced-out sort of way). So I stop. It's hard to go on when you don't have an audience. He just doesn't seem to have much of an attention span."

Observation of Alex in other situations indicated that his attention span was fine. He could attend when he wanted to. Looking away from his mother when she tried to reason with him was his way of getting her to stop saying something he didn't want to hear. Alex did the same sort of thing, only more blatantly, with other children. When a playmate said to him, for example, "You're not being fair! You're supposed to take turns!" Alex would put his hands over his ears.

Unlike younger Stage 0 children (fours, for example), Alex has developed to the point where he's quite aware that other people have viewpoints that may differ from his own; he just doesn't want to deal with them. He seemed determined *not* to give up his Stage 0 view of the world as a place where he could always have his way. Part of his problem was his insecurity; his father lived far away at an age when Alex very much needed a father as a role model, disciplinarian, and source of encouragement. Emotional insecurity often has the effect of slowing down moral development, because development requires openness to change, letting go of an old and comfortable way of confronting your world and taking on a new one. Under the circumstances, Alex's mother would be realistic to expect at least a temporary slowing down of his social-moral growth (Alex's intellectual development, by contrast, appeared to be above normal). She could help Alex both by giving him lots of love and by applying gentle but steady pressure for him to open his mind to the views and needs of others. When she sat him down to talk, for example, she could say:

> "Look, Alex, this can be a short discussion if you listen to me and show me you understand what I'm saying. Or it can be a long discussion. You decide."

"I SHOULD HAVE TOLD A LIE!"

One of the ways a Stage 0 child tries to manipulate situations is to lie. Lying is common and developmentally normal behavior among preschoolers, and at this stage it's morally innocent.

Preschoolers typically tell two kinds of lies. The first are tall tales. When children concoct a story or exaggerate the truth, they're often telling us what they *wish* were true. We should respond accordingly, acknowledging the wish behind their statement. So if a young child says, "I jumped 10 feet high at nursery school today!" we can say, "You *wish* you could jump 10 feet high, don't you? You wish you could jump right over the school!"

A father of a 4½-year-old girl came up with a clever way to deal with his daughter's fanciful fabrications. He explained to her the difference between a "true-true story" (one that's really true) and a "true-false story" (one that you wish were true but really isn't). Then, when he suspected she was making something up, he'd say, "Is this a true-true story or a true-false story?" and she would usually admit that it was the latter.

The other kind of untruth that young kids tell is an "instrumental" lie. Kids tell instrumental lies for the same reason adults do—to gain a good result or avoid a bad one. But since Stage 0 reasoners equate fairness with getting what they want, they don't see anything wrong with telling a lie to achieve that end! A mother told me of how she promised her 3½-year-old daughter, Sara, a small candy treat if she was dry at the end of her nap. The babysitter informed the mother that Sara was in fact wet when she got up, but when Sara saw her mother she ran up to her and said sweetly, "I was dry, Mommy! Can I have my candy?"

One morning when Matthew was 4, I found him still in his underwear 15 minutes after I'd reminded him to get dressed for school. Spying an open comic on the floor, I said, "Matthew, have you been reading a comic?" He admitted he had. "Well," I scolded, "you *should* have been getting dressed as I asked you to!" "Hmmm," he said, "I should have told a lie!" It obviously didn't occur to him that I would frown upon lying as a way out of his predicament.

We can and should tell our preschoolers that it's important to tell the truth and that it makes us happy when they do. We should register our disapproval of lies told to evade responsibility or to place the blame on someone else. But we shouldn't overreact. We should remember that Stage 0 kids don't yet grasp why lying is wrong. For them, lying is just one more way they try to make reality conform to their wishes, one more way they use their developing intelligence to try to control their world.

OUT-OF-BOUNDS BEHAVIOR

A lot of the difficult behavior of Stage 0 kids is anything *but* subtle. Much of it, especially around age 4, is outlandishly provocative.

A mother of a 4-year-old boy, a woman who considers herself a very neat housekeeper, told me of her utter consternation when she discovered her son and his best friend in their game room, peeing against the wall! Another mother described her disbelief when she found her 4-year-old and his friends jumping off the hood of their brand-new car.

A grandmother wrote to an advice column to describe the disconcerting change in her 4-year-old granddaughter. Formerly a well-behaved child, she had taken to "showing off terribly" whenever there was company—posturing, dancing around, and even swearing.[2] A father told me of a time when he had a colleague to the house for dinner and his 4-year-old son ran naked from the bathroom shouting gleefully, "I'm gonna pee on you, Dad!"

You may be lucky enough to escape the wilder forms of showing off and out-of-bounds behavior at this exuberant stage. But if you're not, be assured that they're within the range of what's normal.

Be aware, however, that unmanageable behavior can be caused by many factors, not just developmental change. Lots of times kids misbehave because we unwittingly reward them for doing so—by giving in to whining or temper, for example. Some children's misbehavior reflects distress over a change in their lives (a divorce, for example), or a bid for love and attention, and you'll need to deal with those underlying causes. Some children are constitutionally hyperactive, and you'll want to consult your pediatrician if you suspect that. Other children's hard-to-control conduct seems to be linked to diet. Some kids, for example, seem to get "hyper" when they eat too much sugar. One mother said she couldn't get her 4-year-old to calm down and go to sleep at night until she stopped feeding him a big bowl of ice cream right before bed!

So be sensitive to the many causes of children's difficult-to-manage behavior, but expect a certain amount of trouble at this stage as a natural by-product of development.

HOW TO RELATE TO YOUR CHILD'S MORAL STAGE

In Chapter 1, I pointed out that there are two basic ways you can relate to your child's stage of moral reasoning: (1) You can go with the flow of your child's stage, or (2) You can challenge it.

When you go with the flow of kids' present stage of reasoning, you meet them where they are. You come down to their level. You try to get their cooperation by talking the language of their stage, by fitting into the way they think about the world.

When you challenge kids' present stage of reasoning, you try to get them to look at the world in a new way. You make them work at the cutting edge of their minds. You make them reach and stretch.

Both approaches—going with the flow and challenging—are essential. When you go with the flow, you're accepting kids for what they are and helping them use the reasoning they've got. When you challenge them, you're helping them develop better reasoning and grow toward the next stage of moral development. If we were always challenging our kids to develop, we'd wear them out and ourselves, too. If we were always accommodating to their level, they'd have no reason to develop. Why should a kid change his way of looking at the world if his present way is working just fine? So both challenge and accommodation are needed.

Let's look at the ways you can use both of these approaches at Stage 0.

HOW TO GO WITH THE FLOW AT STAGE 0

Take a Developmental Perspective

This is always the first rule for coping with a difficult stage: remember that it *is* a stage, and it won't last forever! Kids won't always be as egocentric and as out-of-bounds as they are at Stage 0.

Offer Choices When Appropriate

Stage 0 kids, like 2-year-olds, tend to be very strong-willed because they're so centered on what *they* want to do. So another way to go with the flow is to try to avoid an unnecessary clash of wills by offering appropriate choices. For example:

"Tonight is bath night. Would you like to take your bath before dinner or after dinner?"

"Would you guys like to play nicely or go to separate rooms?"

When you give choices within limits, you're letting your child make a decision. And that's a way of accommodating to the spirit of independence at Stage 0.

Offer Positive Incentives

We know that self-interest never runs stronger than it does at Stage 0. So kids at this level are more likely to follow rules and requests if there's something in it for them. (That's true to some extent of human beings at any level, of course, but it's *especially* true of kids at Stage 0.) You can meet them at their level by giving them a positive incentive for obeying. For example:

"When you're done picking up, you can go outside."

"When you finish your dinner, you can have your dessert."

"If you get your pajamas on and your teeth brushed in 15 minutes, I'll read you a bedtime story." (If you have a timer on your oven, you can have your child set it for the allotted time.)

Positive incentives, of course, can also be used to motivate cooperation in older kids. Our younger son is now 9, and I still say things like, "If you're ready for bed by eight-thirty, we'll have time for bedtime reading." What changes as kids develop, as we'll see in later chapters, is that you can make other, higher-stage appeals as well.

I recommend that, as much as possible, you use "natural rewards" for good behavior—things you'd be likely to do for or give to your child in the natural course of events. Allowing your child to choose a favorite breakfast or dinner, or a favorite outing or other activity you do together, is a better reward than "extras" like toys, money, or candy. Natural rewards are less like "bribery," more like a matter-of-fact statement, "If you help us by doing what you're asked, life will be more pleasant for you."

Have Fun Together

Whenever kids' independence is running strong, it's important (and a real challenge!) not to let your whole relationship turn into a struggle to control their behavior. One of the best ways to go with the flow of kids during the Stage 0 period is to take time to enjoy them. Do things that are fun for both of you—whether that means a romp on the playground, getting down on the floor for "imagination play" (let your child show you what to do), playing tag or hide-and-go-seek in the yard, or curling up together with a book. These happy shared times will give both you and your child good feelings, and will help you get through the inevitable hard times.

HOW TO CHALLENGE STAGE 0 KIDS

Reaffirm Old Limits, Teach New Ones

The first and most important way to challenge the reasoning of Stage 0 is to reaffirm old limits and teach new ones as needed.

To see why it's very important to set and enforce limits with Stage 0 kids, try to get inside their minds. What's going on there? They're testing a theory (a stage of reasoning) about how the world works. They're asking themselves, "Is the world really a place where I can get anything I want?" At Stage 0, kids think the world *should* be that kind of a place! Progress beyond Stage 0 requires that this theory be disconfirmed. They need to find out that the world is a place where they *can't* have everything they want, where there are rules they have to obey and consequences if they don't.

As a family counselor I've seen parents who didn't exercise control over an out-of-bounds Stage 0 child, and their child became a tyrant. One mother said she was very concerned about whether her 4-year-old son, Jonathan, was "normal." She described these behaviors:

1. Throwing temper tantrums when it was time to go to bed or nursery school;
2. Demanding that his mother be with him constantly, even that she sit on the edge of the tub when he took a bath;
3. Refusing to eat at mealtimes but raiding the cupboards for between-meal snacks;
4. Tearing up papers and destroying toys around the house;
5. Minding his father but not his mother;
6. Behaving "like an angel" when his mother took him to see a psychologist.

The mother acknowledged that she and her husband were not firm or consistent with Jonathan. When her husband scolded him, she would comfort him. When she scolded Jonathan, her husband would comfort him. When Jonathan screamed about going to bed, they let him sleep with them. Most recently, the mother said, Jonathan's behaviors included dumping the contents of the salt and pepper shakers on a restaurant floor, swearing at the waitress, locking himself in the bathroom, and kicking his Uncle George in the shins.

Was Jonathan a normal 4-year-old? He certainly was—in the sense that he kept testing the limits and trying to manipulate his social world. His abnormally obnoxious behavior came at least partly from the fact that his parents set no firm limits and allowed themselves to be constantly manipulated by him. Jonathan desperately needed to experience structure and expectations from the people in his life.

What could Jonathan's parents do differently? I'd recommend the following four steps, which illustrate a procedure that can help any parents who are having behavior problems with their young child:

1. **Sit down together for a parent conference.**

   Make a list of the behaviors Jonathan engages in that you definitely don't want to encourage and ideally would like to eliminate. (A lot of discipline problems can be traced to the fact that parents do not *get together* and agree upon a set of expectations for their children.)

2. **For each undesirable behavior, establish a rule or rules.**

   The rules should be reasonable and should spell out clearly what's expected of Jonathan, and what happens if he doesn't meet the expectation.

   Next to each rule, write the *reason* for the rule. (I've illustrated this rules-and-reasons list on page 104, using some of Jonathan's behavior problems as examples. Other undesirable behaviors can be handled in the same way.)

3. **Sit down with Jonathan (both parents) and go over the list.**

   This way your changed behavior won't come as any surprise to Jonathan. He'll have the big picture. He'll get the message (even if he doesn't fully believe it yet) that you expect things to be different, that you intend to take charge.

   Ask him to repeat each rule and the reason for it. That way he'll know exactly what you expect of him and why you expect it.

RULES AND REASONS LIST

The Behavior We'd Like to Change	Rule(s)	Reason
1. Screaming at bedtime; demanding to sleep in our bed	1. You must sleep in your own bed. 2. If you scream, we'll have to close your door.	1. Four-year-old boys sleep in their own beds, not in their parents'. 2. We don't like to listen to screaming.
2. Not eating at meals; snacking in between	1. Snacks are allowed at two times only: • When you come home from nursery school, if you've eaten your breakfast and lunch; • At bedtime, if you've cleaned your dinner plate (including vegetables).	1. Snacks are treats. They come *after* you've given your body the nutritious meals it needs to stay healthy and grow.
3. Destroying things	1. If you destroy a toy, you lose all your toys for a week.	1. Toys are not for breaking. If you want to have toys, you have to show that you can use them for playing, not breaking.

Post the Rules and Reasons list where you can easily refer to it.

4. Enforce the rules.

Jonathan, like other children at this and even later stages, will try to get around rules even after they've been clearly established. He'll try to get you to make exceptions right off the bat. He'll plead for "one more chance" when he breaks a rule.

Here's where it's crucial to be firm, keeping in mind that you're helping your child and yourself by following through on what you say. The first few times you do this you may feel like an old meanie, but that feeling will pass.

For example: The *first* time Jonathan destroys a toy, follow through on the consequences. Don't wait for the second toy.

Or take the bedtime example. When you put him in, ask him to tell you the rules about bedtime and the reasons for them. Help him if he has trouble remembering. Then give him a kiss good night, and leave.

If he screams, close the door in accordance with the rule you've just reviewed with him. (He can have a night light—the idea is to help him develop, not to scare him.) *Don't go back*, no matter how much carrying on he does (and, just like younger children, he'll probably do plenty the first time). If you enforce the rule firmly, immediately, and consistently, he'll learn to obey it.

"Dirty" Talk and Swearing

The language of Stage 0 kids is another area that often needs controlling.

Kids at this stage are experimenting with language, trying out things with words that they've never done before. That often includes "dirty" words and "dirty" jokes, which are also a sign of an emerging sense of humor. I've watched two 5-year-olds, for example, repeatedly dissolve into fits of laughter as they called each other "poo-poo face" and shrieked warnings that "a gigantic lady is going to catch you and poop all over your head!" They kept this up for weeks! The father of one of them handled limit-setting for this kind of behavior in a sensible way: "If you guys want to talk like that when you're alone, okay, but don't do it around me!"

How should you handle outright swearing? Parents are usually shocked when they first hear curse words or vulgar language coming from the mouth of their angelic-looking preschooler (sometimes as young as 2), but it's all part of verbal experimentation. That doesn't mean you should accept it, however, and I *don't* agree with the oft-heard advice that you should just ignore bad language and it will go away. It's true that kids are usually doing it for attention, but there are two problems with the "ignore it" approach:

1. It's almost impossible to *completely* ignore such provocative behavior, especially under circumstances where it's embarrassing. If you're talking with your neighbor and your 3-year-

old daughter says, "Oh, shit!", you're going to make some kind of reaction, even if it's only gritting your teeth! And be assured, your child will notice!

2. Ignoring bad language deprives kids of something they very much need for their moral development: clear social feedback when their behavior is inappropriate.

Kids need us to teach them what's acceptable behavior, and why. Bad language is unacceptable because other people don't like to hear it. Or, to put it positively, "Polite people don't talk like that in front of others." (Needless to say, to make that stick, we have to watch our own language!)

If these explanations don't work, then you can add a consequence for bad language—like a time-out, the loss of a privilege, or, if need be, a spanking.

Require Better Reasons From Kids

Another way to challenge Stage 0 kids is to require them to go beyond their natural logic of "I want it, so I should have it!"

Whenever your Stage 0 reasoner says, "It's not fair! I *want* [whatever]," you can respond, "Well, that's not a good enough reason! You can't have something just because you want it."

Gradually, Stage 0 thinkers will get the idea that they have to come up with "objective" reasons for what they want. Their first attempts to do this are humorously lacking in what we would consider logic and are transparently self-serving:

"I should get 4 cookies because I'm 4!"

"I should go first because I'm bigger!"

"I should get the red lollipop because I have a red shirt!"

Primitive as these justifications are, they're a step in the right direction. The fact that Stage 0 kids are bothering to explain themselves at all shows they're beginning to come out of their egocentrism and orient to the expectations of others. They're beginning to understand that you've got to give reasons that other people will accept if you want to get along in life. They're revising their theory of how the world works.

Give Kids Chores

Chores are another challenge for Stage 0 kids. They give a Stage 0 child something that's very important: *a responsible social role in the family.* That's a good antidote to egocentrism.

Make sure the chores you assign include doing things for others (setting the table, for example). And be sure to let kids know how much you appreciate it when they help the family in this way.

The Fairness Approach

A spirit of fairness is really behind all the specific suggestions I've made in this and other chapters. With all of these methods, you're asserting your authority as a parent in a way that requires your child to respect others. But at the same time, you're trying to respect your child as a person with a point of view on the world. Through your words and actions, you're trying to teach the importance of mutual respect. And mutual respect is the essence of fairness.

The "fairness approach" provides a new challenge by introducing the *language* of fairness into this picture. By using the word "fair," you put your concern for fairness up front. Basically, the fairness approach says to a child, "I'm willing to treat you fairly. But I insist on fairness in return."

I believe the fairness approach is one of the keys to fostering moral development and good parent-child relations at all ages. That's why I've devoted Chapter 13 to it in Part 4 of this book. But I want to bring it in now while we're talking about young children, because I believe you can begin to develop your child's sense of fairness even at this level.

Now, it's true that kids at Stage 0 of moral reasoning equate what's fair with what they want. Left to their own devices, they usually don't take anybody else's point of view. But if you *present them* with another viewpoint about what's fair, they'll sometimes respond with understanding. That's because at any stage of development, kids can *understand* moral reasoning that is more advanced than what they can *produce* on their own.

This difference between children's "receptive" moral understanding and what they can produce by themselves is very important for parents to recognize. It's similar to what happens in a child's language development. Think of babies. They can understand many things you say to them long before they can say the words themselves. It would be a terrible mistake never to say anything to babies that they couldn't already say themselves. They'd never learn how to talk! It's the same with moral reasoning.

So begin to talk fairness with young kids. Suppose, for example, your child won't pick up. You can say, "I don't think it's *fair* for you to leave your toys all over the floor. I can't walk through the house without tripping over them!"

Suppose your youngster protests, "But I don't *wanna* pick them up! It'll take too long!"

You can continue the fairness approach by saying, "What if I said, 'I don't want to cook your dinner anymore, or fix your lunch, or wash your clothes! It takes too long!' Would that be fair?"

Of course, if fairness reasoning doesn't get your child to cooperate—and it might very well not at this stage—you can always fall back on other methods (such as asserting your authority—"It's time to pick up your toys"—and insisting on compliance).

Don't overdo fairness reasoning with Stage 0 kids, and remember that reasoning is always more effective when kids know you mean business. Especially at this developmental level, you'll need to use plenty of authoritative control to manage behavior. But by at least introducing the language of fairness, you can begin to develop your child's ability to reason about what's fair.

Peer Interaction

Interactions with age-mates are an important source of developmental challenge for the Stage 0 child. These contacts with friends and other playmates, as I've pointed out in earlier chapters, enable kids to bump up against the viewpoints of others, and those bumps help them become less egocentric.

Simply putting kids together, of course, doesn't guarantee that they'll behave less egocentrically. Often kids who are having a conflict go right on ignoring each other's feelings. I don't think a parent should rush in to settle kids' every scrap—they need to get social feedback from each other—but now and then it helps if you intervene to stir the developmental soup ("Sounds like you're having trouble—how about sitting down and agreeing on a way that's fair to everybody?").

Games

Games are another challenging form of social interaction, one that requires kids to learn to follow rules. And the great thing about games is that kids love to play them.

Any kind of simple board game is good for young children. Here are three things they can learn from such a game:

1. You have to take turns;
2. All players, even grown-ups, have to play by the same rules;
3. You can't have a game if people don't follow the rules.

Simple card games such as "War" are also appealing to young children. So are games that involve physical skills like aiming and throwing. All such games help kids learn to follow rules.[3]

Don't expect Stage 0 kids to follow the rules right away, however. And even after they learn to follow them, expect them to blithely ignore the rules at times in order to do what they want! This kind of "cheating" is like lying at this stage; kids don't think of it as wrong. You should insist that they play by the rules, of course, since that's the challenge that spurs development. Finally, don't expect Stage 0 kids to be good losers; they're definitely not!

Those are some ways to both go with the flow and challenge moral reasoning at Stage 0.

If you're a parent or teacher of preschoolers, you may feel that this description of Stage 0 fits them in many ways but in other ways underestimates their moral capacities. I would agree with you. There's research to prove that children during this developmental period, even without prompting from adults, can rise above self-centeredness. Observation studies of nursery schoolers have found many instances of spontaneous altruism and compassion that indicate a sensitivity to the feelings of others.[4] If one child attacked another, for example, a third child might push the aggressor away from the victim and show intense concern for the

HOW TO RELATE TO KIDS AT STAGE 0

You can go with the flow of your child's
Stage 0 moral reasoning by:

1. Taking a developmental perspective ("It won't last forever!");

2. Offering choices that allow your child to make a decision;

3. Offering appropriate positive incentives for obedience;

4. Taking time to have fun with your child.

You can challenge your child's Stage 0
reasoning by:

1. Reaffirming old limits and teaching new ones as needed, taking pains to spell out rules and enforce them consistently;

2. Requiring kids to give better reasons than "I want to!";

3. Assigning chores that give your child a responsible role in the family;

4. Using the fairness approach to begin to stretch your child's understanding of what's fair;

5. Making sure your child has opportunities to interact with the viewpoints of peers;

6. Playing simple games that help kids learn to follow rules.

hurt child. The early childhood teachers I work with report similar examples of kind and caring behavior on the part of their young charges.

How can we reconcile such observations with what moral development psychology and common experience tell us about the egocentrism of Stage 0 children? The explanation, I believe, is this: Stage 0 kids reason egocentrically whenever their desires *conflict* with someone else's. That's the kind of situation that brings out their self-centered, "I-want-to, it's-not-fair!" reasoning. But there are lots of other situations where young children are not being thwarted in the pursuit of their own desires and are therefore more open to the needs or feelings of others. So the same 3- or 4-year-old who screams "It's not fair!" when he has to stop playing may at another time be very cooperative when asked to help or even be actively solicitous of another's feelings ("Are you sad, Mommy?").

It's also possible that even in conflict situations, young children's moral reasoning may not be *always* Stage 0. You may occasionally see in your preschooler a real flash of fairness, real taking of another's point of view even when needs conflict. These early moral flashes may be like a baby's first word (which is often uttered months before the first real surge of language); they reveal latent capacities, awaiting further development. We should notice and nurture these early demonstrations of goodness in our children, whatever form they take and however fragile and fleeting they may be. They are the seeds from which a stronger, more consistent morality can eventually grow.

We need to be aware, too, that while a child's stage of moral reasoning tells us a lot about his or her moral functioning, it's not the whole story. Kids have individual "moral personalities" which reflect, besides their stage of reasoning, the temperament they bring into the world, their position in the family (firstborns, for example, tend to be high in responsibility)[5], their parents' personalities, their unique socialization histories, their idiosyncratic beliefs and values, their self-concept, their emotional security, and a lot that we don't fully understand.

All this helps to explain why two kids at the same stage of moral reasoning can be so different in the way they relate and respond to their social world. Some children are spontaneously generous; they seem to share easily from their earliest years. Some seem to have a special ability to empathize; they readily enter into the feelings and sufferings of others. Some have a strong sense of loyalty; they make the kind of friend anyone would like to have. Moral shortcomings are similarly distributed: some kids have trouble being satisfied and appreciating what they have; some can't take criticism or ever admit they're wrong; some have great difficulty taking a stand that goes against the tide.

Every child, like the adult he or she will become, is a constellation of strengths and weaknesses. So while you tune in to your child's dominant stage of moral reasoning—which is very important and the focus of this part of the book—see it in the context of your child's total moral personality.

CHAPTER 7

STAGE 1: "YOU SHOULD DO WHAT YOU'RE TOLD"

At Stage 1 of moral reasoning, the tides of independence go out, and the tides of accommodation come in.

Once again, the developmental task kids focus on is fitting in. Once again, there's a shift from self-assertion toward getting along.

All this is relative, of course, since kids are so different. Your Heather may have an independent streak no matter what stage she's in. Your Meg, on the other hand, may be fairly easy to get along with no matter what her stage. A stage of moral reasoning, remember, is only part of a child's total personality.

But whatever your child's personality, Stage 1 brings a change. Kids who are by nature independent and kids who are by nature cooperative both move in the same direction: toward greater co-operation. They're easier to live with than they were at Stage 0.

When Stage 1 makes its appearance varies, of course, from child to child, depending on factors like environment. But as a rough rule of thumb, you can reasonably look for kids to develop this stage sometime between 4½ and 5½ years of age.

HOW STAGE 1 SEES THE WORLD

Stage 1 kids will remind you of 3-year-olds.
Both aim to please.
Both accept your rules and authority.

But Stage 1 kids are more advanced than 3-year-olds in an important way: their ability to put themselves in somebody else's shoes.

In spite of 3-year-olds' general desire to please, they're not very good at taking the specific viewpoints of other people. Suppose a 3-year-old wanted to get his mom something nice for her birthday. He might think one of his *Star Wars* figures would make her a swell present.

Stage 1 kids, by contrast, are able to take the viewpoint of another person. That doesn't mean they always *use* this ability. But they've got it. In any particular situation, they're able to realize that the way other people think or feel may be different from the way they themselves think or feel.

But here's the catch: Even though Stage 1 thinkers can take the viewpoints of different people, they figure that only *one* viewpoint is really right. And that's the viewpoint of adult authority.

Stage 1 reasoners believe that:

• What's right is doing what grown-ups tell you;
• The reason to do what you're told is you could get in trouble if you don't.

Stage 1 is a morality of unquestioning obedience.

Now, it's true you can get kids to obey you at earlier stages of development. In Chapter 2, I talked about how it's possible to get even babies to obey. What's new about Stage 1 is not obedient behavior.

What's new about Stage 1 is that kids have now worked out a theory of right and wrong that sees obedience as their obligation. Now they really believe they *should* obey grown-ups, whether they like it or not. And that attitude, of course, makes obedient behavior at least somewhat easier to get.

As an example of the moral philosophy of Stage 1, I'll share with you a conversation I had with Matthew, just about the time he turned 5. I asked him one night as we were all in the kitchen, "Why should children obey their parents?"

"Because," he said, "children are parents' slaves."

Trying to keep a straight face, I asked, "Why do you say children are parents' slaves?"

A PROFILE OF STAGE 1

At Stage 1 of moral reasoning, kids:

1. Swing away from self-assertion toward greater obedience and cooperation.

2. Can take the viewpoint of another person but think that only one viewpoint is right—that of adults.

3. Respect your authority and believe that:
   - What's right is to do what grown-ups say;
   - The reason to obey is to avoid getting punished.

4. Think that adults are all-knowing and always manage to catch kids when they're naughty.

5. Think that if something bad happens to them, they must have done something bad to deserve it.

6. Tend to tattle a lot, because they see adults as the sole source of morality.

7. Have trouble holding two things—two viewpoints, for example—in mind at the same time.

8. Even though they think they *should* follow rules, often don't when grown-ups and the threat of punishment aren't present because they don't yet understand why rules are needed.

"Because," he said with an air of resignation, "we have to obey your orders."

"Why do you have to obey our orders?" I said.

"I don't know," he said, "we just do."

That's a Stage 1 view of the relationship between parents and children, carried to the extreme!

In the next conversation, 5-year-old Jimmy explains *why* a kid has to obey his parents. I had read Jimmy a story about Peter and the picnic. To help him follow along, I pointed to the pictures on the next page as I read.

PETER AND THE PICNIC

Once there was a boy named Peter. One day his friends invited him to go on a picnic. Peter's Mom said, "You can go, but *first*, you have to pick up the mess in your room!"

So Peter went to his room. But instead of picking up, he read a comic book. When his friends came, his Mom said to him, "You didn't pick up your room, so now you can't go on the picnic!" Peter felt very sad as he saw his friends going off to the picnic. He really wanted to go, but his Mom said no, he had to stay home.[1]

I wanted to find out how Jimmy reasoned about obedience. So I started by asking him, "Do you think Peter should obey his mother and stay home and miss the picnic?"

Jimmy: Yes.

   Me: Why do you think he should obey his mother?

Jimmy: Because he doesn't want to get a spanking.

   Me: I see, he doesn't want to get a spanking. Are there any *other* reasons why he should obey? (*Asking for "other reasons" is a way to find out if a child can come up with better reasoning than he gave in his first response.*)

Jimmy: No.

   Me: What if Peter quietly sneaks out of the house and goes on the picnic? Would that be right for him to do?

Jimmy: No, he'll get in trouble.

   Me: You think he'll get in trouble if he sneaks out?

Jimmy: Yes, because what if the *father* was outside and suddenly he saw Peter sneaking out and gave him a spanking?

Jimmy reasons like another 5-year-old who said, "You should never tell a lie, because somehow, the brains inside grown-ups' heads are *so smart* that they find out!"

In Jimmy's reasoning, we can see two characteristics of Stage 1 thinkers:

1. Staying out of trouble is the *only* reason they can come up with for following a command or rule. That's as far as their moral reasoning goes.
2. They think grown-ups are all-knowing supersleuths who always manage to catch naughty children in their misdeeds!

Stage *0* kids will also say that you should obey your parents if you want to stay out of trouble. They'll say things like, "If your mother says go to bed, you better go or you might get a spanking!" But there's a difference between Stage 0 and Stage 1 in how they see the *legitimacy* of your authority. Whereas Stage 0 might insist that it's not fair to have to go to bed, Stage 1 thinks parents have the perfect right to issue such an order.

Where did Stage 1 kids get such an idea?

For a long time they've observed that grown-ups tell kids "Do this" and "Don't do that." Now, it happens that grown-ups are bigger than kids. Kids notice that it's *big* people who make the rules. Then they go from observing that big people make the rules to thinking that big people *should* make the rules. Grown-ups have this right because they have the power. Might makes right. That's what the Stage 1 reasoner has come to conclude.

This kind of logic—that might makes right—comes through loud and clear in the following conversation with 6-year-old Carolyn:

Interviewer:	What if Peter's mother is taking a nap and doesn't find out that he snuck out to go on the picnic? Would that be okay?
Carolyn:	No way! If she wakes up, she'll get angry. Anyway, his father will see him if his mother doesn't, and his father will yell at him.
Interviewer:	What gives Peter's mother the right to tell him what he can and can't do?
Carolyn:	Because she's bigger than Peter is!
Interviewer:	Can Peter tell his mother what to do?
Carolyn:	No, because he's smaller. She'll get mad at him if he does. He'll get punished.

Here's another difference between Stage 1 and Stage 0 thinking: Stage 0 kids will sometimes say, "It's okay for Peter to sneak out as long as he doesn't get *caught*." That's because Stage 0 kids think that what's right is to do what pleases them. Stage 1 kids won't say that; they believe it's wrong to disobey, period.

At Stage 1, kids have at least a primitive kind of respect for your authority, and that's an important developmental achievement. But it's limited in that if you ask them for the *reason* why they should respect and obey your commands, they keep coming back to fear of punishment (and that's true even of kids who themselves experience relatively little punishment). It won't be until Stage 2 of moral reasoning that they can think of a more mature reason for obeying a parent.

WHY STAGE 1 KIDS DON'T ALWAYS OBEY

It might sound as if Stage 1 kids are obedient all of the time. Alas, that's not true.

Stage 1 kids are *more* obedient than Stage 0 kids—at least when you're standing over them. But when you're not there, it's often a case of "out of sight, out of mind"! Don't be surprised if your Stage 1 child walks off with friends' toys or takes money from your dresser. That's not unusual at Stage 1, and it can happen even if you've been teaching that stealing is wrong.

What's missing at Stage 1? For one thing, an understanding of the practical purpose of rules. Rules make it possible for people to live together, to get along. There's a mutual fairness behind rules that Stage 1 thinkers don't yet grasp. If they did, they'd be able to reason, "I don't want somebody to steal from me, so I'd better not steal from them." Instead, they reason, "Stealing is bad—Mom says so—and if I steal, I might get in trouble!"

Even when Stage 1 kids follow the *dos* and *don'ts* we hand down, rules remain external to them, something stuck onto their minds like bubblegum. *Rules aren't yet on the inside,* not yet inner convictions. And because Stage 1 thinkers don't understand from within why rules are needed in human relationships, rules have no firm grip on their behavior.

That explains the paradox of Stage 1 kids. They believe you have an absolute right to say what goes. But often they turn right around and do just the opposite.

HOW STAGE 1 KIDS THINK ABOUT PUNISHMENT

Stage 1 kids have constructed, just as kids do at every stage, a new moral world view. They now believe in a moral universe of shoulds and shouldn'ts. They also believe that the universe is just. Good is rewarded and bad punished.

Stage 1 thinkers believe so strongly that rule-breakers should be punished (at least other rule-breakers!) that they often recommend severe punishments for even minor misdeeds. Teachers of children at this level are often astonished at the answers they get back when they ask kids what would be a fair punishment for misbehaving in class. Kids recommend, very seriously, things like "no lunch for a week," "no recess for the rest of the year," or "a thousand Indian rope burns"! Stage 1 thinkers prescribe heartless sentences like these even if they themselves never get stiff punishments at home!

Kids at Stage 1 also believe that if something bad happens to you, you must have done something bad to deserve it. Jean Piaget, the great Swiss developmentalist, uncovered this aspect of Stage 1 moral judgment by reading children a story about a boy who stole some apples from an orchard. When he ran across a small wooden bridge with his stolen apples, the bridge collapsed. Stage 1 children said the bridge collapsed *because* the boy had stolen the apples. As children got older, they were more likely to say that the collapsing of the bridge was just a coincidence; it had nothing to do with stealing the apples.

Young children often believe that a cut finger or scraped knee is a punishment sent by God because they did something naughty. Some parents, of course, deliberately encourage such thinking. But even kids whose parents never encourage this idea go through a stage of reasoning this way.

"BILLY'S TEASING ME!"

Because Stage 1 kids see adults as being in charge of making and enforcing all rules, they have a natural tendency to tattle. "Billy's teasing me!" "Richard isn't doing what you asked him to!" "Alexandra took another piece of cake!" This sort of thing can drive parents and teachers batty, but it's predictable behavior at this stage. At the next stage of moral reasoning, Stage 2, kids won't see adults as the sole source of morality and will be *less* likely to run to them to report every wrong. Unfortunately, nuisance tattling doesn't completely disappear even after Stage 1 thinking recedes; other things—like the satisfaction of getting your brother or sister in trouble—keep it going!

For your own peace of mind, you may want to take steps to curb tattling even at Stage 1. I think it's a good idea to teach kids of any age the difference between "unnecessary tattling" and "necessary reporting." Here's how I define that difference:

1. **Unnecessary tattling.** This is telling on someone when:
   (a) You see them doing something relatively minor that they shouldn't be doing, like goofing off when they should be doing chores; or
   (b) They do something minor to you—like calling you a name or giving you a poke—that you should be able to handle yourself.

2. **Necessary reporting.** This is telling an adult when:
   (a) You see somebody doing something seriously wrong, like stealing, taking drugs, or being cruel to another kid; or

(b) Somebody does something bad to you—your older brother bullies you, for example—and you try to deal with it yourself but can't.

Basically, the distinction is between "little stuff" and "big stuff." Obviously, there will be arguable behaviors, like harassment from a sibling, that could go into either category, but the general distinction is still worth trying to teach. We don't want kids coming to us constantly with tales of so-and-so doing such-and-such, but we *do* want them to come to us about serious matters where an adult's help is really needed.

I can tell you something we tried in our family that helped us. Tattling had gotten to be a headache to us and a source of angry feelings between Mark and Matthew. So we got everybody together and agreed to try the following procedure. If, for example, Mark was doing something Matthew didn't like, Matthew would say, "Mark, can we settle this ourselves, or should we file a joint report with Mom or Dad?" The purpose of the "joint report" was so that neither would get tattled on. If the offending party wouldn't cooperate either by settling the conflict or filing the joint report, then, and only then, the other person could come to us alone to report the trouble. When Mark and Matthew remembered this agreement, they more often settled problems themselves. When they forgot it (which they often did), we reminded them. This system didn't end fighting between our kids, needless to say, but it did give us a way to deal with tattling, and we were glad for that.

"YOU CAN'T THINK OF TWO PEOPLE'S FEELINGS AT THE SAME TIME!"

If you had to pick one thing about Stage 1 that stands out above the others, what would it be? It'd be that Stage 1 sees morality as being a one-way street: kids knuckling under to adults. It doesn't yet understand that morality is a two-way street: people following rules and taking each other's viewpoint out of mutual respect.

In this sense, Stage 1 doesn't "have it together." It doesn't see both sides of the parent-child relationship. It doesn't understand that parents should be fair to kids, just as kids should be fair to parents. Stage 1 can't hold two points of view in mind at the same time. Instead, it "centers" on only one viewpoint—that of adult authority—and so decides that being good means doing what grown-ups say in order to steer clear of punishment.

This "centering" on one thing to the exclusion of another shows up in young children's logical thinking as well as their moral reasoning. You can test for centering in your own child's logical thinking by doing the following simple experiment devised by Piaget.

Show your child two identical glasses, each containing the same amount of water. Make sure that your child agrees that the two glasses have "the same amount to drink." Then, as your child watches, pour the contents of one glass into a taller, thinner glass and ask, "Do both of these glasses have the same amount to drink, or does one have more?" Most kids under 6 will say that the taller glass has more to drink "because the water is higher." They think this because they're centering all their attention on the tallness of the new glass and ignoring its *thinness*. With development, kids will come to say that the new glass is both taller *and* thinner, and so has the same amount to drink as before.

We can understand young kids better, and have more patience with them, if we remember how hard it is for them to think of two things at once.

One morning, 5½-year-old Gary wanted very much to take his little green rubber ball to kindergarten. His teacher, however, had told Gary's parents that toys brought from home were causing no end of problems in school (disruptions during circle time, fights with other kids who tried to take them away, searches when they got lost).

"Gary," his father said, "we just can't let you take this to school. It's sure to cause a problem. I know you like to take something, and I understand your feelings of disappointment. But we have to think of your teacher's feelings, too."

At this point Gary looked up in total frustration and said, "But you can't think of *two* people's feelings at the same time!"

GOING WITH THE FLOW
AT STAGE 1

Besides adjusting your expectations to your child's developmental level—standard operating procedure at any stage—how can you go with the flow at Stage 1?

Be The Authority Figure
Your Child Needs

At Stage 0, kids needed you as an authority figure to bring them out of their demanding, egocentric behavior into elementary compliance with the expectations of others. At Stage 1, kids need you as an authority figure because they've constructed a world view in which adults are supposed to be in charge. If adults retreat from their authority role, the world of a Stage 1 child becomes a scary place to be.

In addition, kids between 4 and 7 typically have weakly developed self-control; their emotions often run away with them. When this happens, they really need the kind of external control that only an adult can provide.

A teacher of first-graders overheard the following conversation between Wayne, one of her real behavior problems, and a teacher aide:

Wayne: I don't like Miss Baker.

  Aide: Why not?

Wayne: I don't like what she does when I do something wrong, like hitting.

  Aide: What does she do?

Wayne: She asks me why I did it, what I could have done instead, and what I'm going to do the next time. I have to make a *plan*. It's too hard for me to make a plan! I want *her* to control my temper!

This gave the teacher pause. She decided to try a different approach.

"The next time Wayne was wild—it was the end of the day—I sat him down in his seat. Boom! That was it. The temper ended.

"That week I started taking more control of the class. Things settled down, went smoother. We got more done; the children were more cooperative."

As 6½-year-olds, these first-graders may have been capable of some Stage 2 fairness reasoning, which the teacher tried to appeal to when she asked them to make behavior contracts. But it's pretty clear from their behavior that their dominant orientation was still Stage 1. The teacher was able to get them to behave by providing the firm hand of authority that they needed at their developmental level.

Appeal to Stage 1 Kids' Belief
That They Should Obey

Another way to go with the natural bent of Stage 1 kids is to appeal to their belief that it's right for you to give the orders and for them to obey.

Let me tell another personal story to illustrate this point. When Matthew was in this stage, we stumbled on a way to activate his inclination to obey.

Before our discovery, we'd been having a tough time getting him to obey in situations where he was involved in doing something—playing at a friend's house, for example—and didn't want to stop. He'd respond to our directive—"Matthew, it's time to pick up now; we've got to go home"—by either protesting or trying to "sneak in" a little more of the desired activity. That would try our patience, and a "scene" would often develop.

Then one day we said, "Matthew, *this is a chance to obey*." He did.

After that, we tried to remember to say "a chance to obey" in situations where we anticipated some resistance. When we remembered to do this, to our pleasant surprise, Matthew almost always obeyed without protest (though sometimes we had to repeat firmly, *"a chance to obey"*).

Saying "a chance to obey" seemed to help him categorize the situation as one requiring obedience. It was as if he said to himself, "Hmmm, Mom and Dad are asking me to *obey*, and I'm *supposed* to obey my parents!" When we forgot to say "a chance to obey," we often had the old trouble getting cooperation. The difference that those simple words made was remarkable.

Another thing you can do at this stage—something I also recommended for younger children—is to turn obedience into a challenge. "I want you to the dinner table by the time I count to 10. . . ."

You'll have to experiment to find out what works for you. The underlying idea is to try to bring out the natural tendency to accept your authority that's part of Stage 1 reasoning.

Reinforce Manners and Other Good Behavior

Teaching manners may often seem like a losing battle during the show-off, rambunctious fours. But around age 5, when Stage 1 should start to take hold, you should have an easier time encouraging the simple good manners that I suggested you begin to teach as young as 3. Praise kids for saying "Thank you" and "Please," putting their napkin in their lap, waiting their turn, not interrupting, and so on. The goal at this age is not to have kids remember manners without reminding (they generally won't), but for you to keep sending the message, "Manners are important."

Your praise in general is very important to children at this wanting-to-please stage. Kids will ask, "Am I a good girl?" "Am I a good boy?" You can answer their question in a meaningful and truthful way by referring to specific actions you appreciate: "Yes, you were a good girl when you played nicely with Annie this afternoon." "Yes, you were a good boy when you helped me fold the wash." Don't give false praise, however; kids can always detect that. If kids ask "Was I good?" on a day when they weren't, put the question to them: "What do *you* think? Do you think you were good today?"

One other qualifier: don't praise kids so much for being good that they feel they have to be perfect. You want to encourage obedience, but you don't want to stifle independence. It's wisely been said that every child should have the confidence to misbehave occasionally.[2] Giving kids room to be less-than-perfect individuals is especially important with girls, who, many psychologists believe, are in danger of being "oversocialized" by parents and society. The girl who's a "perfect little angel" as a child isn't necessarily the one who will make a resourceful, independent adult.

HOW TO CHALLENGE KIDS
AT STAGE 1

Use Higher-Stage Reasoning, Not Just Power

I was once asked to do a psychological assessment of a 5th-grade boy—call him "Hank"—who had a pattern of stealing from schoolmates. After talking about other things for a while, I casually asked Hank if he thought stealing was right or wrong. He said, without hesitating, "Wrong." When I asked him why he thought a kid shouldn't steal from other kids, he said, "He might get in trouble with the principal." "Okay," I said, "that's one reason. Can you think of any other reasons why a kid shouldn't steal from other kids?" Hank answered: "He might get caught by the cops and have to go to jail." "Okay," I said, and asked again: "Any other reasons?" Hank said, "Yeah, his father might find out, and he'd get a whippin' when he got home."

The fact that Hank couldn't go beyond Stage 1, fear-of-punishment reasons for not stealing shed light on his own behavior. He obviously didn't take the viewpoint of the victims of his thefts, only the viewpoint of the adult authorities who would be mad if they caught him. As I talked with Hank, he seemed like a "nice" boy; he was certainly respectful to me. But his Stage 1 deference to adults when they were around clearly didn't keep him from doing wrong things when they weren't around.

Like Hank, many kids, even after they've developed well beyond Stage 1, still cite the desire to avoid punishment as a motive for following rules. They do so for a simple reason: adults' power to punish remains a reality of adult-child relationships. But unlike Hank, most 10-year-olds can think of other, more mature reasons for refraining from actions like stealing. What gets them to the level of more mature moral understanding, and what keeps a kid like Hank in Stage 1?

We know from studies of child rearing that some parents rely very heavily on what moral development authority Dr. Martin L. Hoffman calls "power assertion." Power assertion means just that: asserting your power ("Do it because I said so!", "You'll do what I say if you know what's good for you!") without reasoning with a child so as to foster better understanding. And the childrearing literature shows that parents who are high on use of power assertion and low on reasoning tend to have children whose understanding of morality doesn't go beyond fear of punishment.

In order to help kids go beyond Stage 1 punishment reasoning, we need to combine judicious assertions of our authority with exposure to higher-stage moral reasoning. With a first offense, reasoning may be enough. For example, if your 5-year-old son bops his little sister or excludes a neighborhood child from a group game, you could help him think about the effects of his behavior ("How do you think Cara feels when you hit her?" "How would you feel if other kids wouldn't let you play?").

If the behavior occurs again, a mild punishment—or what I urge you to call a "consequence" (because that term emphasizes the connection between a child's misdeed and the resulting penalty)—may be necessary to get your child to take the rule and your exhortations seriously. Even when you do impose consequences, however, it's important to repeat the reasoning process, and to avoid making Stage 1 statements like, "Don't ever let me catch you doing that again!" (which makes it seem as if the main thing is not to get caught!).

In general, when you're trying to challenge kids' reasoning, try to pitch your reasoning one stage above theirs. That may seem hard to do at first, but with practice it gets easier. Here's an example: If you were reasoning with a Stage 1 thinker about stealing, you'd be most likely to "get through" with a concrete, Stage 2 challenge such as: "Would you want somebody to steal from you?" A more abstract Stage 3 reason against stealing—"I want to be able to trust you"—would be less likely to connect. There's certainly no harm in bringing in a more advanced idea like trust; it's better introduced early than late, and the worst that can happen is that it just won't take. So do your best to offer challenges that are one step above your child's reasoning, but don't worry about always being exactly on target. You can, if you like, offer reasons at more than one level. And take your cue from what your child seems to be able to understand.

When you reason with kids, try also to stimulate their moral imagination by dramatizing your point. Kids need help in really *imagining* what it would be like to be in the victim's shoes. To dramatize stealing, for example, you could play-act with your child a theft of one of his or her favorite toys. After "stealing" the toy, ask your youngster: "How would you feel if somebody *really* stole that toy from you? Would it be fair? Why not?"

What are reasonable expectations when you offer kids reasons that are a stage above their own? You can expect them to go through two phases:

1. They'll be able to *understand* the one-stage-higher reasoning as you're talking to them. They may even be able to repeat your words ("Stealing isn't fair, because you wouldn't want somebody to steal from you"). But they won't be immediately able, on their own, to *produce* the higher-stage reasoning in life situations (again, just as a baby can't speak all the language it can understand). The reasoning they carry around in their heads will still be the old stage ("Stealing is wrong, because I could get in trouble").

2. Eventually, with time, social experience, and continued exposure to higher-stage reasoning, kids will be able not only to understand the higher-stage reasoning but also to produce it on their own. When they see the quarter on Mom's dresser, they'll be able to say, "I wouldn't want Mom to take *my* money!"

The 5-year-old daughter of a friend had several times taken things from other children that she wished she could have for herself. Her father had talked to her several times about stealing and why it was wrong. One day she said to him, after admitting that she took a friend's game, "I know I *shouldn't* steal, but I don't know *why*!" Her father had been telling her why all along, but she hadn't yet made the reasoning her own.

One day a light will go on in this little girl's head and she'll be able to say to herself, "*I* know why I shouldn't steal—I don't want anybody to steal from me!" Her father, by continuing to talk to her about why she shouldn't steal, will help her get to that stage sooner than she would without his efforts.

Teach Kids That Certain Things Are Wrong

You may think, "Okay, I can see that the next stage of moral reasoning develops pretty slowly. But what can I do in the meantime about my child's moral *behavior* if she's doing something wrong?"

This is where values teaching comes in. Take the value of honesty, for example. Besides reasoning with kids about *why* it's important to be honest, we should definitely teach them *that* it's important to be honest. We can do that through religious teachings such as "Thou shalt not steal" and "Love your neighbor as yourself." We can read children stories that illustrate honesty. We can set a good example when the opportunity arises—returning extra change to a cashier, for instance, or taking pains to bring something valuable we find to a lost-and-found desk. We can make sure our children return anything we discover they've stolen to its rightful owner, with an apology. In all these ways, we can teach our children important lessons about what's right and what's wrong. This kind of direct values teaching, which I discuss at length in Chapter 15, is something positive we can do in the short run to try to influence kids' moral behavior while we're working on the longer-range goal of helping them get to the next stage of moral reasoning.

Keep in mind, too, that a particular behavior problem, as I pointed out in the last chapter, may be caused by factors other than immature moral reasoning. Some kids steal to try to fill an emotional void with material things. A child will sometimes steal, for example, after a death in the family or loss of a pet. A kindergarten teacher told me of a boy in her class, a child from a very affluent home, who repeatedly stole things from his classmates. An inquiry into his home situation revealed that his father was usually on the road, his mother was preoccupied with her own problems, and the boy hungered for attention and love.

Stealing, lying, fighting, treating other children cruelly—all these behaviors can be triggered by hidden feelings of rejection, envy, jealousy, or anger toward an adult. Kids often use bad behavior to send us a message—"I want your attention!" "I'm mad at you!" "I hate my brother!"—without even realizing that that's the real purpose of their actions. A parent's job in cases like this is not to come down on a child with harsh punishment but to try to get to the bottom of the problem through patient discussion. If you face a persistent behavior problem with your child and can't uncover the cause, don't be embarrassed to consult a counselor or therapist. It's far better to get professional help than to let an unresolved emotional problem jeopardize your child's moral development and personal happiness.

Use a Fairness Approach to Family Conflicts

The fairness approach to conflict, which I briefly introduced in earlier chapters and elaborate in Chapter 13, is helpful at Stage 1 for teaching kids that there's more to fairness than just the viewpoint of adults.

For example, family meetings (no longer than 15 minutes with kids this young) are a good way to challenge Stage 1's assumption that grown-ups dictate all the rules. The spirit of a family meeting is to value everyone's viewpoint, kids' as well as parents', and to solve a family problem in a way that all think is fair.

Some parents worry, however, "Won't my kids lose respect for my authority if I start giving them a voice in decisions?" First of all, family meetings don't mean "majority rules." The idea is to get agreement, not to vote. And the limits of what constitutes an acceptable agreement are set by you, the parent. So you don't lose control through this kind of shared decision-making, but you *gain* input from all family members.

What you *do* lose is a Stage 1 respect for your authority, but that's something you should *want* to lose—and which kids will outgrow anyway if you're treating them like human beings. The unquestioning, don't-argue respect of Stage 1, remember, is based on fear, not understanding. Stage 1 doesn't think, "Gee, I better do what Dad asked, it's only fair." Instead, Stage 1 thinks, "I'd better behave while Dad's around, 'cause I'll get in trouble if I don't!" When Dad *isn't* around, the fear disappears and, very often, so does the obedience.

Treat Kids Like Persons

Perhaps the most natural and effective way to challenge Stage 1 is simply to treat kids like persons. Kids are obviously not the equals of parents, but they *are* persons, with feelings we should listen to and a dignity we should respect. We should speak to them courteously, for example, just as we want them to speak to us. We should give them a fair hearing when they disagree with us. A study by Dr. Diana Baumrind at the University of California at Berkeley showed, in fact, that the most cooperative children were those whose parents didn't give in to whining and crying but did listen to reasonable arguments from their children and occasionally changed their mind on the basis of a well-reasoned appeal.

HOW TO RELATE TO KIDS AT STAGE 1

You can go with the flow of your child's
Stage 1 reasoning by:

1. Providing the firm external control your child needs at this level, when dependence on authority is strong and inner controls are weak;

2. Appealing to kids' belief that they should obey you;

3. Reinforcing manners and other good behavior.

You can challenge your child's Stage 1
reasoning by:

1. Using higher-stage moral reasoning, combined with necessary assertions of your authority, to help kids develop a better understanding of the reasons for rules; avoiding statements like "Don't let me catch you doing that again!" which tend to solidify immature Stage 1 thinking;

2. Teaching kids values which tell them *that* certain things are wrong while you're working on the slower process of helping them understand *why* those things are wrong;

3. Teaching kids two-way fairness by solving family conflicts in a way that considers everybody's feelings;

4. Teaching kids mutual respect by treating them like persons.

If we talk and listen to our kids with respect and try to be fair with them, they'll give up before long their Stage 1 idea that morality is something that big people force on little people. They'll come to understand that the basic rule of human respect binds everybody, big and small. When they've got hold of that idea, they're on to Stage 2.

CHAPTER 8

STAGE 2: "WHAT'S IN IT FOR ME?"

Stage 2 of moral reasoning, for all of its advances over Stage 1, is guaranteed to tax the most patient of parents.

Stage 2 has the two-sided sense of fairness that Stage 1 lacked. But it's a rigid, scorekeeping, tit-for-tat sense of fairness. Stage 2 kids are relentless negotiators, confronting the world with the question, "What's in it for me?"

Gone is the spirit of accommodation that was one of the nice things about Stage 1.

Back is the feisty independence that made kids a handful during the "terrible twos" and Stage 0.

Gone is the belief that parents and teachers know it all. Asked what he had learned in first grade, a 7-year-old answered, "I learned that grown-ups aren't always the smartest people in the world!" At Stage 2, kids become our toughest critics, coming down like a thunderbolt on our every mistake (a feature of Stage 2 that will last for several years!).

Gone, too, is the idea that big people should call the shots. In its place is a passionate belief in equality. Said a 6½-year-old to his mother: "I should have my rights, just like you have yours!"

Once again, the forces of differentiation are back in the saddle. Once again, that means more self-assertion, more friction with the social environment that kids are differentiating themselves *from*. Said 5½-year-old Kelly when her father told her to be quiet in the back of the car: "I am myself, and I can talk if I want to!"

A PROFILE OF STAGE 2

At Stage 2 of moral reasoning, kids:

1. Swing back toward independence and individuality.

2. Believe that everybody has his own point of view and that what's right is to:
   • Follow your own point of view ("Do your own thing") and look out for yourself ("What's in it for me?");
   • Do unto others exactly what they do unto you (both good and bad).

3. Think of themselves as the moral equals of adults ("Kids have rights!").

4. No longer think adults should "boss kids around."

5. Have a rigid, tit-for-tat sense of fairness.

6. Understand the two-sidedness of relationships, and think of their relationship with you as a kind of a deal ("Kids should obey parents so parents will do nice things for them").

7. Tend to sneak if they can't negotiate for what they think is fair.

8. Make constant comparisons ("He's got more than me!") and demand equal treatment.

9. Have a new potential for meanness that stems from their greater assertiveness, reduced fear of adult authority, and insensitivity to the feelings of others.

10. May fail to see an action as wrong unless they can *see* the harmful results (and so often see nothing wrong with lying or cheating).

11. Get into more fights and exchanges of name-calling because they believe they have to pay everything back.

You can see the pattern here. Developmental history repeats itself. Kids go through alternating cycles of independence and accommodation, differentiation and integration, breaking away and going along.

When can you expect Stage 2 to arrive on the scene? Again, it depends. Kids whose home life stresses mutual respect and fairness are going to show Stage 2 sooner than kids who get a lot of "Do what I say or else!" Some kids start to show the first signs of Stage 2 thinking between the ages of 5 and 6. They're moving into Stage 2 at the same time other children are consolidating Stage 1.

By ages 7 to 8, most kids are well into Stage 2. And after they've made the transition to Stage 2, they start to settle down. Some of the steam goes out of their independence. They're at least somewhat easier to get along with than when they were first feeling their Stage 2 oats.

Be prepared for Stage 2 to be around for a long time. Even after kids develop the more flexible reasoning and cooperative spirit of Stage 3, Stage 2 gets used an awful lot. That's true clear through childhood and adolescence. In fact, Stage 2 is alive and well in most of us adults.

HOW STAGE 2 VIEWS THE WORLD

What is Stage 2's theory of how the world works?

Stage 2 believes that:

• Everybody has his own point of view.

• What's right is to:

   Follow your own point of view;

   Look out for yourself;

   Be fair to those who are fair to you.

Let's take a look at each of these beliefs and what they mean for your relationship with your child.

"KIDS HAVE RIGHTS, TOO!"

At Stage 2 kids think, "Wait a minute, just because grown-ups are bigger than we are doesn't give them the right to boss us around all the time! We kids have got our rights!"

Stage 2 kids' belief that they have rights comes directly from a new respect for different points of view, including their own. They reason, "When parents make rules, that's just *their* point of view about how things should be. Kids have their own ideas, and who says they're not as good as parents' ideas?"

This revolutionary logic leads to a kind of "do your own thing" philosophy. Since everybody has his own point of view about what's right, everybody should have the right to do what he wants to!

To illustrate this philosophy and show how the same child's moral thinking really does change with development, permit me to call Matthew once more to the witness stand.

A few years ago, we moved temporarily to Boston, where I had an appointment as a visiting professor. It was a big change for all of us. For eight years we had lived in a roomy house with a backyard in the quiet, small-city community of Cortland, New York. In Boston, we lived in a small, 6th-floor apartment overlooking the trolley line and seven lanes of cars.

It didn't take us long to discover we needed new family rules for big-city living. So during our first week, we had several family meetings to discuss what was allowed and what wasn't in our new environs. The boys' bunk beds (new for them) were not for wrestling; the elevator floor buttons were not for pushing all at once (something the other tenants definitely did not appreciate!); the "WALK" traffic lights were not to be ignored, and so on.

One night, after several such family discussions, Matthew came to us with a picture he had drawn.

"That's very nice, Matthew," his mother said. "Is that us?"

"No," Matthew said with a disgruntled frown. "Can't you see that this mother has long, *blond* hair (my wife's is short and brown) and this kid has *dark* hair (Matthew's is blond)?"

Then he looked off in the distance and said in a detached tone, "This is another family. They don't have any problems."

Judith and I exchanged meaningful glances. Then I said, "They don't have any problems, eh? How come they don't have any problems?"

"Because," Matthew said, "the parents do what they want to do, and the kids do what they want to do."

"Oh, Matthew," his mother sighed, "that would never work."

"It's the *only* way it will work!" Matthew said.

I decided to offer a small challenge to Matthew's prescription for a happy family.

"What if the parents want to do one thing," I said, "and the kids want to do the opposite? What if the parents are tired and want to go to bed and get some sleep, but the kids want to stay up and play?"

Matthew held his ground. "The parents should go to bed," he said, "and the kids should stay up and play."

Matthew's do-your-own-thing philosophy was a classic expression of Stage 2. Everybody has his own point of view, so everybody should be able to do what he wants to. Kids should be free to go their way, parents theirs.

This was obviously a far cry from what he had been proclaiming just 6 months before: "Children are parents' slaves!" Kids had clearly been liberated!

"MIND YOUR OWN BUSINESS"

A teacher shared the following story as another example of Stage 2's go-your-own-way philosophy:

> "My family loves to remind me that when I was a little girl, about 5½, I stole a hot dog from a vendor at a circus. When my father caught me, I said, 'You mind your business, Daddy, and I'll mind mine!'"

The idea that people should "mind their own business" comes directly from Stage 2's theory that we're all individuals with our own point of view and our own interests to look out for. So other people shouldn't butt in!

HOW IS THIS PROGRESS?

Stage 2's do-your-own-thing independence may not seem like progress to parents who have to deal with it. To see just how it *is* developmental progress, let's step back from the stages we've looked at so far and bring into focus an important point: *each stage of moral reasoning is a partial understanding, which gets broadened at the next stage.*

Stage 0 kids, for example, recognize that fairness has something to do with their own desires. They think "fair" means getting what they want. That's a partial understanding—part of the truth but not the whole truth. It *is* fair for people to be able to get what they want and need. But there's a lot more to morality than that.

Stage 1 recognizes that "fair" doesn't just mean getting what you want. There are rules to be followed, like 'em or not. That's another partial understanding, broader than Stage 0's.

Stage 2, opening the lens a little wider, recognizes that there's more to fairness than just following grown-ups' rules. It recognizes that what's a good rule depends on your point of view, and that people should be able to do what *they* think is best for them. That's another partial understanding, broader than Stage 1's. But it's still not the whole story. People's viewpoints sometimes come into conflict. In those cases, as any parent knows, "doing your own thing" is not a very good guide for family living!

In short, each stage has an idea of right and wrong that's partly valid. Each new stage has a better idea, a bigger picture of what's involved in morality. With every stage, kids add another piece to the puzzle.

STAGE 2 FAIRNESS: TIT-FOR-TAT

Kids at Stage 2 take a big step forward in their understanding of fairness. We've just looked at one aspect of that understanding: Stage 2's insistence that kids are people, too, and have "rights" just like parents.

The second aspect of Stage 2's understanding of fairness flows from the first. Feeling like moral equals, Stage 2 kids now see all their social interactions, with parents as well as friends, as a process of making fair agreements, negotiating for what they want, wheeling and dealing. What's a fair deal at Stage 2? Tit for tat. You do something for me, and I'll do something for you. There's nothing noble or altruistic about Stage 2's sense of fairness; self-interest is right up front.

The whole parent-child relationship becomes a kind of a deal in the mind of the Stage 2 thinker. Why should kids obey their parents? Because then parents will do nice things for them. Why should parents do nice things for kids? Because then kids will obey them. Tit for tat.

The "Peter and the Picnic" story presented in the last chapter can also be used to pick up Stage 2 reasoning. I asked 7-year-old Bret why Peter should obey his mother when she said he had to stay home and clean up his room. Bret's answer was straight Stage 2: "Because then his mother will do nice things for him."

The "deal" between parents and kids cuts two ways, of course. If kids do what they're supposed to, they reap the rewards. If they don't, they suffer the consequences. Stage 2 understands and accepts that.

Here's Rebecca, almost 7, responding to the "Peter and the Picnic" story; her answers are especially interesting because they show a mix of Stage 2 and Stage 1 thinking:

Interviewer: Was it fair of Peter's mother to tell him he had to stay home and miss the picnic?

Rebecca: I think so. Because she told him to pick up, and he didn't. The mother made a deal. I think it's fair.

Interviewer: What gives Peter's mother the right to tell him what to do?

Rebecca: She's the boss. If the father's there, then they are both bosses.

Interviewer: Can Peter tell his mother what to do?

Rebecca: No.

Interviewer: Why not?

Rebecca: Because he isn't the boss of the mom. Peter can't be boss because he's smaller.

When Rebecca says the mother "made a deal" and it's fair for Peter to miss the picnic because he didn't keep it, she's talking the language of Stage 2.

When she says, however, that Peter's parents have the right to be boss because they're *bigger,* she's showing Stage 1 thinking: might makes right. Stage 2 reasoning would say: "Moms and dads do lots of nice things for you—*that's* what gives them the right to tell you what to do."

You'll find the same kind of "stage mix" in your own child's answers to these moral stories. As I've pointed out before, stage mix is due to the fact that kids develop a new stage slowly, not all at once, and the fact that even after they're well into the new stage, they often slide back into lower-stage functioning. Kids who are fully capable of Stage 2 fairness will regress in certain situations to a Stage 1 focus on punishment as the sole reason to be good, or even to a Stage 0 show of temper when they don't get what they want.

You may wonder, is interviewing kids about stories like "Peter and the Picnic" the only way you can find out what stage or stages of moral reasoning they use?

No, it's not. Once you develop an "ear" for the stages, you'll start hearing them in the course of everyday affairs. My story about Matthew and his "kids and parents should do what they want to" manifesto was an example of how moral reasoning can come out in natural situations. Especially in conflict situations, Stage 2 kids are often absolutely transparent about their what's-in-it-for-me motivation. When 7-year-old Bruce hit his brother, his mother said she wasn't going to make the cake that Bruce had requested earlier. A few minutes later a very distressed Bruce emerged from his room and said, "Mom, I'm *really* sorry I hit Dickie—because I really want you to make that cake!"

AN EYE FOR AN EYE

What's the flip side of Stage 2's tit-for-tat sense of fairness?

It's a belief in exact revenge. If somebody punches you in the arm three times, you should punch them back three times—no more, no less. If somebody takes one of your pencils, you should take one of theirs, not two.

A 3rd-grade teacher asked her class what would be a fair punishment for a group of teenagers who broke into the zoo in Syracuse, New York, one summer night and killed more than a dozen animals.

"Shoot 'em!" said several children. "Same as they did to the animals."

Said a 12-year-old boy in defense of his behavior of stealing: "People steal from me, so why shouldn't I steal from them?"

Get even.

Give 'em a dose of their own medicine.

Do unto others as they do unto you.

That's Stage 2's version of the Golden Rule.

As you might suspect, this kind of thinking has a big impact on kids' relationships with their siblings and peers. One of the reasons why kids get into so many fights at this stage is that they can never let anything go. *Everything* has to be paid back—every push, every name called, even every dirty look.

"Just ignore it," weary parents say. But that's mighty hard to do at Stage 2. To try to reduce fights at this stage when Mark teased Matthew, we attempted to get Matthew to say, "Mark, I've got superhero skin, and nothing you say can get under it!" It worked for about a day.

Kids at Stage 1, just like Stage 2 kids, will sometimes say, "He hit me, so I should hit him back!" What distinguishes Stage 2's sense of justice from the thinking of lower stages is its *combination* of negative payback and positive payback. Stage 2 believes in getting even with those who do you dirty, but it also believes in paying back those who do you good.

This positive sense of fairness helps kids in their play. You can hear Stage 2 kids saying things like, "I played what you wanted before, so you should play what I want now!" It's possible, with effort, to teach younger kids to take turns, but at Stage 2 kids really *believe* in taking turns.

"BOBBY'S GOT MORE THAN I DO!"

Tit-for-tat fairness, as I've pointed out, really amounts to an expression of Stage 2's passion for equality. Tit-for-tat means equal exchange. That same concern for equality leads Stage 2 kids to define fair treatment as equal treatment—*absolutely* equal treatment. In practice, this translates into a habit of Stage 2 kids that can drive parents up the wall: making comparisons.

"Bobby's got more than I do!"

"How come Paul gets to have a friend sleep over this weekend, and I can't?"

"How come *I* have to wash all these pots, and Jackie gets off so easy?"

Kids as young as 3 or 4 will also sometimes make comparisons ("He's got more ice cream than I do!"), but comparisons become constant with the emergence of Stage 2's obsession with equality. You can point out to a Stage 2 reasoner that things even out in the long run—"You've had a friend stay over on other weekends," "Jackie will wash the pots on another night"—and that might help a little. But just as Stage 1 kids "centered" on one thing at a time, Stage 2 kids center on the "right now." They don't easily take the long view. Even if their intellect grudgingly concedes that things balance out over time, the "deeper logic" of their Stage 2 emotions wants things to be the same right away.

Stage 2 thinkers will also argue that they should be treated as "fairly" as other parents treat their kids. So your 6-year-old may come home from school and say, "All the *other* kids get to watch 'The Hulk,' so why can't I?" Later on at Stage 3, kids will argue that "other parents let their kids do such-and-such" because Stage 3 kids want to be able to do what they think will make them one of the group. But at Stage 2 it's equal treatment, not the freedom to go with the crowd, that kids are demanding. At either stage, of course, our job is to stick to what we think is best for our children, and tell them the reason why.

I don't think, however, that parents should let themselves get drawn into back-and-forth arguing *every* time kids seize on some perceived inequality of treatment. Constantly justifying things, especially with Stage 2 kids (who usually don't drop the issue after one explanation!), wears a parent down. Better you should sit down with kids and tell them how comparisons cause tension in you and conflict in the family and how you'd like to minimize them for everybody's sake. Help them see the ways that you do try to be fair to everyone. At the same time, ask them for their view of what's really fair and unfair in the family. Sometimes kids make nitpicking comparisons because deep down, they resent what they see as the preferential treatment of a brother or sister, and it's important to bring that to the surface.

Periodic talking about nuisance comparisons may help, but a certain amount of this behavior goes with the territory at Stage 2.

THE CONCRETENESS AND CRUELTY OF STAGE 2

Stage 2 is very concrete. It's a world of concrete actions and reactions, give and take, trades and deals. It's an outer world, not an inner world. There's not much talk about "feelings" at Stage 2.

Stage 2 tends to think an action doesn't really hurt anyone unless you can *see* the harmful results. One of the reasons why Stage 2 kids often lie is that they can't see how lying hurts anybody. The same goes for cheating on a test at school. It takes a Stage 3 thinker to understand that lying and cheating destroy something invisible but real: trust between people.

All the names and insults that kids hurl at each other during these years can be chalked up to the combination of Stage 2's thrusting assertiveness and its lack of sensitivity to the inner world of feelings. In defense of their actions, Stage 2 kids will sometimes say, "What's wrong with calling names? Names don't hurt you." Even though kids know *they* don't like to be called names, they don't *see* the hurt feelings they cause when they're on the attack. How much of an increase in this sort of behavior occurs in any particular child depends on the child's personality and the kind of values teaching that's going on in the home. But some increase in verbal whacks against both peers and siblings can be expected at this stage.

Stage 2 can be callous in other ways, too. "Finders, keepers, losers, weepers" is a Stage 2 taunt.

Stage 2's potential for just plain meanness is one of the biggest problems parents face at this developmental level, for two reasons. First, we want to discourage meanness on the part of our own children (more on that later in the chapter). Second, we don't want our child to be the victim of other kids' cruelty. Let me say a few things here about this latter concern.

If you have a child in elementary school, and you ask about how kids treat others at school, you're likely to be appalled by all the stories of how kids ridicule, ostracize, bully, or attack other children. Some schools, in an effort to prevent the playground from becoming a moral jungle at recess, organize games, clubs, and other activities that keep kids occupied in prosocial ways. A few schools go an important step further and do moral education in the classroom to try to help students become kinder, more sensitive people.[1] Unfortunately, most schools (and, school people would say, all too many homes) do not make a deliberate effort to foster children's moral development. I'd urge you, individually or through a parents' organization, to ask your school what it's doing not just to "control behavior" but to help kids develop real respect for others.

Even if schools did a lot more to try to get kids to be decent to each other, however, parents would still have to stay on top of things and help kids learn to cope with the inevitable meanness they'll encounter somewhere along the way. There's no simple strategy that covers all cases. In general, kids should learn how to steer clear of trouble when they can, seek help when they need it (from friends, the teacher, the principal, you), and stand their ground when it makes sense to do that.

I want to say a word here about self-defense. Some parents, who themselves feel an abhorrence of violence, teach their children that they shouldn't hit back if someone hits them. I have to disagree with that advice, even though I think that it's very important to teach children that *aggressive* violence is wrong. I think it also makes sense to teach kids that they shouldn't *automatically* hit back; sometimes the problem can be handled with words, by walking away, or by seeking the aid of an adult. But sometimes hitting back—and that means being willing to risk getting hurt—may be the only way kids can protect themselves from continuing and even worsening abuse.

When our older son, Mark, was in the sixth grade, he became friends with Andy, a small and quiet Korean boy. Andy told Mark that until fourth grade, he had been the object of constant verbal and physical harassment by schoolmates. This had made school miserable for him, until one day he decided he could stand it no longer and took on the ringleader in a fight. After that, the tormenting stopped.

Some adults believe that violence is wrong even in self-defense, but that's an adult morality that I don't think we should impose on children. It makes kids too vulnerable, especially in this day and age, if they can't defend themselves, and being vulnerable may make them fearful and withdrawn. My own view is that every child—girls as well as boys—can benefit from some basic instruction in self-defense (check your local YMCA or YWCA for available programs in your area). Some kids have the desire and need to learn self-defense when they're in elementary school; others are more motivated when they're older. In some families learning self-defense is a shared activity; I know one father who took private karate lessons with his 13-year-old son and found that the practice sessions at home, the lessons, and the stops after lessons for a bite to eat were very positive togetherness time for him and his youngster. At the very least, learning self-defense is a confidence-builder. Kids who feel they can handle themselves don't send out the "vulnerability signals" that make some children prone to attack.

What Should You Do About the Neighborhood Bully?

What should you do if your kids are the object of intimidation or harassment in your neighborhood?

If kids can handle it themselves, fine. But if they can't, don't leave them to suffer needlessly at the hands of their tormentors. Let me share with you a story that illustrates one sensible approach parents can take when their child is the victim of bullying.

Eight-year-old Keith, a shy boy, was several times badly frightened by 10-year-old Jack, who lived at the other end of the street. On seeing Keith, Jack would recruit another boy, shout "Let's get him!" and then chase a terrified Keith. Keith's mother spoke twice to Jack's mother about the problem but met with the response: "My son wouldn't do a thing like that."

When it happened again, Keith's mother asked her husband to try speaking to Jack's father. He called Jack's father, who asked

Jack if what Keith said was true. Jack denied it. The phone conversation between the two fathers then went like this:

Jack's father: My boy says he didn't do it.

Keith's father: Well, Keith has come home more than once very upset, and he says that Jack chased him.

Jack's father: Are you calling my son a liar?

Keith's father: No, but I don't think Keith is lying either.

At that point, Keith's mother suggested that Keith and his father go together to Jack's house so that Keith, still badly shaken, could tell his story and let Jack's father judge for himself who was telling the truth. It was very hard for Keith to confront Jack in this way, but with his parents' encouragement he said he would, as long as his father would stand next to him. Keith's father then called to request this, and Jack's father agreed.

Before Keith and his father left the house, however, Jack's father called back to say that Jack had confessed. He said that he was very hurt that his son had lied to him; he had not lied to him before, as far as he knew. He then came over with Jack to see that he apologized face-to-face to both Keith and his parents. Jack did not harass Keith again.

The moral of this story, I believe, is twofold. First, if you get a call from other parents accusing your child of doing something to theirs, don't assume that your child is innocent or even that he's telling you the whole truth if he protests his innocence. I'd ask the phoning parent if it'd be okay if I talked directly with his or her child in order to get the child's complete version of what happened.

If you're the parent who's doing the calling, step out of the middle as soon as you can and let your child speak for himself. That's good experience for him (or her), and it's easier for the other parent to hear the story from your child. If you don't get satisfactory results on the phone, ask if you can come over with your child. Confronted with his victim under such circumstances, the bullying child will have a hard time telling a plausible lie. Even if he still doesn't own up to his actions, chances are he's not going to want to face this kind of a scene again, and the terrorizing of your child will stop.

I've followed this approach myself when one of my children has been bullied, and have had good results. You might worry, "But I'm afraid if I go to the parents, it could end up being worse for my child." I think it's often worse for your child if you do nothing. If, for some reason, you can't or don't want to deal with the parents, you might try to talk directly with the bully. Keep your cool, of course; I think it helps to plan ahead what you want to say and to use questioning ("Joey says you've been pushing him around. Do you think that's fair? Would you want a bigger kid to pick on you? . . . Can I assume that this is the last time this will happen?"). The important thing is to let the offending child know that there's a parent behind his victim who won't stand for further abuse.

Let me be clear: I'm not saying you should fight all of your child's battles, or even most of them. Kids need to develop the confidence and the skills to make their own way in the world. But if they're being intimidated by bullies, that will reduce their confidence, not build it.

Those are some thoughts about how to deal with the worst expressions of Stage 2 in other kids. Let's turn now to how you can relate to Stage 2, its strengths and its weaknesses, in your own child.

HOW TO GO WITH THE FLOW AT STAGE 2

Whenever kids' independence is running strong, as it is at Stage 2, parents and kids tend to have a hard time of it. At these times, going with the flow of your child's independence becomes especially important for managing behavior and reducing conflict. How can you go with the flow of Stage 2?

Be Tolerant

"Be tolerant, take a developmental view" is by now familiar advice, but I want to underscore it at this difficult stage.

Expect Stage 2 kids to get mad at you and to accuse you of being unfair. Expect them to talk back. Think of it as their *stage* talking back to you. As always, insist on respect—"I speak respectfully to you, so I expect you to speak respectfully to me"—but realize that their fierce sense of fairness is going to make kids sound "fresher" at this stage than they ever have before.

Life gets harder for kids when they reach Stage 2. They've decided that grown-ups don't have the right to boss kids around, and that kids should be able to do what they want to just the way grown-ups do. But they keep banging up against the stubborn fact that grown-ups *do* call the shots and kids *can't* do what they want to! There's a big gap between how they think things should be and how they really are. That can be pretty frustrating.

Let me give an example.

Six-year-old Shawn's transition to Stage 2 was loud and clear. He decided that people either "get their way" or "don't get their way." He began to challenge his parents: "How come parents always get *their* way? How come *you* can do anything you want, and I *can't*?" "*Nothing* ever goes my way!" became his daily refrain. His parents tried in vain to show him how he had his way in the family as much as anybody else.

Shawn also showed a new defiance, another way that Stage 2 kids demonstrate that they've got rights and a mind of their own. One night Shawn was sent to his room after a fit of temper. A few minutes later, he came stomping out and said to his father with clenched fists and tears in his eyes, "Dad, if you send me to my room again, I'm *not* going to go!"

Shawn's father stayed calm. He said, "Shawn, I know you don't like to have to go to your room. And I know you're very upset. But we agreed on a rule about temper. What was it?"

"But it's not fair!" Shawn protested.

His father continued: "Remember the discussion about temper we had the other night? You agreed that if you throw a fit of temper, you have to go to your room for a time-out? Didn't you say that was a fair consequence?"

"Oh, all right!" Shawn said and stomped back into his room.

Shawn's father was firm, but he was tolerant. He didn't get angry at Shawn's defiance. By letting Shawn make his protest, he helped Shawn defuse his angry feelings, while still getting him to honor their agreed-upon rule.

You can deal better with Stage 2 kids if you try to see things from their point of view and understand what they're going through. And take heart from the knowledge that some of the spit and vinegar goes out of Stage 2 after the first year. Kids come to terms with a world where grown-ups are still in charge and kids still have to obey. With a little help from you, they can come to see that it's not such a bad deal.

With a developmental perspective, you can even come to appreciate your Stage 2 child's feistiness for the step forward in development that it is.

Appeal to Reciprocity

Appealing to reciprocity means appealing to equal (tit-for-tat) exchange: "I did that for you, so you should do this for me." If I had to recommend just one strategy for managing kids' behavior at Stage 2, appealing to reciprocity would be it. It goes right to the heart of Stage 2's sense of fairness.

Five-year-old Michael asked his father to read him a story. He did. When his father finished, he said: "Did you like that story?" Michael said yes.

His father continued: "That's being a nice Dad, right, Michael? So you should be nice to me when I ask you to do something, right?"

"Right," Michael said. "You do something nice for me, and I do something nice for you." Then he added: "Or it can go the other way—I do something nice for you, then you do something nice for me!" Michael had reciprocity down pat.

Later Michael's father asked him to help with the dishes. Michael said he didn't want to. "Hey," his father said, "remember how I read you a story when you asked me to? Now I'm asking you to do something for me. Fair enough?" Michael agreed, and complied with his father's request.

You can also use reciprocity in a looking-ahead way that helps kids anticipate the need to return a favor.

For example: Seven-year-old Patty asked her mother if she would take her ice-skating on Saturday morning at the town rink. "Okay," her mother said, "and when we get home and I ask you to help around the house, what will you say?"

"I'll help," Patty said.

As kids get a handle on the principle of reciprocity, it starts to show up in their explanations of why they shouldn't do certain things. "It's not nice to lie," said 6-year-old Charlie, "because people might lie back to you." We can help kids apply the reciprocity principle to undesirable behaviors by asking, "Would you want someone to do that to you? And so, should you do it to them?"

You can use reciprocity to make it clear to kids that it's in their interest to help out. If you're having trouble on a given night getting them to pitch in at dinner time, remind them of the story of *The Little Red Hen*. Since none of the other animals would help her prepare the meal, none of them got to help eat it either. A good Stage 2 lesson in reciprocity.

Sometimes you may want to use reciprocity to "strike a deal": "If you help me all morning with the housework (yardwork, whatever), I'll take you swimming (biking, roller-skating, to the movies) in the afternoon." "If you can go the whole week without fighting with each other, I'll take you to the circus on Saturday." I wouldn't advise you, however, to make a habit of "dealing" to get kids to help or obey. You'll weaken your authority as a parent if you're always "bribing" kids to be good, and they'll get to thinking, "Why should I do this if there's nothing special in it for me?" For this reason, it's generally better to help kids relate your present request to things you've already done for them ("When you asked me to take you out for an ice cream the other night, what did I say?") and future things they'll want you to do ("The next time you ask me to do you a favor, what do you want me to say?"). (Chapter 14 on the ask-don't-tell method of reasoning gives more examples of how to use this kind of questioning at Stage 2.)

A note of realism: Kids don't always hop to and do what they're asked when you make your appeal to reciprocity. In some situations, getting them to accept the implications of reciprocity may be a big struggle. Why is that so at this stage when they're supposed to have a two-sided appreciation of fairness?

Especially when Stage 2 is first breaking through, kids' energy tends to go into asserting *their* needs and desires and making the world accommodate them. They have a supersensitive Unfairness Detector when it comes to finding all the ways that people are "unfair" to them. But they have a big blind spot when it comes to seeing all the ways *they* aren't fair to others and all the ways parents and others do things for them! Appealing to reciprocity helps them open their eyes and practice in their behavior what they now know in their heads to be true: that fairness works both ways. Applying that principle across many different situations is an important kind of horizontal development of Stage 2 moral reasoning. And, as I pointed out in Chapter 1, horizontal (or sideways) development is just as important as vertical (or upward) development. The horizontal extension of a stage is the process by which kids learn to use and generalize the best reasoning they've got.

Be Willing to Negotiate and Compromise in a Spirit of Fairness

Appealing to reciprocity is one way to plug into Stage 2's concept of fairness. Another is to be willing, at least some of the time, to negotiate and compromise when you have a conflict with your child.

In Chapter 13, as I've mentioned, I spell out how to take a fairness approach to conflict resolution. What I want to stress here is the importance of being willing at Stage 2 to go back and forth with kids and work things out in a way you both think is fair.

Now, I know that's not easy. "I get an argument about everything!" is the weary complaint of parents of Stage 2 children. I know that I don't always have it in me to debate with my kids about what's fair. I need to be able to say to them (and I do):

> "Look, there are times, like the end of the day, when I don't have the energy or patience to go back and forth about what's fair. At times like these, parents need kids to just accept what they say."

I think that if there's a lot of fairness communication in the home, kids will accept your appeal when you need a rest.

But why, you may wonder, should you get involved in negotiating what's fair in the first place? Let me offer two reasons why I think a certain amount of this kind of give-and-take discussion is necessary and important to do.

First of all, it's meeting Stage 2 kids where they are developmentally. They really feel they have a right to argue their point of view and to try to organize life the way they'd like it.

Second, if you refuse to talk things over with kids and work them out, you run this risk: they'll do what they want to anyway, only they'll do it behind your back and lie about it if they have to. If kids can't negotiate with adults for what they feel is a fair shake, they'll start to see adults (and later, perhaps, all authority) as something to get around. That's bad for their moral development, and bad for your relationship with them.

I once overheard a 13-year-old boy talking with a group of his friends. "I lie to my parents all the time," he said. "If they want to know where I'm going or where I've been, I just tell them something that keeps them off my back."

Now, most kids are going to go behind your back sometimes and tell lies to cover up, no matter how fair and open you are. That's because there are usually still plenty of things kids would like to do that parents don't or might not allow. But if you're generally willing to work things out with them (and that certainly doesn't mean compromising on everything), they'll have less reason to sneak. They'll know they can come to you with their requests and get a fair hearing.

Being open to kids' appeals and arguments definitely puts a demand on a parent. And at Stage 2, kids will need regular reminders that you'll listen to their point of view but won't tolerate disrespectful talk. But the long-term gains are well worth the short-term strains. You'll be helping them become honest, up-front people, and you'll be laying the foundation for honest communication when your child enters the teens.

HOW TO CHALLENGE STAGE 2

Appealing to reciprocity and working out what's fair accommodates to Stage 2's idea of how the world should work. That's important, as I've said, for parent-child harmony and kids' horizontal moral development. But it doesn't stretch Stage 2 kids, doesn't give them a reason to develop to the next stage. How can you challenge kids at Stage 2 and help them grow toward the next level of moral reasoning?

The best way to understand how to foster development toward Stage 3 is to understand what's missing at Stage 2. What's missing is illustrated by the following story.

Alan, age 10, picked up the newspaper and saw the front-page story about an airplane disaster. To no one in particular he said, with distress in his voice, "Here's a story about a plane crash. All those people killed! Oh, sick!"

His 6-year-old brother, Randy, heard him and said, "Well, just be glad it wasn't you!"

Alan shot back: "Oh, sure, never mind about other people!"

Replied Randy: "Well, you're only supposed to care about yourself!"

What's missing at Stage 2 is caring about others even if there's nothing in it for you. Alan at Stage 3 shows that kind of concern. Randy at Stage 2 doesn't, at least not on his own.

The problem with Stage 2 is not that 6-year-olds think that way. The problem is that a lot of 16-year-olds still think that way. It's easy for kids to get stuck in the Stage 2 groove. "Look out for yourself" moral reasoning coincides with our natural tendencies toward selfishness. The peer group and the behavior of many adults (including much of what comes across on TV and in the movies) tell kids that what's-in-it-for-me thinking isn't bad but is smart, the "cool" way to be. And the longer Stage 2 holds sway, the more it hardens into a callous me-centeredness. A lot of the problems we looked at in Chapter 1—disrespect for authority, vandalism, cruelty to others, juvenile crime—can be traced to teenagers who have acquired many of the powers of adults but are morally still Stage 2 children.

At all developmental levels, our task as parents is to help our children's moral development keep pace with the rest of their development. As they grow toward adolescence, they should be developing beyond Stage 2, into a morality of caring about the needs and feelings of others. At the same time that we're going with the flow of Stage 2 (no small task in itself), we must supply the higher expectations that will help Stage 2 break up and give way to more mature moral reasoning. It's a slow transition, harder for kids than going from Stage 1 to Stage 2. When kids gave up Stage 1, they saw themselves gaining rights; when they give up Stage 2, they gain responsibilities.

I think kids can begin to develop Stage 3 moral reasoning during their middle elementary-school years. Here are some ways we can help them.

Appeal to Love Instead of Fairness

We shouldn't always appeal to tit-for-tat reciprocity when we ask Stage 2 kids to do something. Every so often we should offer a higher-stage challenge by appealing to love instead of fairness.

For example: Suppose you ask your 10-year-old daughter, Emily, to read a story to her 4-year-old sister, Kristen, before dinner. Emily protests, "Why should I have to read a story to Kristen? I was just going to call up Barbara. It's not fair!" You can say:

> "It's a matter of love, not fairness. Sometimes we do a thing because it's only fair, but sometimes we do it because it's the generous, loving thing to do. This is a time when we're asking you to do something out of love."

At first, you can expect kids to grumble and groan when you make this kind of appeal. They'll still be thinking strictly in terms of tit-for-tat fairness. With time, they'll come to understand that love is a different matter: it doesn't keep score, and it means putting aside for the moment what you want in order to do something for somebody else. When I want to get my kids thinking in this direction, I often find it helpful to say, "This is a time when I need you to think of others instead of yourself."

Teach Religious Values

If religious values are important to you, be sure to share them fully with your child. Religion helps to open up a Stage 2 child's view of the world; it calls us beyond selfishness to a communion with something larger than ourselves.

Help kids see the connections between their participation in the family and religious teachings about love. For example:

- "Jesus said we should love each other as much as we love ourselves. What does that mean to you? . . . What's a way that you showed love for someone in the family today? . . . What's a way you can show love for someone tomorrow?"
- "The Talmud says: 'What is hateful to you, do not to your fellow man.' What does that mean? . . . What are some things that people in the family do to you that you don't like? . . . Do you ever do those things to other people?"

I'll say more about religion and moral development later on in the book (particularly in Chapter 15); here I want to indicate its helpfulness in bringing children out of Stage 2.

Talk About Feelings

Stage 2 kids, as we've seen, need a lot of help in becoming sensitive to feelings. Help them think about how they affect the feelings of others by what they say as well as what they do. When kids are mean to a brother or sister, take the time to talk about it. Keep track of what they're doing in the neighborhood and at school. Help them understand the hurt of a child who's locked out of a game or made fun of by others.

All children can benefit from this kind of empathy training, but make a special effort with boys. In their concern with being "tough," they tend to be slower than girls in developing sensitivity to the feelings of others.

Help Kids Orient to
Your Expectations

At Stage 2, kids obey you because (1) they think it's a fair "payback" for what you do for them, and (2) they don't want to get punished. But if they forget about the fair-payback reason, as they often do, and focus just on punishment, they get to thinking "Can I get away with this?" and often take their chances.

Part of helping kids beyond Stage 2 is getting them to think less about rewards and punishments and more about living up to our expectations of them. That means we need to give some thought to when it's wise to impose a negative consequence for wrong behavior, and when it's wise to refrain from consequences in order to get kids to focus on our *disappointment* in their behavior. A young woman remembers the effect when her parents did the latter:

"I once stole some candy from a foodstore and was caught by the manager. He demanded to know my name, and, terrified, I told him. He phoned my parents, told them what I had done, and sent me home.

"As I rode my bicycle home in the dark, I thought about the reception and probable spanking I would receive. Looking scared, I entered the house and was met by a rather calm father and mother. They stressed that they were *very* disappointed in me that I hadn't lived up to their expectations. They said they hoped I would never do it again, because it was wrong to take what didn't belong to me.

"My initial feeling when I was back in my room was that I had escaped with my life. But as I thought about it, I, too, was disappointed in myself. I resolved never to do it again, and didn't."

Had she been punished for her theft, the daughter would most likely have focused on the fact that she got caught. She might have resolved to be more careful next time, not more honest. But because of her parents' talk of their disappointed expectations, she focused instead on their feelings and her feelings about herself. And when kids begin to look within, at the kind of person they are, they're on to Stage 3.

We should also teach kids to feel good about themselves when they do live up to our expectations. With time, they'll come to value our approval as reward enough for good behavior. A father remembers a time as a child when he came home and told his mother that other kids were getting money for their good report cards; what was she going to give him for his good grades? "Not money," she said, "but pride. I am very proud of you for using the brains God gave you to do your best in school."

Stage 2 kids have left behind the old Stage 1 respect for our authority. In its place, they need to develop a new, more mature respect, based on a desire to live up to the expectations and ideals we hold out to them.

Nurture a Loving Relationship

If we want kids to value our approval and be concerned when we're disappointed in them, *we have to first have a relationship of love*. Kids won't give a hoot about the expectations we set if we don't love them and they don't love us.

So be sure to spend regular time with your child, including some time *when it's just the two of you*. Read a book, play a game, take a walk, ride bikes, go shopping, go fishing, or just have a talk at bedtime. Making time for this special kind of togetherness helps us rediscover a whole side of parenting that can get lost in the daily hassles of managing Stage 2 behavior.

And the deepened relationship that is nourished by such contact helps a Stage 2 child come to value your esteem and to care about your expectations.

There are times when it's appropriate to help kids think about the fact that they *have* a relationship with you that extends over time, involves mutual commitment, and is more than just a series of tit-for-tat exchanges. Suppose, for example, your 6-year-old, angry about some "unfairness," comes to you and says, "I'm going to run away!" At this moment, he doesn't want you to take him up on it and say, "Okay, if that's your decision!" What he needs is reassurance that you love him and a way to save face. You can offer both, plus a bigger view of what a relationship means, by saying:

> "Hey, wait a minute. You have no right to walk out. When I get mad at you, I don't walk out. This is a relationship that's binding, pal. We have a commitment to each other. Now let's talk about what the trouble is."[2]

Help Kids Feel Like a Member of a Family

Important at any stage, a strong family life makes a special contribution at Stage 2. Stage 2 kids need to learn to think of themselves as a member of a group. They need to go from thinking "What's right is to do what I want to" to thinking "What's right is to think of others in the family as well as myself."

Any way you can help kids experience the family *as a family,* not just a collection of individuals living under the same roof, will contribute to the development of Stage 3 moral reasoning. Talk together (see Chapters 12 and 13 for ideas for family communication); play together; work together. If it fits into your life style, for example, you might try to establish a tradition of "family work time"—a couple of hours on the weekend, say, when you all pitch in on whatever jobs need doing.

Let me say a word here about allowance. If you pay kids for particular jobs, you aren't helping them develop beyond a Stage 2, tit-for-tat view of helping. I recommend you offer a regular allowance, whatever you think is reasonable, as one of the benefits (like love, food, and shelter) of being a member of the family. And just as we each receive benefits from the family, so, too, must we each make contributions, one of which is helping with the work. Giving kids real responsibilities is never more important than it is at Stage 2.

I'd urge you, too, to write out and post a list of responsibilities for your child. Having responsibilities listed helps to make clear exactly what you expect, orders jobs in a logical sequence, and gives you and your child a common reference point ("You've done most of what's on your list, but you still need to feed Raffles"). Here's a list of summertime responsibilities that one 9-year-old had:

RESPONSIBILITIES

1. SHOWER AND BRUSH
2. PICK UP BATHROOM (PAJAMAS AND TOWELS)
3. MAKE BED
4. DO MORNING DISHES
5. ASK IF THERE'S YARDWORK OR HOUSEWORK I CAN HELP WITH
6. SET TABLE FOR DINNER
7. HELP WITH DINNER DISHES
8. PICK UP TOYS, ETC., IN FAMILY ROOM
9. PICK UP TOYS, ETC., IN YARD
10. FEED SQUIRMY

To be done *cheerfully*.

Kids will still need reminders, of course, and they'll sometimes moan and groan even about chores they've agreed to do. But it's better with a list than without one.

Extend Love Beyond the Family

One way to make love stronger within your family is to extend it beyond your family. As we'll see later, this is an important way to help kids develop from Stage 3 of moral reasoning to the society-wide perspective of Stage 4. But it's helpful even at Stage 2 as a way of getting kids to stop thinking only of themselves and start thinking of others.

Extending love beyond the family can be as simple as doing a good deed for a sick or elderly neighbor. Some families also make a special tradition of helping others at certain times of the year. One family I know does a "Christmas Chain." Three weeks before Christmas, they sit down and cut out links from colored construction paper, one for each day remaining before Christmas. Each family member takes an equal number of links, and writes on each one a way that everyone in the family will show the spirit of Christmas on the day that link is torn from the chain. What each person writes is unknown to the rest of the family, so that each day's link will be a surprise. The links are then shuffled and the chain assembled and hung. Sample links:

- Write a letter to someone who'd like to hear from you.
- Be kind to someone you don't like.
- Pray for peace in a war-troubled country.
- Do a kindness for someone in the community with a special need.

Offer Good Examples

Finally, we can help Stage 2 children grow toward a morality of caring by practicing it ourselves in our family interactions—both in the way we treat our children and in the way we treat each other as adults.

We should also make use of other good examples. There are lots of sources: children's books featuring kind and caring characters (*Uncle Wiggily,* for example), stories about heroism on the part of children or teenagers, articles in the news about a good deed performed or a service rendered, and examples of good deeds that we come across in our own experience.

The more concrete images our children have of people helping people, the more that will seem to be the norm—and the more they'll be drawn out of their Stage 2 view of what's important toward a broader concern for the welfare of those around them.

HOW TO RELATE TO KIDS AT STAGE 2

You can go with the flow of your child's
Stage 2 moral reasoning by:

1. Being understanding of the "back-talking" that comes from Stage 2's fierce sense of fairness (while still insisting on respect);

2. Appealing to tit-for-tat reciprocity ("I did that for you, so you should do this for me");

3. Being willing to do back-and-forth negotiation in order to work out solutions that are fair to both you and your child.

You can challenge your child's Stage 2
reasoning by:

1. Appealing to love instead of fairness as a reason to do what you ask;

2. Teaching religious values that stress the importance of love;

3. Helping kids become more sensitive to the feelings of others;

4. Helping kids focus on living up to your expectations rather than on getting concrete rewards or avoiding punishment;

5. Nurturing a loving relationship that causes your child to care about your expectations;

6. Helping your child feel like a member of a family;

7. Extending love beyond your family;

8. Offering examples, including your own behavior, of kind and caring actions.

CHAPTER 9

STAGE 3:
"WHAT WILL PEOPLE THINK OF ME?"

Stage 3 is a morality of trying to please others by being a "nice" person and living up to their expectations. It's a major milestone in your child's moral development. It's also different from the moral stages we've talked about so far in two important ways.

First, Stage 3 reasoning emerges more slowly and lasts longer. In some kids, it starts to poke through during the middle elementary-school years. In most kids, it's still their dominant stage during the early and mid-teens. Even in many adults, Stage 3 continues to be the major mode of moral reasoning.

The second way that Stage 3 is different is this: It makes kids easier to deal with during childhood but presents new problems for both parents and kids in the teens.

When Stage 3 begins to develop in elementary-schoolers, it's a welcome change from the what's-in-it-for-me spirit of Stage 2. It's easier to get Stage 3 reasoners to cooperate, to accommodate, to accept what you say. There are still conflicts, of course—kids still need to assert their individuality from time to time, and Stage 2 is still alive and kicking. But compared to when Stage 2 was in its heyday, it's smooth sailing.

Then, sometime around 11 (6th grade), the first dark clouds of adolescence usually appear on the horizon. Kids start talking fresh again. Things get a little tense and grumpy. Age 12 typically brings a temporary equilibrium. Then, sometime around 13, the storms of adolescence hit.

In the teens, Stage 3's strength—caring about others—becomes its weakness. Now kids care so much about what others think of them that they can turn into moral marshmallows, willing to do something because "everybody's doing it." The need for peer approval is stronger than ever before.

Part of what makes the Stage 3 teens so hard is that kids now face a double developmental agenda: breaking away from parents *and* fitting into their peer group. Differentiation and integration at the same time.

And just as your teenager faces a double agenda, so do you.

The Stage 3 teens are a time for parents to let go. Parents have to allow kids to define their own identity and at least some of their own values, to make some decisions, to get a sense of themselves as separate persons with a life of their own, to begin to test their wings outside the family nest.

But it's also a time for parents to "hold on." Stage 3 kids are far from mature. They need control as well as freedom, guidance as well as independence, protection from destructive peer pressures as well as opportunities to face the world on their own.

In short, Stage 3 starts easy and gets hard. In the teens, it can be an emotional roller coaster, with lots of highs and lows for both parents and kids. In both childhood and adolescence, you'll probably find yourself doing more moral teaching with your child during this stage than at any other stage of development. And that's as it should be.

HOW STAGE 3 SEES RIGHT AND WRONG

Stage 3 marks the beginning of "conventional" morality. That's because Stage 3 thinkers believe that:

- Being good means being a "nice person" in the conventional sense—doing what people generally expect of a good son, a good daughter, a good neighbor—and caring about your personal relationships;
- The reason to be a good person is so you can think well of yourself and have others think well of you.

This is a big change from Stage 2.

At Stage 2, kids thought, "I should be good to others, so others will be good to me!"

Stage 3 thinks, "I should be good because, well, that's what people who know me *expect* of me. How are they going to feel about me if I let them down, and how am I going to feel about myself?" Social approval and self-approval are opposite sides of the same coin for Stage 3 thinkers. They need the approval of others to feel good about themselves. Stage 2 wanted the con-

---

A PROFILE OF STAGE 3

At Stage 3 of moral reasoning, kids:

1. Believe that:
   - Being a good person means living up to your internalized image of what a "nice person" does;
   - You should be a nice person so others will think well of you (social-approval) and you can think well of yourself (self-esteem);
   - You should treat others the way you would like them to treat you (the Golden Rule).

2. Can think of what others need, not just what's in it for them. When they put themselves in the other guy's shoes, they're capable of good deeds.

3. Are more forgiving and flexible in their moral judgments. They can consider extenuating circumstances; mercy tempers justice.

4. Have a concept of character. During the childhood years, unless adults and TV have made them cynics, they generally accept the idea that grown-ups are wise and good and that following their advice will help a kid grow up to be a good person.

crete goods and favors of other people; Stage 3 wants their good opinion.

Stage 2 thought, "What's right is to look out for number one." That was one of those moral half-truths. It is perfectly natural *and* moral for all of us to look out for our own rights and welfare, even at the highest moral stages. But Stage 3 recognizes that doing the right thing means looking out for the other guy's welfare, too. That's why Stage 3 thinkers talk about what other people "need." Listen to 10-year-old Danny, asked if Peter (in

5. Think of a good relationship as one where people help and trust each other. They're capable of being more responsible family members because they can see things from a group perspective.

6. Are *relatively* easy to get along with as children, but during the early teens may seem to "regress." Feeling insecure about themselves, they become highly critical of others and seem to need peer approval like a drug to feel good about themselves.

7. Have a true conscience, but one with a terrible flaw: it's inner-directed and outer-directed at the same time. It's inner-directed because it has internal standards, but outer-directed because it depends on others to define what those standards should be.

In childhood, if parents make the effort, they can largely determine a child's moral standards. But in adolescence, the peer group moves in as a major competitor for a child's conscience. And because of their intense emotional needs, fragile self-concept, and immature moral reasoning, Stage 3 teens may have a tough time bucking peer pressure. "If everybody's doing it," they reason, "can it be so bad?" But they can, with help, learn to resist that pressure.

the "Peter and the Picnic" dilemma, Chapter 7) should sneak out of the house:

> "I think being sneaky is dirty and rotten. It's better to let people know where you are at all times, so if they need you, they'll know where you are."

A Concern for Character

Danny uses a Stage 3 vocabulary—terms like "sneaky," "dirty," and "rotten"—to describe *character,* the kind of person somebody is. Character is a Stage 3 idea. And Stage 3 kids can now imagine their own character as something that develops over time, for good or for ill. Helen, age 9, shows this ability to think of a future moral self that is affected by present moral actions:

> "You shouldn't sneak out of your room if you're grounded. Maybe when you grow up, you will lie to people. You might be president and lie."

STAGE 3 AND OBEDIENCE

How does Stage 3 affect obedience?

It makes it easier to get kids to obey.

Stage 3 kids are generally more accommodating because they have a new slant on why kids should obey. For one thing, they think it can actually be in a kid's long-range interest to listen to parents. Says 10-year-old Mike:

> "It's good discipline for kids to obey their parents. It's how they're supposed to act. And parents have wise advice. Children should listen to them. If they do, they might grow up to be better people."

At Stage 2, you fought a running battle with kids over what was fair. You'll still get into debates about fairness at Stage 3, but you can also begin to enjoy a new phenomenon. Kids have a new faith that parents and teachers are wise and good and have their best interests at heart. Oh, they may still enjoy catching you and other adults in errors of information and slips of the tongue. But at a deeper, moral level, they now really believe that "father or mother knows best"!

I want to say a word here about respecting children's naive faith in adult authority. Children at this stage do have a natural tendency to look at adults through rose-colored glasses. But it would be a mistake to think, as many people unfortunately do, that we should rip those glasses off and say, "See the world as it really is! See adults—even your heroes—as the dishonest double-dealers or bumbling fools they often are!" Especially during their elementary-school years, kids have a developmental *need* to trust. They need adults to look up to, and they need to believe that adults, especially authority figures, are usually good people, protective and helping and more or less in control of events. If we overwhelm kids with all the evil and chaos in the world (which television news is capable of doing), we risk making them both cynical and insecure.

There'll be plenty of time in adolescence for kids to develop a mature skepticism about authority and social institutions. Even then, it's very important to avoid cynicism by balancing the bad news with exposure to what's good and worth emulating in the world.[1]

THE DAWN OF CONSCIENCE

At Stage 3, morality has a new home.

Because Stage 3 kids have a self-image they want to live up to, they have, for the first time, a true conscience.

You may hear kids at earlier moral stages use the word "conscience." But if you scratch the surface, you'll find that they really mean fear of punishment. An 8-year-old girl once confided to me, "When I do something I'm not supposed to, all day long I have a terrible *conscience* about it!" "You do?" I said. "Yeah," she said, "whenever my mother calls 'Roxanne!' I think she's found out!"

Conscience at Stage 3 is a different matter. It's an inner standard. Nine-year-old Amanda and her mother were discussing the problem of kids stealing lunches at school. "I couldn't steal anything," Amanda said. "Inside of me, I'd know it was wrong."

At the dinner table one night, 10-year-old Larry said, "When I'm tempted to read a comic in bed at night, my conscience says to me, 'You were told lights out. Put it back.' When I feel the urge to take another cookie when I'm not supposed to, my conscience says, 'Put it back. You're only supposed to have one.' It's a voice inside me."

Do Stage 3 kids sound like angels? They're not. They don't always *use* their Stage 3 reasoning. Just as with the rest of us, the voice of conscience is often drowned out by the voice of temptation ("Go ahead and take another cookie!"). But even if kids don't always follow it, a conscience is still a big developmental achievement. Morality, in Larry's words, is now a "voice inside."

STAGE 3 AND THE GOLDEN RULE

At Stage 2, kids believed in tit-for-tat: Do unto others as they do unto you. At Stage 3, they believe in the Golden Rule: Do unto others *as you would have them* do unto you. That's another major breakthrough.

You can find out whether kids understand the Golden Rule by asking them a simple question: "What does the Golden Rule tell you to do if somebody comes up on the street and punches you in the arm?" Kids reasoning at Stage 2 say, "Punch him back. You should do to others the same as they do to you." A boy reasoning at Stage 3 said, "You shouldn't hit back. There's no end to revenge."

Eight-year-old Brenda disagreed with her 3rd-grade classmates who said the police should shoot the teenage vandals who broke into a zoo and killed several animals. Said Brenda: "Two wrongs don't make a right."

Stage 3 thinkers see the shortcomings of a Stage 2, eye-for-an-eye ethic. It doesn't necessarily solve the problem.

Stage 3 doesn't mean you always turn the other cheek, however. As one Stage 3 13-year-old said, "When you're dealing with kids who are mean, sometimes you have to come down to their level. It's the only thing they understand." Many a Stage 2 bully will lay off when his victim returns his blows.

MERCY TEMPERS JUSTICE

Stage 3 thinkers show a new flexibility. They can weigh situational factors, consider extenuating circumstances.

Here's an example of how this new flexibility shows up in kids' judgments about what's fair. The Swiss psychologist Piaget asked kids what should be done if three children were each given a cookie and the littlest one accidentally dropped hers over the bridge and into the river. At Stage 2, kids said, "That's just too bad. They each got an equal share—the two who were careful shouldn't have to give any of theirs to the one who wasn't." At Stage 3, kids said it would be fair for the older ones to give a piece of their cookie to the little girl because "sometimes little kids don't know enough to be careful."

A kinder fairness replaces the strict equality of Stage 2. Mercy tempers justice at Stage 3.

STAGE 3 AND RELATIONSHIPS

Stage 2 thought of relationships as a kind of a deal. You do something for me, I'll do something for you. Stage 3 thinkers still believe in reciprocity, but they've got a broader time perspective. To them a good relationship means that people help each other over the long haul. Immediate payoffs aren't necessary. To a parent, that's a welcome change. You can ask for help with the dishes and not get, "What'll you do for me?" There's a new spirit of cooperation.

Even after kids begin to understand relationships in this new way, it'll take some time—years maybe—before a cooperative spirit gets established as their *dominant* orientation, something you can depend on. Stage 2 will fade slowly. Be patient. Rest assured that with your help, Stage 3 will steadily gain ground.

As kids get better at understanding relationships, they also begin to understand the meaning and importance of trust. They begin to see trust as one of the vital building blocks in any relationship. If you trust people, you know that they'll hold up their end of the stick. Says 10-year-old Kathy, "A friend is somebody I can count on."

Trust makes a big difference in parent-child relations, too. At Stage 3, your child will be on the same wave length when you appeal to trust: "I'm trusting you to keep your promise" or "I'm disappointed—I trusted you to be more responsible."

"IF YOU TELL LIES, NOBODY WILL BELIEVE YOU"

Understanding the value of trust helps kids understand why it's important to tell the truth. I asked Stephen, age 11, "Why do you think a person shouldn't lie?"

Stephen: You could get a bad reputation that way. If you tell too many lies, nobody will believe you.

Me: People would always wonder if you're telling another lie.

Stephen: Right.

Me: Can you think of any other reasons why you shouldn't tell a lie?

Stephen: It makes your life unhappy. If you lie, nobody can trust you, and that's a very sad feeling.

Mind you, even kids who have this Stage 3 understanding of trust are probably going to lie at least once in a while. In fact, the same Stage 3 desire to please that leads kids to do what we want leads them to lie at other times in order to avoid *dis*pleasing us! So don't be shocked if you catch your usually trustworthy 10-year-old in a whopper.

Fear of a parent's anger is no doubt the single biggest cause of kids' lies. So if you want your child to be truthful with you, try to minimize fear of your anger as an obstacle. You might try the following approach. First, stress the importance of trust (and you'll have to say this more than once): "There's nothing more important than trust between parents and kids; it's what makes it possible for us to communicate and believe each other." Then, to try to reduce the fear factor, say something like this:

"When you've done something you shouldn't, and you're afraid to tell me because you think I'll get mad, come to me and say, 'I'm afraid you're going to be angry about this. . . .' That will remind me not to get angry. Depending on what it is, you may have to do something to make up for what you've done. But I promise not to get angry, and I'll be very proud of you for telling the truth."

It's a good idea to repeat this assurance periodically; otherwise kids' old apprehensions are likely to return. And remember that you don't have to let kids off scot-free when they fess up. Sometimes a fair consequence for the misdeed will be appropriate; sometimes just being sorry is enough. The most important thing is to deal calmly with whatever your children own up to, and to congratulate them for having the courage to tell the truth.

Some lying about accomplishments (exaggerating, for example, athletic feats or grades in school) is normal Stage 3 behavior to impress parents or peers. An excessive amount of tale-telling, however, suggests that a child suffers from strong feelings of inadequacy and needs both positive regard from parents and help in finding a different way to try to win recognition and acceptance from peers. (Developing a real skill that peers will admire is one such way.) Similarly, kids who tell a lot of mean-spirited lies about other kids may suffer from lack of peer acceptance and low self-esteem.

So, just as at other stages, a certain degree of troublesome behavior is developmentally normal at Stage 3, but an excessive amount may indicate an underlying problem that needs your attention. As I've said before, don't be afraid to get professional help if the problem seems serious, and you're not having any luck dealing with it.

"HOW DOES MY BEHAVIOR AFFECT THE FAMILY?"

Stage 3's new understanding of human relationships has another positive side: an ability to take the viewpoint of the group.

At Stage 1, kids believed that only one viewpoint was important, that of adult authority ("I should do what Mom and Dad say"). At Stage 2, kids brought together two perspectives, their own and that of another person ("Let's make a deal"). At Stage

3, kids can take the perspective of a whole group and think of themselves in relationship to it. Now, on their own, they can think, "How does my behavior affect the family?"

Rules are no longer just bargains, as they were at Stage 2. Stage 3 understands that rules are necessary to help people live together and get along in groups.

Because of their new perspective-taking ability, Stage 3 kids feel a stronger sense of belonging and accountability to their groups, both family and peers. As a parent or a teacher, you can appeal to this new accountability and try to develop a spirit of "all for one, and one for all."

"I THOUGHT OF HOW HE'D FEEL"

One of the nicest things about Stage 3 is the emergence of a capacity for honest-to-goodness altruism.

Once kids grasp the Golden Rule, they have greater empathy for others. How would I feel if I were left out of the game? How would I like it if somebody made fun of me?

Along with their greater empathy for others comes a greater concern for helping them out. Younger children will sometimes do a "good deed," but usually they're secretly hoping you'll give them a little something for their efforts. At Stage 3, kids really believe that you should do favors for other people and not be concerned about getting a reward. In fact, there is a reward at Stage 3, but it's a new kind: the warm glow that comes from being able to think, "I did a kind thing; I'm a good person."

Ten-year-old Craig came home wearing a smile of satisfaction.

"You look pretty happy," Craig's mother said.

"Yup!" Craig said. "I did a good deed on the way home from the store. I saw the meter maid walking down the street, then I noticed a car with an expired meter. I put a nickel in the meter so the person wouldn't get a ticket."

"Gee, that was pretty nice," his mother said.

"Well," Craig continued, "I thought of how the person would feel if he got a ticket. He'd come out of the store, see the ticket, and say, 'Oh, brother! Just what I need—a ticket!'"

"You feel pretty good that you helped somebody," his mother said.

"Yeah," Craig sighed, "I do."

Craig's mother, in relating this story, hastened to add that this sort of thing didn't happen every day. Craig still fought with his little brother and sometimes dragged his feet when he was asked to help around the house. But he was much more responsive than he used to be when his parents said things like, "We really need your help." At Stage 3, he knew that he *should* be a helpful person.

At Stage 2, kids would say that Craig was crazy to put money in a stranger's parking meter because it wasn't his problem.

Try asking kids what they should do if they see two kids beating up another on the school playground. Stage 2 reasoners will say something like, "It's none of your business." (Unfortunately, a lot of adults still think that way about other people's problems.) Stage 3 reasoners will say, "It *is* your business—you'd want somebody to help you if you were getting beat up by bullies!" Stage 3 kids might not always have the courage to act on what they know is right, but they understand why a person should help.

BE ON THE LOOKOUT FOR STAGE MIX

I want to pause here to remind you that you shouldn't expect your child to be a "pure" Stage 3 (or a pure example of any other stage, for that matter). Kids, like the rest of us, are usually a mix of stages. They usually have a dominant stage that they use most of the time (Stage 2, for example), a new stage that they're growing into (Stage 3, for example), and an old stage (Stage 1, for example) that they're gradually leaving behind. Different situations bring out different stages. When kids are tired, frustrated, or caught up completely in what *they* want, their lower-stage reasoning comes to the fore. That's why it's hard to have a good discussion when kids are upset. High emotion (and the same goes for adults) usually means low moral reasoning.

The trick is to help kids use their best moral reasoning as much as possible by appealing to them at their highest available stage. It also helps to know the lowest stage of reasoning that they still carry around in their heads. That way you won't be surprised when they "don't act their age." You'll understand that they've slipped into a lower-stage way of dealing with the world.

In Appendix B you'll find another moral dilemma (similar to "Peter and the Picnic" in Chapter 7) that will help you get in touch with the range of your child's moral reasoning.

STAGE 3 IN THE TEENS: A NEW BALLGAME

Stage 3 children may frequently "fall from grace" and slide into lower-stage reasoning. But all things considered, life gets easier for parents once kids are able to see the world from a Stage 3 perspective.

Until they hit the teens.

The pattern varies from child to child, but almost always there's more stress and strain between parents and kids once childhood gives way to adolescence. For some parents, the change is almost more than they can believe. Says one mother:

"Barbara is 18 now. Things are good between us, but the years between 14 and 17 were an absolute nightmare. I wouldn't wish it on my worst enemy. Barbara reacted against everything. Before that, we had been very close. She always listened to me, even sought out my judgment. To me, there was a complete regression—from this nice, intelligent girl to a demanding, egocentric 2-year-old. She disappeared into her room and kept the door closed most of the time. If there was a way of sliding the food in, I think she would have stayed in there all the time. It was as if she went to bed one night and left in the middle of the night, and in her place the next morning was this strange person that I didn't like and didn't even want to be in my house."

What's going on here? Why should a nice, cooperative Stage 3 child suddenly regress to what looks like Stage 0?

Teenagers don't always mount a full-scale revolt or do a Jekyll-and-Hyde transformation. But even when they don't, they usually undergo some or all of the following changes, any combination of which can give parents fits: They become moody, argumentative, and sullen; their self-concept does a nose dive;

manners you thought were well established hopelessly deteriorate; they acquire bad habits you never dreamed they'd have; they become obsessed with what other kids think of their every action and with every aspect of their appearance; they no longer seem to have a mind of their own; or they act without the slightest thought to the consequences.

To identify the developmental changes that help explain why teens act the way they do, let's look under the skin of a teenager.

THE INTELLECTUAL REVOLUTION THAT TEENS UNDERGO

Jean Piaget, who pioneered in studying children's moral judgment, also made important discoveries about the intellectual changes that occur as kids graduate from childhood to adolescence. It's a time when they're beginning to develop what Piaget called "formal operational thinking."

Some aspects of formal operational thinking may begin as early as 11 or 12. In a good environment, this kind of thinking will continue to develop throughout the teen years. It's nothing less than a revolution in your child's intellectual functioning, unleashing new powers of thought that have strong social and emotional consequences. Here's what happens:

1. At the formal level of thinking (as opposed to the "concrete" level of childhood thinking), kids can think about their own thoughts. They can go beyond the boundaries of their own concrete experiences. They can dream up possible values, possible life-styles, possible worlds they'd rather live in. They can stand back from life and take stock of it.

2. Kids become acutely aware of themselves as persons. They study themselves in the mirror. They can now put themselves in somebody else's shoes and look at themselves from that perspective. Said one 13-year-old boy: "Sometimes I imagine I'm on a video screen and other people are looking at me, and that influences how I act." Teenagers also imagine how their friends would react to your family's way of doing things. When Mark was 13 and we'd be having a family meeting, he'd shake his head, roll his eyes, and say, "I just keep thinking of what Matt McCarthy would think if he could hear this discussion!"

3. When teens become conscious of themselves, they're usually not happy with what they find. If your 13-year-old is typical, he or she will come down with a huge inferiority complex. "I *hate* the way I look!" is a nearly universal teen complaint. Kids may even wish with all their heart that they could trade themselves in on a whole new model. Says 13-year-old Greg: "I don't like myself at all. I wish I were Jack Casey. He has everything— looks, charisma, sports ability, and he's popular with girls. I don't have any of those things!" Kids struggle with questions of identity: What kind of person am I? What kind of person do I want to be?

4. Acutely conscious of everything around them and feeling bad about themselves, teenagers become supercritics. They're critical of other kids at school. They're suddenly critical of the "childish" behavior of their 6-year-old brother. They're critical of the way you go about being parents. They're even critical of the way you dress or the way you keep or decorate your house. A friend says his 14-year-old daughter announced one day, "This living room looks like a clown's dressing room!" Other parents, compared to you, are nicer, more fair, more "with it." And at the same time that teens are raking you over the coals, they're supersensitive to any criticism of them!

5. Because kids are feeling so vulnerable at this stage, they desperately need peer acceptance and approval. You can offer approval and should. But as one 13-year-old responded to his mother's reassurances, "No offense, Mom, but you just say that because you're my mother—you *have* to love me!" To feel good about themselves, teenagers need to make it in the outside world. For them, that world is the peer group; it's their stamp of approval they so fervently seek. They'll go to great lengths to get it. Once they've got it, they'll go to great lengths to avoid losing it.

A friend's 8th-grade daughter loved gymnastics. She'd gone to gymnastics class at the Y since she was a little girl. Then one day she came home from school and told her father, "Dad, I don't think I'm going to go to gymnastics this year." "Why not?" asked her bewildered father. She said some girls at school had put down gymnastics and said, "What do you want to do *that* for? You won't have any time to talk on the phone!" It took several long conversations with her parents to persuade her to do what she really wanted to do: continue gymnastics.

"I'll Just Slip Away"

Todd, 14, loved acting. He was good at it. He had taken acting classes where he lived before and wanted to join the drama club at his new school. But the "group" at his new school looked down on drama club. It didn't have very high "status." "I'm just on the edge of the group," Todd told his mother. "They just let me hang around. If I join acting, I'll just slip away."

"I Want To Be Popular!"

Mere acceptance, of course, is only barely making it for Stage 3 adolescents. "Being popular" is their big dream. They're sure that popularity is the way to true happiness. "You're too strict, and you're bringing me up to be *prissy*!" 14-year-old Angela complained to her mother in desperate tones. "I want to be *popular*!"

"My Greatest Fear"

I asked an 8th-grader what held him back from sticking up for a teacher he liked that other kids were making fun of. "That's easy," he said. "Fear of rejection."

"My greatest fear," says another teenager, "is being made a fool of."

So those are some of the pressures that teens are under. Pressures that come from changes going on in their minds. Add to that all the changes going on in their bodies, plus the horrendous task of figuring out how to relate to the opposite sex. It's not hard to understand why teenagers are sometimes tough to live with. If we were under as much pressure, we'd be tough to live with, too.

"EVERYBODY'S DOING IT"

The teen years expose the real Achilles heel of Stage 3 moral reasoning: its dependence on the opinions of others. That dependence makes kids vulnerable to the most insidious peer-group pressure of all—the argument that "everybody's doing it."

Think of Stage 3 as a combination of inner direction and outer direction. It's inner-directed in the sense that Stage 3 kids believe they should live up to their inner ideal of a "good person." They don't need external threats or bribes as a reason to be good.

But in another, very important sense, Stage 3 is outer-directed. Stage 3 thinkers want to live up to their image of a good person, but where do they get that image? They get it from people outside themselves. They rely on others to help them decide what's right and wrong.

In the *childhood* years, parents, if they try, can readily supply a child's image of what a good person does and doesn't do. If parents say you should share, help, and care about others, and you shouldn't lie, cheat, or steal, those moral standards become the "voice inside," the conscience of the Stage 3 child. Kids might not always follow their conscience, but it's clear where their conscience comes from: the home.

At 11, 12, or 13—it depends on the child, the family, and the social environment just when it happens—the ballgame changes. Peers gain a new power. Parents have to fight for equal time.

Kids are caught in the middle. They get confused about what they think. Parents and their childhood conscience may say, "Nice people don't steal," but other kids, kids who are like them in a lot of ways, are stealing left and right. Parents and their childhood conscience may say, "Good people obey the law," but half the kids at school experiment with one or another kind of illegal drug. Parents and their childhood conscience may say, "Don't cheat," but their friends cheat on tests all the time. Can these things be so wrong if so many other people are doing them?

Sometimes teenagers deal with their confusion by sticking with the values they learned as a child. Sometimes they deal with it by rebelling against their parents and identifying totally with the peer group. Sometimes they swing back and forth between the two, or come down in between. In any case, it becomes painfully clear just how outer-directed a Stage 3 conscience is.

**"I Feel Other People Are Pressing
Their Views Into Me!"**

"I wonder what kids would think of me if they knew what I was really like," said a 13-year-old who felt he put on a front to please a clique at school.

"What *are* you really like?" his mother asked.

"I don't know," he said. "I used to know what I think, but I don't know anymore." And then, slumping down and pushing his fingertips against his forehead, he said, "I feel that other people are pressing their views into me!"

It's easy to understand how Stage 3 thinkers get started down the slippery slope of sex, drugs, and drinking. Intense emotional needs and immature moral reasoning conspire to make them highly susceptible to the pressure to conform.

HOW TO RELATE TO KIDS AT STAGE 3

How can parents help kids during this difficult part of their journey toward moral maturity?

Rising peer influence during Stage 3 is a natural developmental phenomenon; you couldn't stop it if you tried. But what you can do is to try to make kids strong enough and secure enough to withstand the corrupting influences of the peer group, those influences that run counter to basic moral values.

I think there are four ways to do that:

1. *Maintain a positive personal relationship with your child and a strong family life.*

2. *Help your child develop a positive self-concept.*

3. *Teach your child moral values.*

4. *Balance independence and control.*

In earlier chapters, I talked first about how to go with the flow of a moral stage, then about how to challenge it. Here I'll talk about both at the same time. That's because the four approaches to Stage 3 accommodate kids in some ways and challenge them in others. Using these approaches, you'll give kids support, compensate for the weaknesses of Stage 3, and meet them where they are developmentally. But you'll also help them rise above the limitations of Stage 3 and develop the more independent sense of self that's the bridge to Stage 4 of moral reasoning.

Let's look in turn at each of these four ways to foster your child's moral development during Stage 3.

1. MAINTAIN A POSITIVE PERSONAL RELATIONSHIP WITH YOUR CHILD AND A STRONG FAMILY LIFE

The first way to try to offset the growing power of peers is to try to maintain a positive relationship with your child and a strong family life. How can you do that during Stage 3?

Talk the Language of Stage 3

Don't talk down to Stage 3 kids with Stage 1 threats ("Do it if you know what's good for you") or Stage 2 deals ("If you do this for me, I'll do that for you"). Lower-stage communications don't respect what a Stage 3 thinker is capable of. What's more, they don't encourage Stage 3 kids to develop horizontally by using their new powers of moral reasoning.

Here are a dozen communications that appeal to Stage 3 kids at their developmental level:

1. "Wouldn't you like to have a reputation for being a responsible (caring, sincere, honest) person?"
2. "This is a favor we're asking. Think of it as a good deed."
3. "We appreciate your helping without getting something in return."
4. "How about a little of the old family spirit? If we all help, we can get this done quickly."
5. "Try to stand outside yourself for a minute and look at this from my point of view. What would you do if you were the parent?"
6. "I'm tired and grouchy right now, and I really need your full cooperation. Thank you."
7. "We need you to think of the whole family, not just yourself."
8. "Try to remember what it's like to be 6. It's only natural for Helen to say things that sound silly to you at your age."

9. "How do you think it sounds when you talk to your brother like that?"

10. "We're trusting you to do what we've asked while we're gone. Can we depend on you to do that?"

11. "We expect you to be a responsible person, even when those around you aren't. We probably do expect more of you than some other parents expect of their kids. But we expect a lot of you because we think a lot of you."

12. "Grandma and Grandpa are coming for the weekend. We'd really like you and Brian to make a special effort to mind your manners and get along. Show them you can be considerate, okay?"

A mother told me of a time when her 12-year-old daughter was objecting to the family policy about TV. Matter-of-factly, the mother said, "Vickie, that's just the way we do it in our family. That's just the way we are." The daughter stopped arguing. "It was as if a light went on," the mother said. "Did I tap into Stage 3?" I think she did. Stage 3 stands ready to conform to the norms of the group, once understood as such. At least in the childhood years (before teen independence sets in), that's something you can appeal to in getting kids to accept "the family way."

Another mother did something similar to encourage her 8- and 10-year-old sons to be truthful. "You're a Lieberman," she said. "Liebermans don't lie."

A father, when he found that his 8-year-old son had lied to him about doing his homework, took this tack:

"Andrew, what kind of a reputation do you want to have?"

Replied Andrew, very seriously: "I don't want to have the reputation of a liar."

Father: "So what should you do?"

Andrew: "Tell the truth."

All of these are ways to go with the flow of your child's Stage 3 reasoning. If you're talking in ways that are tuned in to your child's way of looking at things, you'll have a better chance of getting a positive response to your appeal.

If There's a Problem, Try to Solve It

If you're upset with kids about something—not doing chores, tying up the phone, letting their schoolwork slip—sit down and talk it out. The work-it-out strategy isn't new at Stage 3, but it's especially important in the teens, when problems multiply and can easily upset your relationship with your child if you don't take constructive action. Just the act of trying to solve a problem in a way that meets everybody's needs usually does a lot to put things back on an even keel.

Try to resist the temptation, which I think many of us experience, to let things slide in order to "keep the peace" with teenagers. Sometimes we look the other way and hope a problem will disappear—until the whole situation blows up in our faces. Teenagers, of course, are quick to say, "You don't trust me!" when parents confront them about certain issues, such as where they've been, what they've been doing, etc. If your child says that to you, you can reply:

> "Trust isn't blind; it's based on knowledge. I need to know where you are and what you're doing. You're on your way to being an adult, but you're not there yet and you can make some mistakes along the way that can hurt you very much. It's my job to help see that that doesn't happen."

Spend Time Together

In my discussion of Stage 2, I stressed the importance of nurturing a loving relationship with your child by spending some time together when it's just the two of you. That's still very important at Stage 3. With kids or adults, personal relationships need intimacy to stay strong. So make it a point to protect some one-on-one time for you and your youngster.

One of my favorite images of fathering comes from the autobiography of Christiaan Barnard, the doctor who originated the heart transplant:

> "Whenever we were ill, my father got up at night to doctor us. I suffered from festering toenails that pained so much I would cry in bed. My father used to draw out the fester with a poultice made of milk and bread crumbs, or Sunlight soap and sugar. And when I had a cold, he would rub my chest with Vicks and cover it with a red-flannel cloth.
> "Sunday afternoons, we walked together to the top of the hill by the dam. Once there, we would sit on a rock and look down at

the town below us. Then I would tell my problems to my father, and he would speak of his to me."[2]

Stay in Touch

Says the mother of 11-year-old Scott:

> "I hugged and kissed Scott when he was little, but I didn't think he needed that when he got older. This year was more relaxed for me, and I found myself being more physical with him. It was as if a dam broke. I realized he needed it all along. It's made a big difference in our relationship—things are much easier between us now."

Kids don't outgrow their need for physical affection, even in the teens. A little touching—a hug, a tousle of the hair, an arm around the shoulder—can go a long way toward easing tensions and keeping up a flow of good feelings.

Help Kids Develop a Sense of Identity Within Their Family

Strong family roots help kids answer the questions "Who am I?" and "What do I believe?" as they struggle to construct an identity in adolescence. Roots also help them stand firm in the winds of peer pressure.

Some families trace their family tree as one way of helping their kids learn about, and feel connected with, their family's past. Author Heidi Watts, in her essay "Do You Remember When?" describes how parents can create a living family history by reminiscing with their children around the dinner table about shared experiences, good and bad. Other families draw their identity from cherished family traditions, some handed down unchanged through the generations, some adapted to fit new lifestyles.

It's natural for kids in their teens to want to spend more time with their friends. We should honor that and understand the developmental need that lies behind it: friends give teenagers good feelings about themselves at a time when that's terribly important. But I don't think family life should stop in the teens. Kids continue to need adults in their lives, and the family remains an important moral anchor and source of identity.

You may wonder, what about kids who have a fractured sense of family identity? One mother, for example, asked, "What if you *don't* want your children to identify with their father—because you don't think he's a very good role model?"

Says another woman:

> "My parents were divorced when I was 6. My mother was very vague about the reasons for the divorce. She'd say, 'Your father was a wonderful man, but he was weak.' I think I have some of my father in me. Whenever my mother got mad at me, she'd say, 'You're just like your father!'"

Many of us feel that our parents are in us, and they are—including some of their faults. Some of that legacy may be in the genes. We're born, for example, with a certain kind of emotional constitution that makes up an important part of our personality. All that a parent can do to try to modify that sort of inheritance in their child (a short temper, for example) is to make their child aware of it and to encourage the development of habits (ways of controlling anger, for example) that offset it.

I would not recommend, however, running down the other parent in the hope that, once kids realize what a louse he or she is, they'll decide not to be like *that*. Kids should be allowed to develop their own feelings about their parents, based on their relationships with them. We should not sabotage the possibility of a good relationship (which will help a child's moral development) by painting the other parent black. If you feel you have to say something about an absent parent's shortcoming—by way of explaining a divorce, for example—I think it's best to keep it fairly general and try to balance it with what's positive (as the mother did when she told her daughter that the father was "wonderful but weak").

I do think it's important to talk frankly with kids about the moral shortcomings we know they see in us. For example: "Your mother and I haven't been getting along very well lately, and we've said some pretty awful things to each other. I want you to know I feel bad about that." "I've been under a lot of pressure at work lately, and I think that's why I've been yelling at you kids so much. I'm sorry." "I got pretty depressed when I got laid off from my job last month, and I started drinking again. I'm not proud of that, and I certainly hope you won't think that booze is a good way to handle problems."

Especially in the teen years, kids can be very harsh judges when they see us failing to practice what we preach. I think we have a better chance of maintaining their respect if we talk openly with them about the times when we fall short of our own moral standards. As a wise bishop once said, we can have human failings and still be a good example to our children. They don't need to see someone who is perfect, only someone who is trying.

2. HELP YOUR CHILD DEVELOP A POSITIVE SELF-CONCEPT

The second key principle for relating to Stage 3 is this: Do everything you can to help your child develop a positive self-concept.

Says one young woman:

> "My mother was extremely critical of my sister and me when we were teenagers. It seemed as if we never did anything that met with her approval. All through our teens my sister and I lacked confidence in ourselves."

Another mother has a very different memory of her childhood:

> "The climate in our home was always that you could be anything you wanted to be. 'Keep your eyes on the stars and your feet on the ground' was a family slogan. No adversity could keep us from our goals. We were urged to think of our options.
>
> "My mother taught us that it's not important what one has, only how one feels. Though we lived in a tenement, we never felt poor. We were rich in spirit, ability, caring, and laughter."

One mother tore her children down. The other built them up. Why is it so important to build a child's self-esteem during Stage 3? One mother said it well: "Kids who feel okay about themselves, who are at peace with themselves, are more likely to follow their own beliefs." They don't have to rip off or pop pills just because others are doing it.

Dr. Stanley Coopersmith, a University of California psychologist, compared preadolescents who were high in self-esteem and ability to follow their own judgment with youngsters who were low on these dimensions.[3] He found striking contrasts in their home backgrounds:

- Parents of high self-esteem kids showed more love and acceptance of their children through everyday expressions of affection and concern. Parents of low self-esteem kids tended to be very critical.
- Parents of high self-esteem kids were *less* permissive. They set and enforced clear rules; parents of low self-esteem kids didn't.
- There was a healthy degree of democracy in high self-esteem families. They made it a point always to give kids a fair hearing. Not so in low self-esteem families.

Loving acceptance, firm discipline, and respect for their kids as persons—these were the parenting behaviors that enabled a child to think, "I am somebody worthwhile."

Don't Make Comparisons

One thing we should definitely *not* do, something that can run a child's self-concept right into the ground, is to make comparisons.

"Your brother always got good grades, why can't you?"

"Your sister never gave me any trouble—why do you have to?"

"Richard Evans got himself a paper route. Why don't you show a little ambition and do something like that?"

When we make remarks like these, we may think we're telling kids, "You can do better." The message they usually hear, however, is: "You're inferior." Critical comparisons are hard to hear at any age, and in the teens they can be devastating. Moreover, comparisons with a brother or sister often foster intense resentment of the praised sibling.

If you think your kids should be doing better in some way than they are, say so *directly* ("I don't think your grades reflect your ability" or "I think you'd be doing better with your piano if you put in more time")—not by making denigrating comparisons.

Treat Sons and Daughters Equally

One young woman remembers:

> "I was the only girl in my family, and I was the only one who was expected to help with the dishes and the housework. My three brothers never lifted a finger. When I'd complain that it wasn't fair—that they should help—I was told, 'That's women's work.'"

This kind of discrimination hurts the moral development of both sexes. It says to boys, "You have a right to expect women to wait on you and clean up after you." It says to girls, "Your lot in life is to do the work that nobody else wants to do." Girls can grow up with a diminished sense of self-worth as a result of such treatment. We should try to avoid any sort of sexism at all ages, and especially at Stage 3, when kids are more consciously constructing a self-image.

Friends and Self-Esteem

All through Stage 3, but especially in the teens, friends are an important source of a child's self-esteem.

A teenager who has friends, even one good friend, doesn't have to worry as much about dancing to the tune of the peer group. If you have the approval of someone, you don't need the approval of everyone. Friends give a teenager a group within the group, a little island of security on which to begin to develop a more independent sense of self. So support kids' efforts to find friends who accept them for the person they are and invite them to bring their friends home (so you'll know what they're like!).

Help Kids Develop Their Interests and Abilities

One of the best ways to help kids form a positive self-concept and stay out of trouble in the teens is to help them develop their interests and abilities.

Erik Erikson, the famous psychoanalyst, says that children standing on the brink of adolescence face a choice between "industry and inferiority." They can master new skills, learn to win recognition through achievement, and gain the confidence they need to step out of childhood toward the adult world. Or they can despair of their ability to do things, consider themselves doomed to inadequacy, and develop the hostility toward self and others that comes from feelings of inferiority. Whether children strive toward industry or sink into inferiority has a profound effect on their subsequent personal and moral development.

So encourage your child to get involved in some activity that generates "I can do" feelings. It can be an academic pursuit, playing a musical instrument, singing, dancing, acting, drawing, baseball, basketball, tennis, gymnastics, swimming, sailing, skating, skiing, or horseback riding. It can be anything, just so long as it gives your child something to be interested in and good at. If you can help your youngster develop several of these skills, so much the better for his or her self-esteem.

I'm not suggesting, however, that you should ride herd on kids and make they never "waste time." Teenagers *need* to do some things that parents may consider wasting time—talking with friends on the phone, listening to records, daydreaming—partly because such activities have social or introspective value, and partly because they provide a break from all the pressure teens are under. We should respect this need while at the same time helping kids realize that these years are critical for their development as persons. They have the time and energy and just plain raw potential for developing interests and abilities that will serve them all their lives and give them good feelings about themselves right now.

When kids feel good about what they can do, they're better able to tolerate the anxieties that growing up involves. They have less need to seek security through conformity or to escape through drugs, drinking, or sex.

Help Kids Break the Put-Down Habit

We've seen how teens, because of their own insecurities, become supercritical of everyone around them, including their peers. Says a mother: "When our 14-year-old daughter isn't driving us crazy fighting with her younger brother and sister, she's getting on our nerves with her endless catty remarks about kids in her class."

Even though putting down peers and siblings is normal teenage behavior, I don't think parents should just ignore it. I think it's very important to repeatedly make clear our disapproval of put-downs and to help kids understand all the reasons why such remarks are uncharitable, unappealing, and self-defeating behavior:

1. They reveal insecurity; people put others down because they don't feel confident themselves.

2. Even if other people laugh off a put-down, inside they don't like it, won't forget it, and will probably find a way to get even (often by paying you back with a zinger when you're not expecting it).

3. Put-downs cause others to think less, not more, of you; kids who are well liked are ones who make others feel comfortable and good about themselves.

4. At the very time when they are most vulnerable and need most to feel good about themselves, teenagers are destroying each other's self-esteem through put-downs.[4]

A mother told of her efforts to get her 15-year-old son, Blair, to curb his clever sarcasm, which he regularly directed at his school friends and his 7-year-old brother, Bobby. As an experiment, Blair agreed to lay off his usual targets for a week, and to notice each day any effects he could see. Three days into the experiment, a surprised Blair said to his mother:

"Fred King actually thanked me today for not bugging him! Tim also seems more relaxed around me now. Bobby asked me if I can keep this up—not forever, but more like this than before. I can see how sarcasm puts people off. I'd rather have people feel comfortable around me than uncomfortable."

3. TEACH YOUR CHILD MORAL VALUES

A third very important thing you can do to foster moral development at Stage 3 is to teach your child moral values.

At Stage 3, kids have a special readiness to learn such moral values as courtesy, kindness, honesty, and responsibility. They've developed a true conscience. Their conscience tells them to live up to their image of a good person. *That's why it's very important for parents to help kids form an image of what a good person is.*

Don't wait until the teens to start. Lay the foundation of an honest and caring and responsible conscience during the childhood years, before the peer pressures begin to mount. Kids who carry a well-formed conscience into their teens are far better armed to withstand the temptations they'll face than those who graduate from childhood without the benefit of clear moral training.

Chapter 15 presents a wide range of values I think parents would do well to emphasize during the Stage 3 years. Right now I want to focus on a value that represents a real challenge to Stage 3 conformist reasoning, and that's *independence.* By directly teaching the value of independence, you can strengthen kids' ability to be their own person and to resist the worst pressures of the peer group. Here are some ways you can do that.

Be an Independent Person Yourself

Lots of parents unintentionally set the wrong kind of example when they cave in to kids' badgering that "*other* parents let their kids do such-and-such!" To set a good example, parents must show that *they* can resist pressure to conform to *their* peers.

Says a father of three teenagers: "Whenever my kids say, 'But, Dad, everybody's doing it!' I simply say, 'I don't believe in statistical morality. I don't decide what's right by what most people do.'" Besides challenging the moral logic of Stage 3, this father is serving as a model of someone who can stand apart from the crowd.

Parents who are independent people tend to have children who are independent. Likewise, conformist parents tend to have conformist children.

Talk About the Value of
Being Independent

Help kids see that it's really in their own interest to be independent. You can say things like:

"Be your own person. Do what *you* like to do, what *you're* interested in. If you're true to yourself, you'll be happy with yourself. You can't be happy trying to be what you're not."

"Other kids will respect you more if they think you have a mind of your own. It's the independent kids that other kids admire. They definitely won't respect you if they think you're bending over backward to please them."

Help Kids Think of Words to Say

Often kids will resist peer pressure if they can just think of a way to say no and still be "cool." (No kid wants to sound like a goody-goody!) You can help them think of "words to say" when they face tough situations. For example:

To a boyfriend or girl friend who's pushing for sexual relations with the line "Everybody's doing it," a teenager can say: "Well, if everybody's doing it, then you shouldn't have any trouble finding somebody else."

To a group that urges, "Hey, come on, try a little of this [pot, reds, cocaine, angel dust]—you're not chicken, are you?" a teenager can say, "No way—if you want to waste your body on that stuff, that's your business."

Help Kids Understand Themselves

Kids are better able to be independent when they understand the feelings that cause them to conform.

A book like Dr. James Dobson's *Preparing for Adolescence,* written for teens and preteens, helps kids make sense of their feelings. It tells them that virtually all kids in their early teens have acute feelings of inferiority—and that's why they experience such a strong need to seek peer approval through conformity. When kids begin to understand these feelings, the feelings have less of a grip on their behavior.

Help Kids Put Popularity in Perspective

Popularity is the value that keeps a lot of Stage 3 teenagers from being more independent.

Kids need to know that values change. Good looks, sports ability, or a bouncy personality may be highly valued by 14- and 15-year-olds, but they won't count for as much later on. Character, sensitivity to others, the ability to apply yourself and accomplish your goals—those are the qualities that become more and more important the older you get.

It may help teens to know that books have been written, such as *What Really Happened to the Class of '65?*, showing that the kids who "had it made" in high school didn't always make it so big in later life. Kids who weren't so popular in high school, one study showed, tended to *keep on developing*. They turned out to be the more confident and successful adults in their twenties and thirties.[5]

Challenge the "Group Morality" of Stage 3

You can challenge the conformist reasoning of Stage 3 kids by helping them see that "group morality" isn't a very good way to solve moral problems.

Will, who was on the junior high school baseball team, told his mother that the coach had kicked a kid off the team. Kids who thought it was unfair were talking about boycotting practice.

"Do *you* think it was unfair?" his mother asked.

"I'm not sure," Will said. "I just heard about what happened from some other kids. I didn't see it. According to them, Mr. Thompson accused Eric Miller of goofing off when he wasn't doing anything wrong. Then he just told him he was off the team."

"I see," his mother said. "So it's hard to be sure exactly what happened. What do you think of the boycott idea?"

"I don't know," Will said.

"How will you decide what to do?"

"I'll find out what other kids are going to do."

Will's mother tried to get him to examine the inadequacy of this kind of moral thinking. "What if half the kids plan to boycott and half go to practice? What will you do then?"

Will sighed and shrugged his shoulders.

"So can you decide what's right on the basis of what the other kids are doing?"

"I guess not," Will said.

"Right," his mother said. "You have to use your own judgment. Think about what's fair, and what's going to help you, the coach, and the team. Would a boycott help matters?"

"No, not really."

"What else could be done?"

Together, Will and his mother came up with the idea that he could go to Mr. Thompson privately the next day and ask if he'd call a meeting of the team to talk about what happened.

No matter how much you do to encourage independent thinking in the Stage 3 teens, development will be slow. Keep in mind that breaking free of peer-group conformity is often a painful and confusing process for kids. Says 15-year-old Lisa: "It's so hard to know what to do. If you go by your own judgment, things don't go right. If you go by the group, things don't go right." Try to show a sympathetic understanding of the pressures your child feels at this very fragile and vulnerable stage.

4. BALANCE INDEPENDENCE AND CONTROL

Teaching kids the value of thinking independently when they're with others is one way of helping them stay out of trouble and grow toward maturity. Another way is to go slow in granting them independence of action. Balancing kids' freedom with wise parental control, one of the big ideas in moral development, looms very large in the Stage 3 teens.

Stage 3 teenagers, as I've pointed out, still need control, because they're not adults yet. They're still highly susceptible to social pressures and still contending with their own developmental immaturities.

But you may wonder, "How can you control a teenager who doesn't want to be controlled?"

You can't.

The challenge is to get kids to accept control *willingly*.

That's why it's essential to think of independence and control at the same time. *Give kids enough of the independence they desire so they'll accept the control they need.*

Here are some ways to strike that balance.

Base Your Authority on Love

If the parent-child relationship is one of constant anger and hostility, a teenager will resent control and rebel against it. This is another reason why it's so important to keep a good relationship going during these years. If there's little love, kids won't accept your authority, and you'll have little control over their behavior.

Say Yes When You Can, But No When You Have To

Control isn't constriction. Research shows that effective parents set clear rules and high expectations, but they don't hem their kids in. If kids want to do something, and it's not detrimental to them, wise parents try to say yes.

Effective parents are also not afraid to say no. "No, you can't go to R-rated movies. They've got too much sex and violence, and we don't think they're a wholesome influence at your age." "No, you can't go to parties when the parents aren't home. There has to be adult supervision."

Says a father:

> "My 13-year-old son would love to be able to go to rock concerts with his friends. I'm in the advertising business—our firm has even promoted the Rolling Stones' concerts—so I really do feel a conflict when I explain that he can't go because I know what goes on at these concerts. But that's where I come down. I said he could go when he's 15, but even then, I'll have to go with him. He says, 'Oh, Dad!' but so far he's accepted it."

Teenagers don't always stoically submit to our restrictions, of course; sometimes they fuss and fume. But beneath all the sound and fury, they'll usually be glad for the limits. They know it means you care. And if you think they don't know that, then tell them: "You may think I'm unfair and hopelessly old-fashioned, but I'm the way I am because I care very much about what happens to you."

If kids keep protesting a particular decision and insist that you're being unreasonable, hear them out—and see if you can work out a solution that respects both your standards and their desires.

At the same time that you're exercising your authority, let teenagers know that you understand their desire to have more independence and that you accommodate that as much as you can. A 1978 study at Boston University by Robert Azrak found that when parents explicitly acknowledged their teenagers' wish to be more independent—to spend more time with their friends, for example, and less with their family—teens were more willing to accept parents' discipline and to listen to their moral reasoning.

Allow Kids Safe Ways To Rebel

If you give kids freedom in some areas, they don't have to demand it in others. Kids can gain a feeling of independence if they're able to make their own choices when it comes to things like the way they dress, the way they wear their hair, and the music they listen to (though I'd set some outer limits in this last area, since music like punk rock encourages reckless and antisocial behavior). They can do their breaking away in areas like these and still adhere to the basic moral values of respect and responsibility that they've grown up with.

Match Control to Your Child's Needs

Kids are different. Some can handle more responsibility than others and handle it sooner. Says one young woman:

> "My friends all had curfews as teenagers. I didn't. They were always trying to get around them. I would come in earlier than all the others to show my parents they were right to trust me."

Not all teenagers would behave this responsibly without clear limits. You have to know your child.

Kids not only differ in how much control they need; they also differ in how much they'll tolerate. Says the mother of a 16-year-old girl:

"These days if I tell my daughter, 'You can't,' she turns me right off. There's no communication. So instead, I try to get her to *think*. I say, 'Gee, have you really thought about that?' Or 'Before you do anything, would you please talk to me first?' She does think about it, and we do talk. We usually don't end up that far apart."

Every child is a unique human personality, with changing moods and needs. The general principle is to balance independence and control. But you have to find the *particular* balance that works for you and your child at this point in your child's development.

Don't Control Through Destructive Guilt

If you say to Stage 3 kids, "I'm disappointed in you," they may respond, "You make me feel so guilty!"

If your child says that, I'd recommend responding, "*I'm* not making you feel guilty; your conscience is. Guilt is a healthy sign that you've got a conscience that knows the difference between right and wrong. You can feel good about that."

Parents should understand that guilt is a natural expression of a child's maturing sense of moral responsibility. It's not a bad thing. What's important is to teach kids not to wallow in guilt but to say to themselves, "Okay, I didn't measure up. I feel bad about that, but I'm going to do better." Handled in this way, guilt is a constructive moral experience.

Destructive guilt is another story. It can cause a child to say, "I'm a bad person. I can never make up for the wrong I've done." The other side of this kind of guilt is intense anxiety: "I don't dare do anything to displease my parents. I couldn't stand to lose their approval!"

Parents should not use destructive guilt to control kids. It may block their development of a mature independence—and even cause them eventually to reject all morality as a "guilt trip" that stunts people's growth and robs them of happiness.

Use Indirect Control

Control doesn't always have to be direct. Some of the most positive and effective forms of parental control are indirect.

HOW TO RELATE TO KIDS AT STAGE 3

You can both go with the flow and challenge Stage 3's moral reasoning if you:

1. Maintain a positive personal relationship wih your child and a strong family life.
   - Talk the language of Stage 3 to get cooperation.
   - If there's a problem, try to solve it.
   - Spend time together and stay in touch physically as well as verbally.
   - Help your child develop a sense of identity within the family.

2. Help your child develop a positive self-concept.
   - Treat your child with love, firmness, and respect.
   - Don't compare your child with others.
   - Treat sons and daughters equally.
   - Support kids' efforts to find friends who help them feel good about themselves.
   - Help kids develop their interests and abilities.
   - Help them break the put-down habit.

3. Teach your child moral values, especially the value of independence.

4. Balance independence and control.
   - Base your authority on love.
   - Say yes when you can but no when you have to, and acknowledge teenagers' desire to be more independent.
   - Allow your child safe ways to rebel.
   - Match control to your child's needs.
   - Don't control through destructive guilt.
   - Use indirect control.

Parents who encourage their son's interest in music are exercising indirect control. So are parents who encourage their daughter's dedication to gymnastics. So are parents who expect their children to study hard and do their best in school. Encouragement and expectations of this kind help to channel kids in positive directions. A busy, involved child or teenager is one whose life needs relatively little external control.

So give kids some space, but stay involved in their lives. Some independence, but enough control.

Those are the four ways we can help our children at Stage 3: maintain a good personal relationship and a rich family life; help them develop a healthy self-concept; teach them moral values that offer an image of what a good person is; and balance independence and control.

All of these approaches will help to bring out the best of Stage 3—its capacity for cooperation and caring—and help kids develop horizontally by using that capacity in their relations with others. All will help kids become stronger, sturdier people who can survive the inner vulnerabilities and outer stresses of the Stage 3 teens. And all will help them turn another corner and move toward the next stage in their growth toward moral adulthood.

CHAPTER 10

STAGE 4:
"WHAT IF EVERYBODY DID IT?"

Teenagers who develop Stage 4 moral reasoning take a giant step toward what we normally think of as adult morality.

Stage 3 was a morality of personal relationships. At Stage 3, kids asked, "What does it mean to be a good son (daughter)? A good friend? A good member of my group? What do the people I know expect of me?"

Stage 4 has broader horizons. At this stage, teenagers can think of themselves not only as having personal relationships but also as being part of one or more "social systems." Now they can ask, "What does it mean to be a good member of my community? My church? Society? What do these social systems require of me, and everybody else?"

At Stage 3, kids wanted to live up to the expectations of the important people in their lives. Those expectations helped make Stage 3 kids more sensitive and caring people.

But those same expectations hemmed them in. They were a kind of moral straitjacket, keeping kids from really being their own persons.

Stage 4 breaks out of that straitjacket. It says, "Wait a minute, there's a lot more to morality than doing what my friends and parents expect of me. There's a whole society out there. I'm part of it, and so is everybody else. We've all got to obey the law and meet our obligations, or the whole thing will fall apart."

In this way, Stage 4 is more independent than Stage 3. If you feel a *duty* to your community or country, you've got a basis for bucking your immediate peer group. Everybody around you, for example, may be loafing on the job, but you put in an honest day's work because that's what you think makes a society work. Conformity to your peers isn't your highest calling; responsibility is.

Seen this way, Stage 4 is a swing back toward differentiation, toward asserting your individuality. There's a stronger sense of self, of being in the driver's seat, of setting your own agenda at Stage 4.

And yet, Stage 4 is also an important step toward greater social integration, toward taking your rightful place in a bigger social system. There's a more active sense of social obligation than there was at Stage 3. People shouldn't just go along; they should actively contribute to their community and society. They're part of it, they benefit from it, and so they should do their share. Differentiation and integration come into a more mature balance at Stage 4.

Why is Stage 4 so important? Why worry about developing it in kids?

It's at Stage 4 that kids truly understand what it means to be a good citizen. That's why Stage 4 morality is the essential foundation of a democratic society. You can't have government of, by, and for the people if the people don't care what shape the country's in. You can't even have a good community where you live if there aren't Stage 4 citizens who care about more than just themselves and their own family.

When do kids begin to show Stage 4? As always, it depends. Large numbers of teenagers graduate from high school still unable to see beyond the "me and my group" morality of Stage 3. Many stay at that level, even as adults. But with the right kinds of experience, kids are capable of developing at least some Stage 4 awareness during their teens, often during high school and sometimes as early as the junior high years.

"WHAT IF EVERYBODY DID IT?"

Stage 4—or the lack of it—relates to a moral problem that's a growing concern in nearly every community: teenage shoplifting.

A PROFILE OF STAGE 4

At Stage 4 of moral reasoning, kids:

1. Believe that being a good person includes carrying out their responsibilities to the social systems they feel part of.

2. Believe that the reason to fulfill their social responsibilities is to help keep the system going and to maintain self-respect as "somebody who meets my obligations."

3. Are more independent of peer pressure than they were at Stage 3, because being a responsible person is now a higher priority than pleasing people around them.

4. Can see the ripple effects of an action like stealing, cheating, or lying by thinking, "What if everybody did it?"

5. Care about people in their system that they don't know personally as well as those they do know.

6. Believe that cooperation is essential for the survival of society.

7. Have a need for a creed that gives them answers to questions about life, society, and their role in it.

8. Understand what it means to be a good citizen.

Talk to teenagers who shoplift and they often say, "So, what's a little ripping off? These store owners make enough profit to cover their losses." That's Stage 2 reasoning: "I'm looking out for myself [by ripping off], and they're looking out for themselves [by making big profits]." Or a teenager might try to justify shoplifting with Stage 3 logic: "Look, practically everybody shoplifts some of the time. All my friends do it. I don't want to look like some kind of a goody-goody."

Kids at Stages 2 and 3 don't *necessarily* steal, of course. If they've learned at home that stealing is wrong and honesty is important, they'll come up with reasons at their stage why they *shouldn't* steal. At Stage 2, a child can think, "I shouldn't steal if I know what's good for me"; at Stage 3, "What would my parents think of me if they found out I stole?"

Stage 4, however, is a stronger bulwark against stealing than the lower moral stages. Stage 4 thinkers, standing on higher moral ground, can see more. They can see the ripple effect, the wider social consequences, of an action like shoplifting.

Whereas Stage 3 often tries to justify an act by saying everybody's doing it, Stage 4 stands that moral logic on its head and asks, "What if everybody *really* did it? What if everybody shoplifted?" Here's Roland, arguing with his 8th-grade classmates, most of whom think shoplifting isn't so bad:

> "If everyone goes around shoplifting, do you know what kind of life that would be? Everybody would just be walking off with everybody else's stuff. The only thing that holds society together is the government, and you can't have government if everybody doesn't follow the rules."[1]

These 8th-graders were debating "Sharon's Dilemma": what should Sharon do when a store security officer demands the name of her companion and good friend, Jill, who has just slipped out the door with a shoplifted sweater? (Appendix B gives the full form of this dilemma, along with questions for drawing out moral reasoning.)

Two kids who spoke completely ignored the issue of stealing. They saw the whole issue as a matter of Stage 3 loyalty to a friend.

Harold: She should say, "I don't know her." She should lie for a friend.

Irene: I agree. Friendship matters more than a rule. I would value somebody I could talk to a lot higher than a material thing like a sweater.

Contrast Harold's and Irene's reasoning with that of Perry. Like Roland, he shows a Stage 4 concern for the far-reaching consequences of an action like stealing:

Perry: It's just not fair if everybody steals. You can't *live* if everybody is stealing. I say that if you lie and don't tell on your friend, you will probably keep your crummy friend who left you standing there in the store. But even if you tell and lose your friend, somewhere along the line you will get some other friends, because I am sure that one or two people in this world are straight.

Does Stage 4 say "to heck with friends"? Not at all. Friends are important at any stage of development. Friendship is still important to Perry, for example, but it's not the *only* thing that's important. Respecting other people's property rights is also important, and so he wants friends who are straight and who will share his sense of social responsibility. He's like a 14-year-old girl who decided she wasn't going to be friends anymore with a "popular group of kids" because "the only way they can get themselves up is by tearing other people down."

In Sharon's dilemma, does Stage 4 reasoning demand that you turn in your friend? Not necessarily. You might be very concerned about preserving the friendship and about doing what's good for your friend. You might try to get her to turn herself in. You might try to persuade the store owner not to press charges but to give her a chance to make amends somehow. You might even take the rap yourself and then try to get your friend to go straight.

But at Stage 4, no matter how much you cared about your friend, you'd also be concerned about the rights of the store owner and the bigger moral issue involved, namely, the social consequences of stealing. You might think, as one 15-year-old did, of "how old people and poor people are going to have to pay higher prices for things they need because of all the shoplifting that goes on." You might think about how everybody suffers from the inflation that shoplifting contributes to. At Stage 4, you'd see the big picture.

I want to underline the point that higher moral stages don't toss out the concerns of lower stages. Instead, each new stage folds the old-stage values into a wider understanding of what's right and what's wrong. Stage 4 doesn't forget about the personal relationships that are so central at Stage 3; rather, it makes those relationships part of a bigger moral vision that's concerned about the welfare of all members of society.

You can see how important Stage 4 is for a healthy society. Stage 4 helps you be good to people you don't know and may never even see. It keeps in mind two questions: *How will my actions affect other people in the system?* and *What if everybody did it?* If I dump my poison waste in a handy hole or river, will somebody else be drinking polluted water? What if everybody got rid of their waste that way? If I litter, who will have to pick up after me? What kind of an environment would we have if everybody used the world as their wastebasket?

At Stage 4, for the first time, kids understand human interdependence. They understand that we're all in the same boat, the same social system, and that "no man is an island." They realize that people, even people who are total strangers, have to cooperate with each other for the sake of the common good. That's a big idea, and a very important one in a youngster's moral development.

THE MANY FACES OF STAGE 4

I don't want to convey the impression that Stage 4 moral reasoning is concerned only with the big social system out there. Stage 4 thinkers also feel obligations to smaller "systems" closer to home.

Take the issue of smoking marijuana in school. A Stage 2 thinker might say, "Whether you smoke pot in school is your own business. It's no skin off anybody else's nose." At Stage 3, kids would tend to focus on their parents' or friends' feelings about it. But at Stage 4, kids could identify with the school as a system. They could ask, "What kind of a school would we have if everybody came to class stoned?"

A person's sense of religious identity also changes at Stage 4. At Stage 3, religion is like a personal relationship: I might go to church, for example, because I want to please God or my parents and because doing that helps me feel like a good person. At Stage 4, I can think of the community as well as the personal side of religion. I can feel a membership in a body of believers, a faith community through which I worship my God and live out my beliefs.

How you think about your family relationships—husband and

wife, parent and child—is also affected by Stage 4. Consider one of Kohlberg's fictitious moral dilemmas about a man named Heinz, whose wife is dying from a rare form of cancer. He can't raise the money to pay the exorbitant price a greedy druggist is charging for the medicine that might save his wife. So Heinz becomes desperate, breaks into the store, and steals the drug. Was he right or wrong to do that?

At Stage 3, people may talk about the husband having a "duty" to his wife to do something, but it's a duty based entirely on their personal relationship. Says Bob, "It's his duty to take care of his wife somehow, even if he doesn't love her anymore. He must have loved her once, and they've been through a lot together." See if you can spot the difference between Bob's Stage 3 viewpoint and Patrick's Stage 4 reasoning:

> "When you get married, you take a vow to care for the other person 'in sickness and in health,' and therefore you're morally obligated to do so. Even if you don't get married in a church, you still take on this kind of responsibility, and you're committed to help each other in the eyes of society. What kind of a world would it be if even husbands and wives didn't feel any obligations to each other?"[2]

Patrick, like Bob, is concerned about the personal relationship between a husband and wife. But unlike Bob, he puts that relationship in a wider social framework. As he sees it from a Stage 4 perspective, when you get married, you make a promise, a commitment, to take care of each other, and society counts on you to keep it. "Vows" and "oaths" are not just private matters; such commitments are the very foundation of a workable society. As one young woman says, "Promises are kind of like the law. You rely on people to keep them. If somebody says 'I will do this,' they will do it. If you couldn't trust people to keep their word, I think we would all go crazy."

How does Stage 4 look at the obligations that exist between parents and children? As a parent, you may be good to your kids because you love them and they love you. But at Stage 4, you also believe you have a responsibility, as a member of the community, to bring up healthy, decent, caring human beings. If parents don't take that responsibility seriously, we all suffer the consequences.

If you're a grown son or daughter, you may respect and care for your parents because they've done a lot for you and you love them. But what if they haven't been so good to you? What if something has happened to cause a rift, and your feelings toward your parents are mixed with hurt or anger? At Stage 4, you'd still feel an obligation to care for them. You'd recognize that all children have an obligation in decency to be concerned about their parents' welfare, no matter what the personal relationship between parent and child.

CONSCIENCE AT STAGE 4

At Stage 3, social approval was the tail that wagged the dog of conscience. If other people thought well of me, then I could think well of myself.

At Stage 4, it's the other way around. Self-respect comes first. Now a person thinks, "If I do what's necessary to respect myself, other people will respect me, too. If I carry out my obligations, people will respect and admire that. If they don't, that's their problem."

Barbara, 19, expresses the priority Stage 4 places on self-respect. Asked why a promise should be kept, she answers: "If you don't keep a promise, you lose respect for yourself because you don't have the integrity to keep your word. Other people will likewise lose their respect for you."[3]

To be "a person of honor," someone whose word can be trusted, becomes a moral ideal at Stage 4.

THE NEED FOR A CREED

Teenagers, says psychoanalyst Erik Erikson, have a deep need to "redefine their identity" as they approach the challenge of being an adult. They wonder, "What should my role in society be? Where do I fit in? And what kind of a society do I want to fit into?"

Teenagers who grapple with questions like these develop what Erikson calls an "ideological mind." They have a hunger for ideology, a need for a creed. They seek a system of ideals and beliefs that will guide their search for identity, dispel their confusion, and enable them to sort out what's good and bad in their lives and society.

All of this is an expression of Stage 4. And it explains the fiery moral idealism, the religious fervor, and the political zeal that frequently burst forth in the mid to late teens. Kids at this stage of development can imagine a better world, one that's much more appealing to them than the mess they think we've made of this one. Sometimes their idealism takes the form of a "we've got all the answers" attitude and simple solutions to complex problems. But even this immature form of idealism is an advance in moral maturity when measured against the restricted world view of Stage 3.

HOW TO HELP KIDS DEVELOP STAGE 4

Obviously, all of us have a stake in helping kids develop Stage 4 of moral reasoning.

If people don't develop to Stage 4, we end up with politicians who put special interests above the common good, businessmen who put profits ahead of people, and citizens whose moral vision and sense of responsibility stop at their doorstep. If people don't develop some Stage 4 reasoning, they lack the perspective to see the whole, to see that all of our lives are linked, and to see that each of us has a duty to care about the welfare of the society we live in.

What can a parent do to help kids to Stage 4?

I won't pretend that it's easy, in these days of narrow self-interest, to develop a Stage 4 perspective in kids and get them to use it. But I do think there are at least three kinds of things a parent can do to help kids cross the bridge from Stage 3 to Stage 4.

First, you can continue to foster kids' spirit of *independence,* their sense of being their own person, just as you did during Stage 3. Second, you can help them become *aware of society,* of the social systems (neighborhood, school, church, community, country) they belong to and how these systems depend on all of us to behave responsibly and do our part. Third, you can encourage kids to *participate in social roles* that give them firsthand knowledge of the more complex social systems that lie beyond their family and peer group.

A spirit of independence, an intellectual awareness of a wider social world, and real experience in that world—those are the factors that will help kids move on to Stage 4. Let's take a closer look at what a parent can do in each of these areas.

DEVELOPING INDEPENDENCE

All the ways you encouraged independence during the Stage 3 teens (by being an independent person yourself, talking about the value of being your own person, helping kids understand the social pressures working on them, putting popularity in perspective, encouraging kids to use their own moral judgment instead of the group's, etc.) will help develop the kind of moral backbone that's part of Stage 4.

As kids move out of the early teens and into the high school years, you can continue to encourage their growth toward independence. You can let them make more of their own decisions, while still exercising influence and control when you think it's needed (as it will often be). You can ask questions that help kids make good decisions—"What do you think will make you happy in the long run?" "What alternatives are open to you?" "Can you think of another way to solve that problem?" "How would you judge the pros and cons of doing that?"—and you can say directly what you think is wise. But, when you think it's appropriate, let the bottom line be, "Think about it, and then decide what you think is best. I'll respect your decision if I know you've given it serious thought."

You can also help Stage 4 along by talking about self-respect. About how self-respect doesn't come from conforming to what others want you to do, but from living up to your expectations of yourself, your own sense of responsibility or obligation. When your youngster is struggling with a moral decision, you can say, "Imagine that none of your friends will know what you decide. What decision would you make then? What decision would give you good feelings about yourself?"

Don't be surprised, though, if you have mixed feelings about your child's growth toward independence. Parents often feel "left behind" as their kids begin to lead their own lives and seem to need them less and less. Even if intellectually we think, "But I *want* my child to be independent!" our children's emancipation can be hard to accept emotionally.

Our job at these times is to resist the temptation to keep our kids dependent on us or to feel sorry for ourselves because we no longer play the same kind of role in their lives. Just as our kids are developing, so we can develop as parents—and evolve a new relationship, one that respects our child's development into a young adult.

HELPING KIDS SEE THE BIG PICTURE

How can you help kids develop an intellectual awareness that they're part of a bigger society? That they have obligations, as members of various social systems, to people they may never know personally?

Here are some ways to try to do that.

1. **Encourage kids to learn about the wider world around them.** Anything that raises kids' consciousness about what's happening outside their own circle of friends and family helps prepare the ground for Stage 4 thinking. Reading a newspaper can do that. So can watching the news or, better yet, any of the shows that do in-depth reporting and analysis of important current events. TV specials such as *Holocaust* and *Roots* are examples of programs that acquaint kids, in an emotionally powerful way, with the forces of good and evil as they operate and collide on a broad social scale. Books with a social dimension, either fiction or nonfiction, are an especially good way to help kids begin thinking about the relationship between the individual and society.

2. **Talk with kids about social and moral issues that have a Stage 4 dimension.** Kids can learn information about society without necessarily developing higher-stage moral *reasoning*. So it's important to help them develop a more complex understanding of the information they learn. You can help kids develop a Stage 4 understanding by talking with them about social and moral issues that make it very clear that our lives and fates are intertwined.

Help them see how the actions of an individual—an assassin's attempt on a president's life, for example—can send shock waves through an entire social system. Help them understand how society is a web of individuals, interest groups, and social institutions connected by countless crisscrossing strands; touch any part of the web and the whole thing quivers. Banks raise interest rates; fewer people take mortgages to buy homes; builders have less work; construction workers get laid off; the public bill for unemployment compensation goes up, and so do the taxes that all of us pay. Energy becomes a national priority; the federal government relaxes pollution controls; coal-burning electric utilities several states away send large amounts of sulfur dioxide into the air; acid rain falls on the mountain lakes in your state and kills all the fish.

Issues close to home, ones that arise within small social systems like your neighborhood or community, are good for kids to cut their Stage 4 teeth on. Issues that are controversial tend to stir the most thought. If there's a problem in your neighborhood because young tenants party and play their stereos as if no one lived within 10 miles, talk about that. If there's a controversy in your community because the state wants to build a regional waste-treatment plant that many people think will threaten your water supply, talk about that. If drugs, drinking, and reckless behavior on the part of teenagers have been a problem at rock concerts in your area and irate citizens are proposing an ordinance to ban such concerts in the future, talk about that. If, as happened in one community I know of, Halloween has become such a menace, both to trick-or-treaters (who wind up with razor blades in their apples) and to homeowners (who wind up with broken fences and trampled lawns), that many people want a law that keeps kids off the streets on Halloween, discuss that. Who has what rights in such conflicts? What's fair?

Moral dilemmas like these, which pit the interests of one group of people against those of another, teach kids how complex even small social systems are and why you have to step outside your own reference group (go beyond a Stage 3 perspective) in order to solve societal conflicts.

Difficult societal moral dilemmas that raise the question "Who shall decide?" are good for horizontal development and stretch Stage 4 moral reasoning once it begins to emerge. Who should decide in the case of a terminally ill person whether to continue or withdraw life-support systems—the family, the hospital, or the courts? Who should decide whether a 3-year-old boy with leukemia will have chemotherapy treatments—the parents who are opposed to such treatments, or the doctors, who say the treatments are essential for the child's survival? Should the state be able to dictate to conscientious parents how they must care for the health of their child? If not, does that mean parents have absolute power over the life and death of their child? Doesn't society have a responsibility to protect the child, knowing that even well-meaning parents don't always act in their child's best interests?

You may be thinking, "Good grief, I'm not sure what I think about these moral dilemmas myself—how am I supposed to guide my child's moral thinking?"

Fortunately, we don't have to have our minds made up about a moral dilemma in order to help kids develop their moral reasoning. In fact, it's often better if we aren't 100 percent sure of what we think. The idea isn't to give kids the "right answer" to tough moral dilemmas, but to get them to think more complexly, to look at all sides of an issue, and to examine the logical implications and social consequences of taking this or that position.

You'll know kids are starting to develop Stage 4 thinking when they say things like, "Dad, if you carry that argument to its logical conclusion . . ." You can help kids develop that kind of thinking by using it yourself and by complimenting them when they use it, even if they're making a point against what you happen to think about an issue.

Says a mother who had had a series of conversations with her 15-year-old son about difficult moral dilemmas:

"Through these dilemma discussions, I find I have a new respect for Marty's thinking. I have always felt close to this boy—I've shared a great deal with him—but around these dilemmas I've talked with him as one adult to another on issues which have no easy answer. It has strengthened our communication at a time when I appreciate that, and when he may need it, too. And I find that I trust his judgment."

Social Studies Dilemmas

Your child's social studies courses are another source of grist for the Stage 4 mill. A good social studies curriculum is full of social-moral issues that can help kids develop Stage 4 thinking about social systems and the role of the individual in society.

How did Hitler come to power? Who made it possible for him to carry out his evil social policies? Should nuclear power plants be abolished or expanded? Is busing fair? Should public employees such as teachers, firemen, and air controllers, ever be allowed to strike? If not, what should be the consequences if they do?

Ask kids if they discuss controversial issues like these in their social studies classes at school. They should; they're missing out on an important opportunity to develop Stage 4 reasoning if they don't. In a social studies class where students did debate such issues, one lively discussion centered on the question of whether the United States should have boycotted the 1980 Olympics in Moscow. Most students, reasoning at Stage 3, focused entirely on the individual athletes, how they had trained for many years and would have been terribly disappointed if their dreams of winning a gold medal were shattered.

A few students, however, raised Stage 4 issues: What about world peace? What would happen if a country like Russia could invade Afghanistan and suffer no consequences from other nations? At the time, Iran held 50 Americans hostage. Hadn't Russia taken a whole country hostage? In World War II, men risked and often lost their lives for a higher cause. Couldn't the Olympic athletes be asked to make a smaller sacrifice for a higher cause?

What Is Our Obligation to Strangers in Distress?

Stories about bystander unresponsiveness in emergency situations are another excellent way to get kids thinking about their responsibility to their fellow human beings.

You may remember the story about Kitty Genovese, a 28-year-old woman who was murdered in New York City in 1964. She came home to her apartment after working late one night and was attacked by a man with a knife. She screamed. Lights went on in the apartment house; someone shouted, "Let that girl alone!" and the attacker fled. But when the lights went out, he came back and stabbed her again. Another scream, more lights, and once more the assailant fled. But when the lights went out again, he brazenly returned, found Kitty Genovese lying at the foot of the apartment stairs, and this time killed her. "A simple phone call," a police detective said later, "would have saved that girl's life."

What is our obligation to strangers in distress? Certainly, Stage 4 would say, we're obliged to come to their aid when there is no grave risk to ourselves. Many European countries, in fact, have a Good Samaritan law which actually *requires* citizens to render aid of some kind when they can do so without endangering themselves.

But what about when helping would involve real risk to life or limb? Here's a moral dilemma written by a high-school student that pits personal safety against concern for the welfare of another:

> "You are driving through the country, on very isolated roads. As you take a turn, you see two men beating up a lady. You don't know any of them. If you drive by, nothing will happen as far as you are concerned. If you stop, you will probably get beat up, but the lady will be left alone. Should you stop?"[4]

At Stage 4, you recognize the right of a person to safeguard his own life. But there's another pull: you know you just can't turn your back on a fellow human being in distress. You have to do *something*. What kind of a society would it be if we all just minded our own business and said to heck with everybody else?

Here's a drug dilemma, also written by a high-school student, that raises this same issue in another form:

> "I knew of a guy who is just a bit more than a casual acquaintance. Anyway, this person is selling an illegal drug, PCP (modified form of a horse tranquilizer). He is a big pusher of this drug. I have read many articles and medical journals on this type of drug. I have concluded that PCP has violent side-effects. I am very much against this drug, but what am I going to do? I have spoken to him countless times on not selling the drug—especially to

younger teenagers. So I have only two options: I could totally ignore it, or inform an official."[5]

Ask your child, "What do you think this kid should do? What would the consequences be if he informs on the pusher or keeps quiet? What would you do in his shoes, and why?"

Personalize Stage 4 Reasoning

Whenever possible, it's important to personalize Stage 4 reasoning. Show how it's relevant to issues in your own life and that of your child.

You can talk about how your feelings of obligation as a member of society and your community lead you to look out for your neighbors, give time to community service, vote in elections, contribute to charities, be honest when you pay your taxes, and so on. You can be frank about conflicts you may feel: how it's not easy to be completely honest on your income tax at a time when the government wastes a lot of money and you're just making ends meet. But you think, "What are the consequences if everybody cheats? And if people cheat on their income tax, what's to keep them from cheating in other areas of their life? Do I want to be part of that, when I believe one of the biggest problems in society today is that people aren't as honest as they used to be?"

You can help kids see the relevance of Stage 4 thinking to the immediate world they live in. Why shouldn't kids cheat on tests? (How can a school ever know what students are really learning if a lot of them cheat? What happens to your self-respect when you cheat?) What's wrong with pranks like setting off a false fire alarm? (What happens to the fire department's ability to protect people from real fires if they're chasing down false alarms?) Why shouldn't kids shoplift even little things? (What would happen to prices if everybody did it?) Why shouldn't you cut class at school? (Would you want to try to run a school where people came to class only when they pleased?)

In short, life is full of Stage 4 moral issues that stretch kids' social awareness and sense of responsibility beyond the borders of their own social circle.

THE IMPORTANCE OF REAL EXPERIENCE IN THE WIDER WORLD

Kids can develop an intellectual awareness of society and their social responsibilities in it through the kinds of discussion we've just talked about. But the horizontal development of a stage of reasoning—getting it into kids' bones so it becomes second nature for them to *use* it—always requires more than just talk. For Stage 4 to really take, kids need to have *lived experiences* in the wider social world. To feel part of society, they need to take part in it.

How can a parent help in this area?

You can't—and shouldn't try to—orchestrate all of your child's participation in the world outside the family. That would be tipping the balance away from independence and too far toward control.

But you can be aware of experiences that are good for the development of Stage 4. Some of these experiences you can provide; some you can encourage; some you can model by your own example. In all cases, you can support whatever kind of responsible social participation your child does pursue.

Let's look at some examples of real-world experiences that help kids understand and feel part of the larger human community.

A job. Parents have long recognized that holding a job is one of the best ways kids can learn to stand on their own feet. But besides helping kids become more independent, a job is a chance to step into a responsible social role in the larger world.

It doesn't have to be a full-time job. Part-time work, like having a newspaper route or clerking at a store, or a seasonal job, like working at a summer camp or supervising a playground, enables kids to take on significant social responsibility outside the home.

I remember Mark's first job as a paper boy for the *Boston Globe*. He was 12; he had to get up at 5:30 to deliver the morning paper before school, and the first few times out were not without mistakes, frustration, and more than one temptation to throw in the towel. But after a few days he began to get the hang of it and feel better about the venture. One morning, as he came to the end of his route, he spotted a *Boston Globe* delivery truck at a traffic light. He took a deep breath and said with satisfaction, "Now, when I see that truck, I feel like I'm part of the *Globe*!"

When kids hold a job, they have a real role, however small, in society. People they don't know personally are counting on them to do their work. They can come to understand that workers are like links in a chain: if somebody doesn't do his or her job, the whole enterprise fails. A reporter covers a story; a printer turns it into a page of newspaper; a truck delivers the bundles of papers to their various distribution points; the local distributor drops them off at the carriers' doors; but none of these efforts has the intended result if a news carrier doesn't get the paper into the hands of the readers.

The teen years are an important time not only for kids to enter the world of work but also for them to begin thinking about and preparing for the kind of work they'd like to do for a living. Kids should be thinking, "What kinds of jobs are there that I might like to do? What sorts of careers do I have an aptitude for? What kind of education or training will I need?"

A parent can help kids find answers to questions like these. You can suggest that your youngster talk to the guidance counselor at school about career possibilities or, if there's a college nearby, stop in at the career planning office there. You can help your youngster get a realistic picture of his or her aptitudes by arranging for individual vocational testing at a college or with a psychologist in private practice. If your son or daughter wonders what it would be like to be a teacher, lawyer, doctor, nurse, banker, or baker, you can take a trip to the library to see what books you can dig out on these careers. Or you can try to find somebody in your town who's in that line of work and who'd be willing to sit down with your child to talk about it. You can also visit colleges and universities together and talk with people there about different fields your child may be interested in.

The purpose of helping kids think about the work they'd like to do is not to push them into an early vocational choice. They should take as long as they need to make up their minds about what they want to do with their lives. But what's important while they're still at home with us is to help them develop a positive attitude toward the value of work, an image of themselves as responsible, productive adults, and goals for the future that inspire them to make the most of their present opportunities. Kids are less likely to drift through the high school years if they see a relationship between the math or English course they're taking now and the chemist or journalist they might like to become.[6]

Kids need this kind of encouragement today more than ever, because work doesn't enjoy the status it once did. A lot of people scoff at the "work ethic," and a lot of kids have grown up with negative attitudes toward working. I think that's very unfortunate, both for them and for society. When people don't think work is important, they don't work as hard at their jobs, they take less pride in their work, or they don't bother to work at all, and all of us pay the price.

A healthy person, Freud said, is one who is capable of both love and work. We help our children grow into morally mature adults if we raise them to see work as a source of personal dignity and a way to contribute to the human community. They should realize that any job well done, whether it's repairing cars or repairing people, growing food or growing children, contributes to the quality of life for us all. They should understand, in the words of essayist Lance Morrow, that "all life must be worked at, protected, planted, replanted, fashioned, cooked for, coaxed, diapered, formed, sustained. Work is the way we tend the world." From a moral standpoint, work is one of the most basic ways we enter into and enhance the lives of others, and that's why it's one of the major stepping stones to Stage 4.

A helping role in the community. An excellent way for kids to grow into responsible members of society is for them to take on an active helping role in their community.

There are lots of ways kids can get involved in service to their community. There are Big Brother and Big Sister programs that pair up teenagers with children who need a one-on-one relationship with somebody they can look up to. There are crisis-counseling centers, where teens can listen to and try to help troubled peers. There are opportunities for young people to spend time with old people in nursing homes or to help in day-care centers or programs for handicapped children. There are opportunities to do valuable volunteer work in hospitals. Teenagers who extend their circle of caring in these ways are already taking their place as responsible citizens of their society.

High schools committed to fostering good citizenship some-times provide students with chances for social involvement as part of their schooling. At the same time that students are learn-ing in courses about law and government, they're out in the community trying to make a positive contribution. They might be interviewing and going to bat for senior citizens who are having trouble getting around or heating their homes. They might be participating in a drive to clean up the city's river or get a law passed requiring a deposit on throwaway containers. Students who get to participate in projects like these, and too few do, are getting front-lines training for the kind of active citizenry that a healthy democracy demands.

Often kids are led into helping roles beyond the family by the example we set. If we're involved in giving our time and energy to help our neighbors, church, or community, chances are that kids will get the message that this is part of being a responsible person. They may even want to have a hand in the very work we're doing. I recently met a father who serves on the am-bulance squad of the volunteer fire department in his town. So, I learned, does his 17-year-old son.

Many families talk with their children about ways to extend concern for others beyond the family circle. Some families, for example, discuss at the dinner table how they tried that day to show kindness toward someone not a member of the family. Some families, at Thanksgiving or Christmas time, bring a bag of groceries to the local Salvation Army as a small way of sharing what they have with others who are less fortunate.

The human community that we belong to goes, of course, beyond the boundaries of the community where we live. Kids can develop a Stage 4 sense of responsibility by helping those whose lives may never directly intersect with their own. Some families, for example, encourage their children to give a portion of their allowance (the kids decide how much, and often give more than parents would have expected) to a charity of their own choosing. In one family, the 14-year-old son learned from a ser-mon in church about New York City's Covenant House, a haven for teenage runaways who have been seduced or coerced into prostitution. He decided he wanted to send a portion of his monthly baby-sitting earnings to help those kids.

Living away from home. Another way for kids to feel part of the wider world is to live in it.

Teenagers can certainly keep developing while they live at home, and they don't automatically develop just by leaving it. But leaving the nest is usually a step toward adulthood and helps kids develop the broader view of life and society that's characteristic of Stage 4.

Going away to college, for example, can be a very important growth experience for young people. They become part of a new social system. They have opportunities to take on new social roles and responsibilities, like serving as academic advisor to younger students, "buddy" to an incoming freshman, supervisor or counselor in a dorm, member of the student government, or volunteer in the various community work programs typically associated with a college. Courses in moral philosophy and social ethics challenge students to examine their beliefs about what's right and wrong and to reflect on moral issues in their own lives and in society at large.

The moral education kids receive at college may well be the most important part of their education. For that reason, it's a good idea to encourage your child to consider colleges with a known tradition of caring about students' total development, their values as well as their intellect.

Involvement in politics. Political activism is one more way kids can develop a Stage 4 perspective and a felt sense of being part of society.

Boning up on the issues, finding out how political parties work, seeing a political campaign from the inside, going door-to-door for a candidate—these experiences can be an exciting and enlightening baptism in the social arena. Political involvement teaches kids, better than all their textbooks and courses, the nuts and bolts of democracy. They learn how to work within the system, how to channel their idealism and try to make their voices heard. They can learn that their candidate or position might not always carry the day, but that the system, when it's working, gives everybody a fair shot.

Holding a job, helping in the community, taking on the responsibilities of living away from home, getting involved in politics—

all these are ways kids can develop and extend Stage 4 moral reasoning. All are ways of constructively participating in the real human affairs of the wider world around them. This is learning by doing—learning to think and act like a responsible member of society by doing the things that responsible members of society do.

For all of its virtues, however, Stage 4 is still not a fully developed morality. But before turning to Stage 4's shortcomings, and how Stage 5 overcomes them, I want to make three more points about this very important stage in your child's moral development.

First, don't expect too much. Even if kids are showing signs of Stage 4 understanding in their early or mid-teens, they'll still think and act like Stage 3 conformists much, if not most, of the time. Stage 4, like every other stage, is slow to grow, even under the best circumstances.

Second, you don't have to wait till the teens to lay the groundwork for Stage 4. Even young children can learn that there's a bigger world out there, that a lot of people in it are hurting, and that we should do what we can to help them. Eleanor Roosevelt, who lived a life of compassion and humanitarianism, indicates in her autobiography that the seeds of her social conscience were planted early:

> Very early I became conscious of the fact that there were people around me who suffered in one way or another. I was five or six when my father took me to help serve Thanksgiving dinner in one of the newsboys' clubhouses which my grandfather, Theodore Roosevelt, had started. My father explained that many of these ragged little boys had no homes and lived in wooden shanties in empty lots, or slept in vestibules of houses or public buildings or any place where they could be warm.[7]

When the country of Cambodia was threatened with massive famine, one elementary school I know of enabled its students to participate in the relief effort by having a sale to which kids donated their old toys and games. When the city of Atlanta was being terrorized by an elusive child murderer, schoolchildren across the country wrote to send their concern, their prayers, or

HOW TO HELP KIDS DEVELOP STAGE 4

1. Help kids develop an independent conscience based on self-respect and a sense of social responsibility.

2. Help them become aware of the social systems (school, neighborhood, community, country) they belong to and the obligations involved:
   - Encourage them to learn about what's happening in the world around them.
   - Discuss social and moral issues that get kids thinking about the relationship between the individual and society and the responsibility all of us have to cooperate for the common good.
   - Show how Stage 4 concerns (e.g., "What if everybody shoplifted?") are relevant to your life and theirs.

3. Encourage and support their own initiative to seek firsthand experiences that help them act and feel like responsible members of society, such as:
   - Holding a job;
   - Serving their community;
   - Helping people outside their community;
   - Getting involved in political or citizen action;
   - Taking on the responsibilities of living away from home.

4. Encourage them to develop goals for their future, an image of themselves as contributing members of society, and a positive attitude toward work as a way of contributing to the welfare of others.

5. Prepare the ground for Stage 4's development in the teens by making kids aware, even as children, of the needs of others in society and the importance of being a concerned citizen.

6. Encourage kids to think of a college education as an important chance to develop their values as well as their intellect.

money they had raised to support summer camps for Atlanta's black children. During the Christmas season, children in some classrooms are made aware of their community's effort to raise money for poor or tragedy-stricken families, and have the opportunity to contribute from their allowance to a class donation.

By making kids aware at an early age of the suffering of others and meaningful ways they can help, we obviously won't develop 8- and 9-year-olds who have Stage 4's sophisticated understanding of social systems; that understanding requires the intellectual powers available to a teenager. And in recommending that we raise the social consciousness of children, I'm not suggesting we should inundate them with information about all the wars, famines, natural disasters, and other tragedies of the world; their young minds and emotions aren't ready to handle that. What I am saying is that kids are more likely to begin to develop a Stage 4 awareness, as they should, in early to mid adolescence if they have had at least some exposure as children to human needs beyond their own family and to the idea and importance of being a concerned citizen.

Finally, I don't want to convey the impression that Stage 4 calls people to be saints, always working out in the community, always sacrificing to help others, and never thinking of their own needs. Stage 4, like the other moral stages, includes legitimate self-interest. In fact, Stage 4 is an enlightened way of looking out for our own welfare by looking out for each other. "Cooperation, not conflict," writes anthropologist Ashley Montagu, "has been the most valuable form of behavior for human beings taken at any stage of their evolutionary history. Without the cooperation of its members, society cannot survive."

That is the great insight of Stage 4.

CHAPTER 11

STAGE 5: "RESPECT THE RIGHTS OF EVERY PERSON"

When you hear a person described as "a man [or a woman] of principle," you're probably hearing about somebody who's at Stage 5 of moral reasoning.

At Stage 5, there's a new basis for moral decisions: *the principle of respect for the rights of individual persons.* The right to speak the truth as you see it. The right to equal treatment under the law. The right to be treated with respect for your dignity as a person. The right to life itself.

Stage 5 makes a sweeping claim: *these rights are universal.* Every person possesses them, simply by virtue of being human. Every government, every social system, has an obligation to respect and protect them. It's these inalienable human rights that make us moral equals, no matter what our station in life.

How is that different from Stage 4?

At Stage 4, you feel an obligation to *your* social-moral systems (your community, your country), not to the principle of respect for the rights of all individuals.

Stage 4 asks, "What does it mean to be a good member of my social system? What are my responsibilities to other members of my system?"

Stage 5 asks, "What does it mean to be a human being? What are my responsibilities to any other human being, people who don't belong to my system as well as people who do?"

For Stage 4, the bottom line is, "Does this action help keep the system going?" For Stage 5, the bottom line is, "Does this action respect the rights of the individual people affected?"

In practical terms, how does reasoning at Stage 5 make a difference in moral behavior?

In a lot of situations, it doesn't. Stage 4 and Stage 5 both think

---

A PROFILE OF STAGE 5

At Stage 5 of moral reasoning, people:

1. Believe that what's right is to show the greatest possible respect for the human rights of every individual person, and to support a social system that protects those rights.

2. Believe the reason to be good is the obligation of conscience to be faithful to the principle of respect for all human beings.

3. Can mentally stand outside their social system and use the principle of respect to judge the morality of the system's actions.

4. Value democracy as a way to seek liberty and justice for all.

5. Don't impose their personal values on others but do hold every individual responsible for respecting the rights of others.

6. Feel a Good Samaritan obligation to be concerned about the welfare of all members of the human family.

7. Believe the end doesn't justify the means.

8. Understand that respect for persons requires keeping commitments.

9. Believe that all persons, no matter what their status, deserve to be treated as moral equals.

it's important to respect rules and laws. Stage 4 and Stage 5 both think it's important to keep your word and be honest in your dealings with others. Stage 4 and Stage 5 both think you should take care of your family, help your neighbor, and contribute to your country. Stage 4 and Stage 5 both think we should all do our part to maintain a social system that benefits people.

To understand when Stage 5 does make a difference, and why loyalty to a principle of respect for persons is better than loyalty to a social system, we need to look at what happens when the system is wrong.

WHERE STAGE 4 FALLS SHORT

As long as the social system that Stage 4 believes in is working to benefit people and protect their rights, Stage 4 is a perfectly good way of moral reasoning. But what happens if the system isn't working for everybody's benefit? What if somebody's rights are getting stepped on?

What should you do, for example, if you're a citizen living in Nazi Germany and the system you've always been loyal to says, "Jews are less than persons and shall be treated accordingly"?

What if you're a white person and your system says, "Blacks are inferior and shall be kept in their place"? Or you're male, and the system says, "Women shall not be granted the same rights and opportunities as men"?

What if you work for a big company and the corporate system says, "Payoffs to politicians, fighting dirty with the competition, and cutting corners on product quality are all part of the game, all necessary to keep profits up and people employed"?

What if you consider yourself a patriotic citizen, but your country is waging a war you think is wrong, and the system says, "Stand up for the flag"?

How does a Stage 4, system-oriented morality handle problems like these?

One way is to define the problem out of existence. A Stage 4 reasoner could decide, "I'll trust in the authorities. The system must be right." You figure if the system is good, its decisions must be good. The voice of the system becomes the voice of your conscience.

Or you might think the system is wrong in this case but you should go along anyway. You think people should subordinate their personal conscience to the system. You reason:

"What would happen if everybody raised a big ruckus every time they disagreed with something?"

"My company deserves my loyalty."

"My country, right or wrong."

Or you might, at Stage 4, decide to drop out of your present system and get a new one. You denounce "American imperialism" and join a radical leftist group. Or you denounce "American weakness" and join the far right. You might reject the "materialistic" culture of your parents and become a Moonie. But if you swore the same kind of allegiance to your new system that you did to your old, you'd still be reasoning at Stage 4.

So, one way or the other, Stage 4 tries to solve moral conflicts by putting loyalty to a system before individual rights and conscience. And that's because at Stage 4, *the rights of individuals and the voice of personal conscience are less important than the smooth functioning of the system as a whole.*

In the last chapter, we looked at the good side of Stage 4 responsibility to the system. Stage 4 "solid citizens" are the backbone of any society. They "give a damn." They care about the state of the social ship.

But Stage 4's virtue is also its vice. It's loyal to a fault. It doesn't have an independent standard, a higher moral principle, by which to evaluate the norms and rules of its system. It opens the door to great moral dangers by letting a social system take the place of a personal conscience based on respect for the rights of individual human beings.

I know of no more chilling demonstration of those dangers than the experiments carried out in the early 1960s by Stanley Milgram.

THE ANATOMY OF OBEDIENCE

You may have read about Milgram's experiments[1] or seen them dramatized in a television play *(The Tenth Level)* a few years ago. A Yale University psychologist, Milgram was interested in the phenomenon of obedience. He knew that the Nazis had, on command, slaughtered millions of innocent persons. But what about Americans? Would we obey an authority figure who told us to inflict pain on an innocent victim? Or would we rebel?

To find out, Milgram ran an ad in the New Haven newspaper that offered $4.50 to anyone who would participate in a "study of memory." He got volunteers from a variety of age levels and from all walks of life; subjects included postal clerks, high school teachers, salesmen, engineers, laborers, and several persons who held doctoral or other professional degrees.

Imagine that you volunteered for this experiment. When you arrive at the laboratory, the experimenter introduces you to another "volunteer" who is, unbeknownst to you, his assistant. You and the other person draw lots to determine your role in the experiment; but it's rigged so that you get to be the "teacher" and the other person the "learner."

The experimenter then leads you and the learner into an adjoining room. There the learner, looking a little nervous at this point, is strapped into a chair and electrodes are attached to his wrist. The experimenter explains that the learner's job is to try to memorize word associations, like "blue" and "box." Your job is to motivate learning by administering a punishment, an electrical shock, each time the learner makes a mistake. The experimenter explains: "Although the shocks can be extremely painful, they cause no permanent tissue damage."

You're taken back to the original room, where you sit down before an imposing shock generator, with shock levels ranging from 15 to 450 volts. Your instructions are to increase the shock by 15 volts with each additional mistake by the learner. The experimenter then gives you a sample shock—45 volts—and the jolt convinces you that the generator is for real.

The experiment begins. The learner makes one mistake after another, and each time, following your instructions, you increase the shock. The learner doesn't complain at first, but when you reach 120 volts, he shouts to the experimenter that the shocks are becoming painful. When you reach 150 volts, he cries out, "Experimenter, get me out of here! I won't be in the experiment any more! I refuse to go on!" Since the learner is on the other side of the wall, you don't realize that you're hearing pretaped responses, and the learner isn't really getting shocked at all. To you, the responses coming through the wall are very convincing. And each time you increase the voltage, the learner's response is more anguished. He screams with pain. He pleads to be released. He cries out that he can stand the pain no longer. Finally, he falls silent.

If at any point you express a reluctance to continue giving the shocks, the experimenter says firmly, "The experiment requires that you continue," or, "You have no other choice; you *must* go on."

How long will you obey?

Before running the experiment, Milgram asked psychiatrists to predict how many people would obey to the very end and give the full 450 volts. They said that fewer than one percent of the subjects would do so—and that those who did would be psychologically disturbed.

In fact, two thirds of Milgram's subjects, 26 of 40 persons, did as they were told and gave the highest level of shock, 450 volts.

How are we to make sense of Milgram's findings? What was going on inside the people when they gave the shocks? Were they enjoying it? Hardly. Milgram reports that "subjects were observed to sweat, tremble, stutter, bite their lips, frown, and dig their fingernails into their flesh. These were characteristic rather than exceptional responses."[2]

Most subjects said after the experiment that they felt terrible about giving the shocks but felt they were doing their moral duty by following instructions. They felt like agents of the experimenter, extensions of his will. They saw him, not themselves, as ultimately responsible for the suffering of the victim.

Despite a lot of controversy about the ethics of Milgram's experiment, other psychologists repeated it and found the same high levels of obedience among their subjects. These studies turned an uncomfortable light on one of the grave dangers of "system thinking": you can pass the buck. You're not ultimately responsible; the system is. You can say, "I was only doing my duty. I don't make the rules; I just follow them."

CONSCIENCE AT STAGE 5

Stage 5 says *no, you can't abdicate personal moral responsibility*. The buck stops with you.

That's what we told the Nazi war criminals at the famous Nuremberg trials. We said they couldn't excuse their actions by claiming, "I was just following orders." They were accountable, as individuals, to something that transcended the orders of their superiors and the laws of their nation. They were accountable to a universal moral standard: the principle of respect for human life and dignity.

Let's go back to the Milgram experiment. If you were Stage 5 and a subject in that experiment, how would you reason?

You might go along for a while, figuring that you and the learner had both made a commitment to the experimenter that you should keep. Keeping personal commitments or "social contracts" is very important at Stage 5. But as the learner screamed, you'd think, "I know we agreed to do this, but I don't think either of us knew what we were getting in for. The learner is in pain and demanding to be released. Forcing him to continue violates his rights. No experiment justifies that." At Stage 5 you could say to the experimenter, as one woman did, "No, I don't think we have to go on. We are here of our own free will."

A Stage 4 reasoner might also question the Milgram experiment, since Stage 4 doesn't *blindly* obey authority (blind obedience is Stage 1). Stage 4 might ask, "Is the experimenter a qualified psychologist? Will the knowledge gained from this experiment help society?" If Stage 4 reasoners think an authority is *not* legitimate, not working within the system to help the system, they don't feel obligated to cooperate. Stage 4's shortcoming is that it lacks a higher moral principle by which to judge the actions of even legitimate authority.

You may remember the My Lai incident in Vietnam. In 1969, in the village of My Lai, a U.S. Army platoon massacred over 100 men, women, and children. At his trial Lt. William Calley, who gave the orders to shoot, defended his actions in terms of duty to the system as he understood it:

"I was ordered to go in there and destroy the enemy. That was my job on that day. That was my mission I was given. I did not sit down and think in terms of men, women, and children . . . I felt, and still do, that I acted as I was directed, and I do not feel wrong in doing so."[3]

One soldier, Michael Bernhardt, refused to participate in the My Lai killings. In a subsequent interview, he showed clear indications of Stage 5 reasoning:

"I c.n hardly do anything if I know it's wrong. . . . The law is only the law, and many times it's wrong. It's not necessarily just, simply because it's the law. My kind of citizen would be guided by his own laws. These would be more strict, in a lot of cases, then the actual laws."[4]

That kind of talk makes Stage 4 thinkers nervous; they think, "What if everybody went around following 'their own laws'? It'd be bedlam." But Stage 5 is not a prescription for social chaos. Notice that Michael Bernhardt states that the laws of conscience are *stricter* than the laws of the land. Stage 5 recognizes that in any given situation, morality may demand more of us than the law.

The higher law that Stage 5 responds to is respect for the rights and worth of individual human beings. But I want to make it very clear that this respect for human rights and dignity leads Stage 5 reasoners to have the greatest respect for law in general. Stage 5 reasoners feel obliged to obey the law whenever it's morally possible to do so. They know that law, imperfect as it may be, is the best means we have for keeping social order and protecting our individual rights.

In fact, it's Stage 5 thinking that produces constitutions, efforts to create a society of law that maximizes everybody's chance to get a fair shake. If a particular law isn't working to protect people's rights, Stage 5 thinkers try to change it. Down through history, our great moral leaders—people like Abraham Lincoln, Susan B. Anthony, and Martin Luther King, Jr.—have fought to bring the law of the land into closer accord with the dream of "liberty and justice for all."

"THE END DOESN'T JUSTIFY THE MEANS"

Stage 5, of all the stages, has the clearest understanding of a very important moral principle: the end doesn't justify the means.

Suppose there's a riot in your city and widespread looting. The mayor orders police to shoot looters on sight. Should you support that policy?

Stage 5 would say no. Looters are criminals and should certainly be brought to justice, but they still have rights. It would be wrong to shoot and endanger their lives, even if that would stop looting in the future.

Terrorism is another example of failing to see that the end doesn't justify the means. Terrorists take hostages, bomb, maim, and kill—all in the name of righting some wrong or bringing about their idea of a better world. But their loyalty is to their cause, not to people. They'll use any means to achieve their end. If they come to power, they rule as dictators, imposing their vision of the good society.

Stage 5, by contrast, is not fanatical; it never sacrifices people's rights to a cause. At Stage 5, if you have a moral goal, you have to find a moral way to get there.

STAGE 5 AND DISSENT

Every so often, the Gallup Poll asks Americans to come out for or against their constitutional rights, disguised slightly in the form of questions like, "Should the government be able to stop a newspaper from publishing 'sensitive' material?" "Should a large group of people be allowed to rally to protest government policy?" "Should police be permitted to wiretap the phones of dissenters suspected of disloyalty?" Every time Gallup asks, an overwhelming majority of people express a Stage 4 preference for order over freedom and, in effect, vote down the Bill of Rights.

At Stage 5 a person thinks, "Conflict is built into democracy. Dissent and debate are what the system is all about. People have different points of view and a right to express them. No group has the right to impose its ideas on everybody else. Democracy gives us all a chance to say what we think and a way to settle our differences fairly."

Stage 5 makes democracy safe for diversity. It grants people the liberty to lead their lives according to their conscience as long as they don't violate the rights of others.

Stage 4, by contrast, doesn't see clearly that safeguarding individual rights is the reason for setting up a democracy in the first place. That was the issue during Watergate. People who wanted to "save the system" (protect national security) did things that violated the very rights that a democratic system is supposed to protect. Liberals and conservatives alike agreed that the government could not logically commit crimes against individuals in the name of democracy.[5]

At least one of the Watergate participants spoke publicly about a change in his thinking that amounted to a rejection of Stage 4 logic (placing national security above individual rights) in favor of a Stage 5 respect for rights. Egil Kroh, before being sentenced for his role in directing the break-in at the office of Daniel Ellsberg's psychiatrist, rose and made the following statement:

> "It is only recently that I have come to see the effect that the term 'national security' had on my judgment. However national security is defined, none of the potential uses of the information we sought could justify the invasion of the rights of individuals that the break-in necessitated. The understanding that I have come to is that these rights are the definition of our nation. To invade them unlawfully is to work a destructive force upon the nation.
>
> "I hope that young men and women who are fortunate enough to have an opportunity to serve in government will recognize that the banner of national security can turn perceived patriotism into actual disservice. When contemplating a course of action, I hope they will never fail to ask, 'Is this right?'"[6]

There's a new patriotism at Stage 5. It doesn't say, "My country, right or wrong." It says instead, "When my country's wrong, I must stand up for the right." Its loyalty is to the principle on which any democracy is founded: respect for the rights of all persons.

"WHOM SHOULD I HELP?"

There are two sides to a morality of respect for individual persons. One says, "Don't hurt. Don't interfere with other people's rights." The other says, "Do help. Offer aid to those in need." But whom am I responsible to help?

Each moral stage, of course, gives a different answer to that question. Stage 2 tells me that I should help those who help me, tit-for-tat. Stage 3 tells me I'm a member of a group and should be nice to others if I want them to like me. Stage 4 stretches my sphere of responsibility; it tells me I'm a member of a social system and that I and others have to do our part to keep the system going. But Stage 4 doesn't tell me what my obligations are to people *outside* my system.

Stage 5 does. Its answer to the question "Whom should I help?" is an ancient one. It's contained in the parable of the Good Samaritan.

The Good Samaritan parable, as we know, tells the story of a traveler who was attacked by robbers who stripped him, beat him, and left him half-dead. Later, a priest came along, saw the man, and passed by on the other side of the road. A Levite did the same.

Finally, a Samaritan saw the man and had compassion. He bound up his wounds, took him to an inn, and cared for him. The next day before leaving, he gave the innkeeper two denarii and instructed him, "Take care of him, and whatever more you spend, I, on my way back, will repay you."

What's most significant about the Good Samaritan is not the risk he took or the lengths he went to to help a stranger. What's most significant is that he was a *Samaritan,* traveling in a land where Samaritans were traditionally despised. He went out of his way to help a Jew, despite the mutual hatred that existed between Jews and Samaritans for hundreds of years.

The unstinting altruism of the Good Samaritan exemplifies a Stage 5 respect for persons. If you respect people, you value them. If you value them, you feel a measure of responsibility for their welfare, the kind of responsibility you'd want any human being to feel for any other human being. It doesn't matter whether you have a personal tie to the individual in need or belong to the same social system. It doesn't matter if you're part of a different age group, sex, race, religion, class, or nation. It doesn't even matter if an ancient enmity divides your group from the other person's. At Stage 5, you can look beyond these personal characteristics and see, as the Good Samaritan did, those inner qualities that make all men and women human, and therefore responsible for each other.

Earlier, I stressed Stage 5's *independence,* its ability to stand apart and follow its conscience when the going got tough. Here I'm stressing Stage 5's *interdependence,* its sense of connection and obligation to fellow human beings. Aren't these two tendencies opposed?

Not at Stage 5. At this point in human development, the processes of differentiation (standing apart) and integration (fitting in) that we've traced all through the stages achieve their fullest expression and best balance. At Stage 5, I am most fully an individual, most able to assume personal moral responsibility, most able to make independent moral judgments in the face of pressure to conform. But it's precisely my heightened sense of myself as a free and responsible individual that makes me most respectful of other individuals, most open to them, most aware of the common humanity that binds us together. At Stage 5, being an individual and being in community are really two sides of the same moral experience.

"WHY SHOULD I KEEP MY COMMITMENTS?"

A big part of being a member of the human community is keeping your commitments. You'll remember that keeping commitments, meeting obligations, was very important at Stage 4. That's one of the values that gets carried over to Stage 5.

There's a difference, however, in how Stage 4 and Stage 5 answer the question, "Why should I honor my commitments?" Take the matter of promises. Asked "Why should a promise be kept?" a Stage 4 reasoner focused on the chaos that would result if everybody went around breaking promises. "If you couldn't trust people, we'd all go crazy."

Stage 5 also thinks trust is essential for stable human relationships. But Stage 5 sees a deeper issue: respect for the individual. Listen to this interview with a Stage 5 reasoner:

Q: Why should a promise be kept?

A: It's necessary to hold the fabric of human relations together. Promises concern the value of a person, his dignity. A promise affirms a person. A broken promise seems to disintegrate people and their affirmation of one another.

Q: Why is it important to keep a promise to someone you're not close to?

A: It's a sign of respect for the other person's worth. It shows you consider him or her to be a person of worth.[7]

Does Stage 5 say you can never break a promise?

No. We all make promises in the present, not knowing what the future will bring. Sometimes we can't keep a promise, however much we want to. But the breaking of a promise must be done for a very good reason, and in a way that maintains respect for the other person. If you can't take Bobby to the carnival as planned, you explain the reason and try to make good on the promise in another way. If you can't keep your promise to your spouse to do something you've agreed upon, you seek your partner's consent to a change in plans.

HELPING KIDS TO STAGE 5

People rarely reach Stage 5 before their twenties. Developing this sophisticated level of moral understanding requires, even more than Stage 4, lived experiences in the adult world. It requires facing moral conflicts, making moral commitments, and reflecting on moral experience. It requires a thinking involvement with social issues and the kind of social awareness that comes from firsthand experience as a member of society.

So our part as parents in developing Stage 5 is a preparatory one. We can till the soil and sow the seeds. But the full development of a mature, principled morality must be done by kids themselves, under the sun of the wider world.

What can we do to lay the groundwork for that development?

HELP KIDS RESPECT THEMSELVES AS INDIVIDUALS

If kids are to respect other people as individuals, *they need to respect themselves as individuals first.* How can we help them develop a respect for their own worth and dignity as persons?

One way is to make the family a place where kids are accepted for the unique individuals they are becoming, a place where their rights as people are acknowledged and respected. John, 27, remembers his family as that kind of place:

> "There was a lot of freedom to debate things in our family. I remember standing around the kitchen arguing openly with my parents, going back and forth about some issue or a rule I disagreed with. I grew up with a very strong sense of my right to speak my mind."

University of California at Berkeley researcher Norma Haan, in a study of nearly 1,000 college students, looked at the relationship between students' level of moral reasoning and their perception of their fathers. Students who scored at the principled level (Stage 5) on moral dilemmas gave their fathers high marks for "letting me take chances and try new things." Principled young women, in particular, remembered their fathers as encouraging their independence and "not pressuring me to be like other people." This pattern contrasted sharply with the perceptions of students who scored at lower stages of moral reasoning. They tended to remember their fathers as wanting them to make a good impression and discouraging them from trying anything that might mean failure.

Other studies have found the same thing: principled young people, who stand up for their rights and the rights of others, come from families that encourage independence and self-expression.[8]

That certainly doesn't mean abandoning our responsibility to exercise parental authority. But we need to keep in mind that the kind of authority that develops principled moral reasoning is *fair and rational* authority, authority that explains itself and lets kids explain their point of view. Says one principled young man: "The basic idea in my family was that with any order given, I should be able to ask for a reason and get a rational response."

COMBINE RESPECT WITH LOVE

Everything we do to raise good kids, including helping them to Stage 5, has to build on a foundation of love.

But it appears to be a special kind of love that nurtures the growth of principled morality. That was the key finding of one of the first major studies of moral development in this century.[9]

Back in the 1940s, Robert Peck of the University of Texas and Robert Havighurst of the University of Chicago set out to study the character development of boys and girls in a typical small Midwestern city. They followed the children from their 10th to their 17th years (1943–1950). Their research was done before Lawrence Kohlberg's work on stages of moral reasoning in teenagers, but Peck and Havighurst postulated a developmental sequence of "character types" that were remarkably like the moral reasoning stages that were later identified by Kohlberg.

Their most mature character type sounds a lot like Stage 5. They called it "rational-altruistic." A rational-altruistic person, they said, "has a stable set of principles. His moral horizon embraces all mankind. He is honest with all, kind to all, and respects the integrity of every human being."[10]

Peck and Havighurst didn't expect the teenagers in their study to reach this rational-altruistic ideal, but they wanted to learn about the kids who came closest to it. What kinds of families would they come from?

In the 34 families they studied over the seven years, Peck and Havighurst found three distinctly different ways that parents went about loving their children. One kind of love was highly permissive. It didn't demand obedience or respect but instead gave kids approval no matter what they did. You can easily guess what kind of kids this love produced: "me-firsters" whose only thought was to get what they wanted.

A second type of love was possessive. It was blind to the characteristics that made a child a unique individual. Possessive parents often "projected" onto their children their own unfulfilled wishes, regardless of whether those wishes fitted their child's hopes or temperament. They were also highly controlling and often severe in their discipline. This possessive, over-controlling love produced conformist teenagers who couldn't think for themselves and who were more concerned about following the letter of the law than about helping their fellow human beings.

The third type of love both understood and accepted the child as an individual. Parents who gave their child this kind of love also loved each other in the same accepting way. They gave each other and their kids a chance to be themselves. All family members had a voice in decisions that affected them and the life of the family. In the words of the researchers: "These parents have no need to irrationally project frustrated hopes onto their children or otherwise treat them as objects for personal satisfaction rather than as individuals in their own right."

Not surprisingly, it was this third type of family that produced the teenagers who came closest to the ideal of the rational-altruistic person. These teenagers weren't perfect, but they were, in the researchers' words, "the most morally effective adolescents in the study. They conform to moral precepts because they want to and because they understand them. They enjoy life thoroughly and actively, having as healthy a respect for themselves as they do for other people."[11] In the outside world, these young people extended to others the same kind of respectful regard on which they had been nourished in their families.

In raising principled kids, love and respect turn out to be very close allies. Respect touches more deeply when it's warmed by love. And "I love you" is more ennobling when it carries the message "I respect you for the person you are."

BE A PRINCIPLED PERSON

The importance of love, respect, and balancing independence and control is strongly suggested by the studies of principled young people. So is the importance of another big idea: setting a good example by the way we lead our lives.

As a case in point, let me share with you an effort to delve into the backgrounds of young persons whose moral principles led them to take courageous action on behalf of others.[12]

David Rosenhan, a Stanford University psychologist, was curious about the young Americans who got involved in the civil rights movement of the sixties. He identified two groups. The first he called "fully committed"; they had given a year or more to front-line civil rights work, sometimes at personal risk. The second group Rosenhan called "partially committed"; their involvement was limited to one or two low-risk "freedom rides," and their commitment seemed more talk than action.

Partially committed students, the interviews disclosed, usually disliked their parents. They frequently remembered them as "hypocrites" who preached one thing and practiced another. One young man, for example, went on a tirade about how easily his father condoned dishonesty when the victims were people he didn't like.

Fully committed civil rights workers, by contrast, typically looked up to their parents as persons who lived by their moral ideals. One young man remembered vividly how his father had carried him on his shoulders in a parade to protest the execution of two political dissidents believed by many to have been framed for murder. Another recalled how his father, outraged by Nazi atrocities, had signed up for service in World War II despite bad health and old age.

The people I interview tell similar stories. There was the young woman who remembered how her mother stood alone in befriending a new minority-group family whose entry into the neighborhood the other neighbors had tried to block. Another young woman, a dedicated teacher who also opens her home to people needing a meal or shelter, remembers her mother's moral courage:

> "My mother had a tremendous sense of justice. She was always involved in causes. One of my earliest childhood memories is that of my mother being arrested for leading a PTA crusade. She said they wouldn't leave the capitol steps until they saw the governor.
>
> "It was my mother who taught me from my earliest years always to stand up for what I thought was right. I don't remember much talking about it. The beauty was in what she did. My mother is the corner I've woven my web in."

Besides trying to be principled persons ourselves, it's important to expose kids to other examples of people who have tried to live by their moral principles. A book such as *Profiles in Courage* provides many instances from the pages of history. And once in a while a movie comes along, such as *Chariots of Fire* or *A Man for All Seasons,* that presents an inspiring portrait of moral integrity. In *Chariots of Fire*, Scottish track star Eric Liddle sacrifices what he believes to be his one chance at a gold medal in the 1924 Olympics rather than violate his religious principles by running on Sunday. In *A Man for All Seasons* (a wonderful play as well as a film), Sir Thomas More stands virtually alone, despite imprisonment and threat of death, in his refusal to swear to the oath declaring Henry VIII the head of the Church in England. When his friends and family plead with him, unable to understand why he won't take the oath and save his life, More tries to explain:

> (To his friend Norfolk) "I will not give in because I oppose it—*I* do—not my pride, not my spleen, nor any other of my appetites, but *I* do—*I*!"

> (To his daughter) "When a man takes an oath, Meg, he's holding his own self in his hands. Like water. And if he opens his fingers *then*—he needn't hope to find himself again."[13]

If we would raise principled children, we should let them see principles in action.

DEVELOP PRINCIPLED REASONING THROUGH MORAL DISCUSSION

Some principled young adults remember their parents' actions more than their words. But there's also evidence that strong words are part of many homes that breed a deep sense of justice and compassion.

Says one young man, deeply involved in social activism: "There was a lot of talk about justice in our family. Dad would comment about things he'd read about in the paper. We'd talk about discussions I'd had in school."[14]

One way to foster kids' awareness of human rights is to talk about cases where someone's rights have clearly been violated. All of us regularly come across things that offend our sense of justice and arouse our moral indignation. We should share with kids our thoughts and feelings about such matters. One mother described at the dinner table a magazine article she read on the sexual harassment of women at work and her feelings about women being treated with anything less than full respect. A father read to his children from a newsletter, *Klanwatch,* that reported dozens of incidents of terrorism and violence carried out against blacks by a resurgent Ku Klux Klan. It saddened him, he said, to think that this kind of hateful racism was still alive in the country. The more we talk about values like equality, human dignity, and social justice, the deeper they'll penetrate into kids' moral consciousness.

Family conversation should also include discussion of controversial moral issues where rights come into conflict. Abortion is a case in point. Whose right is greater: the fetus's to live or the woman's to decide whether she wishes to give birth? What about busing? Does the right of nonwhite children to a good education (which many people think means integrated schools) outweigh the right of parents to choose where to send their child to school? What about quotas? In the famous Alan Bakke case, was the University of California at Davis Medical School right to reject Bakke while accepting minority students with lower test scores under an affirmative-action program intended to compensate for past discrimination?

Contested moral issues like these force kids to come to grips with the human rights involved. And they teach them that people may agree about the broad principle of respect for persons but disagree sharply about how to apply it.

TALK TO KIDS ABOUT THINKING FOR THEMSELVES

I'd also urge you to talk to your teenagers about thinking for themselves, the way you did when they were at Stage 3 and needed to learn to stand apart from the peer group. Only now they need to learn to think critically about social systems. Talk with them about what happened in Nazi Germany. Chances are it'll be covered in school, but they should know it's important to you.

Tell them about the Milgram experiment, and ask them why they think so many people obeyed. Talk about personal moral responsibility and how you can't pass the buck by saying, "I was just following orders." Talk about the kind of patriotism that loves the ideals its country stands for and wants to make those ideals a reality. Talk about the role of dissent in a free and democratic society.

Talk, too, about "causes," and about what happens when people swear total loyalty to a cause and stop thinking critically. Cults are a good example of this. Cults demand absolute, unquestioning adherence to the tenets of their "system." I recently spoke with a mother who, with the help of a parents' organization, had finally extricated her son from a religious cult led by a 40-year-old ex-carpenter who called himself "Jesus Christ Lightning Amen." The cult forbade marriage, sex, and material possessions, and wandered barefoot through the countryside and cities begging and scavenging for food.

"While Dave was with them," the mother said, "they had a complete hold over him. Psychologists are wrong when they say it's just a phase kids go through. I tried to talk with him once for two hours, and there was no reaching him. He just smiled and called me 'Sister.'

"Now he says, 'How could I have been taken in?' He's still angry about it. He was vulnerable because he was so idealistic. They don't get the street kids—they're too savvy."

Cults, like many other causes, don't tolerate critical thinking and freedom of choice because they don't respect the individual. Recent books, such as *Lord of the Second Advent* by Steve Kemperman and *Moonwebs* by Josh Freed, charge cults with using sleep deprivation, denial of privacy, malnutrition, and other manipulations to indoctrinate their members and reduce their ability to think for themselves. As parents, we may not be able to completely protect our children against people who would manipulate them for their own ends. But by alerting them to such dangers, talking with them about respect for individual persons and what that means, and developing their critical thinking through moral discussions, we can try to make them "savvy" in a morally principled way. (Parents whose children are current or former cult members can go to the following organizations for referral to counselors, lawyers, and parent groups that can help: Citizens Freedom Foundation, P.O. Box 86, Hannacroix, N.Y. 12087, 518-756-8014; and the American Family Foundation, P.O. Box 336, Weston, MA 02193, 617-893-0930.)

Our Judeo-Christian heritage, unlike fanatical cults, strongly affirms the dignity and sacred value of every individual person. If you're a religious family, you have a powerful resource for helping kids develop a principled respect for persons. Religion deepens respect for the human person by asserting that we all have within us a holy spark and are all children of a common Creator who calls us by name to goodness.

With its emphasis on our common origin, destiny, and purpose in living, religion can also teach kids that while we are individuals, we are also one. We are members of a single human family. As such, we are meant to care for each other.

TALK ABOUT MORAL RELATIVISM

We should also talk with kids about "moral relativism." Moral relativism is the belief that *all* moral values are relative: "There's no right or wrong, it's all a matter of opinion." You might regard this way of thinking as patently illogical; after all, if all values are relative, then somebody like Hitler could say, "Sorry, folks, but by conquering countries and carrying out genocide I'm just acting on my personal values."

Nevertheless, Kohlberg's longitudinal study found that about 20 percent of his middle-class subjects, sometime between late high school and their second or third year of college, went through a period of really believing in moral relativism. Their uncertainty and confusion were very genuine; sometimes they weren't even sure about their relativism! Said one young man in his twenties: "I don't think there's any moral law which is always right, and which always has been for all time. But then . . . I don't even know if that's true."

Sometimes relativism takes a form that sounds like Stage 2 selfishness (though it's a lot more intellectually sophisticated). Says Brian, a college sophomore:

"When I was in high school, I was trying to please the norms of society and, in essence, conforming to the prevailing thought about moral right. I was concerned about other people and society in general when I was younger. Now I think more of a moral responsibility to oneself. Self-concern takes precedence over morals."[15]

Brian is in a moral twilight zone. He's beyond Stage 4; he can stand outside society and be critical of its morals. He can ask, "Why be moral, anyway? Who's to say what's right or wrong?" But he hasn't yet constructed a new morality, the principled respect for persons of Stage 5, to replace the Stage 4 morality he's thrown overboard. Because relativists fall between these stages, Kohlberg has dubbed their position "Stage 4½."

Some relativists sort things out. They come to understand that many values *are* relative, but some values, like respect for human rights, are not. By age 25, Brian had moved beyond relativism to Stage 5.

Interviewer: What does the word morality meant to you now?

Brian: I think it is recognizing the right of the individual, the rights of other individuals, not interfering with those rights; act as fairly as you would have them treat you. I think it is basically to preserve the human being's right to existence; I think that is the most important.

Interviewer: How have your views on morality changed since the last interview?

Brian: I think I am more aware of an individual's rights now. I used to be looking at it strictly from my point of view, just for me. Now I think I am more aware of what the individual has a right to.[16]

Radical value relativism is not, however, a necessary passage from Stage 4 to Stage 5. It may be the result of "diversity shock"—going to college, for example, and meeting up with all sorts of people who believe all sorts of things about sex, God, politics, and morality. For kids who have been exposed to only one "system" of morality or truth, that's a bucket of cold water in the face. They go from thinking, "There's only one right system—mine," to thinking, "If so many people believe so many different things, it must all be just a matter of opinion. There's no real right or wrong."

Kids shouldn't collide with value diversity for the first time when they leave the nest. While they're still at home, we can talk with them about the many perspectives and beliefs that abound in a pluralistic society. We can teach them the basis of our belief system and the critical challenges that have been put to it. We can teach them that they can appreciate the insights and values of other systems—other religions, for example—without necessarily abandoning their own. And we can teach them that even though some values are personal choices that we wouldn't impose on others, there are other values—such as respect for persons—that are universal, binding all people everywhere.

THE PAINS OF GROWING UP MORALLY

I don't want to give the impression that, by taking all the right precautions, you can take all the storm and stress out of this part of your child's passage to moral adulthood. You can't. There'll be growing pains for your child and for you. You may even find that your child's late teens and early twenties are your toughest years as a parent. Here are some of the tensions and conflicts that parents may experience during this period (and experience varies widely):

• Children who were "good kids" in their earlier teens—not the ones who were into drugs or arrested when they were 15—may suddenly go off the track. A mother in a small rural community told of her anguish as her son, a good student and a responsible, considerate person during high school, got a job with a construction company after graduating, started drinking heavily, became verbally abusive toward his family, and totaled both family cars.

• Kids go away to college and come home different people. They may have different ideas about sex and marriage; they may reject our politics or life-style; they may stop going to church. Parents find themselves paying out thousands of dollars a year to finance a college education that's changing their child in ways they don't like!

• Kids are done with school, sometimes working, sometimes not, but they're still living with you. They're willing to eat at your table but not to live by your rules. Says a mother: "I worry about my 19-year-old daughter staying out late. But what do you say when she points out that none of her friends has a curfew and she doesn't want one either?"

• You don't like something your grown child is doing, but you don't know whether to butt in or butt out. Twenty-two-year-old Tony was living with his girl friend. His father had decided not to make an issue of that but was disturbed because he felt Tony was treating the girl badly. He wondered, should he say something? When do you stop being a parent?

I won't pretend there are easy answers to these kinds of questions and concerns. But it may help you get through a difficult period with your older child if you keep the following in mind:

1. Moral development during this period of life often involves questioning values and beliefs that went unquestioned during childhood. It's not easy to take when kids question values—religion, for example—that we hold dear and have tried hard to pass on. But we should remember that adult moral maturity requires independent critical thinking. If we want our children to become principled moral reasoners who can stand back and evaluate the norms and values of the society around them, we should expect that they'll practice their developing powers of moral reasoning on what's close to home.

Remember, too, that values discarded for the present aren't necessarily discarded forever. Kids often come home in later years to values they pushed aside in young adulthood. In the meantime, we can talk with them, adult to adult, about the values that guide their lives. If we have religious faith, we can also pray for them. But the bottom line is that they're becoming their own persons, a process we couldn't stop if we wanted to.

2. Even when our children are adults, we don't stop being their parents. We continue to love them and to want to help them in ways that we can. Sometimes the best thing is not to interfere—not to offer counsel, for example, unless it's asked for. At other times it may be wise for us to take the initiative. In either case, it's essential to let our children know that we respect the fact that they are now adults. The father who thinks his 22-year-

old son is treating his girl friend badly, for example, might broach that delicate subject as follows:

> "You're an adult now, and you're in charge of your own life. I can't tell you how to run it. But I wouldn't be honest if I didn't tell you my feelings about something that concerns me. I think of you as someone who can be kind and loving, and so I'm troubled by some of the ways I see you treating Ann."

Sometimes our intervention has to be more forceful—as in the case of the 19-year-old who began drinking heavily and behaving recklessly. As long as kids are living under our roof, we have a responsibility to ourselves and to them to require them to behave decently toward us and to follow reasonable rules. Sometimes we'll have to sit down and work out reasonable rules together in a spirit of fairness and compromise (see Chapter 13); sometimes, when drugs or alcohol is in the driver's seat, we may need to seek outside help (see Chapter 18).

3. Time is sometimes the best problem-solver. Says a mother:

> "I went through hell with my teenage daughter. For a while, I thought I had raised this surly, self-centered individual. But now she's 21, and she's turned out to be the most thoughtful, tolerant person. Sometimes I can't believe it, and I say to myself, 'Where did this come from?'"

Frequently, the cause of our children's offensive behavior has nothing to do with us, and the cure isn't anything we can provide. They need time—time to work through a difficult developmental transition, time to find out who they are, time to find a direction for their lives. The challenge for us in the meantime is to be there when they need us and to keep the door open to a relationship that will mature as our children do.

One point in closing about Stage 5 of moral reasoning.

Developing a capacity for principled moral reasoning doesn't guarantee that we use it. Sometimes our higher principles carry the day; sometimes they don't. Often we do something less than noble and then find reasons later to rationalize our behavior.

HELPING KIDS TO STAGE 5

1. Develop kids' respect for their own rights and dignity by:
   - Encouraging them to speak their minds;
   - Allowing them the independence they need to become their own persons;
   - Using parental authority in a fair and reasonable way.

2. Avoid permissive or overcontrolling love. Love kids in a way that respects them as individuals. Give them a voice in the family.

3. Try to be a principled person yourself; expose kids to other examples of people acting on moral principle.

4. Have discussions that help kids develop principled moral reasoning:
   - Talk about cases where someone's rights have clearly been violated.
   - Discuss controversial moral issues where rights come into conflict.
   - Talk with kids about the importance of thinking for themselves.
   - Show how religion affirms the sacred value of the human person and our obligations to each other as members of the human family.
   - Talk about "moral relativism" and prepare kids to deal with value diversity.

5. Make kids aware that it's not always easy to act on principle but that the effort to do so is the struggle for character.

Partly that's because of our human capacity for selfishness; partly it's because we're creatures of a social environment that does not always summon us to be our best moral selves.

A recent book, *When Dreams and Heroes Died,* by Carnegie Foundation Fellow Arthur Levine, takes the measure of the moral climate in which young people today are preparing for their adult lives. Levine studied college graduates of the 1970s. He concluded that they have a "*Titanic* mentality." They think the ship of society is headed for disaster, but they want to go first class. Their goal in life is not to better the world as they find it, but to make a lot of money, have status, and live well.

Our children should understand that morality is the subordination of selfishness.[17] They should know that it can be tough to be good in a world that says looking out for number one is the smart way to go. And they should know that living out their moral principles may be the toughest challenge they'll face in their lives. It is, as psychologist Roger Brown so aptly puts it, the struggle for character.

PART 4

CONCERNS THAT CUT ACROSS AGES AND STAGES

CHAPTER 12

HOW TO GET KIDS TO TALK TO YOU

Says a mother:

"Our 13-year-old son has become very quiet. He's not sullen or disrespectful; he just doesn't talk. When I ask questions, I get one-word answers. 'How's school?' 'Okay.' 'How was the game?' 'Good.' When he's home, he spends most of his time in his room, with the door closed. I don't know what's going on in his head."

Says a father:

"Our family has gotten so activity-oriented that there's hardly ever a chance to just sit down and talk. Somebody's always rushing off to a lesson or a practice or a game or something. Sometimes I feel I know the people I work with better than I know my own children."

Much of what's involved in raising good children comes down to communication. We show respect for our children by how we talk to them. We need to be able to communicate effectively in order to teach them the values we cherish, help them learn to reason about right and wrong, and let them know we love and appreciate them. We need to communicate in order to encourage their independence and provide them with guidance and control.

So at any age or stage of moral development, communication is important. If our communication with our children is good, our overall relationship will be good, and they'll be more open to our influence as moral teachers. And if the lines are open about things in general (school, friends, problems, feelings), it'll be easier to discuss sensitive moral issues when we want to talk about those.

In a recent study of 250 children, ages 4 to 17, almost all the children said they wished their families talked more.[1] And yet when parents and kids do talk, they often don't get beyond nonconversations like: "What'd you do in school today?" "Nuthin'." Parents ask: "How can I get my child to really *talk* to me?"

Let's look at some ways.

CONVERSATION STARTERS

To draw kids out, we may have to be more imaginative about how we start conversations. For example, a specific request to "tell me two things you did in school today" usually works better than the question "What did you do in school today?" The latter can easily be answered with "nothing"; the former can't.

It also helps to vary our approach. Beginning a conversation with the same old question is about as interesting as serving the same old lettuce and cucumber salad at the start of every meal. The box on page 253 suggests some alternative ways you can try to get a conversation going with your child.

DO THINGS WITH KIDS

A father said to me recently, "I think all this emphasis on communication is phony if you aren't taking the time to *do* things with your children. That's when you have your best conversations—when you're doing something together that you both enjoy."

Said a mother who has raised three children:

"I think it's very important to spend time with children *individually.* I always tried to do that. We used to take walks. And we'd have long conversations when we were doing the dishes. That's a good time for talking; your hands are busy. It's a lot easier

TEN WAYS TO START A CONVERSATION WITH YOUR CHILD

1. How was today on a scale of 1 to 10 (where 1 is terrible and 10 is terrific)? What made it that way?

2. What was the high point (low point) of your day?

3. Tell me the good news and the bad news about school today (work today, practice this week, camp this summer).

4. What's a thought or feeling you had today?

5. What happened today that you didn't expect?

6. (If your child seems preoccupied) I'm wondering what you're thinking about. Would you be willing to talk to me about it?

**The following conversation starters
may be especially helpful if you haven't seen your
child for a period of time:**

7. Tell me about something good that's happened since the last time we talked.

8. What's something you've done recently that you're proud of?

9. What's on your mind these days?

10. What are you looking forward to these days?

to talk in a situation like that than if somebody sits you down and says, 'Now let's have a talk.'"

I want to underscore this point: meaningful conversation with kids depends less on using the "right techniques" than it does on having a good relationship. And good relationships require time together—time invested, for example, in shared activity. As the mother's memory of talk during dishwashing shows, shared activity can be work as well as play. One father described a fall afternoon when he and his teenage son spent several hours working together—moving a compost heap—in their back yard:

> "Sandy was thirteen, and the new school year had gotten off to a pretty rocky start. Problems with peers, insecurity about his place in the group, that sort of thing. As we shoveled dirt and sod that afternoon, we had one of the best conversations we'd had in a long time. We talked about a lot of things: his teachers and how he felt about them, some kids at school who were giving him a hard time, a girl he used to like and a new one he thought he might like, and a discussion of drugs they had in health class. I felt close to him at the end of that day."

Food can be a good facilitator of communication. One father says he and his teenage son have some of their best conversations over a sandwich or a pizza after they've seen a movie or play together. A mother says she connects with her teenage daughter when they go out to lunch together. Says a mother of two elementary schoolers, Penny, 8, and Jeff, 6:

> "We have some of our best conversations when the kids have a snack after school. I hear about who their best friend is this week, the fight they got in on the playground, and the time their teacher yelled at them when it wasn't their fault. Last week Penny told about the problem of things disappearing in her classroom, and we got into a discussion of why some kids steal, why it's wrong to steal, and what you could try to do to get kids to return something they stole."

The idea that I want to stress here is that we shouldn't expect good communication with kids to occur in a vacuum. It needs a natural context. And that means spending time with our children.

ASK KIDS WHAT *THEY* WANT TO TALK ABOUT

One way to get kids talking is to ask them what *they* would like *us* to talk about. *Families* magazine, an unfortunately short-lived publication on parenting and family life, carried an excellent article titled "Conversations Kids Crave," in which educational psychologist Torey Hayden reported the results of her study of what several hundred children and teenagers really wish their parents would talk with them about.[2] Eight topics emerged as kids' major concerns:

1. **Family matters.** This was first on kids' lists. When there's a problem in the family (money troubles, job pressures, conflicts between parents, impending divorce, death), kids don't want to be in the dark, wondering what the problem is. They want their parents to tell them. And when there are decisions to be made that affect them (allowance, bedtime, vacations), they'd like a chance to talk it over.

2. **Controversial issues.** What is sex like? What's a "homo"? Why do drugs make you high? Is it ever right to tell a lie? Kids have lots of questions like these that they wish parents would talk to them about. They don't like it when parents say, "You're too young," or "It's too hard to explain."

3. **Emotional issues.** "In every group of children who participated," says researcher Hayden, "someone brought up the fact that he wishes his parents would tell him they love him." (That finding reminds me of a 12-year-old girl who told me, "I love my father, and I'm sure he loves me, but he never *says* so!") Other kids simply wanted their parents to talk about their feelings in an open and sincere way.

4. **The big whys.** Says 6-year-old Lance: "I want to know about a lot of things. I wish they'd talk to me about God. And what it's like in heaven. I want to know about space and night and people on other planets. I want to know why people are made. And how come they fight."

5. **The future.** Many kids approaching adolescence want to talk about what it's like to be a teenager. Older kids wonder about college and careers.

6. **Current events.** Many kids are keenly aware of world events and want to discuss them at home. Kids hear a lot about the threat of nuclear war, for example, and need to talk out the anxieties that that subject arouses. (One survey of elementary school children found that nearly half of them believed that nuclear war would occur within their lifetimes.)

7. **Personal interests.** Kids said they wished their parents would show interest in what they do and like (their hobbies, sports, friends).

8. **Parents themselves.** Kids wonder how we behaved and felt as children. They especially like to hear stories—about a time we were scared or a time we got in trouble, for example—that reveal our emotional side or human failings. Says 12-year-old Megan: "I figure my mom and dad must know an awful lot about how it feels to grow up. I wish they'd tell me. How did my mom feel when she got to be a teenager?"

Said one 10-year-old boy who was interviewed: "There's a lot of good stuff to talk about. All I really care about is that we talk about something. That's all that matters."

TALK AT BEDTIME

Since most kids will do anything to postpone the moment of sleep, bedtime is an excellent chance to ask, "What's on your mind?" or to tell them what's on yours. I would sometimes find out what our kids were thinking about by asking, "If God were here right now, what question would you ask Him?"

If you're having trouble with your teenager, try a bedside conversation. When the lights are out, barriers tend to fall away. It's easier to speak the language of the heart.

A mother told of the terrible time she was having with her 16-year-old daughter. Then one night, after another bitter argument, she went into her daughter's bedroom and sat down on the edge of the bed. Her voice trembling with emotion, she said, "Susan, I love you. Why can't you say that you love me?" Tears welled up in Susan's eyes, she hugged her mother and sobbed, "I do love you! I do love you!" They held each other and cried. After that, the mother said, their relationship was much improved.

PLAY A COMMUNICATION GAME

There are a number of noncompetitive, nonthreatening communication games on the market that will help you enter the inner world of kids and help kids better understand you.[3] The game I know best, one we've often played as a family and that I recommend to parents in workshops, is "The Ungame." Just about all families report strong feelings of closeness and deeper knowledge of each other after playing this game.

"The Ungame" was developed by Mrs. Rhea Zakich, a California homemaker and mother of two boys. Mrs. Zakich had throat surgery and was ordered by her doctor not to speak a word for three months. During her sentence of silence, Mrs. Zakich says:

> "I began to realize that as a family, we had not shared our feelings on many subjects. I had not instilled in my children the things that were important to me. Even my husband didn't really know me. I wrote down every question I wished people would ask me, and all of the questions I wanted to ask and couldn't."[4]

These questions became the basis for "The Ungame." In the game, players draw a card and either respond to it or, if they prefer, draw another. Sample cards:

> *What four things are most important in your life?*
> *Share one of the happiest days of your life.*
> *What is something that really bugs you?*
> *What feelings do you have the most trouble expressing?*
> *Why do some kids use drugs?*

When kids respond to questions like these, they often reveal things that tend not to come out in ordinary conversation. In response to the card *What do you think about when you can't fall asleep?* for example, 7-year-old Melanie said, "Having a mink coat and a diamond ring." Her mother comments:

> "The sales company I work for rewards personnel who have high sales with mink coats and diamond rings. Many times I've said, 'Oh, wouldn't you like Mommy to win a mink coat?' I now think I've mentioned this too much in the family. I realize our children are learning values from us all the time without our realizing it."

Says another mother:

> "I learned my 11-year-old son couldn't express himself when he pulled the card that asks you to say something you like about yourself. I think more comments from me in the future concerning his good points would help him in this regard."

You may be thinking, "That kind of game may work for other families, but mine would be too self-conscious to take it seriously." Many parents share that apprehension before they try the game but have been pleasantly surprised by the results. Says a mother of three boys:

> "There was much embarrassed giggling at first. But when the kids saw how thoughtfully and seriously their father and I answered the questions, they settled down and followed our example. I enjoyed the quiet—no arguing, no unkind words. By the end of the game, there was a real sense of belonging—a feeling that this was family, where we accepted, respected, and loved each other."

THE FAMILY DINNER HOUR

Says a father of two boys, 12 and 9:

> "When the kids have soccer practice, we eat early. For us, dinner is one of the times of the day when we're certain to all be together. Part of the kids' identities comes from what we do as a family, and there's a value system I want to be part of their lives. Dinners with the family give them a support base."[5]

The dinner hour is a golden opportunity for the kind of family communication that draws kids out, deepens relationships, and makes a difference in their moral development. Not that dinners will be idyllic islands of intimacy, free of all strain and strife. But with a little effort, they can more often be a grace note in the day, an experience in what it means to be civilized, and a time for the meaningful contact with each other that we'd all like to have more of.

How can you make that happen? Here are some things you can try.

1. **Establish "manners for talking" as well as manners for eating, and review them at the beginning of the meal.** Civilized conversation doesn't just happen. It needs cultivating. The quality of dinner conversation can be significantly better if you call to mind three manners for talking:

- Don't interrupt.
- Listen to and look at the person who's talking.
- No put-downs.

Make it clear that a meal is a sharing of thoughts as well as a sharing of food. You'd like respect for both.

2. **Open the meal with a ritual that helps to set a tone.** Rituals express shared values and create a feeling of oneness. Grace, for example, joins a family in recognizing that a meal, like other blessings in life, is not to be taken for granted. Some families link hands around the table as they say the grace; some vary the grace from time to time and occasionally make up their own graces to keep the words from losing meaning.

3. **Instead of free-for-all conversation, have a topic.** Choose something that everyone at the table (kids, parents, stepparents, grandparents, guests) can respond to. Any of the questions I suggested earlier for starting one-to-one conversations with kids can also be used to get a dinner discussion rolling. The box on page 260 gives some other possibilities.

If your children are old enough, try the topic, "What's in the news?" Don't underestimate kids' capacity to develop an interest in local, national, and world happenings. Americans who visit countries like England, for example, are often surprised at how much children as young as 8 and 9 know about the leaders and current events of their country. And remember that by developing kids' knowledge about society, you're laying a foundation for their eventual development of moral reasoning about social systems.

One mother of elementary-age and junior-high-age children stimulated their interest in the news through the following game. During the week, each family member cut out a picture from the newspaper and posted it on the refrigerator. On Friday, everybody brought his or her clipping to the table, and the rest of the family tried to guess who was in the picture and what it was

TOPICS FOR DINNER DISCUSSION

1. What did you do today (this week) that you feel good about?

2. What was the best thing that happened today (this week)? Or: What stood out for you?

3. What was something you learned today?

4. What's a way you've helped someone recently?

5. What's a way someone has helped you recently?

6. What's a new experience you had this week?

7. What's something you did today that you never did before?

8. What's something you're thinking about but haven't told anybody about yet?

about. That was the springboard for further discussion of people and events in the news.

4. **Try one-word topics.** Take turns suggesting one-word topics that people can comment on in any way that they like. Possibilities: television, movies, friends, school, careers, teachers, parents, sports, heroes, clothes, dating, love, marriage, and God. You can also raise moral issues such as lying, sexism, prejudice, cheating, shoplifting, drugs, and violence.

Open-ended subjects like these tend to bring out related experiences people in the family have had. They're also a good way to find out what kids are thinking.

5. **Vary the format.** A "jumping in" style of conversation is the most natural and spontaneous—people piggybacking on each other's comments, speaking when the spirit moves them. But it's often good to go around the table, so that nobody dominates the discussion and everybody, even a quiet child, has a say.

6. **Play "Circle Questions."** Go around the table, each family member asking a question of the person on the left (any ques-

tion, with the proviso that the person may pass on the first one and request another).[6] If there's time, you can reverse the direction and do another round. For example, you might ask your 8-year-old son, "Who's your best friend in school these days?" He might ask his teenage sister, "Do you like that boy who called last week?" She might ask her mother, "How did you and Dad meet, and how did you know you wanted to marry him?" Mom might ask Dad, "How did *you* know you wanted to marry *me*?" And so on.

Circle questions help parents and kids get better at asking good questions in conversation and brings out a lot of information in a short time.

7. **Build feelings of positive regard.** Kids open up when it's safe to do so, when they feel their disclosure won't be laughed at or otherwise put down. You should discuss with kids why putdowns don't help family communication. But often the best way to get kids to stop saying negative things is to create a positive atmosphere. One way to do that is to start dinner conversation with "appreciation time." Ask, "What's something that somebody in the family did for you recently that you appreciated?" (You can mention more than one person.)

8. **Discuss moral dilemmas.** Here's a way to have lively dinner conversation and expand kids' powers of moral reasoning at the same time. In our family, we've found the advice columns ("Dear Abby" is the one our paper carries) to be a good source of real-life moral dilemmas that are both challenging to the mind and easy on the stomach.

One of us reads the letter aloud but not the advice. A 16-year-old girl has had an accident with the family car through her own fault; should her father carry out his threat to take away her driving privileges for a whole year if this ever happened? Should a 12-year-old boy be able to invite to his overnight slumber party a neighborhood girl who's "one of the gang"? Should an 8-year-old girl be allowed to talk every night on the phone and go to the movies with a "boyfriend" she says she "loves"? Should a boy tell his teacher he saw a classmate defacing school property? What should a mother do when she finds a pornographic magazine in her 16-year-old son's room? Only *after* we all say what advice we'd give and why, do we read Abby's.

Try moral dilemmas like these sometime when grandparents are at the table. The value perspectives of another generation can further enliven the discussion and give kids an even richer mix of views to think about. (See Appendix C for a sample "Dear Abby" letter and questions you can use to stimulate family discussion.)

9. **Discuss a personal problem.** If dinnertime has a "sharing and caring" atmosphere, kids will often feel secure enough to bring up a real problem they're facing. Or you can draw troubles out by asking, "Who's having a problem these days?" Your kindergartener may be upset about a classmate who keeps hitting him. Your 6th-grade daughter may feel pulled between two girls she likes but who don't like each other. Your 8th-grade son may be unsure about how to deal with a kid at school who keeps putting him down. Or the problem can be one you're having—a tough situation you're facing at work, for example. The purpose of the discussion is for you to put your heads together and brainstorm possible ways of dealing with the problem.

Discussions like these give family members a chance to serve as a real support system for each other. And they can improve sibling relationships by giving kids a chance to render valuable help to each other. Many times a brother or a sister, who may have recently gone through a similar problem, can come up with ideas that a parent might not think of. By experiencing this kind of mutual assistance, kids are also learning something that's important for their moral growth and personal happiness: that they can give effective help to someone who has a problem[7] and can go to others for help when they have a problem of their own.

Some of these ideas may not be your family's cup of tea, and any attempt at "organizing" dinner discussion might feel funny at first. It may help to introduce a new idea by saying, "Dinner is one of the few times we're all together, and it's important to me to use the time to really talk with each other. Here's something I just learned about that I thought would be good to try for a change." Kids may groan at first, but they quickly adapt. In time, having a focused dinner discussion will feel like an old shoe. And moving in this direction certainly shouldn't rule out spontaneity; not every dinner discussion needs to have an official topic or deliberate format.

The important thing is to think of mealtime as an opportunity to be in touch with kids about all sorts of things, moral matters included. And regardless of what you discuss, civil conversation—listening with respect, asking a question that shows interest in another, sharing honestly and tactfully one's thoughts and feelings—is itself a lived moral experience, and a vital part of a child's moral development.

That kind of conversation, we should also remember, is an art. Like any important human skill, it takes *years* of practice to develop. Most adults are still developing it. So don't lose heart when, despite your best efforts, kids interrupt, don't listen, complain about the food, and call each other names. It only means your family is normal. Keep at it. The habit of trying to make meaningful contact at the table will carry you over the rough spots, and there will be nights that convince you that all the effort is worthwhile.

THE DIRECT APPROACH

Parents who try one or another of these approaches—varying conversation starters, doing things with their children, asking kids what they'd like to talk about, bedside chats, communication games, and real conversation at the dinner table—usually find that communication with their kids improves. But you may have a naturally quiet youngster who's still hard to draw out. Or your once-talkative son or daughter may suddenly retreat into a cocoon of privacy while they work through the growing pains of the teens.

If your most imaginative efforts to get your child to talk to you aren't bringing satisfying results, try the direct approach. *Tell* your child that it's very important to you to be in touch. You can say, for example:

> "Look, I don't want to be always pressuring you to talk to us when you don't want to. I want to respect your privacy. But it helps me a lot if I know what's going on in your life. I really need to feel in touch. Parents are like that—they worry if they don't know what's going on with kids. Can you understand that feeling?

. . . So I'd really appreciate it if you'd talk to me or your father when you're in the mood. Okay?"

Even if your youngster is not exceptionally quiet, you may still want to make a direct appeal for more communication. When Mark got into his teens (and he's not a quiet kid), there'd be times when I'd grow weary of asking him questions ("What's happening at school these days?" "What are you reading in English?" "How was the test?" "How was the game?"). One day, as we were riding in the car and I launched into my routine inquiries, I stopped and said:

"You know, sometimes I feel like an interrogator. I ask all the questions, and I think you must get tired of answering them. You never ask me any. It's all one-way. I'd like it if you asked *me* a question once in a while. What do you say we take turns—you ask me a question, and I'll ask you one."

He responded with a good-natured "Sure," and asked me how my courses at the college were going that semester. I enjoyed telling him about that. Then I asked him something. It felt like a real conversation. So now I sometimes strike up a conversation by saying with a smile, "Ask me a question."

Taking turns asking questions can also be a way of catching up on each other's lives if you've been out of touch with your child for a while. Like circle questions at the dinner table, it brings out a lot. Most important, mutual questioning *balances* the interaction and promotes real sharing. It teaches kids that conversation, even with parents, should be a two-way street. With a little training in the art of asking questions, they'll be less likely to grow into the kind of adult who is always talking about himself and never asking about anyone else.

Don't be afraid to work at communicating with your child, but don't overdo it either. Just as there can be too little communication in a family, there can also be too much. People need psychological rests from each other, alternating cycles of privacy and contact. Some need more privacy, some more contact. Be sensitive to the individual personality of your child. Remember that kids, just like grown-ups, will have times when they just don't feel like talking and secrets they want to keep.

BEING A GOOD LISTENER

If we want kids to talk to us, we should listen when they do.

All of us know from personal experience how important it is to be listened to. Really *listened to*. When others give us their full attention, truly try to understand what we're saying and enter into our thoughts and feelings, we feel affirmed, valued, cared about. We want to talk to them. We know we've got an audience.

With kids, as we've seen, it may take more than a receptive ear to get them talking. You may have to do a lot of priming the pump. But once they begin to talk, how much they open up depends a lot on how well we listen up.

A few people seem to be naturally good listeners; the rest of us have to try. How can we get better at listening to our kids?

1. **Listen with your whole self.** We often do a half-eared job of listening to others. We're half listening, half thinking about something else. Try to develop the discipline of listening with your whole self. Really focus on what your child is saying to you. Maintain good eye contact; a lack of eye contact communicates a lack of interest. You can't always give such concentrated attention, of course, and not all conversation with kids demands it. But serious conversation does require this kind of whole-self listening.

2. **Don't interrupt constantly with questions and comments.** We all know how irritating it can be to have somebody repeatedly interrupt us when we're trying to get something out. Hold your questions and comments until kids have a chance to speak their piece.

3. **If you can't listen right now, set a time when you can.** It's best, of course, to listen to kids when *they* want to talk. But if you can't really "be there" at the moment, you can say, "I must get this finished, but I'll be with you in 15 minutes." Or, "I'm in a rush right now, but let's talk at bedtime." What's important is to send the message, "I care—you are important to me, and I want to listen to you."

4. **Acknowledge feelings.** When we tell somebody, "What a bummer of a day!" we don't want them to say, "Oh, come on—

look at the bright side!" And yet when our child says, "Andy can't come over to play—what a lousy day!" we're likely to say "Stop whining!" "Cheer up—you can find something else to do!" or "That's life—you've got to learn to accept disappointments." We all know what kids do then; they complain all the louder. They didn't get understood the first time, so they try again.

If we know that kids and other people cling to their feelings all the more when we try to change them, why do we respond in this way? I think our intentions are good; we want the other person to be happy. So we rush in and try to "fix" their unhappy feeling. But it often has the opposite effect of what we intend; it only makes them feel worse.

Now, it *is* possible to help people feel better by helping them look at things differently or take steps to solve their problem. But when kids or others tell us their feelings, THE FIRST THING THEY WANT FROM US IS UNDERSTANDING. *After* they feel understood, they may be willing to let go of their original feeling a little bit, look at the situation more positively, or do something to change it.

You can show kids you understand them by *bouncing back* their feelings. I call this "empathic listening" because it conveys empathy. Empathy is a moral response. Listening empathically shows you care enough to put yourself in the other person's shoes and to *let that person know* you understand what he or she is saying or feeling. And that's the difference between empathic listening and silent listening; bouncing back a person's feelings *shows* that you understand.

Suppose your third-grade son comes home very angry at his teacher because she kept the whole class in during recess. Here's how you could use empathic listening in a situation like that:

Michael: Mrs. Barber makes me so mad!

    Mom: Sounds like you're pretty angry with her about something. (empathic listening)

Michael: Well, you would be, too, if you had to stay in the whole recess when you didn't do anything!

    Mom: She kept you in for recess?

Michael: She kept the *whole class* in—just because *some* kids were noisy lining up for lunch!

Mom: You feel it wasn't fair that she punished everybody because of what some kids did. (empathic listening)

Michael: That's right—*I* wasn't goofing around, so why should I
have to stay in?

Mom: That really makes you mad. (empathic listening) I can
understand your feelings. (pause) Why do you suppose
Mrs. Barber kept in the whole class? (in a curious tone)

Michael: I dunno—she was pretty mad.

Mom: Well, do you think she could have picked out the kids
who were talking from the ones who weren't?

Michael: No, kids would just say, "*I* wasn't talking!"

Mom: So why do you think she kept in the whole class?

Michael: 'Cause she couldn't tell who was bad from who wasn't.

Mom: I think you're right. And what do you suppose she
hopes will happen the next time?

Michael: Kids won't be noisy, because they don't want the whole
class to stay in on account of them.

Mom: So you can understand why Mrs. Barber did what she
did.

Michael: Yeah, I guess so.

Mom: Still, it's tough to miss recess.

Michael: Yeah.

Michael's mother didn't try to banish his feelings. She didn't
say, "Don't make such a big deal out of missing one recess!" or
"I'm sure your teacher had a good reason to keep you in." Instead, she respected his feelings. She listened empathically to
his anger at what he considered unfair treatment. Once Michael
felt his feelings were understood, he was willing to try to understand his teacher's—but feeling understood had to come first.
This is another example of a larger truth in moral development:
Our children will be better able to consider the needs of others
when their own needs have been met.

Empathic listening may sound simple, but it actually takes a
long time before it becomes natural. Many parents have been
helped by Thomas Gordon's book, *Parent Effectiveness Training,* which has several chapters on how to use this important
communication skill (he calls it "active listening").[8] I'd also recommend the recent and inexpensive book, *How to Talk So Kids*

Will Listen and Listen So Kids Will Talk, by Adele Faber and Elaine Mazlish.

Two caveats about empathic listening:

1. Don't overdo it. It'll sound phony if you go around bouncing back everything everybody says, and besides, kids don't need empathy all the time.

2. Research shows that with young kids, empathic listening often *intensifies* their feeling instead of defusing it. So if you say to your crying 3-year-old, "You're really sad because I have to leave now," he might cry all the harder! I've found that with young and even older kids, it's often helpful to make a statement of *direct understanding,* with as much sympathy as you can muster. For example: "I understand your feelings, Charlie, I really do." You can tell what works for you by paying attention to how your child responds.

CREATE A CLIMATE FOR COMMUNICATION

A good flow of communication also depends greatly on the overall moral climate in your home. Are respect and love in the air? Or is the atmosphere thick with anger and accusation?

You can build up a more positive climate for communication by reducing negative communications. Here are four destructive patterns to try to avoid:

The Boot Camp Approach. Parents routinely order kids around in a way they would never dream of treating another adult:

> Shut your mouth!

> Get over here!

> Do what I say!

> Because I said so!

Threats. A close ally of the Boot Camp Approach:

> You'll do it if you know what's good for you!

> Hit your brother one more time, and I'll smack you good!

> Don't make me lose my temper, young lady. . . .

> Your father will hear about this when he gets home.

Put-Downs. Imagine your response if another adult said any of the following to you:

The trouble with you is you're just plain lazy!

Your manners are atrocious!

You're acting like a baby!

Why don't you watch where you're going?

How many times do I have to tell you not to do that?

When I want your opinion, I'll ask for it.

I've had all I can take of you for one day!

Sarcasm. Sarcasm is saying things you don't mean. It should be forever stricken from human discourse. It usually offends, often cuts deeply, and almost never leads to productive dialogue. Common examples of the kind of sarcasm that is used with children (the real message is in parentheses):

Nice going (you jerk)!

Thanks a lot (for nothing).

That's great, just great (awful, just awful).

How did I have such a smart (stupid) kid like you?

You're a big help (headache)!

You're so innocent (guilty).

Beautiful (terrible).

Many of our communications with kids aren't flagrant violations of respect like these, but they are negative nonetheless and take a toll over time. Things like constant criticism or just plain yelling when you get to the end of your rope around eight o'clock at night. None of us can eliminate these negative interactions, but I know it gets me down as a parent when they start to make up *most* of the interactions I have with my children.

One way to try to keep negative interactions in check is to keep score. Divide a sheet of paper in half and head each column *plus* and *minus*. Every time you and your child have a positive interaction, make a mark on the plus side. Every time you have a negative interaction, make a mark on the minus side. You'll find that just keeping track helps you increase the positives and decrease the negatives.

The best way, though, to keep negative interactions from being your whole relationship is to start creating more situations where there's good feeling and good communication between you and your child. Situations where you can just *enjoy* each other. Most negative interchanges come when we're in the role of trying to *control* our kids—trying to get them to do something or stop doing something. That goes with the territory, but it's absolutely essential to have times when we're not in that role. One of the reasons I've liked putting our kids to bed is that when we read together, there's no managing, just plain enjoyment.

Educator John Holt writes:

> At its very best, the family can be what many people say it is, an island of acceptance and love in the midst of a harsh world. But too often family members take out on each other all the pain and frustration of their lives that they don't dare take out on anyone else. Instead of being a ready-made source of friends, the family is too often a ready-made source of victims and enemies, the place where the cruelest words are spoken.[9]

I'll always remember a workshop on parent-child communication by a family counselor, 20 years in the business, who began by saying, "I've sometimes treated my own son worse than my enemies and often not as nice as my friends." No matter how much we know and how much we try, all of us can expect to fail many times. We'll say words that wound, and we'll need to be able to turn to each other for forgiveness.

But we can also do better. We can make the most of our opportunities to communicate with our children. We can try different ways of drawing kids out. We can be more attentive and empathic listeners. We can create a better climate for communication by trying to treat kids with courtesy and respect. We can make sure they know that we love them. If we do, the lines will be open between us and our children, and we'll have a better shot at helping them grow into good and decent people.

CHAPTER 13

THE FAIRNESS APPROACH TO CONFLICT

The fact that even young children say "It's not fair!" shows how basic fairness is to our sense of right and wrong. At each stage of moral development, you can capitalize on kids' desire to be treated fairly. You can solve or at least alleviate the conflicts between parents and kids that so often eat away at a good relationship, cause mounting tension, and lead to a breakdown in communication. All the things you're doing to keep up a good flow of communication between you and your child will be more effective if you try to take a constructive approach to handling conflicts.

This chapter describes the "fairness approach" to solving conflicts. This approach requires parents to respect kids by considering their point of view. It teaches kids to reason morally—to think of others' needs as well as their own. That's a big part of what's involved in progressing through the moral stages: getting better and better at considering everyone's needs when solving a problem.

The fairness approach also gives kids necessary practice in the skills of conflict resolution: expressing a viewpoint, listening to the other person, and finding common middle ground. These important life skills will help kids translate their moral reasoning into fair behavior in their human relationships.

FAIRNESS WITH TEENAGERS

Fairness is crucial in the teens. As one mother said, "*Everything* becomes an issue!"

With teenagers or with younger children, there's no single "script" for using a fairness approach; the *spirit* of fairness, your sincere effort to be fair, is more important than the particular words you say. And you should approach problems in a way that you're comfortable with, one that's suited to your personality and your style of interacting with your children. You may prefer, for example, to keep discussions short, simple, and informal. But if you're facing a conflict with your child that's been tough to solve—of the kind that parents commonly experience with teenagers—you may find it useful to take a more structured approach that helps you break out of the old communication pattern that isn't working.

To illustrate a relatively structured application of the fairness approach, let's look at how one mother used a 3-part, sit-down fairness discussion to deal with a classic problem. Richard is 16; his bedroom, his mother says, "is a disaster area." Nagging and yelling have not persuaded him to pick it up.

PART 1: ACHIEVING MUTUAL UNDERSTANDING

The key idea of the first part of a sit-down fairness discussion is to *take turns being understood*. You can't be fair if you don't understand each other's feelings.

Here are six steps to mutual understanding:

1. **State the purpose of the discussion: to solve the problem fairly. Get an agreement to participate.** (This step puts the goal of being fair up front.)

> Mother: Richard, we're having a problem about your room. I'd like to sit down with you and see if we can come up with a solution that we both think is fair. Okay?
>
> Richard: I don't know if it'll work, but we can try.

2. State your intent to get both points of view about the problem out on the table. (This emphasizes the goal of mutual understanding.)

Mother: I'd like you to understand my feelings about this problem—and I'd also like to understand *your* feelings.

3. Describe the problem as you see it.

Mother: Richard, it really bothers me that your room is almost always in total disarray, that things are so often lost because of this, and that it is virtually impossible for me to vacuum, dust, and keep clean.

4. Ask your child for his feelings about the problem.

Mother: Okay, I've told you my feelings. Now I'd like to get your feelings about it.

Richard: It isn't as bad as you think, Mom. I know where most everything is, and I don't see the point of cleaning it up unless we're having company.

5. Paraphrase your child's point of view, so he knows you understand it.

Mother: Okay, Richard, let me make sure I understand your feelings. You think your room isn't all that messy, and you don't see the reason for picking up unless company's coming.

Richard: Right.

6. Ask your child to paraphrase your viewpoint, so you know he understands you.

Mother: Richard, would you tell me what you think my feelings are?

Richard: Okay, Mom; you think my room is a total disaster, things are always getting lost, and you can't clean in there.

PART 2: SOLVING THE PROBLEM

Once you're both feeling understood, you're ready to solve the problem.

7. Together, make a list of possible solutions to the problem (you don't have to agree yet—just consider possibilities).

STEPS IN A SIT-DOWN FAIRNESS DISCUSSION

PART 1: ACHIEVING MUTUAL UNDERSTANDING

1. State the purpose of the discussion (to solve the problem fairly).

2. State your intent to get both points of view out on the table.

3. Describe the problem as you see it.

4. Ask for your child's feelings about the problem.

5. Paraphrase your child's feelings to show understanding.

6. Ask your child to paraphrase your feelings.

PART 2: SOLVING THE PROBLEM

7. Make a list of possible solutions to the problem.

8. Write an agreement stating the solutions you both think are fair.

9. Plan a follow-up discussion to see how your agreement is working.

PART 3: FOLLOWING THROUGH

10. Have a follow-up discussion to evaluate your plan.

Mother: Okay, I think we understand each other. Let's make a list of some ways we could solve this problem fairly. Let's just put down whatever ideas come to us; once we've got a list, we'll see which ones we can agree on, okay?

Richard: Sure.

Richard and his mother came up with this list of possible solutions:

(1) Don't bug Richard about it.
(2) Richard will pick up clothes every day, put dirty ones in hamper, and clear dresser.
(3) Clean only when company comes.
(4) Clean thoroughly once a week.
(5) Make bed every day.
(6) Find new places for stuff (games, etc.) that doesn't belong in Richard's room.

8. Write an agreement stating the solutions you both think are fair.

Mother: Let's go through the list and see which ones we both think are fair. Then we'll write them up into an agreement and sign it to show we're serious about this, okay?

Richard: You really think we have to write it out like some sort of a contract?

Mother: Well, it might seem like a big deal, but you know how memory is. This way we'll have something to remind us and to refer to if there's any question about what we each agreed to.

Reaching agreement usually involves some give-and-take; you won't necessarily see eye-to-eye about what's fair right off the bat. You may have to do some empathic listening (more paraphrasing of each other's feelings). Try to keep the discussion calm and focused on the question, "What solutions are really fair to both of us?"

Here's what Richard and his mother settled on:

AGREEMENT

1. Richard will make his bed daily, do a thorough cleanup once
   a week (not every day), put away clean clothes promptly,
   and put all dirty clothes into the hamper promptly.

2. Mom will stop bugging him, help him find places for stuff
   that doesn't belong in his room, and vacuum and dust following his weekly cleanup.

   Richard   *Mom*

**9. Plan a follow-up discussion to see how your agreement is
working.**

> Mother: I'd like to plan a time when we can sit down again for a
> few minutes and talk about how our agreement is work-
> ing. What's a good time, do you think?
>
> Richard: How about a week from today?
>
> Mother: You think that's soon enough?
>
> Richard: Yeah. I think we really need to give it a week.

Richard and his mother agreed upon the following Saturday to
discuss how the plan was working.

PART 3: FOLLOWING THROUGH

10. Have a follow-up discussion to evaluate your plan.
Don't skip this step; not many plans work without it. Start out
by praising progress. Then ask, if necessary, "How can we make
our agreement work better?"

> Mother: So how do you think our plan has been working?
>
> Richard: Pretty good. I made my bed every day but yesterday.
>
> Mother: I've appreciated that—and the fact that your dirty un-
> derwear isn't strewn all over the floor. How do you feel
> I've been doing?

Richard: Great! You didn't yell at me all week. And it was great to get some of that junk cleared out of here.

A fairness approach, as I've pointed out, doesn't always have to involve a structured, sit-down discussion leading to a written agreement. Sometimes it can take the form of a quick, on-the-spot verbal agreement ("If you want to play ball tonight, get your homework done now. Fair enough?") But if the problem is a tough one, the step-by-step structure can help. And the written commitment helps you remember exactly what each of you agreed to.

DON'T GIVE UP

If your fairness discussion heats up or hits an impasse, don't give up. Take a break and come back to it.

Sixteen-year-old Sharon and her mother had a running conflict over when she should be in the house on weeknights during school vacation. Sharon wanted a regular curfew of eleven-thirty. That seemed late to her mother. They tried a fairness approach and got through the mutual understanding part. But feelings ran high when they tried to solve the problem.

Sharon: Mom, I don't feel I can agree to your solutions! It's still all *your* way!

Mother: Sharon, I understand how you feel. Maybe we can reach a compromise. What do you think would be fair?

Sharon: Some nights I might come home around nine o'clock but I'd like to know I could stay out to eleven or eleven-thirty if something came up—like the movies or a party. I am 16 years old, and I have always come home on time. Don't I always tell you where I am?

Mother: Sharon, please try to take my point of view. Why do you think I want you in earlier?

Sharon: You don't want me hanging around street corners. You're afraid something terrible is going to happen to me!

Mother: Don't you think those are good reasons for concern on my part?

Sharon: But I don't hang around street corners! Anyway, times have changed, and you should, too! You don't know what's going on!

Mother: I feel I *do* know what's going on, and that's why I worry as I do!

"After some more back and forth and no compromise," the mother says, "I suggested we take a break, try to come up with some new suggestions, and talk again later."

The second discussion, several days later, went better. The mother began, "I've thought over the things you said. I do trust you. Yes, you have been responsible in the past, and it is time I gave you more responsibility for making decisions." Sharon and her mother agreed on this compromise:

1. I will tell Mom and Dad where I'm going, with whom, and what I'm going to do.
2. I will call home if I'm going to be late, or if I'm going to a place other than where I said I'd be.
3. Eleven o'clock curfew every night, with the stipulation that if nothing is going on, I will come home earlier or stay home.
4. Eleven-thirty curfew if it's a special evening, like a party.
5. Mom and Dad have the option of saying no to an activity if they don't think I should be there.

Sharon's mother comments: "We both felt great about this approach, and agreed to use it for other problems. It gave me a way to relate to Sharon on more of an equal basis, not just as an authority figure. I think it made her feel important to have her suggestions thought about and accepted. I was convinced our discussions were a success when one of her friends came to me and said he wanted to know about fairness discussions because his parents agreed to have one with him!"

You may wonder, "Am I giving away my authority as a parent if I enter into this kind of negotiation with my child?" That's a good question, and I'd like to make two points in response to it.

1. A fairness approach does inject an element of equality into parent-child relationships, in that you treat kids as persons who have needs and feelings that deserve respect. But being fair with kids doesn't mean that parents and children are complete equals;

they're not! *You* are the authority figure; *you* have the right and the duty to set standards and hold your children accountable to them. If you believe you have that right, your children will know it and respect it. If you *don't* believe it, they'll know that, too. Kids who don't recognize your authority, who think they are the full equals of adults (and we see all too many kids today who think like this), will use "fairness" arguments defiantly to try to steamroll over adults and get their way.

It's crucial, then, for parents to have confidence—as most parents once did—in their basic moral authority, their right to set expectations for their children. When it comes to applying those expectations to particular situations (what's a reasonable curfew?), there's room for give-and-take. But such fairness discussions must occur against a backdrop of strong parental authority.

2. Although the need for parents to be moral authorities hasn't changed, the effective way to use our authority has changed. In the old days, when authority of any kind spoke—whether it was parents, police, the church, or the government—kids and people in general were more likely to accept authority's edicts without challenge. These days all of us—adults as well as kids—expect authority to be fair, and protest vigorously when it isn't. That's a big change in the culture, and it very definitely affects our relationship with our children. Teenagers, for example, frequently rebel against parental control when they think parents are being arbitrary and dictatorial. They are much more likely to accept parental limits when they think their parents are making an effort to be fair.

Take another look at the fairness agreement that Sharon and her mother worked out. By listening to her daughter's views and compromising where she thought it reasonable, Sharon's mother in the end exercised a good deal of control, *which Sharon willingly accepted*. Their fairness agreement granted Sharon a measure of freedom but within some very clear limits (she had specified curfews, and she acknowledged her parents' right to say no to a particular activity).

Think of the fairness approach as a way to strike the balance between independence and control—between your child's desire to be independent (which is itself healthy and part of moral development) and your responsibility to exercise a necessary degree of control. At the same time, a fairness approach engages kids in the kind of dialogue that develops their sense of fairness, and that's an important part of their long-range moral development. And because kids today *expect* to be treated fairly, a fairness approach is more likely to work than simply dictating what goes.

GET AT THE PROBLEM BEHIND THE PROBLEM

Sometimes the problem that's causing a conflict between you and your child turns out to be a symptom of something deeper. The real problem may be a need that isn't being met.

Twelve-year-old Becky said she wanted a phone of her own in her room. Her friends all had their own phones, she said. Becky's mother said absolutely not. It was an unnecessary expense; Becky could use the family phone, like everyone else.

Becky kept it up. Her mother grew increasingly impatient with her demanding behavior. Finally, she tried the fairness approach. Becky revealed during the discussion that she didn't care all that much about having a phone! What really bugged her was always having to take hand-me-downs from her two older sisters. She wanted something new, something that was just hers.

Once her mother understood Becky's real need—not to feel like a second-class citizen in the family—the conflict could be solved in a way that was acceptable to both. They agreed that Becky could have a new bike for her upcoming birthday.

How can you find out if there's a deeper problem behind a conflict you're having with your child? Sometimes the real problem will surface once you start talking, especially if you're listening empathically. Other times you may have to "go fishing"—to ask questions and watch your child's response.

For example: Suppose your 4-year-old Katie is mean to her 2-year-old sister, Bethanie. You could go fishing with questions like:

"Katie, I want you to tell me the truth. I won't be mad at you, I promise. Do you sometimes feel jealous of Bethanie when I spend time with her?"

"Do you secretly wish you were the only one and could have all of Mommy's time and love just for yourself?"

"When you're mean to Bethanie, is it because you're mad at me, too?"

Your child might not come right out and say, "Yes, that's it!" But you can usually tell when you've hit a chord. If Katie nodded, looked down, or filled up when you asked her any of the above questions, you could take those nonverbal responses as signs that you'd touched on the truth. Then you could say something like:

"I see. Well, I can understand that feeling. You know, lots of children feel that way about their little brother or sister. It's hard to share a Mommy with someone else."

This kind of discussion achieves three things:

1. You gain a better understanding of your child;

2. Your child gains a better understanding of herself (kids don't always know why they're acting the way they are);

3. Once your child understands her feelings and knows you understand them, too, it's easier to solve the problem in a way that answers the underlying need.

In Katie's case, a solution might go something like this:

"I want you to know I understand your jealous feelings. I'm not angry with you for having them. But I can't let you push Bethanie or take away her toys, because that's not fair to her. So when you get these jealous feelings, you come and whisper them to me. I'll give you a big hug and remind you of how much I love *you* and how special you are in our family. Okay?"

Very often, especially with young children, the problem behind the problem is a need for attention and love.

GETTING PAST
FEAR OF PUNISHMENT

When you first try the fairness approach with young kids, it may take a while to get past the fear-of-punishment part of their immature moral reasoning.

That's what happened to the mother of Phillip (7) and Ben (5). Her situation:

> "My husband no longer lives with us, but we manage pretty well. The kids are generally good if it's just us. But as soon as I get on the phone, they go bananas. It's as if they have joined forces against me and whoever is at the other end of the conversation. Since I seem to be on the phone more and more with parents of the children I teach, homeroom mothers, teachers, and friends, this poor behavior has become the prime cause of conflict in our home."

When the mother tried the fairness approach with Phillip and Ben, this is the sort of dialogue that ensued:

Mom: In a fairness discussion, the three of us will work together to solve the problem.

Ben: I don't get it.

Phillip: If you keep your big mouth shut, you might understand, Dummy.

Ben: You shut up yourself!

Mom: I want *both* of you to be quiet and listen. Now, the prob-
lem is that it upsets me when you guys get wild when I'm on the phone and I can't carry on a conversation. What are your feelings about this?

Phillip: Are you going to tell Daddy about this?

Ben: Are you?

Phillip: I haven't been so bad.

The mother comments: "This type of reasoning on the part of the children went on for what seemed like an endless time. It was very hard to get the idea of the meeting across to them. I was astonished to see how punishment oriented they were."

But the mother persisted: "We need to come to an agreement that is fair for all of us. I want to understand your feelings about this problem." Finally, there was a breakthrough:

Phillip: Mom, I hate it when you get on the phone and talk forever. It really makes me mad.

Ben: Yeah, the other night you talked on the phone when you said you would play a game with us, and then there wasn't time.

Mom: You feel I spend too much time on the phone?

Phillip: I could never stay on the phone as long as you do, and I wouldn't want to.

Ben: You don't love me when you're on the phone.

Phillip: She always loves us!

Ben: You're not home that much, so when you are you should want to be with me.

"The more we talked," the mother says, "the better I understood their feelings of rejection when I talk on the phone. I explained that I often do get carried away—but that with working and going to school and taking care of our home, I hardly have time to see my friends, and this is often my only way of keeping in contact with them."

Once they understood each other's feelings, Phillip, Ben, and their mother were able to brainstorm solutions to the problem. Once again, the kids showed a lot of Stage 1, punishment-oriented thinking ("Mom's the boss"; "We should be grounded"). Gradually, the problem-solving became more positive, and they came to an agreement (see next page), signed by all and posted.

"During our follow-up meeting two days later," the mother says, "we agreed that we had stuck to our plan. The kids played together or did things independently when I was on the phone, and I made calls shorter. We also agreed there had been less arguing and less hassle."

AGREEMENT

1. If Mom has promised to do something with us, she will tell the person she is busy and will call back later.

2. We will make a list of things to do while Mom is on the phone.

3. Mom will make her calls shorter.

4. If Mom has to be on the phone for a longer time, she will tell us, and we will behave.

Mom   *Phillip*   BEN

USING FAIRNESS TO HEAD OFF TROUBLE

You can use a fairness approach to anticipate trouble and head it off at the pass.

Michelle, 4, liked to be read to at bedtime. When her father finished one story, however, she would plead for another, then another after that. If he simply said "Good night" and walked out after one story, she cried, and bedtime ended on a sour note.

Michelle's father used the fairness approach to strike a bargain *before* reading. He said: "Michelle, I'll read you a story, but first you have to promise you won't ask for another when I'm finished."

Michelle promised. That ended the afterstory negotiations.

You can probably think of lots of situations when you can use the fairness approach as an ounce of prevention to prevent a predictable conflict.

"Billy, you may go to the store with me, but only if you promise not to ask for a toy. You may have a gumball, but no toys. Agreed?"

"I'll take you to the playground, but only if you agree to leave when it's time to go and not cry that you want to stay longer. Fair enough?"

If your child forgets the deal when the time comes, simply ask, "What did you promise?"

IF A HABIT IS HARD TO BREAK

Some problem behaviors are hard to change because they've become such a habit. If you're up against that kind of situation with your child, and nothing else is working, you might try "counting and charting." Developed by behavioral psychologist Ogden Lindsley, this technique is a simple way to make even small improvements in behavior concretely visible to you and your child.

Here's what you do: Present the idea of a chart to your child. Explain that it will be a secret between the two of you, unless or until your child wants to reveal it. At the end of each day, you'll record on the chart the number of times the problem behavior occurred. The goal: to show a decrease in the behavior by the end of the week.

Sample Chart

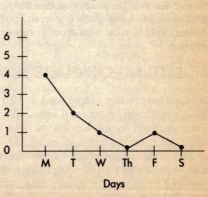

Number of times the problem behavior occurred

Days

Let me give an actual example.

Lonnie, 7½, sucked her thumb much of the time. Threats and bribes had failed to get her to stop.

In their fairness discussion, Lonnie's mother explained that she didn't want Lonnie to suck her thumb because other kids teased her about it and that caused bad feelings and fights, the dentist said her teeth were crooked and couldn't be straightened until she stopped sucking, and she already had to go to a speech therapist for a "tongue thrust" due to the sucking. Lonnie explained that she liked sucking her thumb because it relaxed her, and it was very hard to stop because she'd been doing it for so long.

Lonnie agreed to try to stop, recording on a chart the number of times she sucked her thumb each day. She was to keep count on her own; her mother promised not to say anything. At the end of the week, there would be a "surprise" if there had been improvement.

At the week's end, the mother had this to report:

"Each night, Lonnie was eager to fill in the chart. I never questioned her as to whether she had recorded the correct number. I saw her suck her thumb only once during the week, and that evening she marked down one. She always sucks her thumb while she watches television, and this past week she did not. Each night she became more excited about the plan, and also more confident she could succeed.

"I think this approach worked where others had failed because Lonnie was in on the planning of the chart, and she was the one to fill it in without being watched or questioned. We ended this week feeling closer to each other about a sensitive issue than when we began it."

SETTLING CONFLICTS BETWEEN KIDS

A fairness approach can be used quickly to settle many of the conflicts that crop up between kids—either siblings or friends.

Five-year-old Brian wanted to play with his 10-year-old brother, John, for the half hour before dinner. John wanted "private time." An argument started. With brief mediation by their father, they reached a fair compromise: 15 minutes of play together and 15 minutes of private time.

Owen and Andy, both 7, were good friends. But often they couldn't agree on what to play and ended up frustrated and cross with each other for "wasting time." Owen's mother suggested they sit down first thing and each make a list of what they'd like to do. Then they'd agree on a "fair plan" that included activities from each of their lists. When they remembered to do this, their time went much more smoothly.

Eric, Jimmy, and Dickie liked to do a lot of the same things. But when the three of them got together, they argued constantly about what to play first. Eric's father suggested they draw lots. The person who pulled number 1 would choose the activity for the first half hour (e.g., "play Micronauts"), the person who drew number 2 would choose the second activity (e.g., "draw"), and so on. They all thought that was fair.

Karen, Brenda, and Rhoda were playing tag on the backyard gym set. From the house Karen's father heard, "Cheater!" "I called time out!" "That's cheating!" "Oh, yeah, *you're* the cheater!"

When the father arrived on the scene, Karen said, glowering at Brenda, "She thinks she can just make up any rules she wants!"

"Did you all agree on the rules before you started?" the father asked.

"No," Karen said.

"Well, maybe that's why you're having this problem. How about taking a minute to agree on fair rules?"

That solved the problem.

Sometimes you can motivate kids to settle their own conflicts by offering them a choice:

> "Can you guys solve this problem fairly, or should you call it quits for today?"

> "Can you settle the argument about the TV, or does it need to be turned off?"

You can also help kids solve their own disputes by teaching them "words to say" when conflicts arise, such as:

> "Wait a minute—what's fair?"

> "Let's compromise."

Sometimes kids will say, "Okay, we'll say that next time," but when next time comes and tempers flare, they fall right back into old habits. To help them break out of their well-worn pattern, have them act out the very situation that causes a conflict and actually say the words they would use to try to settle it fairly. Rehearsing a new strategy in this way (and plan on doing it more than once) increases the chances that kids will integrate the new behavior into their response repertoire.

Venerable child-rearing advice tells parents not to intervene in kids' arguments. There's wisdom in that: We should give kids a chance to work out their own problems; we should avoid getting emotionally embroiled in our children's conflicts; and we should beware of being manipulated by kids who provoke a fight, get hurt, and then play the role of the innocent victim in order to get an older brother or sister in trouble with Mom or Dad. So use your judgment about when to stay out of a conflict and when to get involved. If kids are truly having a hard time solving a problem on their own (and there are plenty of adults who have trouble solving conflicts fairly), a parent's question or suggestion can be a valuable lesson in fairness.

QUESTIONS PARENTS ASK ABOUT THE FAIRNESS APPROACH

Q: What should you do if you make an agreement, but your child doesn't keep it?

If that happens—and it will—the most important thing is to let kids know that you *expect* them to keep their fairness agreement. There are several ways to do that.

1. **Remind them of their agreement.** You can figure that kids are going to forget their agreement more often than not, and you'll have to remind them of it. This is especially true with teenagers, who are notoriously absentminded (they have so much else to think about!). It's the fate of parents of adolescents to have to issue endless reminders; we might as well accept it and issue them calmly. "Hey, don't forget the trash." "Please hang the wet towels on the rack."

2. **Ask them to make a self-reminder.** Tell kids you'd rather you

didn't have to remind them about so many things; it makes you feel like a nag. Then suggest: "How about making a little sign or note to remind yourself and putting it where you'll see it?" Or you might post the fairness agreement itself in a visible spot.

This is hardly foolproof—kids forget to look at the reminder—but it's worth a try.

3. Have a follow-up discussion to evaluate how your agreement is working. Sit down with kids and get them to think about the commitment they made and whether they're keeping it. Don't start out by reading them the riot act. Just ask, "What was our agreement?"

4. Enforce the agreement. If kids refuse outright to honor their agreement, you'll have to enforce it. This is more likely to happen with younger children.

For example: Anthony, 5, came home from nursery school hot and dirty. Knowing he didn't like to take a bath, his mother offered him a choice (which had worked before): "Would you like to take your bath right now or after playing for an hour?"

"After playing," Anthony said.

But when the hour was up, Anthony said he didn't want to take his bath.

> Mother: Anthony, what agreement did we make?
>
> Anthony: I want to change my mind. I want *two* hours to play.
>
> Mother: Is that fair?
>
> Anthony: Yes.
>
> Mother: Is it fair to break a promise?
>
> Anthony: Yes.
>
> Mother: Would you want *me* to break a promise I made to *you*?
>
> Anthony: I didn't really say the word *promise*.
>
> Mother: Okay, mister, it's time for your bath (calmly picking him up and carrying him crying to the tub).

By reasoning with Anthony, his mother let him know that she expects him to keep his agreements. When he continued his Stage 0 efforts to squirm out of the deal, she reinforced her expectation of fairness by enforcing the agreement they had made.

5. **Revise the agreement to include "fair consequences" for not keeping it.** Suppose 16-year-old Sharon didn't keep her curfew agreement to be home on school vacation weeknights by eleven o'clock. She comes in on Tuesday night at midnight without having called to say she'd be late. You ask her if she thinks she's living up to her agreement, and she says no and apologizes. Then on Thursday night the same thing happens.

You could say, "Look, our agreement isn't working. We agreed it's not fair for you to make your father and me worry by coming in late. So I think from now on it would only be fair if there were some consequences for not living up to the agreement. What do you think would be a fair consequence for coming in late?" Or you can propose what you feel is a fair consequence.

I'd encourage you, as I did earlier in the book, to talk about "fair consequences" rather than "punishment." As one 8-year-old said, "A punishment is something a parent does to you. A consequence is something you do to yourself."

Kids will usually agree to pretty stiff consequences when you ask them what's fair, so you don't have to worry about their getting off too lightly. And whenever you can, try to keep the consequence logically related to the offense. If Sharon doesn't handle her freedom responsibly, a logical consequence would be losing that freedom for an agreed-upon length of time.

By getting kids to agree in advance upon fair consequences as part of the "contract," you'll have an easier time enforcing it if that becomes necessary ("What did we agree was a fair consequence for not keeping the agreement?"). You won't have to feel like a "meanie," as many parents do when they impose a unilateral punishment. When kids break a rule for which there's an agreed-upon consequence, they are choosing, by their behavior, to accept that consequence.

Q: What if you're having a problem that immediately erupts into an argument when you try to talk about it?

Sometimes a subject may be such a sore point, rubbed raw by so many past arguments, that it's very hard to discuss it rationally. In that case, you might try writing a letter to your child and leaving it on his or her pillow. For example:

Dear Beth,

   I'm writing you a letter because I've decided it's the best way for me to express my feelings about a subject that's difficult for both of us. Please understand that I write out of love and concern for your welfare. (I know what you must be thinking: "You worry too much, Mom!")

   I know you're under a lot of pressure, and our bringing up the issue of your grades only adds to it. We don't want to hassle you, but we would like to help if we can. Because we know you want to go to college, and we know your grades don't reflect your potential. *We* don't need high grades to know how smart you are, but colleges do.

   In the past, we've ended up arguing when this comes up. I wonder if we could try another approach. I'd like to start by listening to your feelings.

   What do you say?

   I love you very much.

Mother

   A thoughtful, heartfelt letter can be a great door-opener when a tough-to-talk-about problem comes between parents and kids (or, for that matter, between husbands and wives).

   You may decide, after talking about the problem, that the most sensible thing to do is to get outside help—such as a counselor or therapist. Ask someone you trust, perhaps your family doctor, for a recommendation.

Q: What if you don't feel you can compromise?

   Remember, a fairness approach is a *spirit* of fairness in how you handle conflicts with kids. It's not a rigid formula for 50-50 compromise. If you don't feel you can, with integrity, "give in" on a particular point (say, your son's going out with his girl friend on school nights), see if you can respond to your child's feelings in some other way (say, by having his girl friend over for dinner on a weeknight). And point out to kids that you're trying your best to be fair, trying to grant them as much independence as you can while still being a responsible parent.

Q: Can't you ever just lay down the law?

Parents and kids would both go crazy if they had to negotiate everything. There are lots of times when you can and should use your parental authority to simply invoke a rule ("To bed by eight-thirty"), state a request ("We need everybody's help with the dishes"), or give a command ("Pick up your toys"). Kids will generally accept your assertions of authority as being fair as long as you give a reason when one is needed, grant them a fair hearing when they want one, and try to work out fair solutions when real conflicts arise.

Be clear when you need simple obedience or cooperation: "This isn't a time for negotiating; this is a time to do what you're asked."

Q: What if your child does something you think deserves a consequence even though you haven't agreed ahead of time on a consequence for that behavior?

Suppose you pick up your 6-year-old at his friend Sammy's, and he throws a temper tantrum while you're talking to Sammy's mother because he doesn't want to go home. You haven't made a prior agreement that says "No temper tantrums when I come to pick you up, or else no going to Sammy's for a week"—but you certainly don't want to let such a performance pass without a consequence.

First, make sure your child understands how you feel and why.

Then ask, "What do you think would be a fair consequence for what you did?"

Then agree on what you think is fair.

Kids often think only of negative consequences, some of them overly harsh (not playing with Sammy for a whole month, for example). Help them think of *positive* consequences. Kids should learn that when they do something wrong, they should try to set things right—and there are three ways to do that:

1. Apologize, and say *why* they're sorry ("I'm sorry, Mom, for upsetting you by acting the way I did");
2. Promise to try to do better ("The next time you pick me up at Sammy's, I'll come without getting mad");
3. *Show* they're sorry by offering to do something positive to make amends.

I think it's a good idea to teach kids to ask, "How can I make up for it?" when they've done something to hurt or upset another person. (Remind them to say that if they forget.)

If your 6-year-old makes positive reparation for his tantrum and then throws another one the next time you pick him up, you can switch to a negative consequence, such as not being able to go to Sammy's for an agreed-upon period of time. But try positive fair consequences first.

Asking kids to choose fair consequences for their misbehavior requires them to *think* about what they've done and so develops their moral reasoning. It also avoids the problems of parent-imposed punishment, such as kids feeling mad at you (instead of sorry for their offense) or free to do it again after they've "paid the price." With young children, you may have to impose some punishments (like a time-out or the loss of a privilege) because of their limited ability to do back-and-forth moral reasoning. But work toward getting kids to accept more of the responsibility for thinking about what's fair when they've done something wrong. They're more likely to improve their behavior if they have to "punish themselves" when they misbehave.

HOW TO USE THE FAIRNESS APPROACH IN FAMILY MEETINGS

A family meeting is a roundtable discussion involving all members of the family who are concerned about or affected by a particular issue. A family meeting doesn't have to deal just with "problems"; you can use it to plan time together (a Sunday, a work project, a vacation trip) and to try to prevent problems from occurring ("How can we make this be a good week?"). But when family problems do arise, a sit-down discussion in a spirit of fairness is often the sanest way to handle them—and one that helps kids grow morally at the same time.

A mother describes the problem that led to her family's first meeting:

"In our family of two parents and three boys—Jack (11), Greg (10), and Wayne (8)—there is almost always a conflict about TV vs. bedtime. Our boys are very active (baseball, Scouts, music lessons, homework, etc.), and we are concerned that they get enough sleep. They, however, feel that they are entitled to some leisure time at the end of the day—which means watching TV and getting to bed later than we'd like."

This problem cropped up again on a Saturday night when the parents were planning to go out and leave the kids with a sitter.

> **Dad:** Boys, you had a very busy day today with baseball and the Boy Scout yard sale. You may watch TV until nine o'clock, and then it's bedtime.
>
> **Greg:** Oh, Dad, we always have to go to bed early!
>
> **Jack:** You treat us like babies.
>
> **Wayne:** It's Saturday night. "B.J. and the Bear" is on!
>
> **Mom:** Let's have a fairness meeting.
>
> **Everyone:** What's that?
>
> **Mom:** Well, we have to solve this problem, right? (General agreement.) Okay, Dad and I will tell you how we feel about the problem, and you can each tell us how you feel. Everyone will get a chance to talk, and no one is allowed to interrupt. Hopefully, we can agree on a solution.
>
> **Jack:** Okay, I'll go first. I think we should get to stay up until ten o'clock because it's Saturday night, and we don't have school tomorrow.
>
> **Greg:** Everyone else gets to stay up late.
>
> **Wayne:** "B.J. and the Bear" is my favorite show.
>
> **Dad:** You were all very busy today, and Wayne, you are just getting over an ear infection. I think you need more rest.
>
> **Mom:** I object to letting you stay up until ten o'clock because you always goof off for 45 minutes upstairs. That means ten-forty-five, and I feel that's too late. . . . Does anybody have anything else to add? (No one volunteers.) Okay, let's think of some possible solutions.
>
> **Dad:** I'll compromise on nine-thirty.
>
> **Wayne:** But that's in the middle of the show!
>
> **Greg:** We can stay up until ten o'clock, sleep late in the morning, and go to late church.

Dad: We have some yardwork to do tomorrow that I'd like to get started on before most of the day is gone.

Jack: How about if we promise to go to bed right after the show at ten o'clock?

Mom: It will still take some time after ten o'clock to get ready for bed.

Jack: We'll get our pajamas on *before* the show, and then we'll be ready to go right to bed.

Wayne: That's a good idea.

Greg: I vote for that!

Dad: We're going out tonight. The sitter will be here. Can we trust you to honor this decision?

Boys: Yes, we promise.

The mother comments:

"Since we weren't going to be home at ten o'clock we weren't sure how this would work. Our boys have been known to 'goof off' when the baby-sitter is here.

"When we got home, we were very pleased to hear that they had kept the agreement. They were in bed at ten o'clock and asleep shortly thereafter. This experience really delighted us, because we were able to reach a solution, and the boys, on their own, showed us that they could be trusted. The next day my husband and I praised them for the way they handled their part of the bargain. They felt good about themselves and are eager to try this new approach again."

Family meetings don't always go so smoothly. Contrast the meeting I've just described with another family's first attempt. The mother sets the scene:

"Jenny (15) had just had an altercation with Gary (12). Gary was calling me unfair. Dad arrived home from work upset to hear Jenny and Gary going at it again."

The meeting began:

Gary: I'd be happier if no one would fight, and everybody around here would try to be a little nicer.

Jenny: I'm always being dumped on! I'd be happier if Mom didn't *baby* Gary and didn't yell at *me* about friends and school problems. When you don't trust me, that gets me mad. I also don't like it when you complain about my room and clothes.

Mom: I'd be happier if I could stop being a nagging mother.

Dad: (to Jenny) I think it's only reasonable for us to expect you to care about how your room looks.

Jenny: Every kid gets their room dirty!

Dad: I'd be happier in this family if there was a more positive atmosphere.

"The animosity was so strong," the mother says, "that I was reluctant to pursue any of the issues we had raised."

A SAFE WAY TO BEGIN FAMILY MEETINGS

The family that solved the bedtime-with-the-baby-sitter problem succeeded with an impromptu discussion for their first meeting. Depending on the problem, that might work for you, too. But if you think a spur-of-the-moment meeting might be risky for your family, as it was for the parents of Jenny and Gary, here's a sequence you can follow that will stack the deck in favor of a successful first family meeting.

Laying the Groundwork

1. Choose a practical problem that you think your family can handle in a first meeting. (Possibilities: morning hassles, chores, bedtime, TV policy, making meals more pleasant, kids getting along, kids wanting to be with their friends instead of going on family outings.)

2. Decide who's involved in the problem, tell them you'd like to discuss it to try to find a solution that's fair to everyone, and set a time to meet that's agreeable to all.

3. Take individual soundings before the family meeting. How do your kids feel about the problem? How does your spouse feel? Don't try to solve the problem in these conversations—just try to listen and understand.

4. Do something before the meeting that generates good family feelings. If you're going to talk right after dinner, for example, you might do "appreciation time" during dinner—or play something like "The Ungame" the night before (Chapter 12).

5. If, for any reason, the scheduled meeting time arrives and the family atmosphere isn't good, postpone the meeting. Find another time when you'll have a better chance of a successful meeting.

Conducting a Family Meeting

1. Begin the meeting by stating the purpose. For example:

> "School mornings have been a real hassle lately. By the time I get you kids out the door, I'm in a bad mood. I'd like to talk about this problem and see if we can find some solutions that are fair to everybody. Okay?"

2. Set ground rules for discussion. Very important.

> "I'd like this to be a *positive* discussion where we listen to each other and respect each other's opinions. The purpose isn't to blame anybody; it's to solve the problem.
> "First, we'll go around and each tell how we feel about the problem.
> "Then we'll each suggest ways to solve the problem and try to come to an agreement.
> "No interruptions and no put-downs. Agreed?"

3. After the ground rules are understood, go around the table, giving each person a chance to state his or her viewpoint about the problem without interruption. (You don't always have to follow this round-the-horn format, but in the beginning it's a good way to draw everybody into the meeting and keep parents from doing all the talking.)

4. When all have stated their viewpoint, use empathic listening to review what each has said, so everyone feels heard and understood (don't make any judgments).

5. Go around the table, asking each person for suggestions for solving the problem. Write them down. Again, no interruptions.

6. Read back the proposed solutions.

7. Discuss proposals until *all agree* on solutions that are fair. (Avoid voting, which produces winners and losers.) Make a list of who will do what and when. For example:

1. Jamie and Laura will lay out their clothes the night before a school day, starting tonight.
2. They will get dressed right away when they get up.
3. Dad will help with breakfast (cook the eggs).
4. Mom won't yell, but will remind everybody of the agreement if they forget.

8. To show everybody's commitment, sign the agreement and, if you like, post it for easy reference.

9. Set a time for a follow-up meeting to see how your plan is working.

10. Have a follow-up discussion. Start positively by recognizing progress on the problem even if there's still room for improvement.

Try to keep the pace of the meeting brisk and the length under a half hour; long, drawn-out meetings put everybody off. After you've led a few meetings, rotate responsibility for leading the meeting (you'll have to coach kids through the steps the first time they do it).

You don't always have to go through such a structured process. Family meetings can be as short as 5 to 10 minutes. Once your family gets the hang of them, you can even use them as a quick way to restore calm and reason when things start to get out of control. If a day is getting off to a bad start, for example, a short family meeting can get it back on the track ("How can we each help this be a good day?").

How Do Family Meetings Aid Moral Development?

How do family meetings help kids' moral development? First of all, they challenge kids to take the perspective of the group—to think of what's good for the family as a whole, not just for themselves. That's an important part of Stage 3 moral reasoning, and a step toward the Stage 4 ability to think of the good of society.

Second, such discussions bolster kids' self-respect by giving them a say in family life, a forum where their ideas are heard and respected.

Finally, by sharing responsibility for solving family problems, kids are sharing responsibility for the making of a good family life. In a real sense, they become cocreators of the family. As a result, they're more likely to identify with the family and its basic moral values. And at a time when kids face dangerous peer pressures, that identification with positive family values is very important.

Says a father after several months of having family meetings:

> "Looking back, I think one of our most important achieve-ments has been learning to share our ideas and listen to and respect each other's point of view. Not every family meeting has been a storybook success, but some important decisions affecting the family are now being arrived at by all the members, not just Mom and Dad. We've decided that when anyone is having a prob-lem, that person may call a meeting so that all of us can try to help. We're becoming a closer family."

FAIRNESS BETWEEN PARENTS

One of the best ways to create a climate of fairness in your home is to take a fairness approach to the differences you have with your mate. When kids know that the two of you respect each other enough to try to settle your conflicts fairly, you have a lot more credibility when you ask them to be fair.

Husbands and wives have used the fairness approach to reach mutually acceptable decisions about matters such as:

- Parenting issues, such as what kinds of rules and expectations should be set for kids, and how to handle the religious upbring-ing of children when parents have different beliefs;
- Fair sharing of housework;
- The amount of time one partner spends on "personal activities" (going out with friends, watching football, etc.) versus "to-gether time" with spouse or family;
- Problems with relatives;

- Problems about money;
- How to spend a vacation;
- Priorities for getting work done around the house or yard.

IF YOU'RE A
DIVORCED PARENT

If you're a divorced parent, a fairness approach can also help you in the area of discipline. Divorce tends to upset many things, including the balance between children's independence and parents' control. A divorced father, for example, if he's the one who's left the home, may think he should "make up" to the kids for the divorce, and so may be reluctant to say no to them during visits or to exert proper control over their behavior. A divorced mother, if she's the one with custody, may worry about losing control over the children and become overrestrictive, especially with boys. A fairness approach—"We need to have some fair rules, ones that respect my needs and yours"—helps maintain the balance between independence and control.

FAIRNESS AND BLENDED FAMILIES

If you marry into a family where there are stepchildren, a fairness approach can help you with the period of adjustment that blended families often go through.

Says stepmother Jeanette Lofas, coauthor of the book, *Living in Step*: "The usual problem [in step families] is that the adults have different parenting styles, resulting in the total nonstructuring of the family. There are no clear-cut chores. No one knows where they fit in."

Family fairness meetings won't bring instant solutions to such problems; new relationships need time and love to grow. But gathering everybody around the table for a fair discussion is a way to develop a sense of being one family and to work out living arrangements that respect the needs and feelings of all.

A fairness approach isn't magic. It doesn't change human nature. People may start yelling at each other in the middle of a family meeting or a one-on-one fairness discussion. If that happens, you can try to calm things down by asking people to do empathic listening ("What do you think I'm saying?" "Tell me what you think my point is") or to express their feeling in an *"I need"* statement ("I need to be able to ask for help around the house and not get complaints" "I need to be treated as an individual, not constantly compared to Valerie").

If you're like most parents, no matter how fair you try to be with kids, you'll lose all patience and blow up from time to time. I certainly do. But your first reaction doesn't have to be your second reaction. When you've simmered down, you can say, "I was angry before. I'd like to talk this over now, fairly." Sometimes it helps to recruit a third party, like the other parent, to serve as an impartial mediator.

After a while, fairness will be "in the air," part of the moral atmosphere the family breathes. Says a mother of four children:

> "Just using the word 'fair' has helped to defuse a lot of emotional situations in our house. Attitudes in our family are improving. There's less dictating by us, more input from the children."

Says another mother:

> "In our first family meeting, my 13-year-old daughter and her 11-year-old brother solved a long-standing conflict by agreeing that whenever *either* has a friend over and wants to be left alone, they must communicate this in an adult way, and the other must say 'Okay' and leave. Several days later, I overheard Leslie being fair with Tommy about an entirely different conflict they often have. I was delighted."

A fairness approach shows kids that reason rather than power can be used to solve conflicts. It teaches them not only that they should be fair but also *how* to be fair. It thereby equips them to deal effectively with the many conflicts they'll encounter as they make their way through their widening social and moral world.

CHAPTER 14

THE ASK-DON'T-TELL METHOD OF REASONING WITH KIDS

Parents complain:

"I tell my kids something, and it goes in one ear and out the other."

"I'm tired of sounding like a broken record."

"I've reasoned with my kids till I'm blue in the face. It doesn't work."

What parents haven't heard, time and again, that they should "reason" with their children?

The problem with "reasoning," however, is the way we tend to do it. Too often, it's the *parents* who are doing all the reasoning. We talk, and kids listen—if they do that.

How can you get *kids* to do the reasoning?

Ask questions.

The whole idea of the ask-don't-tell method is simply this: *Get your child to do the reasoning by asking questions instead of making statements.*

When we ask kids questions—

"What will happen if you keep that up?"

"How would you feel if somebody did that to you?"

"What am I thinking?"

—we capture their attention and get the wheels turning. A question, by its very nature, requires a child to think.

We've already seen how asking "What's fair?" helps parents and kids solve conflicts (Chapter 13). But there are many other ways you can use questions to get kids to cooperate and at the same time develop their moral reasoning.

Reasoning with kids by questioning doesn't, of course, mean you should never tell them straight out what you think is right or wrong. Teaching by telling, the focus of the next chapter, is one of the most important ways you can influence your child's moral development. But there's a time to tell and a time to question. This chapter looks at the times when it makes sense to ask instead of tell.

ASK QUESTIONS THAT MAKE KIDS AWARE OF THEIR BEHAVIOR

You can use questions to make kids aware of their behavior. A simple "What are you doing?" is often enough to get kids to stop what they shouldn't be doing or start what they should be doing.

1. Parent: What are you doing?
   Child: Interrupting.

2. Parent: What are you doing?
   Child: Jumping on the furniture.

If "What are you doing?" doesn't get results, you can add, "What should you be doing?"

Parent: What are you doing?
Child: Reading a comic.
Parent: What should you be doing?
Child: Getting ready for bed.

ASK QUESTIONS THAT HELP KIDS REMEMBER THE RULE

You can use the ask-don't-tell method to get kids to remember and apply a rule.

Suppose your 4-year-old son comes into the kitchen, right before dinner, and says, "I want a cookie." How should you respond?

You could simply say, "No, it's too near dinner."

But what if your child persisted and said again, "I want a cookie!"?

You could stick to your guns and repeat: "No cookie before dinner."

At that point your child might escalate the power struggle by crying or throwing a tantrum. Depending on your stamina, you might hold the line or give in. If you held the line, you'd probably face more crying. If you gave in, you'd face many more requests in the future for cookies before dinner.

What else could you do besides fighting a war of wills or folding under pressure? Instead of *telling* your child the rule, you could ask questions:

Parent: What's the rule about cookies before dinner?

Child: No cookies before dinner. But I want a cookie!

Parent: When *may* you have a cookie?

Child: After dinner. But I want one *now*.

Parent: But what's the rule about cookies before dinner?

Child: Oh, all right!

By questioning, you don't have to impose the rule; kids come up with the rule themselves. And that helps to "depersonalize" the issue. It's not you they're banging up against. It's the *rule* that says, "No cookies before dinner."

Think of everyday situations in which you could use the "What's the rule?" question. There are lots of them. For example:

1. Parent: What's the rule about picking up when friends are over?
   Child: Do it together before they leave.

2. Parent: What's the rule about playing ball?
   Child: Outside, not in the house.

3. Parent: What's the consequence for hitting?
   Child: Sit in the chair for 15 minutes.

Sometimes questioning reveals that kids aren't very clear about what the rule is. In that case, our job is obviously to teach the rule. To do that effectively, I recommend these three steps:

1. State the rule.
2. Ask your child to *repeat* the rule.
3. Ask your child to *apply* the rule—either to the present situation or a hypothetical situation—to see if he really understands it.

For example:

Norman: Mom, I wanna watch "Eight Is Enough" but Billy keeps changing it to some other stupid show!

Mom: What's the rule about conflicts over TV?

Norman: I don't know . . . talk it over?

Mom: Remember the last time this happened? You said you'd turn the set off until you *agree* about what to watch. Okay, what's the rule?

Norman: I know, I know.

Mom: Well, you forgot it once. I want you to tell me, what's the rule?

Norman: (big sigh) If you're having a fight, turn it off till you agree what to watch.

Mom: Okay, so what should you do right now?

Norman: Turn if off till we agree what to watch.

HOW TO QUESTION SO KIDS WILL LISTEN

As adults, we respond differently to the same question, depending on how it's asked. ***"What are you doing???"*** gets a different response from "What are you doing?"

The same is true with kids. To maximize your chance of a positive response to your questions, I recommend that you:

- Keep your voice at normal or lower-than-normal volume;
- Speak in a respectful tone of voice rather than a demanding or threatening one;
- Ask only *one* question at a time (adults often ask a child several questions at once, which can be confusing).

WHAT SHOULD YOU DO IF QUESTIONING DOESN'T WORK?

What should you do if you ask questions and your child just doesn't answer?

If that happens, repeat the question. If you still don't get an answer, say firmly, "You're not responding to my question. Answer my question, please."

By that point, most kids will respond. But if you still didn't get a response, you could say, "The next time you ask me a question, do you want me to respond?"

As an example, consider the following exchange between 6-year-old Henry and his father. Henry didn't finish his dinner. But now that it's bedtime, he wants a snack and starts to get out the milk and cookies. The long-standing family rule is, "You have to finish your dinner if you want a bedtime snack."

Father: Wait a minute, did you finish your dinner tonight?

Henry: But, Dad, I want a snack!

Father: I understand that, but what's the rule about snacks?

Henry: It's not *fair!*

Father: It's entirely fair. We've had an understanding about bed-

time snacks for a long time. Now, what's the rule? I'd like
an answer to my question.

Henry: (reluctantly) Finish your dinner if you want a snack.

Father: Thank you. That's right. And so what should you do tomorrow night if you want a bedtime snack?

Henry: Eat my dinner.

What if Henry had persisted in his refusal to answer his father's question about the rule? In that case, his father should
simply enforce the rule.

USE QUESTIONS TO GET COOPERATION WHEN THERE'S NO ESTABLISHED RULE

Not every problem situation that comes up is covered by a
rule. How can you get kids to cooperate when there's no established rule to appeal to?

Use questions to help them see that it's in their own interest to
cooperate.

Let's assume you've taken your 5-year-old to the playground,
and now it's time to go home. Your child says, "I don't wanna
go!" You point out that it's late and you've been there a long
time. Your child says, "We have *not* been here a long time! I
hardly got to do anything!" You feel your blood pressure rising,
grab your child by the hand, and announce with a tug, "We're
going home!" Your child starts crying. You wonder why you
bothered to come to the playground in the first place.

Here's how questioning could help your child see that he's
hurting himself by not obeying:

Parent: (bending down and speaking in a low, firm voice) Look, if
you cry and make a big fuss when it's time to leave, will I
want to come to the playground when you ask the next
time?

Child: No.

Parent: So what should you do now?

Child: Leave.

Parent: Right. Then I'll have a good feeling about bringing you
again.

QUESTIONS THAT GO BEYOND SELF-INTEREST

Appeals for cooperation shouldn't always be pitched to a child's self-interest. If kids are going to develop beyond Stage 2 moral reasoning, they need opportunities to do the right thing without thinking, "What's in it for me?"

A father was driving in heavy traffic. The kids were cutting up in the backseat. In a situation like this, a parent's first impulse is to say something like, "Will you knock it off back there! It's hard enough to drive in this traffic without you kids acting like a bunch of wild animals in the backseat!"

This father resisted that impulse.

Father: What can you guys do to help me?
   Kids: Be quiet.
Father: Thank you.

The father appealed to his kids at a higher level than self-interest. He asked them to consider his needs.

Here are some other situations where a simple question can orient kids toward others' needs:

SITUATION	QUESTION
The family is on vacation. When they arrive at the first motel, the kids start arguing about who's going to sleep in what bed.	"How can you kids help us have a happy vacation?"
Eight-year-old Lester is dawdling instead of getting ready for school.	"How can you help this be a good morning instead of a grumpy morning?"
As dinner is being served, the kids start calling each other names.	"How can you guys make this a pleasant meal instead of a tense one?"

USE QUESTIONS TO HELP KIDS THINK OF CONSEQUENCES

Questions can also help kids develop a moral imagination—an ability to see the consequences of their behavior. Here's an example:

John is a very active 7-year-old boy. Each morning he and his 9-year-old sister walk two blocks to get the bus to school. One day the bus driver reported to John's parents that John and two other boys had been throwing stones into the road as cars were driving by.

John admitted throwing the stones. His parents asked him about his behavior.

His father said, "John, do you think anything might happen to anyone else if you throw stones while cars are driving by?"

"Yes," John said.

"What could happen?"

"The driver could stop and yell at us." John then asked in a small voice, "Are you going to spank me, Daddy?"

"No," his father said, "but I think we should talk about this some more. What would happen if you threw a stone and frightened a driver and caused him to go off the road?"

"He'd get hurt."

"How would you feel if you were the driver, John?" his mother asked.

"I might hurt all over with a broken leg if I hit a tree."

"And how could you prevent that from happening to a driver?" his mother said.

John looked down. "By not throwing stones," he said.

"Yes," his mother said.

There was a short silence. Then John's father said, "You know, John, your mother and I feel very bad that you were throwing stones. We want to hear from you what you intend to do about this situation."

"I won't throw stones in the road again," John said. He kept his promise.

John's parents relied on questioning, plus a direct statement of their concern, to help him understand why throwing stones at cars was wrong and resolve not to do it again. Consider some less effective ways they might have handled the same situation and the moral lesson John might have learned in each case:

PARENT'S RESPONSE	JOHN'S MORAL LEARNING
Shaming: "Don't you know any better than that? Throwing stones at cars is something we'd expect from a 3-year-old!"	"Mom and Dad don't think very much of me. I guess I am pretty dumb."
Embarrassment: "What kind of home will people think you come from?"	"I should be worried about what the neighbors think—not about what could happen to a driver."
Intimidation: "Do you realize what could happen if a policeman saw you doing that?"	"If I'm gonna throw stones at cars, I'd better be sure nobody's looking."
Punishment: "You lose all TV for a week. I hope this will be a lesson for you."	"I'd better not throw stones again if I know what's good for me."

John's parents, as we saw, used none of these approaches. They didn't shame him, express embarrassment, scare him, or punish him. Instead, they handled the matter in a calm but serious way that conveyed their concern and disapproval but left John's dignity intact. Rather than tell John why his actions were wrong, they asked a series of questions that got *him* to do the thinking about possible consequences of his behavior. Rather than forbid him ever to do it again, they got him to make his own statement of the right course of action in the future.

You can also stretch kids' ability to imagine the consequences of their actions by asking, "What if everybody did it?"

That line of questioning was used to good advantage by the mother of 6-year-old Mary Ann. One of Mary Ann's responsibilities was to make her bed, which she usually did without a fuss. One day, however, her mother noticed her bed unmade.

Mother: Mary Ann, you didn't make your bed this morning.

Mary Ann: I know.

Mother: Why didn't you make it?

Mary Ann: I didn't want to.

Mother: But isn't making your bed one of your responsibilities?

Mary Ann: I know, but I don't *want* to make it anymore. I just don't *feel* like it.

Mother: I see, you just don't feel like it.

Mary Ann: Yeah, it's *boring*!

Mother: It's boring. Well, suppose I said I didn't feel like cooking anymore because it was boring to me. Suppose I said I didn't want to make dinner tonight. What would happen then?

Mary Ann: Daddy would fix it.

Mother: What if *everyone* in the family decided they weren't going to do any more work? Nobody would cook meals, wash clothes, pick up things, do dishes, clean rooms, empty the garbage, fix things when they're broken, or feed the cat and dog. Would that be a very good situation?

Mary Ann: No.

Mother: Why not?

Mary Ann: Nothing would get done.

Mother: So do you think everybody should do their jobs?

Mary Ann: Yes.

Mother: And what about making your bed—do you think you should do that job or not do it?

Mary Ann: Do it.

You might think, "That's a lot of trouble to go to to get a kid to make her bed! Why not just tell her to get in there and make her bed, period?"

You might get her to make her bed with that approach. In any situation, the method you use depends on your goals. If your goal is simply to get Mary Ann to make her bed that day, then a direct command might do. But if your goal is to develop Mary Ann's moral reasoning—to get her to understand *why* she should make her bed, why it's only fair, and what the consequences would be if everybody stopped working because they "felt like it"—then the questioning approach is the way to go.

DOES QUESTIONING WORK WITH TEENAGERS?

What about teenagers? Does the ask-don't-tell method work with them?

It depends.

The teens, as we've seen, are a time of heightened consciousness—of oneself and others. Part of a teenager's sharpened awareness is an awareness of how you go about being a parent. And once they realize how you try to influence or relate to them, they may resist what they see as your "strategies"!

Parents who do a lot of empathic listening, for example—bouncing back what their kids say to them—sometimes find their teenager saying things like, "Don't use that listening stuff on me!" When Mark turned 13, he began saying things like, "Dad, you're so psychological!" Sometimes, when I'd use a questioning approach, he'd say, "Dad, never mind the questions—just give it to me straight!"

Although teenagers usually won't sit still for long, lawyerlike chains of questions, they're not as likely to object to single questions such as:

"Hey, what's it time to do?" ("Homework.")

"What's going to happen if you and Debbie keep bickering?" ("You'll get upset.")

"What's the effect of your talking on the phone for an hour at a time?" ("Nobody else can use it.")

"What should you be doing?" ("Taking out the trash.")

"Are we going to solve this problem by yelling?" ("No.")

Questions can also get teenagers to think about the consequences of their behavior—something that's often far from their minds. A mother tells this story about her 16-year-old son:

"I was very troubled by Gene's behavior toward his girl friend, Linda. He'd always been a good kid. But from the time he started going with Linda, he treated her badly. In a careless sort of way. He didn't do the little things that show respect for a girl. Kept her out later than her parents approved. Sometimes they came home having had too much to drink.

"He knew I disapproved of all of this—I said so—but that didn't seem to have much effect. Finally, I confronted him. I asked him two questions: 'How do you think Linda's family is going to react to her doing these things?' and 'How do you think she's going to feel about their reactions?'

"For some reason, that seemed to stop him. He didn't say much at the time, but later he brought it up. He had really been thinking about what I said.

"He looked at me with this 'Now I get it' expression and said, 'Are you saying that what I'm doing will ultimately affect how Linda feels about herself, and that will affect our relationship?'

"After that, he changed. He's a different person with her now."

Lecturing didn't reach Gene. Questioning did.

Suppose you try the questioning approach with your teenage son or daughter and they say: "Just tell me what you think. That's what you want me to know anyway, right?"

Level with them:

"Look, I'm not playing games. I *do* have feelings about this, and I'll tell you what they are if you want to know. But I'm asking you questions because I want *you* to think about this—because I want you to really think about what might happen. I'm trying to get you to use your best judgment."

Teenagers appreciate straight talk. So give it to them.

ASK QUESTIONS THAT HELP KIDS TAKE ANOTHER'S POINT OF VIEW

Nothing is more important in moral development than being able to put yourself in the other guy's shoes. People steal from others, cheat them, demean them, ignore their cries for help, and do violence to them at least partly because they don't put themselves in the place of the victim.

Asking questions is one of the best ways to develop kids'

ability to take the viewpoint of others and the habit of using that ability in their social interactions.

Five-year-old Russell had been playing at the house of his friend, Josh. Playing ended when Russell hit Josh with a toy. Russell's parents used the ask-don't-tell approach to help Russell enter into Josh's feelings.

Father: What happened today when you were playing with Josh?

Russell: Well, Josh wouldn't play with me. He just kept playing with Maskatron. I *tried* to get him to play with me, but he just kept playing with Maskatron! So . . . I got one of his tinker toys . . . and hit him on the head.

Mother: Do you think that was right to do?

Russell: No.

Mother: Why not?

Russell: Because it hurt him.

Father: Yes, I think it hurt him in two ways. It no doubt hurt his head. But how else do you think it may have hurt him?

Russell: It hurt his feelings.

Father: Why might it have hurt his feelings?

Russell: He might think I don't like him.

Father: And how would that make him feel?

Russell: Sad.

Mother: Russell, what should you do the next time you're trying to get Josh to play with you and he's not paying any attention?

Russell: Not hit.

Mother: Yes, but what can you do to solve the problem you're having?

Russell: I don't know.

Mother: Here's a suggestion. Go off and start playing something by yourself. That might get Josh curious, and he might come over to see what you're doing. Okay?

Russell: Okay. But what if that doesn't work?

Mother: Well, I guess you'll have to say, "Look, Josh, if we can't agree on something to play together, I might as well go home."

Father: What can you do right now to help yourself and Josh feel better?

Russell: Call him up and say I'm sorry. (He did.)

Note that at the close of their conversation, Russell's parents helped him find a better way to handle his problem with Josh in the future. They also helped him think of what he could do right then (call and apologize) to set things right. That provided an upbeat ending to their conversation, which is important. The purpose of questioning is not to leave a child feeling guilty but to sensitize him to the feelings of others in a way that will motivate appropriate moral behavior.

HOW TO GET KIDS TO TAKE YOUR POINT OF VIEW

Since one of the most important relationships kids have is with their parents, they should learn to take a parent's perspective. Questions can help them do that.

Imagine you've taken your 6-year-old son to the store to buy a toy he's wanted. At the checkout counter, he picks up a candy bar and says, "Can I have this?" The following dialogue ensues:

Parent: No, we came to get a toy, not candy.

Child: But I want a candy bar!

Parent: I said *no*! You're lucky to have the toy.

Child: *Please* . . . I'll share it with Robert?

Parent: No! Now, don't ask me again or I'll lose my temper, young man!

Child: (cries)

Parent: (loses temper)

How to avoid this all-too-familiar scene? Ask a question that forces your child to take your point of view. For example:

"How would you feel if *you* were the parent and you made a special trip to get your little boy a toy, and then he made a big scene at the checkout counter because he couldn't get a candy bar, too?"

Questions like this compel kids to reverse roles. They have to get outside their skin and climb into yours. You can continue the challenge by asking:

"What would you say to your little boy if you were the parent?"

Here are some other situations where you could use the ask-don't-tell method to get kids to take your perspective:

SITUATION	QUESTION
You call your kids to dinner and they don't come.	"How do you think I feel when I work hard to fix a nice dinner, and you don't come when you're called?"
You ask your 16-year-old daughter for help with the Saturday housework, and you get complaints and protests.	"If you were giving advice to parents on how to get their kids to help around the house, what would you tell them?"
You've asked your 8-year-old son to pick up his room, and a half hour later it's still a mess.	"What am I thinking?"
You discover your 10-year-old son lied to you about where he was that afternoon.	"How do you think I feel when I find out you've lied to me?"
Your 15-year-old son comes in an hour after his Friday-night curfew.	"How would you handle this situation if you were the parent?"

HOW TO USE QUESTIONING TO DEFUSE AN EXPLOSIVE SITUATION

Perspective-taking situations can be especially helpful in defusing a situation where you're particularly upset about something your child has done.

Says a single-parent father of three teenage boys:

"I've brought up my three sons pretty much on my own. We've talked frankly about girls and sex. I've told them my feelings about the importance of respecting any girl they got involved with. We've talked about what it means to treat her like a person, to respect her feelings, to never exploit a situation.

"We've also had an agreement that they could bring a girl to the house when I wasn't there as long as they respected my feelings about what was appropriate behavior. There was a pretty clear understanding about that. Maybe I was too liberal, I don't know.

"Well, anyway, one night I came home and found my middle son, Art, involved with his girl friend in a way that was way out of bounds. They were embarrassed, and I was furious. I told my son to take Carol home, and I would talk with him in the morning.

"I was still just as angry when the morning came. Art came into the kitchen as I was fixing breakfast. I took a deep breath and said, 'Art, why am I upset with you?'

"He said, 'Dad, I know why you're upset with me. You trusted me to respect the agreement we had, and I didn't. I have no excuse, and I don't blame you for being mad.'

"After that, I felt a lot calmer, and we had a good, long talk."

Suppose, instead of asking a question ("Why am I upset with you?"), the father had begun by discharging the anger and betrayal he was feeling:

"Art, I'm extremely upset with your behavior! We've talked many times about this matter. We had an agreement, and I trusted you to keep it. And now you've flagrantly violated that trust. You've embarrassed me, your girl friend, and yourself. I don't know if you're mature enough to handle the privilege I gave you."

Telling Art these feelings would have put him on the defensive. He would not have been likely to reply, "Gee, Dad, you sure are upset with me. I guess I really let you down." Most likely, father and son would have ended up more alienated than when they started out.

The father's asking "Why am I upset?" worked far better than venting his feelings for several reasons:

1. It was much easier for the father to keep his emotions under control by beginning with a question, which immediately shifted responsibility for talking to his son.

2. Since the father wasn't attacking, the son didn't have to defend.

3. The question gave Art a chance to show awareness of his father's feelings—and thereby to make up at least in part for the insensitivity he had shown by violating his father's trust.

ASK KIDS TO TAKE THE VIEWPOINT OF PEOPLE THEY DON'T KNOW

In figuring out what friends or family members feel, kids can draw on their own direct experience with these persons. It's harder to step into the shoes of a relative stranger.

Asking kids to take the viewpoint of someone they don't know personally is an excellent way to expand their perspective-taking ability. Some examples:

"If you were the janitor, how would you feel about having to remove all the wads of gum that kids stick under their desks?"

"If you were the bus driver, how would you feel about kids cutting up when you were trying to drive?"

"If you were a substitute teacher, how would you feel about kids acting in a rude and disrespectful way?"

"If you were a store owner, how would you feel about shoplifters?"

HOW TO GET BETTER AT ASKING KIDS QUESTIONS

Here's a way to practice the ask-don't-tell method. Stop, before you speak to your child, and convert your would-be statement into a question. You can practice this "instant conversion" technique by doing the following exercise.

On the list on page 319 are assorted statements that parents commonly make to kids in various situations. On the right are possible questions that could be asked in the same situations.

Cover the right side and try your hand at replacing each statement with a question. (There's no one "right" question for a given statement—you could ask any of several questions.)

INSTEAD OF SAYING . . .	ASK . . .
1. It's time to go—get your shoes and jacket on.	1. It's time to go—what should you do to get ready?
2. That kind of language around the house is totally unacceptable!	2. How do I feel about that kind of language around the house?
3. No, you can't stay out after dark—you know that.	3. What's the rule about staying out after dark?
4. If you keep fighting about the TV, it's going to go off!	4. What will happen if you keep fighting about the TV?
5. Don't throw the ball in the house—you could break something or hit somebody.	5. What are two reasons why you shouldn't throw the ball in the house?
6. I asked you to turn down the record player!	6. What did I ask you to do?
7. Put the wet towel back on the rack.	7. What if everybody left their wet towels lying around on the bathroom floor?
8. You're not cooperating the least bit!	8. Are you cooperating?
9. I don't think you guys are going to be ready when it's time to leave.	9. What am I thinking?

INSTEAD OF SAYING . . .	ASK . . .
10. If you don't get your pajamas on now, you're going to miss your bedtime snack.	10. Would you like to get your pajamas on now or miss your bedtime snack?
11. You're causing a lot of tension by your whining and complaining!	11. What are the effects of your whining and complaining on the rest of the family?
12. You've been on the phone for more than an hour—it's time to get off!	12. What's the rule about using the phone?
13. Remember your manners.	13. What are you forgetting?
14. It's 6:30—you said you'd be home from the movies by 5:30!	14. Why am I upset?
15. Tell your sister you're sorry you hit her and promise you won't do it again.	15. What should you do after you've hurt someone?
16. I get so aggravated when you get out of bed after I've put you in!	16. How do I feel when you get out of bed after I've put you in?
17. Share some of your popcorn with your little brother.	17. How would you feel if your brother was eating popcorn and wouldn't share any with you?
18. Stop fighting and take turns!	18. How can you solve this problem?
19. Stop screaming!	19. What can you do instead of screaming?
20. You didn't do what you were asked.	20. Did you do what you were asked?

INSTEAD OF SAYING . . .	ASK . . .
21. Sarcasm won't get you anywhere.	21. How can you take a more positive approach to this situation?
22. You're making this a miserable morning!	22. How can you help make this a happy morning instead of a miserable one?
23. Any more bickering about the car and nobody gets to use it!	23. What will happen if you continue bickering about the car?
24. When you make demands instead of asking nicely, I don't feel like doing anything for you.	24. When you make demands instead of asking nicely, how do I feel?
25. Cover your nose when you sneeze.	25. What should you do when you sneeze?
26. You can help by bringing in some of the groceries.	26. How can you be helpful in this situation?
27. That should teach you not to hit when you don't get your way.	27. What lesson can you learn from this experience?
28. I'm at my wit's end—I don't know what to do with you!	28. What would you do if you were the parent?
29. I get terribly worried when I think you're going to parties where there are going to be a lot of drugs.	29. What do you understand to be my feelings?
30. I've tried reasoning with you about this, but we don't seem to get anywhere.	30. If your friend and her mother were having this problem, what advice would you give them?

Once asking questions becomes second nature, you'll find your own situations where questioning is a helpful way of dealing with your child. One mother came up with a simple question to cope with her 2-year-old's habit of going into a full-scale cry whenever he didn't get his way. As soon as the crying started, she'd say, "Martin, do you want to cry?"

"No," Martin would sniff.

"Well," his mother would say, "then don't."

With that, the mother says, the tears would usually stop.

Questioning, of course, doesn't always produce wonderful results. It's a tool in a parent's repertoire, like any other. And when it doesn't work, we need to be ready to try something else (such as a straightforward explanation, a fairness discussion, or a simple command).

Just as with other methods, questioning also has diminishing returns if you overuse it. So ask questions when it makes sense to do so, and make a direct statement when it feels natural to do that.

THE LONG-RANGE GOAL
OF QUESTIONING

There's a long-range goal of questioning. It's to get kids to ask questions of themselves. That's really what a conscience is: the habit of asking yourself questions about right and wrong.

The most serious moral problem in society today may not be that people ask moral questions and reach the wrong conclusions. It may be that they don't ask moral questions at all. We cheat on our income tax, steal from work, slander our neighbor, abuse our spouse, or neglect our parents or children without ever stopping to ask, "Is this right?" We don't use the moral reasoning we have.

Questioning is one way to get kids to use their moral reasoning. The more they use it, the more they'll develop it to higher stages. And the more they use it, the more it will get to be force of habit, second nature to think in terms of right and wrong.

If we start questioning early and do it as a matter of routine as our kids are growing up, it'll be easier for them to ask questions themselves when they hit their teens. Questions like:

"What's the rule (or law) in this situation?"

"What will be the consequences if I do this?"

"Do I have to go along with the group?"

"What other choices do I have?"

"Is it smart to take this drug?"

"Is it right to cheat on this test?"

"Is it fair to take advantage of this girl (or boy)?"

When we've helped our kids develop the ability to ask these kinds of questions, we've helped them a long way down the road to moral maturity.

CHAPTER 15

TEACH BY TELLING

For as long as your children are with you, you are—or can be—their most important moral teacher.

Part of moral teaching, as we've seen, is asking kids questions that make them think. But another part of your role as a moral guide, a terribly important part, is telling them what *you* think. You'd be selling kids short, cheating them of something very necessary in their moral development, if you didn't give them direct moral instruction.

For a long time, parents understood that they had this duty to teach their children right from wrong. In recent times, however, many parents lost sight of how important it is to do this kind of deliberate moral teaching. They became nondirective with regard to their children's moral upbringing. They didn't "impose" their values. They didn't guide and instruct.

That created a values vacuum in the home. Television, the movies, advertising, and the peer group rushed in to fill it. Kids ended up getting plenty of values, but from all the wrong sources. We began to see children who had been raised by the culture instead of their parents, kids who were ill-tempered, ill-mannered, and generally unsocialized in their behavior toward both peers and adults.

I think parents are coming back to the time-honored view of their role as moral teachers. That means believing that they do have a moral heritage to give to their children, one that children might not come to on their own. It means realizing that each generation benefits from such a heritage, a set of values passed on to us by our parents. We may alter those values or add to them, but we start with a foundation.

WHEN YOU TEACH BY TELLING

Here are a few things to keep in mind when you step into the role of moral teacher:

1. How well kids understand a certain moral value depends in part on their stage of moral reasoning. A child at Stage 1, for example, can understand concrete behavioral traits like "obedience" and "cooperation" more easily than abstract qualities like "trustworthiness" and "loyalty." Similarly, a child at Stage 3 can understand trustworthiness and loyalty more easily than the higher-level concept of "integrity."

   But even if a young child doesn't fully grasp the reasoning behind a particular value concept, early exposure to the value helps it "take" when more mature moral reasoning comes along.

2. Remind kids that you don't think you're perfect and all-wise. One mother disarms her kids by saying, "You know, I've never been a mother before, so sometimes I make mistakes." You do have wisdom to impart to kids, but do it as a guide on the side, not a sage on the stage.

3. Don't get discouraged when it seems as if you're talking to the walls. Especially in the teens, as family psychologist Carl Pickhardt points out, "not listening" is a pose of independence that kids adopt, all the while carefully taking in what we say.

4. Remember that kids' values won't be a carbon copy of yours. If you're helping them grow toward maturity, they'll learn to think for themselves. But if you're teaching moral values all through their growing years, and making an effort to practice what you preach, chances are good they'll turn out to be more like you in their basic values than they are different.

WHAT MORAL VALUES SHOULD WE TEACH KIDS?

What is the moral heritage, the fund of wisdom, that we should try to pass on to our children?

Each of us has to decide that. But fortunately, we don't have to start from scratch. Here are 18 values that have stood the test of time.

1. Believing in yourself. James R. Jeffreys was born in 1932 with *osteogenesis imperfecta*—brittle bone disease. Doctors predicted he would not live more than a year. If he did live, they said, he would eventually be totally disabled, and would never be able to lead a productive life.

James Jeffreys did live. He rolled his wheelchair two miles a day to and from high school to get an education. By the age of 21, he owned his own shop and was a successful cabinetmaker.

He went on to become a prizewinning drag-racer as well. Using a car equipped with special handheld controls, he has won 14 racing awards.

He married a nurse. Together they had two natural children and then adopted seven more when they found there was a 50 percent chance that their own offspring would inherit brittle bone disease. One of their adopted children is blind; one was crippled by polio; one has a spinal disorder; one was born with no legs, and one suffers from diabetes. Four of the children are bi-racial, and two are Korean.

In the course of his lifetime James Jeffreys, who stands four foot three, has had over 100 fractures.

In 1977 he was named "Outstanding O.I. Adult of the Year" by the American Brittle Bone Society for overcoming his own disabilities and adopting seven children. The governor of New Jersey, where Jeffreys was born and still lives, proclaimed it "James R. Jeffreys Day," stating that "The life and career of James R. Jeffreys serves as an inspiration and a source of strength to all persons afflicted with physical handicaps."

Jeffreys talks about how he tries as a father to help his children develop a positive self-concept:

> "I'm convinced that a person isn't really handicapped until people begin to tell him that he is. I try to teach my children that there's no such thing as 'can't.' My parents taught me not to give up, to always try a thing first and to believe I could do it."[1]

James Jeffreys's story is remarkable, but there are others like it. Dr. John Gilmore, when he was a professor at Boston University, wrote a book called *The Productive Personality* in which he reported his concentrated study of three areas of human productivity: academic achievement, scientific creativity, and leadership. Throughout history, Dr. Gilmore found, highly productive people have been characterized by a "hopeful attitude," and at the core of that attitude was an unwavering belief in themselves.

Self-esteem, as we've seen, relates to moral behavior as well as personal success. It's easier to respect others when we respect ourselves, easier to be good to other people when we're feeling good about ourselves.

So we should teach our children to believe in themselves. And we should teach them that one of the greatest enemies of self-esteem is comparing ourselves with others. We can always find somebody who seems smarter, more talented, more successful than we are. Kids should know that everybody—even someone at the "top"—is prey to this demon of comparison. Teach them to measure themselves against themselves ("Am I getting better?"), not against anybody else.

2. **Courage.** Author Jenkin Lloyd tells this story:

> "Years ago there was a columnist named Ernie Meyer, who wrote for one of the Wisconsin newspapers. On the day his mother died he wrote his masterpiece. He captioned it: 'She Taught Me to Love the Storm.'

> "Ernie Meyer described how, as a small child, he was terrified by thunder and lightning. He used to hide, trembling, in his bedroom closet. But his mother would come for him and lead him by the hand down to the front porch, where the display of heavenly violence could be seen in full force. There she described the glory of a firmament that could produce these things, and spoke of what a privilege it was for puny man to have his life enriched by this power, even if there was danger in it. Gradually, Ernie learned to love the storm. And all the things that make storms in life—controversy, reverses, criticism—no longer terrified him."[2]

We do our children a great service if we can help them develop the courage to face the storms of life. Without courage in the face of adversity, many kids give up, turn to drugs or drink, or even end their lives. Suicide is now the third leading cause of death among teenagers.

When life deals kids a setback, they have trouble keeping perspective. You can help them cope with adversity by helping them see beyond it. Says one man: "My mother taught me to say to myself, no matter how bad things were, 'This, too, shall pass.'" The wisdom of the ages is full of such sentiments: "The lowest ebb is at the turn of the tide," "It's always darkest before the dawn." These may be old saws to us, but there's valuable philosophy in them from which kids can draw strength in a moment of need.

Moral courage—doing the right thing in the face of personal risk or social pressure—is the hardest kind. Robert Kennedy said it was rarer than bravery in battle. But if we try to help kids develop a core of inner strength, we help them develop this special kind of courage, too.

3. **Excellence.** There is the story of the cabinetmaker who was showing a customer how beautifully finished even the backs of the drawers were in a small chest he had just completed.

"Why do you take such pains with the backs?" the customer asked. "No one will ever know."

The cabinetmaker moved his fingers lovingly over the top of the chest and replied, "*I* will know."[3]

People used to believe that "any job worth doing is worth doing well." Somebody taught them that.

4. **Fairness.** We've seen how the fairness approach to conflict can be used to teach the value of fairness.

Says a father: "I remember my mother telling my sister and me, 'Fair and square, learn to share.' This saying stuck with me, and I've used it with my own children."

Says a mother: "I don't remember how old I was, but my mother gave me a key chain with a small ruler on it. On the back was written, 'Do unto others as you would have them do unto you.' It was a constant reminder because it was always with me, and I can remember being very aware of trying to live up to that."

If we teach kids the Golden Rule, and how to apply it to personal situations and societal problems, we've taught them all they need to know about fairness. With time and experience, that principle will come into full flower as a belief in universal justice.

5. **Freedom.** Kids should know that freedom is one of the great

human values, and a cornerstone of our democracy. They should learn to respect other people's freedom as much as they value their own. And they should learn that freedom always has limits: "Your right to swing your fist ends where my chin begins."

6. **Faith.** Kids need something to believe in. We can't "give" them a dream. But, as author Ardis Whitman points out,

> We can listen lovingly and respectfully to a child's plans and hopes, however naive they may seem, and whenever possible, help to make them come true. We can also open our children to the world of books, music, and art, because these are the lodging places of many a good dream. And, finally, we can offer them a religious faith, the most spacious of all things to believe in.[4]

Religious faith alone won't necessarily make a child good, and there are many children who manage to be good without it. But faith can help a child grow up with positive moral values. It can serve as a bulwark against a culture that preaches a pleasure-now, this-is-all-there-is view of life. Traditional religion tells us who we are, why we're here, and where we're going. It says we're children of God, we're meant to serve God by serving each other, and if we do, we're destined for eternal happiness with Him in the next life.

When a child believes in a good God, Whitman says, "life becomes much clearer. It's like finding a path through a dark wood."

In a recent national survey of more than 300,000 American families, fully two-thirds said that a belief in God or a higher being is "very important" in their family life. "Time after time," the study reported, "parents made it obvious that religion is the major influence on their attitudes and behavior." One family's comment was typical: "When spiritual and religious foundations are strong, many other threats to family life can be surmounted."[5]

Said a mother: "I find that our religion helps a great deal in the moral upbringing of our children. I tell them that they're ultimately accountable to God, not me, for what they do."

What if you don't believe in God yourself, or aren't sure what you believe?

A 5-year-old girl asked her mother: "Is there a God? And if there is, what is He like?"

"I don't know," her mother said. "You'll have to figure it out for yourself as you grow up. Everyone has to."

Be honest with kids: tell them that questions about God are big questions, ones that thinking people struggle with all their lives.

Many parents who aren't sure of their own religious beliefs nevertheless take their children to church or synagogue and send them to religious classes or schools. They reason: "I'm not sure what *I* believe, but I want my child to have a chance to make up his own mind, and I want him to have the benefit of a good moral framework while he's growing up." I think that's sound reasoning. Kids aren't likely to value religion if they're never exposed to it.

Suppose you are a religious, church-going family and your teenager announces, "I don't want to go to church. I don't think you have to go to church to love God."

You can say (without getting your hackles up):

> "I can understand how you might not find much meaning in church right now. But suppose you said school was boring and you wanted to quit. Even if you were old enough to quit under the law, we'd be copping out as parents if we said, 'Okay, if that's how you feel, go ahead and quit.' We think that you need an education, and that the older you get, the more you'll think so, too.
>
> "Well, we feel the same way about church. We go because we need it. Without it, we wouldn't take time to worship God. We hope that someday you'll come to see the value of going to church, too. But until you're older and can make your own decision about this, we feel it's our job to keep you involved."[6]

Some families find that teenagers are more willing to attend religious services if they can choose which service to go to or even go by themselves sometimes instead of always with the family. Says one 15-year-old boy: "Mass has a different effect on me when I go by myself. When you're with your family, you sort of blend into the group. When I'm there alone, I feel as if the priest is talking to *me*."

Some families don't identify religion with church or temple or even with belief in God, but still consider themselves religious. For them, religion has to do with values like ritual and tradition, reverence for life, faith in life's meaning and fundamental goodness, and celebration of our membership in a single human family.

I spoke with a Jewish father, a man who said he didn't have a clearly worked-out concept of God but felt that religion was an important part of his life and that of his three sons. "I'm very happy that they made it through adolescence without getting mixed up in drugs, drinking, or any kind of serious trouble," he said. "To what do you attribute their success?" I asked.

He answered: "Bar Mitzvah."

"What was it about Bar Mitzvah?" I asked.

"They got a powerful dose of Old Testament Law," he said. "Bar Mitzvah is the first time a young person is invited to join the grownups in reading and interpreting the Bible. It's hard to say; there are so many influences. But I think they got the message that becoming an adult is joining the ongoing quest for righteousness, for holiness, for understanding how the old moral traditions apply to modern situations. I think all of this also helped them develop a strong sense of ethnic identity, and that helped them withstand negative peer pressures."

7. **Forgiveness.** One of the great religious teachings is that we should forgive those who do us wrong. The Christian religion, for example, teaches that God forgives us in the same measure as we forgive others. Kids should also understand that the act of forgiving helps them in another way, too: nursing a grudge prolongs a hurt; when you forgive, you can forget.

8. **Humility.** Humility is another virtue with roots in religion. True humility is recognizing the truth; there's no false modesty in it. If you're good at using words, solving problems, or organizing things, you know it. But you recognize that your talent is a gift and that you've been given it for the purpose of doing good.

The world around us tends to encourage humility's opposite: pride. The great English writer, C. S. Lewis, pointed out that pride is essentially competitive; it's the pleasure of feeling you're better than somebody else. Lewis called pride "the worst vice, a spiritual cancer that eats up the very possibility of love, or contentment, or even common sense. . . . If I am a proud man, as long as there is one man in the whole world more powerful, or richer, or cleverer than I, he is my rival and my enemy."[7]

So, in addition to helping kids believe in themselves, teach them to be humble. Teach them never to look down their nose at another person, or to envy someone who has something they don't. Teach them to recognize and be grateful for the gifts that are theirs. And teach them what Confucius said about error: "A man who commits a mistake and doesn't admit it is committing another mistake."

9. **Happiness.** Happiness is the habit of taking pleasure in life. Is it a virtue? Says psychologist Nevitt Sanford: "If you don't know how to enjoy life, you're going to be a burden to other people." The kind of home that teaches a child how to enjoy life, Sanford says, is the same kind that teaches him how to be moral.

If we would teach our children the art of being happy, we should teach them that happiness is in large part a state of mind. Said an anonymous sage: "Happiness is not having what you want, but wanting what you have." Said Martha Washington:

> "I am determined to be cheerful and happy in whatever situation I may be. For I have learned from experience that the greater part of our happiness or misery depends on our dispositions and not on our circumstances. We carry the seeds of the one or the other with us in our minds wherever we go."

And an anonymous poet wrote:

> Two men looked through the prison bars.
> One saw mud, and the other saw stars.

Help kids also understand the profound relationship between happiness and goodness.

You can't be happy in life unless you're good—unless you get outside yourself and serve others. Tell your child the story about the great psychiatrist, Alfred Adler.

When people came to Adler suffering from depression and feelings of worthlessness, he would ask them, "Do you wish to be cured?"

They would answer, "Yes, certainly."

And Adler would reply: "Then I will prescribe for you a therapy guaranteed to bring results: For two weeks, every day, do something to bring happiness to another person."

10. **Honesty.** Honesty is *the quality of being able to be trusted.*[8]
Honest people don't lie, don't cheat, don't steal. They don't try to weasel out of deals. You can count on them to keep their word.

Teach kids that a reputation for being honest is one of the most valuable assets they can have.

Help them think clearly about violations of honesty. Why is it wrong to lie or break an agreement? Because it violates trust, and trust is essential in any relationship.

Why is it wrong to cheat in school? Because cheating is a lie (it misrepresents your knowledge); it's a violation of your teacher's trust in you; and it's unfair to all the people who aren't cheating.

Why is it wrong to steal? Because there's a person behind the property. Theft violates that person.

Since shoplifting is a major problem among teenagers today, it's a good idea to consider what you would do if you found that your child had taken something from a store.

A father remembers what his mother did:

> "I was 11. It was a hot summer day, and I asked my mother if I could have some lemonade. She said we had no lemons. I said if she gave me the money, I'd go to the store and buy some lemons. She said we had no money to buy them.
>
> "So I walked to the store—half a mile—stole the lemons, and brought them home. I presented them to my mother saying, 'Now we can have lemonade.' She said, 'Where did you get the lemons?' I told her. She then made me walk back by myself, return the lemons, and tell the store owner what I had done.
>
> "The message to me was that no matter what we lacked, we did not have the right to hurt another person to get it. I never stole again."

When kids are caught stealing, lying, or cheating, they're usually too ashamed or afraid to take corrective action on their own. They need a parent's push. At moments like this, teaching by telling means getting kids to bite the bullet and do what's necessary to clear their conscience and set things right.

The highest form of honesty is *integrity*, the quality of being honest with yourself. It's captured in the statement: "The measure of a man's character is what he would do if he were never found out."

11. **Love.** All of us want our children to learn the importance of love. How can we teach it?

First, remember that up through Stage 2 of moral reasoning, kids confuse love with fairness. Teach them the difference. Fairness meets the other person halfway. Love goes the extra mile. Love is generous; it doesn't ask, "What's in it for me?"

Second, teach children the difference between love as a *virtue* and love as a *feeling*. "Love your neighbor" doesn't mean you have to feel lovingly toward that kid in the next row who calls you a jerk. You don't even have to like him. We're required to love others in the same way that we love ourselves. That means we seek their good, wish them well, do them no harm, help them if they're in need—all the things, in short, that we do for ourselves even if we don't like ourselves at any particular moment.

Third, teach kids that love usually doesn't take the form of grand gestures but of small deeds. Setting the table without being asked. Reading a story to your little sister when you'd rather do something else. Obeying promptly. Controlling your anger when your brother calls you a name. Playing with a kid at school who doesn't have any friends.

Says one man: "From my father, I remember one very important moral teaching: 'If you can't say something good about someone, don't say anything at all.' He also said that when you compliment someone, they remember it, and when you put them down, they remember that, too."

St. Paul described love this way:

> Love is patient. Love is kind. Love is not jealous. It does not put on airs; it is not snobbish. Love does nothing rude; it is not self-seeking; it is not prone to anger; it does not brood over injuries, but rejoices along with the truth. Love covers over everything, believes everything, hopes for everything, puts up with everything.
>
> Love never fails.

12. **Learning.** In 1978 *Family Circle* magazine published the results of its investigation into the backgrounds of 50 highly successful Americans, people who had reached the top of their field in business, politics, science, the arts, or entertainment. The interviewers found what others had found before them:

that the parents of successful people place a great emphasis on learning. Most began reading to their children before they were 2 years old—and read several times a week. Books were an important part of the home; families that couldn't afford to buy them borrowed them from local libraries. Forty-five of the 50 famous offspring got some sort of training to supplement their formal education. And they grew up in homes where there was real conversation: discussion about politics, science, literature, art—whatever stimulated interest.

For the parents of these successful children, the interviewers reported, "to be alive meant to be growing, developing new skills, learning; they took courses, read books, visited museums, entertained friends, had hobbies, got involved in politics. And they encouraged their children to develop a similar zest for learning."⁹

"There's nothing to do!" is the chronic complaint of kids who get into trouble because they're bored. When we teach kids to value learning, we teach them that there's everything to do. And we broaden their minds and enlarge their spirits in the bargain.

13. **Patriotism.** Patriotism is love of country. It's one of those values, like religion, that calls us and connects us to something beyond ourselves. It's a value that has unfortunately declined sharply among young people over the last decade, and one that needs strengthening if our democracy is to remain strong.

Patriotism was the dinner topic at our house recently when our older son, Mark, had a friend over. This boy, an intelligent and thoughtful 15-year-old, said quite sincerely, "When you hear about things like Watergate and Abscam and all the other rotten stuff going on in the country, you say to yourself, 'What's there to be patriotic about?'" Kids need to realize they can feel good that in their country corruption is something to get upset about. As a Canadian once said to me, "You Americans may be embarrassed about Watergate, but up here we admire you for caring enough to clean house and not being afraid to wash your dirty laundry in public." Watergate was a great scandal in this country only because Americans take the ideal of honest government seriously.

Kids should know that their country had a beginning most rare in human history: it was founded on moral ideals. It was, as Lincoln said, "conceived in liberty," based on the revolutionary idea that all people are moral equals, that they all have the same inalienable human rights, and that the government has no business governing unless it's safeguarding those rights. These ideals have served as the conscience of the nation, telling us that slavery was wrong, that our treatment of Native Americans was wrong, that denial of the vote to women was wrong; they've told us, in short, how we've needed to improve as a society if we want to be the kind of country we say we are. These ideals, we should teach our children, form the core of a "thinking patriotism," one which constantly judges the country's conduct at home and abroad against the high standard of its own moral principles. This mindset is the very opposite of the "my country, right or wrong" thinking that gives patriotism a bad name.

I think it's also easier for kids to feel patriotic if they know something about their country's heroes. They should know about the people who have embodied the best of the national character, people whose lives were extraordinary examples of determination, resourcefulness, courage, or compassion. Men and women such as Abraham Lincoln, Harriet Tubman, Ben Franklin, Elizabeth Cady Stanton, John Chapman (Johnny Appleseed), Helen Keller, Jackie Robinson, Eleanor Roosevelt, and Martin Luther King, Jr. Kids should know, too, that heroes were human, with limitations that often reflected the times they lived in. But they were also giants.

Finally, I think young people can feel good that their country is unexcelled in the opportunities it provides people to become all that they are capable of being. Recently I asked a young man in his late twenties, who had come to the United States two years ago, for his impressions of the country. In the city where he was living, he said, people were on the whole not as courteous as they were in his native country. "But," he said, "it's true what you hear: this really is a place of opportunity. I come from a working-class family. Back home, if I said that I wanted to be a fashion designer or an airline pilot, people would laugh at me because I didn't have the right background. Here I would be taken seriously. I'm not saying it would be easy, that there wouldn't be any obstacles; but here you have the feeling that, if you're willing to work hard, anything is possible."

14. **Respect.** Respect, as we've seen, lies at the very center of

moral development. It comes in many forms: respect for law and legitimate authority; respect for people's rights; respect for human dignity; respect for the environment and life in all its forms.

I think of a father of two elementary-school-age children who was concerned about how much kids put down others at school, especially those who are "different." He says:

> "We've talked a lot about prejudice. The kids come home with stories about incidents at school. We've stressed over and over that people are human beings, no matter what their accent or the color of their skin. That prejudice is a cruel and stupid thing. That it can hurt people very much. That kids who are prejudiced toward someone who's different would never want to be treated that way themselves.
>
> "We think the message is getting through. The other day Ruth, our 6-year-old, came home very proud of herself. She told how she had stood up for a Japanese boy that some kids were making fun of and pushing around on the playground."

Another father remembers how he learned respect for the environment:

> "I grew up in Montana. My family spent a great deal of its vacation and leisure time camping. Often we would see no other campers for days; we would hike into places that had almost no sign of human life ever having been there. My parents taught me to respect the right of others to a litter-free environment. I remember how important it was for us to leave our campsite spotless. I still feel today that it is my responsibility never to litter or pollute."

And I think of a mother who tells this story:

> "We visited some friends last summer. Our boys—David (10) and Bret (9)—had gone out to play in the woods with our friends' 12-year-old son, Billy, who proceeded to chase a frog and then stone it to death. Without knowing about the incident, we agreed to have Billy come back home with us for an overnight.
>
> "In the car on the way home, the three boys were talking in the backseat. Billy said, 'That was pretty funny about the frog, wasn't it?' I felt an uneasiness in the back and realized that the boys hadn't said anything in response. So, I turned and asked what had happened that was funny. Billy blithely related the story.

"Thunderstruck, I asked if he meant that he had *killed* the frog. When he said yes in a surprised tone, I asked him why he had done it. He said it had been fun and, again, seemed very surprised by my question. I asked the boys about their part, and they said they had just watched.

"I asked how the frog looked, how it must have felt, and said how disappointed I was that this had happened. I said we had always felt that life was very special and should be preserved if at all possible. I related the joy we have gotten out of watching the birds or from following a bee or snake or cat in its travels. I related how careful we were to capture spiders and put them outside rather than killing them inside. Finally, I said that we were entrusted with the care of the animals of the world, and that God would want us to treat them in a kind manner, not inflict suffering.

"Billy said, 'Gee, I'm really sorry. I didn't think you'd feel that way.'"

Later, the mother says, she and her husband talked with just David and Bret. Their father said:

"You know, I think if someone had told Billy that it wasn't right and he should stop, he would have. If he had realized you didn't like it, he would have stopped. In any situation like this, it's up to you, somehow, to try to turn it around."

Billy learned, from this mother's reaction, that some people think it's very wrong to be cruel to animals. David and Bret learned that concern for what's right requires more than silently witnessing someone else's cruelty.

15. **Sin.** Sin obviously isn't a virtue, but awareness of it is.

A well-known psychiatrist, Karl Menninger, wrote a book a few years ago titled *Whatever Became of Sin?* Dr. Menninger didn't think that people had stopped sinning, only that they had stopped calling it that.

When I was a boy, we learned in catechism class that there were Seven Deadly Sins: Pride, Greed, Lust, Anger, Gluttony, Envy, and Sloth. I think it's a good idea to make kids aware that these human tendencies are still very much with us. They explain why we can reach high levels of moral reasoning and still behave like scoundrels.

There's another big idea about sin, one that David and Bret's parents touched on in pointing out the wrongness of doing nothing while Billy killed the frog. And that's the idea that sin comes in two forms: sins of *commission* and sins of *omission*. The Gospels, as ethicist Daniel Maguire points out, make it clear that "the primary form of sin does not involve what we do, but what we *don't* do!"[10] In the Last Judgment scene, for example, all the sins that Jesus names are sins of omission ("I was hungry, and you did not feed me. I was thirsty, and you did not give me drink . . .").

We should teach kids, early on, that to fail to act is to act. We're responsible for both.

16. **Sportsmanship.** Many of us encourage our children to participate in sports. Sports can build self-esteem, offer an experience in being part of a team, and provide challenges that test and develop a youngster's self-discipline. They can also be the opportunity for kids to develop a quality of character that is universally admired: good sportsmanship.

Most of us grew up with the famous lines by sportswriter Grantland Rice:

> *When the One Great Scorer comes*
> *to write against your name,*
> *He marks—not that you won or lost—*
> *but how you played the game.*

Unfortunately, too many people today act as if winning the game is the only thing that matters. Kids pick up that value. They insult their opponents. They curse out their own teammates for making a mistake. A first-grader came home dejected from his soccer game. "What's wrong?" his father asked. "I think I'll quit soccer," he said. "I missed a kick today, and the other team scored a goal. Everybody was yelling at me. They said, 'You stink!'"

A school principal complained, "We're trying to teach kids to be halfway decent with each other. But we get parents who will come to their kids' hockey game and tell their kids to 'go out there and beat the hell out of those son-of-bitches!' And so that's how the kids behave."

Kids need to hear from us—from coaches, parents, and teachers, and hear it over and over till it sinks in—what it means to be a good sport and how important it is. We also obviously need to model good sportsmanship by our own actions. If we make this kind of an effort, it will show in kids' attitudes and behavior. It's no accident, for example, that Penn State's football team (number 1 in the nation in 1982) has a reputation for good sportsmanship. Listen to the philosophy of their coach, Joe Patterno:

> "Our boys are taught not to make jackasses of themselves and to do nothing to degrade an opponent. In the end zone, they do not spike the ball or throw it. They hand it to the official.
> "I also teach them not to rant and rave at officials. And that goes for me, too. When I coach a perfect game, then I'll criticize the officials."[11]

Chris Evert Lloyd, a tennis champion and a fierce competitor, explains how she developed her determination to play the game "like a lady":

> "From the time I was 6, my father drilled into me the importance of being controlled on the court. 'You've got to take the bad with the good,' he said. 'If you lose, don't be a bad sport about it. Just be gracious.'"[12]

Sports don't automatically "build character." But, depending on what we teach our children, they can.

17. **Thinking.** It doesn't matter how much moral reasoning kids have developed if they don't stop to use it. How can we teach them to think first and act later?

Asking kids questions, as we saw in the last chapter, is one way to get them to think about the consequences of their behavior. But there's something else we can do, and that's teach kids a systematic way to make moral decisions, one that forces them to think carefully. Here's a step-by-step process I recommend—which kids are capable of learning at Stage 3 and up. When making a moral decision, ask three questions:

1. *What are my options?*
2. *What are the likely consequences of the different things I might do?*
3. *What's the best decision—the one that's consistent with my values and results in the most good for everybody involved?*

(With younger children, you can simplify this by asking, "What else can you do? . . . What would happen then? . . . So what do you think is best?")

Let's apply this decision-making process to an actual moral dilemma faced by an 11-year-old boy named Eddy.

Eddy was a new kid in school. After a month of feeling friendless, he finally struck up a friendship with Doug and Barney. One day, on the way home from school, Doug spotted a package in the mailbox of an apartment building. He grabbed it, said "Let's go!" and they all took off for Eddy's house.

In Eddy's bedroom, Doug opened the package and found two gold-plated medallions. "Oh, cool!" Barney said. Eddy said, "Okay, I think we'd better take them back now—it's against the Ten Commandments to steal!" Whereupon Doug replied, "Well, I'm not very religious!" Then Doug and Barney each took a medallion and went home.

Eddy knew that stealing was wrong, and he felt involved. But he didn't want to lose Doug and Barney as friends. He didn't know what to do.

You might try reading Eddy's dilemma to your kids to see how they would solve it. What Eddy did was to bring it up that night at the dinner table (which had been the occasion of previous moral discussions). "I have a moral dilemma," he said. "A real one."

He told his parents what had happened—a decision in itself. They praised him for his honesty and courage in doing that. Then together, they tried to think of the options for dealing with the problem and the probable consequences of each.

1. Eddy could do nothing. That wouldn't jeopardize his friendship with Doug and Barney. But he'd still feel guilty (he said), the person who owned the medallions would never get them back, and the same kind of situation with Doug and Barney might happen again.

2. Eddy could try to talk Doug and Barney into returning the medallions. This time he could give a new reason, like "How would you like it if some kids ripped off a package from your family's mailbox?" If that didn't work, Eddy could drop Doug and Barney as friends. But that would leave him without friends at school, and it wouldn't solve the problem of how to get the medallions back to their rightful owner.

3. Eddy's parents could call Doug and Barney's parents. That might get the stolen property returned, and their parents would know what Doug and Barney had been up to. But there was no telling how the parents would handle the situation, and Doug and Barney would be mad at Eddy for sure.

4. Eddy's parents could talk with Doug and Barney and ask them to take back the medallions. That wouldn't get them in hot water with their parents, it might have some positive influence on their future behavior, and it would keep alive Eddy's chance for a continuing friendship with the boys.

Eddy and his parents agreed that option 4 was the best course of action. It was consistent with their values regarding stealing and the responsibility to do something when you see somebody else stealing. It took into account Doug and Barney's perspective and Eddy's desire to try to keep his friendship with the boys as long as they didn't continue to steal.

The next day, Eddy's father wrote the following note to Doug and Barney, and Eddy delivered it to them at school:

Dear Doug and Barney,

At dinner last night Eddy told us about something that was bothering him very much. He said that you had taken a package from someone's mailbox, opened it here at our house, and kept the medallions it contained. (This was hard for Eddy to tell us, since he considers you his friends.)

This concerns us very much. We talked for a long time last night, trying to find a way to deal with this problem that's fair to everybody involved.

We decided that we'd like to talk with you today after school at our house. Please bring the medallions with you.

We look forward to seeing you at 3:00.

Sincerely,
Mr. and Mrs. Cook

Doug came to the house that afternoon to deliver his medallion. Barney didn't come, but sent his medallion with Eddy.

Doug and Eddy, after talking with Eddy's father, wrote an unsigned note of apology to the owner of the medallions, wrapped it up with the medallions in the package, and returned it to the mailbox from which it came. Eddy, Doug, and Barney remained friends.

The "What-are-my-options? What-would-be-the-consequences?" approach obviously requires time. That's why it's so important to teach kids to *take* time to think before they act. And raise the question "What are your options?" often enough in your house so it becomes second nature for them to ask it when they confront a problem.

Coaching kids through options-and-consequences decision-making shows how natural it is to combine asking questions and sharing our own thoughts when we teach children. A mother of three teenagers says she combines asking and telling in this way: When her children are considering what she believes is an unwise course of action, she asks them, "How do you expect to feel about yourself after you do that?" (The issue might be whether to tell a lie, fake a book report, cut practice, break a date because someone else has called, etc.) That usually gets them to reconsider. Then she often adds why she thinks a different course of action would be better.

There are a few other things I would teach kids about making moral decisions: Don't try to do it when you're angry or tired; beware of "rationalizing" (making up reasons for doing what you want to do); don't be afraid to seek the advice of someone whose judgment you respect; and try to make a decision that you wouldn't be ashamed of if the whole world were to know it.

18. **Understanding.** A sympathetic understanding of others is a quality that will help kids in all their human relationships. We can't be fair or loving or helpful toward others if we don't understand their needs.

A mother remembers:

"When I was in second grade, someone in my class started stealing things. The teacher asked whoever it was to stop and to see her after class. The next day the teacher said no one had come to see her, so at recess she searched the desks and somehow found out who was the culprit.

"When I told my parents that night how surprised I was that Donna was the thief, they said how hard it must be for her. She had every material thing she needed, but her mother had recently died and she missed her terribly. We talked about how if the class pitched in—if kids were friends with her—she might feel better. I realized that a person's behavior was more complicated than I had ever dreamed and that we really should care about people and try to understand them."

A father remembers his father's teaching: "Never judge a man until you have walked a mile in his shoes."

READING AS A WAY OF TEACHING KIDS VALUES

In urging you to teach by telling, I hope I haven't given you the image of a long-faced parent perched on a soapbox, delivering a nonstop sermon about right and wrong. Actually, I don't think it's a bad idea to get up on your soapbox now and then. But much of the moral teaching you do can be more subtle than that. Good teachers are fond of saying that kids often learn best when they don't know they're learning.

One of the most enjoyable ways for children to learn about values—and for you to foster them—is from the pages of a good book.

Books can teach kids to have faith in themselves. In her wise and helpful book, *In the Beginning There Were the Parents*, Dolores Curran has a delightful chapter called "Read It Again, Mom." It begins with this story:

He was late walking. He was late talking. All the other kids in the neighborhood rode trikes before he did. He caught up, but he was always the last one in the group to achieve the normal. He sensed his parents' anxiety, as children always do, and he tried harder, but it just discouraged him.

Then one day his mother bought him a book: *Leo the Late Bloomer* by Robert Kraus (Windmill Books, Inc.). It became his bible. "Read it to me," he demanded daily, and his parents did. This delightful story of Leo, a young lion who doesn't bloom as early as his friends, became his solace. It calmed the boy's fears that he wasn't as good as the other children, and it helped his parents understand the depth of his feelings.

"A simple five-dollar book did what dozens of visits to the pediatrician couldn't do," said his father. "It showed him he wasn't alone in his problem and gave him hope that he would bloom someday, too."[13]

Teaching values through literature, as Curran points out, is one of the oldest teaching methods used by humans: "From Old Testament stories through *Pilgrim's Progress* to Horatio Alger, cultures have used this method to inculcate morals and values."

Books not only give children characters who are like them to identify with and take comfort in. They also, as Boston College educator Kirk Kilpatrick points out, give a child characters to *aspire* to be like—"others who are better than himself, who are just like he might become if he fulfills his potential for goodness." Even in the most virtuous of societies, Kilpatrick says, adults have realized their personal shortcomings and the need to offer children examples of moral wisdom and moral courage beyond themselves. Stories meet that need. They satisfy a child's hunger for heroes.

Other books teach quieter virtues. The "Little House" series by Laura Ingalls Wilder, for example, not only gives children a wonderfully realistic record of America's pioneer past, but also paints a rich portrait of a family whose happiness lay not in material possessions but in shared activity and love. These eight books tell of human decency, hard work, religious faith, and abiding kindness in ways that live in a child's imagination.

And therein lies the magic of literature: it captures the imagination and, in so doing, touches the heart. All of us have experienced the power of a story to stir strong feelings. We can talk to children in abstract terms about deceit and hatred and loyalty and love. But when they come face to face with these qualities enfleshed in unforgettable characters like the wicked White Witch and the great and gentle Aslan in C. S. Lewis's *Chronicles of Narnia,* they feel repelled by the evil and drawn, irresistibly, to the good. Teaching morality through stories recognizes that developing virtue is an affair of the emotions as much as it is an affair of the mind.

Most parents know that few interactions with children are as satisfying as reading aloud. And yet a hundred things seem to encroach on that special time. For a good source of ways to "win the battle for family reading," consult the excellent book, *How to Grow a Young Reader: A Parent's Guide to Kids and Books* by

John and Kay Lindskoog (David Cook Pub. Co., 1978). This inexpensive paperback is also an invaluable guide to over 400 books for children of different ages and includes short descriptions of best books of all kinds, including old classics, modern fantasy, realistic fiction, biography, and literature that nurtures religious values.

Try to work in a weekly trip with kids to the library. If your child has a special problem like lying or being very shy or feeling unattractive, ask your librarian to recommend books on the problem.[14] For children who have experienced a divorce in their family, Dr. Richard Gardner's *The Boys and Girls Book About Divorce* offers them practical advice on how to understand their feelings about divorce and deal with changed relationships.

Good books have a special value for teenagers. They offer them a temporary retreat from the stresses of those years, a chance to experience worlds that they don't have to cope with, and, in the case of some books, an opportunity to see how other young people work through the issues of identity, independence, sex, parent-child conflict, and the responsibilities of approaching maturity. "Books got me through high school," says one young woman. "I don't think I would have made it without them."

Books like Elizabeth Speare's *The Bronze Bow* and *The Witch of Blackbird Pond,* and Madeleine L'Engle's *A Wrinkle in Time* and *A Wind in the Door,* show young people struggling with moral dilemmas or facing moral dangers and offer inspiring lessons in courage, friendship, and love. And such stories are wholesome and captivating for both teens and younger children. In our family, we've enjoyed reading them aloud on a trip in the car or around the table with a big bowl of popcorn.

Kids who get hooked on books have a lifelong legacy. Through the world of literature, they can continue to explore on their own the richness and meaning of life, the joys and conflicts of the human heart, the endless struggle of good against evil.

In Appendix D I've provided an annotated list of books that I think are good for fostering values.

PARENTS WHO MADE A DIFFERENCE

Since our children grow up to be their own persons, free to choose their own path, we can't be sure what long-range impact our moral teaching will have. But when we begin early to teach the values we cherish, and when we do so over many years, our potential influence, I believe, is very great indeed.

Let me tell you a story about people whose parents had such an influence on them. It is a tale of moral heroes: persons who risked their fortunes and their lives to save Jews from Hitler's genocide.

The story begins in 1961, during the trial of Adolph Eichmann. The trial, revealing as it did the ghastly machinery of the death camps, projected a horrendous image of man. A striking exception was the testimony given about a Christian who had rescued Jews from one of the Nazi camps.

Rabbi Harold Schulweis of Oakland, California, saw in this testimony "a glimmer of redemption." He wrote a magazine article urging that rescuers be identified and honored. On Christmas day, 1962, NBC commentator Chet Huntley presented a network television documentary in which some rescuers were identified and their stories told.

With the help of this publicity, Rabbi Schulweis was able to recruit and fund a team of psychologists to study the backgrounds of the rescuers. Where did they grow up? What were their families like? What led them to take such risks to save the lives of people they did not know?

One such courageous individual was a once-wealthy German businessman. In the interview, he reported how he had first become involved in the business of rescue:

> "I was believing in 1942 that the war will be another year. It cannot be any longer. It's impossible.
> "I was then a rich man. I had about 300,000 or 400,000 marks, and I started with one person, then six people, from there to 50, then 100. . . . People came to me, asking me very bluntly and very frankly, 'Will you save me?'"[15]

The first request for help came from his secretary. The Germans, she said, were going to kill her Jewish husband. He thought at first that she was crazy and said: "Germans don't do things like that!" But she insisted that they would, and so he agreed to keep the husband in his office over the weekend. As he became convinced that the fears of Jews were justified, he became more and more deeply involved. By the war's end, he had spent four years and all of his fortune to save more than 200 Jews.

"My Mother Said To Me When We Were Small . . ."

Here is what this man told the interviewers about his family:

> "I come from a poor family. My mother came from Hesse, which was mainly small farmers. . . . I believe that is part of my personality. You inherit something from your parents, from the grandparents. My mother said to me when we were small, and even when we were bigger, 'Regardless of what you do with your life, be honest. When it comes to the day you have to make a decision, make the right one. It could be a hard one. But even the hard ones should be the right ones.' I didn't know what it means. . . ."[16]

He went on to talk about his mother in glowing terms, about how she had told him to live, how she had taught him morals, and how she had exemplified morality for him.

> "Always in life she gave me so much philosophy. She didn't go to high school, only elementary school, but so smart a woman. Wisdom, you know."[17]

This man's childhood proved to be the rule among rescuers rather than the exception. Other rescuers remembered their parents in similar ways: as strong, good people who both preached and practiced morality.

What lesson can be drawn from the findings of this remarkable study? It lies in the words of the German businessman: "My mother said to me when we were small, 'When it comes to the day when you have to make a decision, make the right one.' I didn't know what it means. . . ." To this young German boy, the message of his mother was unclear. But as he grew in years, he grew in understanding of what she was telling him, and it helped to guide his adult life.

So even if our children don't fully understand what we tell them when we tell them, our words may have lasting value nonetheless. They may echo in our children's minds in years to come.

And as they look back through the lens of a more mature stage of development, our words may take on new and deeper meaning. As a parent, I find hope and comfort in that possibility.

So talk to your children about what you believe. Teach by telling.

CHAPTER 16

TELEVISION AS A MORAL TEACHER—AND WHAT TO DO ABOUT IT

There was a child went forth every day,
and the first object he look'd upon,
that object he became,
and that object became part of him for
the day or a certain part of the day
or for many years or stretching cycles
of years.

—Walt Whitman,
Leaves of Grass[1]

Television. We call it a lot of unflattering names: the idiot box, the boob tube, the flickering blue-eyed parent, the plug-in drug. And yet we have allowed it to reshape our personal lives—our reading habits, our eating and sleeping patterns, how much we entertain and visit friends, the way we interact as families—more than any other technological innovation of the twentieth century.

Most serious, we may have allowed TV, without even realizing it, to replace us as our children's primary moral teacher.

When parents hear the statistics on how much time kids spend in front of the TV set, most are shocked.

- Preschoolers watch an average of 4 hours a day. Before kindergarten they will spend more time watching TV than a student spends in four years of college classes.

- The average elementary-school child watches 30 hours of television a week.
- Junior high school kids watch even more.
- By the time they graduate from high school, kids will have spent some 15,000 hours watching television, compared to 11,000 hours in the classroom.

Sure, there are good programs for kids—shows like "Little House on the Prairie," "Wild World of Animals," "Mister Rogers," "The Muppet Show," and "Sesame Street." But what else are kids watching, and how does it affect their values and behavior?

In the college courses I teach, teachers tell me that almost without exception, children in their classes say "The Dukes of Hazzard" is their favorite TV show. A spoof of Southern law and order, "The Dukes" features bootleggers and parolees as the "good guys" who race cars, have hilarious smash-ups, and regularly outsmart the stupid and corrupt law-enforcement officials.

One kindergarten teacher asked her children, "Who would you like to be if you could be anybody?"

Their overwhelming response: the Dukes of Hazzard.

This teacher continued: "They come in Monday morning singing the theme song, calling each other by the characters' names, and buzzing about what happened in the latest episode. This week Jeremy said to Shawn, 'Did you see him making out?' Shawn replied, 'Yeah, and did you see the way he ripped off her blouse?'"

So powerful are the visual-action images that shows like this present that kids don't even have to watch them regularly to be profoundly affected. Says a mother of a 3-year-old: "I slipped *once* and let Timmy watch 'The Dukes of Hazzard.' Five months later he's still acting it out—racing and smashing cars and calling himself Bo and Luke."

Another kindergarten teacher asked her children, "What do you do after school?"

Most answered: "I sit with Mom and watch the soap opera until the cartoons come on."

"You don't go out and play?"

"No."

"I wasn't surprised by that answer," the teacher says, "because they live out this stuff in the classroom. In the housekeeping corner they play 'Guiding Light.' A typical play session will start like this: 'You're pregnant by him.' 'You're running away with her.' 'You get shot.'"

In case you haven't seen the soaps lately, here's what the kids are watching on a typical week of "Guiding Light":

> Amanda tells Derek to start divorce proceedings for her and Ben. If Alan continues to avoid Hope, she will dissolve her marriage and deny the baby she's carrying is Alan's. Ed and Rita agree on a legal separation. Rita prepares for romantic interlude with Alan. Mike suspects Alan has a mistress. . . . In an attempt to win Ross back, Vanessa takes overdose of pills and liquor and calls Ross to save her, but he is not home. . . . Nola succeeds in getting Floyd to spread rumors to Tim about Kelly. . . . Breaking into Andy's apartment, Joe steals Andy's bank statements.[2]

And that was tame compared to some. Here's a slice of life from "Days of Our Lives" (same week):

> After signing divorce papers and being institutionalized at Bayview sanitarium, Lee says she just wanted to be loved. In a crazed state, Kellum loads gun intending to kill Alex, Joshua, and Max. . . . Alex wants Sister Marie to leave the church for him. . . . Marlena is raped by Kellum.[3]

Neil Postman, professor of communications at New York University and author of the recent book, *The Disappearance of Childhood,* reminds us that one of the main differences between adults and children used to be that we knew things that they didn't. But TV, with incredible swiftness, has changed all that. Drug addictions, incest, promiscuity, corruption, adultery, violence, and sadism are all becoming as familiar to kids as they are to adults. All of this flies smack in the face of what was until recently part of our civilization's wisdom: that childhood is a period to be protected and nurtured, a time of innocence and curiosity and trust, very necessary for children's healthy development.

Young children, of course, are not the only ones who stand to be disillusioned and corrupted by TV saturation in the seamy side of life. Teenagers, at a time in their moral development (typically, Stage 3) when they're highly impressionable, can easily develop a warped picture of human relationships from a constant diet of such fare. Says a mother of a 14-year-old girl: "All of my daughter's friends watch the soap operas religiously the first thing when they get home from school, and I mean *religiously*. Then they get on the phone and talk about it for an hour. I told Karen I didn't like her watching that stuff, but she didn't want to be cut out of the action."

And it's not just the soaps or an occasional trashy show that present kids with values that are contrary to what most parents believe. Observes the publication *Television and Movie Facts for Parents:* "A few years ago the television 'good guys' with whom youngsters identify—the lawyers, detectives, doctors, policemen, and policewomen—began, as if somebody gave a signal, to 'sleep around.' If the chief heroes and heroines appear to be happy, successful, *and* sexually promiscuous—and viewing America seems to approve—why would a teenager be inclined to be strict with himself?"[4] If kids are watching such shows week in and week out, they're getting regular reinforcement for the immature moral reasoning that says, "If everybody's doing it, can it be so bad?"

OTHER VALUE LESSONS KIDS LEARN FROM TV

Besides casual attitudes toward sex and the idea that the promise of fidelity shouldn't be taken too seriously, what other value lessons is TV teaching?

1. **If you're having trouble getting what you want, try violence or crime**. By age 12, the average American child will have viewed approximately 100,000 violent episodes on TV and seen 13,000 persons violently destroyed.

Cartoons—the mainstay of children's programming—contain, per hour, an average of 26 incidents of physical force intended to hurt or kill.

Nobody has yet counted the incidents of robbery, arson, bombing, forgery, smuggling, and psychological terror that kids are exposed to on the screen. And with the advent of Home Box

Office, an alarming number of children are viewing new levels of graphic violence (not to mention sex). A second-grade teacher in an average middle-class community told me recently:

> "I did a survey. Of the 22 kids in my class, all but 7 have Home Box Office. Of those that have it, only 4 say they have any restrictions on what they can watch. The rest describe in vivid detail all the violence, sex, and gore they watch on Home Box, often with their parents in the room."

I think far fewer parents would let their kids watch violent TV if they realized the effects it can have on kids' attitudes and behaviors. Here's what the research shows:

• At the University of North Carolina Child Development Center, researchers paired 10 preschoolers who were alike in their television and play habits. For the next 11 days, one child in each pair was shown a violent Saturday morning TV show, while his partner was shown a nonviolent show. No change occurred in kids who watched nonviolent fare. But the preschoolers who watched violent programming showed a sharp increase in aggression, some even *tripling* their violent behavior (kicking, hitting, choking, etc.).

Drs. Jerome and Dorothy Singer, directors of Yale University's Television Center, report similar findings from their year-long study of nursery schoolers: 3- and 4-year-olds who watch the most violent television are most likely to get into fights and disrupt others' games in nursery school.

• A study of juvenile offenders commissioned by ABC television found that 22 percent confessed to having learned their criminal techniques from TV shows.

• In an extensive investigation of the roots of childhood aggression, University of Illinois psychologist Dr. Leonard Eron and his colleagues studied 875 8-year-old children in a county in upstate New York. Ten years later, in 1970, they did a follow-up on 475 of these children. Here are their major findings, reported in their book *Growing Up To Be Violent:* (1) Childrearing practices appear to contribute to children's aggression; parents who were high in their use of physical punishment or low in love for their children tended to have the most aggressive youngsters; (2) Although parents seemed to play a part in shaping a child's aggression, TV violence appeared to play an even stronger one: *the single best predictor of how aggressive a young man was at age 19 was the amount of violent television he watched at age 8.* (There was no such relationship for girls in this study.)

In 1977 Dr. Eron and his associates began a second study. They measured the television-viewing habits and aggressive behavior of 750 6-to-10-year-olds in the Chicago area and followed them for three years. In the February 1982 issue of *American Psychologist* Dr. Eron reports that girls now show the same effect as boys: the more violence they watch on television, the more aggressive is their behavior. Moreover, Dr. Eron indicates, this relationship between TV violence and children's aggression has recently been confirmed for both sexes in parallel studies being carried out in Finland, Poland, and Australia.

• In 1982 the National Institute of Mental Health (NIMH) issued a major report, *Television and Behavior,* summarizing over 2,500 studies done since 1972 on the influence of television. The results of these studies—drawn from many different countries—led the NIMH to conclude: there is now "overwhelming evidence" of a causal link between children's watching television violence and their performance of violent acts.

Such statistical generalities pale by comparison to the reports we read of individual cases where kids have copied what they saw on the screen.

In sentencing two teenage boys for holding up a bank and keeping 25 persons hostage for seven hours, a Los Angeles judge noted with disgust that the boys had seen the whole scheme laid out on "Adam 12" two weeks earlier.

In a Long Island community, police arrested an 11-year-old boy who admitted burglarizing homes for more than $1,000 in cash and valuables. His accomplice was a 7-year-old friend. The boy said he learned the burglary technique by seeing how it was done on television.

In Columbus, Ohio, a 14-year-old boy shot his 11-year-old brother to death in the chest. They were using their father's handgun to act out a scene from the movie *Dirty Harry,* shown on TV the night before.

In California, four children used a bottle to sexually assault a 9-year-old girl. The incident occurred three days after the assaulting children had seen NBC's prime-time broadcast of *Born Innocent*, in which reform-school girls "rape" another young girl with the handle of a plumber's plunger.

At least some of the people in the TV industry are beginning to admit that TV does in fact breed violence in children and teenagers (though that admission hasn't yet led them to curb violent programming!). Here is Brandon Tartikoff, president of NBC, quoted in *The New York Times:*

"Television did have an effect on me right from the beginning. In first grade, I was a member of a four-kid gang that went around imitating TV westerns. We'd disrupt class to play out scenes, picking up chairs and hitting people over the head with them—except, unlike on TV, the chairs didn't break, the kids did. Finally, the teacher called my parents in and said, 'Obviously, he's being influenced by these TV shows, and if he's to continue in this class, you've got to agree not to let him watch television any more.' So, from first to second grade there was a dark period during which I didn't watch TV at all. And I calmed down, and the gang broke up."[5]

2. **Violence isn't anything to get upset about.** Even if all kids don't copy the violence they see on TV, they may develop a ho-hum attitude toward violent behavior in others. In one study, kids shown an aggressive television show were subsequently slower to stop a fight between younger children than were kids who had not seen violent programming.[6] The National Institute of Mental Health study reports that looking at violent scenes for even a brief time makes children more willing to accept the aggressive behavior of others. One experiment demonstrated that kids who are high TV users actually show less physiological reaction (measured by sweating and pulse rate) to violence than do children who are low TV users.[7]

Says one 11-year-old boy: "You see so much violence that it's meaningless. If I saw someone really get killed, it wouldn't be a big deal. I guess I'm turning into a hard rock."[8]

3. **Put-downs are funny.** There's always been wisecracking on TV, but with the flood of situation comedies, it's reached a new

high (or low). When Archie called Edith a "ding-a-ling" on "All in the Family," he helped to usher in the Era of the Put-Down. TV laugh tracks teach kids that these insulting remarks are funny and "cool." And parents and teachers will attest that kids' putting each other down is a major cause of interpersonal problems at home and at school.

4. **It's a rotten world.** George Comstock, writing in *Character* magazine, argues that television gives kids a jaundiced view of society—which may help to explain why they have so little respect for authority figures and traditional social institutions. In its news coverage, for example, TV focuses almost exclusively on the bad news—the riots, the strikes, the congressman facing a bribery charge, the disgraced president waving a last farewell. It thereby portrays a world of turmoil and dishonesty to which cynicism may seem the appropriate response. In its entertainment shows, television often depicts established authority as corrupt; a recent study by Robert and Linda Lichter, two George Washington University sociologists, found that businessmen, professionals, and policemen plan or commit nearly half the criminal offenses portrayed on TV.

Not surprisingly, television also heightens anxiety. A 1979 study by the Foundation for Child Development in New York found that children who are heavy TV viewers are more fearful of the world and more apt to have bad dreams than kids who see less television.

5. **Adults are dolts.** The next time you watch "family" comedy shows, ask yourself: Who's smarter here, the grown-ups or the kids? As *Newsweek* quips, TV has gone from "Father Knows Best" to father knows *least*. When they're not depicted as dumb, parents are often represented as narrow-minded, racist, or self-centered persons. We could hardly be surprised if kids brought up on such stereotypes failed to look upon adults as a source of wisdom and advice.

6. **Women are inferior.** While blacks and other minorities have generally improved their TV image, women still take a beating. Female TV characters, one study showed, are twice as likely as men to display incompetence—both in programs and in commericals.

7. **Life is entertainment.** Kids who spend 30 hours a week

sitting in front of a television set are spending a good portion of their time being passively entertained. As a result, they're less likely to be able to amuse themselves or to develop the disciplined capacity for hard thinking and hard work that a productive life requires. They're more likely to think that gratification in life should be as quick and as easy as turning on a show.

8. **Drinking is where it's at.** A University of Michigan study found that even though kids can now see up to 40 sexual encounters a week on TV, they can see even more drinking. In crime shows, alcohol is consumed on the average of four times an hour. Thirty-three percent of all beverages drunk on TV are alcoholic. The highest rate of alcohol consumption occurs during prime time and on the top ten shows. Meanwhile, communities all across the country face the problem of kids who drink more and at an earlier age than ever before.

9. **Things make you happy.** In TV commercials (the average child sees 20,000 a year) and in programs, kids are constantly shown all the material things there are to have and led to believe that these things, once possessed, will make them happy. TV materialism may even lead kids to think they're *entitled* to all the goodies that everybody else seems to have. Recall the common teenage justification for shoplifting: "We have a right to the material things in life."

Obviously, we can't blame everything on TV. Kids can get bad examples and shoddy values from lots of sources. But we're fooling ourselves if we don't think that television is part of the problem.

WHAT'S *LOST* AS A RESULT OF TV

By now you may be ready to holler, "Enough! I'll make sure my kids watch only *good* shows, and I'll even turn down the sound on the commercials!"

Unfortunately, as Marie Winn points out in her persuasive book, *The Plug-In Drug,* the problem isn't just *what* kids watch; it's *that* they watch.[9] Why is this so? Because whenever kids are watching TV, they're *not* doing something else—not reading, not studying, not exercising, not playing with their friends, not using their imaginations, not pursuing hobbies, not practicing a musical instrument, not learning new skills, not spending time with their families.

Any and all of these activities have *lasting* value for kids' development. By comparison, even educational TV runs a poor second. Studies show, for example, (and you may want to test this out for yourself) that viewers typically learn and retain very little from even the best educational shows.

When kids don't read, and don't do the kind of thinking that reading requires, they're missing out on an important source of moral values and a chance to sharpen the powers of thought that are part of moral judgment.

When kids play less with friends, they're missing opportunities to learn to share, take another's point of view, play by the rules, and solve conflicts fairly.

And when kids spend little time interacting with family members because everybody's too busy watching TV, they suffer the most serious impoverishment of all.

It's estimated that in the average American home, the set is on for 6 hours and 48 minutes a day.

Urie Bronfenbrenner, Cornell University's expert on the family, helps us stand back and see the grip that TV has come to have on our family life:

> Like the sorcerer of old, the television set casts its magic spell, freezing speech and action and turning the living into silent statues so long as the enchantment lasts. The primary danger of the television screen lies not so much in the behavior it produces as the behavior it prevents—the talks, the games, the family festivities and arguments through which much of the child's learning takes place and his character is formed.[10]

One survey, cited in *Television and Movie Facts for Parents,* found that parents across the country "talk seriously" to their children less than 3 minutes a week!

It's a hard fact to face, but kids for whom TV is their constant companion may feel a stronger attachment to the tube than they do to us. In a study by Dr. Jung Bay Ra of Longwood College, Virginia, 44 percent of the 4- to 6-year-olds interviewed said they liked TV more than they liked their fathers. A few years ago, *Bill Moyers Journal* asked elementary-school-aged children, "If you had to give up one of these for the rest of your life, which would you give up: watching TV or talking to your father?" About half of the children answered, "Talking to my father."

"SO WHAT CAN I DO ABOUT TV?"

What can we do to keep TV from dominating our family life and taking over as our children's major moral teacher?

First, be mindful of the fact that watching begets watching. Research shows that parents who are heavy watchers tend to have children who are heavy watchers. Parents who are light watchers tend to have children who are light watchers.

Besides curbing your own TV behavior, how can you regulate your child's?

A St. Louis father invented the Plug-Lok (available in stores), a plastic device that fits over the plug end of the TV set's cord and locks on with a key. Since he started using the Plug-Lok, the father says, his son watches TV less and reads more.[11]

Some families have reduced TV viewing by keeping the set in a hard-to-get-at place, like a closet (definitely *not* in a child's bedroom). Some have quit altogether, cold turkey, retiring the set to an attic or basement graveyard.

Still other families have brought about the demise of TV by simply neglecting to repair a set on the blink, or taking it to the repair shop and leaving it there.

I've never heard of a family that wasn't delighted with the results of restricting or eliminating television in their home. Says one mother:

> "It was like an awakening. The children began to choose to play games. Randy, who had never really read any more than he had to, is now into novels. I became more involved in hobbies and community activities. I guess we all began to realize that our time is valuable and that we should spend it on things that are important to us."[12]

Single-parent mothers tell of their panic when the TV set broke right before a weekend and of marveling at their family's ability to survive and even flourish without it.

SHOULD YOU BE DEMOCRATIC ABOUT TV POLICY?

I don't think parents are obligated to be democratic about curtailing TV. Kids may be too hooked to see the wisdom or fairness of a decision that means giving up any of their shows. But I'd encourage you to at least try a family meeting about TV and see if you can get everybody's consent to a new approach. Here's a scenario:

1. Get your spouse to support you in an effort to limit TV; it's much easier to make a change if parents present a united front.

2. Keep a TV log for a week, recording who watches what for how long.

3. At a family meeting, share the results of your record-keeping, which will probably show more TV-watching in a week than even kids will attempt to justify.

4. Propose a "let's-see-what-happens" experiment: NO TV FOR 2 WEEKS. You can settle for one week if you can't swing two, but two is better because it provides a longer period for new patterns to evolve. You can make it a challenge, pointing out that this "pull-the-plug" experiment has been tried by many schools and families across the country, and they've been able to go the 2-week stretch.

5. Brainstorm other things you can do, individually and as a family, during the TV moratorium (see box on page 362 for possibilities). It helps to think of these alternatives-to-TV ahead of time, since some kids (and many parents!) actually show "withdrawal symptoms" (restlessness, irritability) when they're cut off from their daily dose of the tube. And post your list of possible activities on the refrigerator so kids can check for ideas when they "don't know what to do."[13]

6. Get together after the moratorium to assess the results of your no-TV experiment: "What did we each do with our time? How do you feel about life without TV?"

At this point, you may be one of those families who like their new life-style so much that they decide to kick the TV habit for good. Most families, however, aren't ready to bury the set, so

INSTEAD OF WATCHING TV . . .

1. Read (a book, a magazine, the paper), together or alone

2. Play (inside or out)

3. Exercise (take a walk, ride your bike, jog, play a sport)

4. Help with the housework or yardwork

5. Have a friend over, or visit a friend

6. Do a good deed for a neighbor

7. Do your homework

8. Practice a musical instrument

9. Listen to the radio, records, or tapes (tapes of old radio shows are great for stimulating imagination)

10. Finish an unfinished project

11. Play a board game

12. Work on a hobby

13. Cook something special together

14. Go to a movie, play, concert, or museum

15. Go on a hike or picnic

16. Go somewhere you've never been before

17. Visit someone who's sick or shut in

18. Write a letter to someone who'd like to hear from you

the next step is usually to work out a TV-on-a-limited-basis policy.

Here are various TV rules that different families have arrived at:

- No TV on school nights; 3 to 4 hours on weekends.
- No TV in the morning before school, and no TV during meals (one teacher's survey found that 50 percent of her children's families watched while they ate dinner).
- A daily maximum of *a half hour* for 2nd-graders and under, and a maximum of *1 hour* for 3rd-graders and up. (Some schools have helped parents out by sending a letter home asking families to follow these guidelines; subsequently, the schools find that students are less sleepy, concentrate better, and get along better with classmates.)
- A weekly maximum—such as 5 hours—for each family member.

The only problem with the last two strategies is that several family members watching different shows at different times means the set may be on much of the time! Then it becomes an enforcement hassle to make sure that Bobby isn't watching Kathy's program, etc. And TV is still fragmenting the family, pulling you away from shared activity.

I can tell you an approach that's worked fairly well for our family. When our kids were 4 and 9, we finally got to the point where we felt TV was controlling us rather than the other way around. There wasn't time to read to the kids before bed (they'd be watching TV up to the last minute); they were cranky and "logey" after Saturday cartoons (didn't feel like doing anything, work or play); my wife and I were wasting who-knows-how-many hours watching meaningless shows ourselves, and so on.

So we had a family meeting and agreed on a "specials only" policy that would hold for all of us. If there was going to be a "special" on—a "Charlie Brown" cartoon, a holiday special, a National Geographic program, a good documentary or docudrama—the interested family members could watch it.

The kids went along with this agreeably enough—it was the Christmas season, and there were plenty of specials coming up. But after Christmas the TV stayed off for weeks at a time, and nobody seemed to notice. We made exceptions to the specials policy when we lived in Boston for two years and the kids didn't have as much freedom to go out; then we allowed a couple of "regular" shows a week. We've also allowed TV while you're getting a haircut and when you're sick. Sometimes our kids will poach a little TV when we're not home or when they're at a friend's, and we have to insist on some selectivity when an occasional flood of "specials" comes along. But on the whole, this policy has worked for us.

MONITOR *WHAT* KIDS WATCH

Whatever restrictions you place on how much TV your kids see, I urge you to take a very strong stand on what they watch. If you're not sure what they're watching, watch with them. Ask yourself, "What values are they learning from this show? Is this what I want them to learn?"

I know how hard it can be to take away a TV show that a child loves. When Mark was 4, he was absolutely crazy about an afternoon cartoon called "Gigantor." It featured a little boy, Billy, who controlled a giant robot and used him to smash villains like invaders from outer space. We weren't happy about all the violence, but since Mark looked forward to it all day, we couldn't bring ourselves to "deprive" him. Until, that is, his nursery school teacher complained that Mark was constantly running up and down the classroom, arms outstretched in robot style, shouting "GI-GAN-*TOR*!" That got us to push the button. To our amazement, he didn't even seem to miss the show he had loved so much.

But what if your child wails, "All the *other* kids watch this show and talk about it at school! I won't even know what's going on!"

Hold the line. Here's a mother of 10- and 12-year-old boys who made that very plea to her:

> "The kids complained and said we weren't being fair when we wouldn't let them watch shows like 'The Dukes of Hazzard,' 'Dallas,' 'Three's Company,' and other programs that the kids at school all seem to watch. My husband and I told them that we're concerned about their minds and that we don't want them filling them with that kind of stuff.
>
> "They still complained, but then one day Brian said about one of his friends, 'His mother must not care very much about him, because he can watch anything he wants.' I said to myself, 'Well, that's progress.'"

If you have young children, keep in mind that studies find that children who watch shows like "Mr. Rogers" are less aggressive, more cooperative, and more imaginative than kids who watch a lot of action, cartoon, and game shows. And try to resist the temptation (to which we all have at least occasionally succumbed) to use TV as a babysitter. The formative preschool period is the best time to head off the TV addiction before it starts. If, during these years, you can establish habits of creative play, exercise, and reading (plunk them in a chair with a book instead of in front of the set), you'll be making a long-range contribution to your child's mental, moral, and physical development.

Many families have found particular shows—dealing with issues like divorce, friendship, drugs, stealing, prejudice, and parent-child conflict—to be a good catalyst for family discussion, especially with teenagers. One mother remembers watching a show about an elementary schoolteacher who taught his 6th-graders about Nazi Germany by running the classroom, on a trial basis, as a small Nazi-like society. "We talked about the moral questions that raised for weeks after," this mother says. Other families report stimulating dinner discussions after shows like "Holocaust" and "Roots." Programs of this sort, as I pointed out earlier in the book, can help a youngster develop a Stage 4 awareness of society and its moral problems.

My bias, though, is to keep TV from being a *regular* part of family life. With rare exceptions, even good TV, minute for minute, is not as valuable for either kids' development or family life as the creative, helpful, and productive things we do when we're not glued to the set.

Says a mother of three boys:

"When I told a friend that we were watching almost no TV anymore, she said, in a shocked way, 'Really? What do the kids *do*? Don't they fight a lot more?' I said that on the contrary, they fight less. They don't argue about who's going to watch what, and I don't have to keep hassling them to turn the set off. And there's not the constant background noise of the television. I can't believe the *peace*!"

So by taming the one-eyed dragon, we may reduce the battles that upset our homes. And we have a better chance of winning the most important battle: the one for our children's minds.

CHAPTER 17

SEX

Says Becky, a college sophomore:

"I started going steady when I was a junior in high school. My friends kept hounding me, 'What's wrong with you? Didn't you lose your virginity yet?' I just wasn't ready to have sex with my boyfriend—to me, it was a big thing. But finally I lied and said, 'Yes, I did.' It was the only way to get them to leave me alone."[1]

A mother overheard her 17-year-old son telling his older brothers about the terrible time he was having with a 16-year-old girl at school. She threatened to throw herself off a cliff if he didn't relieve her of her sexual frustrations. His brothers advised him to stop seeing the girl, and he did.[2]

Says Mary, a 15-year-old in an affluent suburban community:

"I was part of a group in junior high school that was into partying, hanging out, and drinking. I started to have sex with my boyfriend, and it was a real downer. It was totally against what I was, but it was important to be part of a group. Everybody was having sex. I couldn't handle the pressure."[3]

Commentators on social change in America speak of the rise of a "sexual fascism." This attitude puts enormous pressure on young people to get with it and go all the way. In the name of sexual liberation, it denies them the right to say no.

Even without direct peer pressure, however, teenagers would still face a whole host of influences that beckon them toward early sexual involvement. They live in a culture that uses sex to sell things. They see sex on TV. They see it graphically portrayed on the movie screen—sometimes between people their own age, often between persons who barely know each other. They hear it seductively promoted in popular songs like "Please Go All the Way," "Take Your Time (Do It Right)," and "Lay, Lady, Lay."

Whatever the reasons, teenage sexual activity has increased sharply, especially among girls.

- In 1980 two Johns Hopkins University professors, Drs. Melvin Zelnik and John Kanter, released the results of their study of the sexual behavior of 1,717 girls aged 15 to 19. They found that by 1979, 49.8 percent of girls in that age group had had premarital sex—compared to 30 percent in 1971, when they began their study.
- One-fifth of all 13- to 14-year-olds have had intercourse, according to a *Boston Globe* article on teenage pregnancy (August 5, 1979).
- According to Susan Cronewett, author of the California State Department of Education *Curriculum Guide for Sex Education in California Schools,* an estimated 1 in 10 California teenagers will have a case of venereal disease before finishing high school.
- One million teenage girls—one out of every 10—get pregnant each year, and 600,000 teenagers give birth each year. The number of illegitimate births to teenage mothers has more than doubled since 1960 and is increasing most rapidly for girls under 14 (source: *Newsweek*, September 1, 1980).

Certainly, not all young people are rushing into early and irresponsible sexual activity. But the trends are enough to make any parent worry—and to wonder how sexual morality changed so fast. It wasn't that long ago that sex was supposed to be something that happened between adults who had made an enduring commitment to each other—which usually meant people who were married. Sexual union was part of the total union between two persons. Sexual intercourse before marriage was wrong because it divorced sexual love from the lasting love relationship it was meant to express.

WHAT CAUSED THE "SEXUAL REVOLUTION"?

How did we get from "wait until marriage" to where we are now?

In part, widespread teenage sex is a legacy of the sixties. In that stormy decade adolescence emerged as a culture unto itself, hostile to adult authority and influence. The youth culture rejected the establishment ethic of "work today, enjoy tomorrow"; it wanted whatever adults had, including sex, now.

This general rebellion against authority also loosened the hold that religion had had over the sexual conscience of young people. When they stopped asking "Is this a sin?" a major impediment to premarital sex was removed.

But even before the sixties, a sexual revolution had been brewing in the country, and not just among the young. Some think it began with the studies of Alfred Kinsey in the late forties and early fifties. Kinsey shocked America with the first explicit, public discussion of sexual behavior—the sex histories of 18,000 persons—and revealed that many more people were doing many more things than anyone had supposed. Moreover, by their tolerant attitude toward nonaccepted sexual practices, Kinsey and his colleagues seemed to be saying (although it wasn't their intent), "All these sexual goings-on are okay." Moral questions were not raised and so seemed irrelevant.[4]

Kinsey was followed in the sixties by Masters and Johnson, who carried the detached, scientific study of sex a big step further. They actually observed and measured the physical responses of 700 human subjects during masturbation, artificial intercourse, and natural intercourse. Here was sex studied as a biological act—or, as Masters and Johnson put it, "a natural physiological process, comparable to other natural functions such as respiratory, bowel, or bladder function." The effect of Masters and Johnson, argue psychologists Robert Hogan and David Schroeder, was to amplify Kinsey's implied message: "sex can be regarded purely objectively"—you don't have to have any moral hang-ups about it.

Pop Freudian psychology added further to this "demoralization" of sex. People knew Freud had said "repression" is bad; it can mess up your mind. Translation: If you have sexual impulses, better not repress them. Let it all hang out.

Few people realized, however, that this interpretation confused "repression" with "suppression." A *repressed* thought or desire, Freud said, is one which is pushed into the unconscious, usually at an early age, because it's too painful to bear—and which may erupt in later development in the form of a neurosis. A *suppressed* desire, by contrast, is one which is consciously controlled or resisted, like a temptation. Suppression is healthy; repression is not.

What Freud advocated was *talking* about our sexual instincts (which the Victorians he saw in therapy were afraid to do), not indiscriminately acting upon them. He saw sexual self-control as essential for civilization. A proper respect for the power of sex has in fact traditionally led cultures all over the world to establish moral rules about sexual behavior. But Freud's real message got garbled along the way, and the fuzzy thinking that "it's bad for you to 'repress' your sexual urges" became another ally in the sexual revolution.

Finally, the pleasure-now hedonism that had been the trademark of the youth culture became a cultural norm for a large part of adult society as well. You only go around once, so get all you can. That applied to sex, along with everything else.

As a result of all these cultural changes, sex and morality, once so closely identified, have become completely separate in many people's minds. Sex for some persons has become a kind of "moral free zone"[5] where anything goes. And worst of all, this kind of thinking has worked its way into literature for kids. One book for teenagers, for example, flatly states—as if it were a virtue—its intention to treat sex "without moral judgment." It then goes on to describe casual teen sex, serious sex, sex with others, sex with yourself, sex with the opposite sex, sex with the same sex, saying yes, saying no, "waiting" for religious reasons, waiting because you're too busy right now to sleep around—all served up to the young reader, cafeteria style, with the advice: "Trust your own feelings . . . do what feels right for *you*."

I don't think many parents are terribly happy with that message as a guide for their growing children. A national poll commissioned by *Time* magazine a few years ago asked adults of all ages, races, and religions, "Is it morally wrong for teenagers to have sex relations?" Sixty-three percent said yes, it's morally wrong. Among those over 35, the condemnation rose to 76 percent.

Most parents sense, correctly, that kids desperately need moral guideposts that tell them *not* to yield to their every sexual desire. They know, too, with a moment's thought, that telling teenagers to "trust your own feelings" in matters of sex is poor advice for two reasons. First, most teens are at a time in their moral development, Stage 3, when their feelings (wanting to be accepted, liked, considered "normal") make them *highly vulnerable to peer pressure.* Telling them to trust these feelings is throwing them to the wolves of their developmental weaknesses. Second, common sense tells us that when sexual desire is running strong, "feelings" are the *last* thing to trust as a guide to a wise decision. "It feels so right, it can't be wrong" is exactly the kind of thinking that has gotten many a teenager (and many an adult) into a jam that less emotional moral judgment may have kept him or her out of.

HOW CAN PARENTS HELP KIDS DEVELOP RESPONSIBLE ATTITUDES TOWARD SEX?

What can we do as parents to help our children develop morally responsible attitudes toward their sexuality?

Let me start with some don'ts.

1. **Don't cop out.** Avoiding the whole issue is a great temptation. We may be uncomfortable talking with our kids about sex, and it's easy to say, "They'll cover that stuff in school." The fact is, though, that most schools still do little or no sex education. And school can't do adequately what you can do in the home—teach a clear moral framework for guiding sexual behavior.

Right now, if the statistics are to be believed, most of us aren't teaching kids the bare facts about sex, let alone values. A study of 1,400 parents of teenage girls in Cleveland, for example, found that 60 percent of mothers had never explained menstruation to their daughters and 92 percent had never discussed sex. Another study, called the Gilbert Youth Survey, found that only 1 out of 8 families teach their children any kind of sex information at all—and most of those that do, talk about plants and animals instead of human beings!

We may think that kids today "know it all" about sex, but even in this day and age great numbers are abysmally ignorant. And very often it's the kids who experiment earliest with sex who are found to be the least informed about physiology and reproduction. Author Grace Naismith cites the case of a girl who had sex with her boyfriend and then sneaked one of her mother's birth control pills in the belief that it would keep her from getting pregnant. Another young girl who got pregnant said, "I thought it was safe if we did it standing up."

If you need any extra motivation to get off the dime and talk with your kids, keep in mind a study cited by sex counselors Phillip and Lorna Sarrel: Teenagers whose parents discussed sex openly with them were more likely to postpone sexual involvement than those whose parents never talked with them.

2. **Don't wait till the teens to talk about sex.** It'll be much easier for both you and your teenager to talk about sex if it's been an open subject all along. It's important, for example, to talk with a girl about ovulation, menstrual discharge, breast growth, and the like sometime around 10 years of age, *before* these things happen to her. Similarly, it's helpful to talk with a boy about hair growth, voice changes, onset of the ability to ejaculate, wet dreams, etc., before they happen to him. The same thing goes for the topic of intercourse—it's a lot easier to discuss with kids for the first time if you do it before they're embroiled in the self-consciousness and sexual development of the early teens.

And sex education shouldn't always be the kind of hushed-tones, high-drama affair where the parent takes the child aside and announces solemnly, "There's something I've been meaning to talk to you about." A good deal of sex education can go on in the living room or around the dinner table. A magazine article about teenage sex, a TV documentary about unwed mothers, a movie or TV show whose sexual values you take issue with, a girl at school who got pregnant—lots of things can serve as a springboard for talking about sex in the same natural way that you talk about other matters of interest and concern.

With young children and preteens, you may find that sitting down and reading a good "facts of life" book for youngsters is a comfortable door-opener to discussion. Ask your librarian or pediatrician to suggest some books that would be appropriate for your child's age. I'd recommend, however, that you carefully read any facts-about-sex book yourself before sharing it with your child. Ask yourself, "Does this book support or at least not contradict what I think is a sound moral attitude toward sexuality?"

3. **Don't think it's ever too late.** If your son or daughter is 15, going steady, and you haven't said boo about sex until now, better late than never. If you feel awkward about broaching the subject, say so: "Listen, I've made a mistake in not talking with you sooner, and I feel funny about bringing it up now. But I'll feel a lot better if I talk to you about this. . . ." One way to make it a conversation instead of a lecture is to ask some questions: "I'm curious to know what they're teaching in school about sex, babies, boy-girl relationships. . . . What do you discuss in health class?" Or, "What are kids saying these days? Do they put pressure on each other to get sexually involved? In my day there was a lot of bragging about who did what with whom—do you hear any of that?"

4. **Don't send mixed messages.** The mother who says to her 16-year-old daughter, "I don't think you should have sex, but just in case, I'm going to get you a prescription for the pill" is sending two messages: "Don't," and "I expect you to." The literature on adolescent sex is full of stories of young girls, outfitted with birth control by "enlightened" mothers, who look back with regret. "I wish I had waited until I met someone I really cared for," says Martha, who went on the pill and lost her virginity at 14.[6]

5. **Don't fall into a "biology is destiny" mentality.** Many parents think, "They hit puberty at 12—how can we expect them to wait till they're married?" But plenty of young people *are* waiting. And even if your child doesn't wait until marriage, you may be able to tip the scales in favor of delaying sexual involvement until a mature relationship comes along.

6. **Don't communicate a green-light attitude toward sex because you don't want your child to feel "guilty."** True, a lot of us were taught about sex in ways that made us feel guilty about things that now seem positively innocent. So it's understandable that some parents favor sexual freedom for kids, thinking, "I don't want them to have to suffer through the hang-ups I had." But there's a middle ground: we can advocate responsible self-control regarding sex without heaping on the guilt.

7. **Don't think that what's okay for you is okay for kids.** We read stories these days that make our toes curl: like the one about the mother who rented a motel room for her 17-year-old daughter and her boyfriend so their first sexual experience would be "nice," or the parents who invited their teenage son's 17-year-old girl friend to join them on an extended motor trip and got the kids their own room when they stopped overnight at motels. But even parents who don't push kids into sex may have a permissive attitude toward it because they think, "How can I discourage my child from enjoying something I think is normal and good?"

The answer is that what's good for adults isn't necessarily good for kids. There *should* be a double standard for adults and kids in matters of sex. Many adults have all they can do to handle the feelings and responsibilities that go with sexual involvement; such feelings and responsibilities can easily overwhelm immature young people.

Thinking "what's right for me must be right for my child" keeps some parents from even discussing sex with their children. A divorced mother, for example, says:

> "Although we've never discussed it, my 16-year-old daughter knows I've had affairs. I'd rather she did not get involved in sex for a while, but I feel almost embarrassed to tell her that. She might bring up *my* sex life, and I don't know how I'd deal with that."[7]

The way to deal with her daughter's challenge would be to say:

> "Look, I'm an adult and you're not. That makes all the difference. So what goes for me doesn't go for you. Some day you might be in my shoes talking to your daughter. And you'll want her to understand that she doesn't need sex in her life when she's 16 years old."

8. **Don't think, "I fooled around when I was a kid—I'd feel like a hypocrite if I told my teenage son or daughter not to!"**
First of all, compared to our generation, kids today clearly face a greater push, from their peer group and the whole society, to experiment sexually. Because they're more vulnerable, they have a greater need for support, for sound reasons from an adult

they love and respect why they should resist those pressures. If your youngster confronts you with the question, "What did *you* do when you were a teenager?"—and you did have some sexual experiences you now think better of—you can say:

> "What I did isn't necessarily right or what you should do. I made a lot of mistakes when I was young. The older you get, the more you know what's good for you. That's why I'm advising you to wait until you're an adult to make these decisions."

9. **Finally, don't be overrestrictive.** That says to teenagers, "I don't trust you—you can't handle any responsibility." They may rebel against your authority and then live down to your worst expectations. Clinical psychologist Daniel Sugarman tells the story of Anne, a 17-year-old girl whose parents hemmed her in with rules. She had to come home immediately after school; she couldn't date. One day she ran away from home and hitchhiked to the next city. Her first pickup took her to a motel, and nine months later she had his baby.[8] Sexual "acting out" on the part of some teenage girls is really rebellion against overcontrolling parents. If we treat teenagers like children, they may do something to prove we *can't* control them.

So much for the *don'ts*. What are the *dos*?

First, remember that kids are whole people. Their sexual values and behavior will, to a considerable extent, reflect the total person they are. That means if we're doing a good job to raise kids who, in general, are considerate of others, honest with themselves, open to our influence, and emotionally secure about who they are, chances are that these qualities will carry over into the realm of sexual behavior as well. That's a reason to relax a little.

Second, decide what you want to communicate to kids about sex, love, marriage, and morals. Parents are obviously going to differ about the particulars, just as our kids may end up thinking somewhat differently from us. But I think there are some core ideas that most of us believe in enough to want to pass on to our children. Here are the ones that I would nominate:

1. **Sex is good.** That's the starting point. Kids won't listen to our admonitions about sex if they think we regard it as something dirty. If you're a religious family, you can point out that "sex was

God's idea, not ours."[9] It's part of His plan for us, part of what causes us to bond together, raise families, and carry on the race. It's also a part of our individual human personality, part of the way we express our personhood. But, like everything else that's good in creation, sex can be abused. Here's the place to be up front about whatever religious beliefs you hold about sex and marriage. For example, one father, a Catholic, said to his 14-year-old son:

> "It's pretty old-fashioned these days to talk about waiting until marriage to have sexual relations. Chastity is an unpopular virtue, because it's hard. Even St. Augustine, who was quite a lady's man in his youth, is supposed to have prayed, 'Lord, make me chaste—but not just yet!'
>
> "Jesus made it pretty clear in the Gospels that sexual intercourse is for married people. He said that a man and wife are to be considered 'one flesh,' one in spirit, one in body. Married persons remain separate individuals, of course, in that they have different thoughts and personalities, but in a very deep way, they're united. And the trouble with intercourse before marriage is that it separates sexual union from the total union that it's meant to be part of. When sex is part of marriage, it's part of something that's holy and blessed by God.
>
> "Of course, I can tell you these things, but ultimately it's between you and God. Think about it, pray about it, and He'll help you know and do what's right."

2. Sex is a continuum. Most discussions—this one included—use "sex" as shorthand for "sexual intercourse." But the dictionary gives "intercourse" as the fifth meaning of sex; before that it defines sex as "the attraction drawing one sex toward another" and the "manifestation of that attraction in life and conduct."

I think it helps young people to think of sex in this broader sense—as a continuum. From this perspective, sexual feeling and expression are not an all-or-nothing proposition; they're a dimension of a relationship that increases gradually with each stage in the relationship. Using this framework, you can say to your child (regardless of what your religious views are):

> "Look, it's only one end of the continuum—sexual intercourse and the kind of intimate touching and love-making that are a natural prelude to intercourse—that you shouldn't get involved

with now. That's a very special kind of intimacy meant for a very special relationship, one that's for keeps. You make yourself very vulnerable when you make love with someone, you give yourself completely, so you need to be as sure as you can be of that person's love.

"That's why people have always said, 'Wait until marriage.' When two people get married, when they make that kind of public and lasting commitment to each other, they're as sure as they can be of each other's love. They join their bodies because they've joined their lives.

"In the meantime, you're free to enjoy the rest of the continuum—from holding hands to snuggling to holding and kissing someone you've come to care for. The emotional and sexual feelings that accompany those forms of affection are healthy and good, and don't let anybody tell you you're missing out on the big time. *They're* the ones who are missing out. You'll have moments and memories of tenderness and innocence and romance that they'll never have. Savor them.

"You may regret being sexually intimate too soon, but you'll never regret waiting."

3. **No matter what your religious beliefs, the decision to have sexual relations is a serious moral decision.** Whatever you say and whatever kids decide about "waiting," they should understand that the decision to be sexually intimate with someone may have profound consequences, for themselves and their partner. That makes it a *moral* decision.

There are, for example, very real risks involved in premarital sexual relations.

• The girl can get pregnant, even with birth control (which an estimated 75 percent of sexually active teenagers don't use[10]). Eighty percent of school-age girls who get pregnant never finish high school. Only 40 percent marry the father, and they are twice as likely as any other group to get divorced. Teenage mothers are seven times as likely to attempt suicide as teenage girls without children.

• Either the boy or the girl can get one of more than a dozen sexually transmitted diseases that may involve severe pain and injury. Teenagers should know that if you are sexually intimate with another person, and that person has a venereal disease, you stand to catch it. Untreated venereal disease can cause sterility in *both* males and females (and that happens to 16,000 teenagers a year). Young people should know, in particular, about the increasing danger of herpes, which now afflicts an estimated 20 million Americans (compared to 5 million just three years ago). You can get herpes through a single contact, and once you get it, you have it for life.

• Either the boy or the girl can get emotionally hurt, especially the girl. It's not fashionable these days to talk about differences between the sexes, but people who work with teenage boys and girls (for example, psychiatrist Beverly T. Mead, writing in *Medical Aspects of Human Sexuality*) report that males and females do in fact tend to have different expectations regarding sexual encounters. Teenage girls—and there are, of course, exceptions—tend to think of sexual intimacy in stereotypical Stage 3 terms: as "a way to show you care." Teenage boys—and again, there are exceptions—tend to take an opportunistic, Stage 2 approach to sex: as a chance for pleasure and "scoring." (Those of us who have sons should, of course, explicitly and repeatedly repudiate this exploitative attitude toward sex, and teach them to treat any girl with the same respect they'd want a boy to show their own daughter if they had one.) The girl who expects a sexual interlude to be tender and loving may feel cheated or used, especially if the boy doesn't show a greater romantic interest in her after the experience. Often, he doesn't—and may even head in the opposite direction. "I never expected the guy to marry me," says a 14-year-old girl in San Francisco, "but I never expected he would avoid me in school."[11]

Girls should know that even in later years they may have very different expectations of sexual intimacy—and hence much more vulnerability—than their boyfriends. Jane, a University of Arizona graduate interviewed by journalists Kenneth and Betty Woodward, says, "I told myself I was going to stay a virgin until I was married." But once in college, she found the pressures more than she could resist. Finally, she says, "I met somebody I thought I loved enough to give up my virginity for. But the whole time we made love the TV was on. And when it was over, he just switched to another channel and lit up a joint. God, was I angry! Here I had made the ultimate sacrifice, and he didn't even care. I was hoping through the whole thing that he'd say, 'I love you.'"

Many studies, according to sex counselors Howard and Martha Lewis, show that a large percentage of women who had premarital intercourse expected to marry their partners. Only a small percentage of men had the same expectation.

Girls who feel betrayed after sexual intercourse may experience two kinds of emotional repercussions: lowered self-esteem and difficulty with future relationships. Trust, once badly shaken, may be hard to rebuild.

• There's another risk that requires the perspective of maturity to realize: *premature sexual involvement can hinder a youngster's development as a person.*

Sex can be emotional dynamite. For teenagers, who tend to be intensely emotional anyway, a sexual relationship can easily become obsessive, filling their lives.

I think of a 17-year-old girl who wrote to "Dear Abby" not long ago. She said she and her first cousin "discovered early the difference between the sexes, and experimented with that difference frequently." They started when they were 13, went all the way when they were 15, and kept their passionate love affair a secret until recently, when they were discovered by a parent in bed together. The girl wrote Abby that they wanted to get married and signed herself "Lovers for Sure."

You don't have to be a psychologist to imagine the hold that this secret sexual love had on these youngsters, the spell that it cast, the easy security it gave them during the difficult teen years. They had a haven, a port in the storm. Just as some teens handle anxiety by turning to drugs, they could handle theirs by turning to each other and sex. They weren't learning other ways to cope with life's pressures.

Teenagers who are absorbed in, preoccupied with, an intense sexual relationship are turning inward on one thing at the very time in their young lives when they should be reaching out—trying new experiences, forming new relationships, exploring new ideas, developing interests and skills, taking on wider social responsibilities. All these things are important nutrients for their development as persons—including their moral development, and the developing they do during these years will affect them all their lives. We should help kids to think of their teens in this way, and to want to develop their full potential.

Girls should bear in mind, too, that the risk of closing the door on other interests and relationships is likely to be greater for them. Says New York psychiatrist Samuel Kaufman: "A girl who enters into a serious relationship with a boy very early in life may find out later that her individuality was thwarted. She became part of him and failed to develop her own interests, her sense of independent identity."[12]

Most teenagers, surveys show, subscribe to the popular idea that "any kind of sexual activity is okay as long as you're not hurting anybody." What kids often fail to realize, however, is that there's more to the question "Am I hurting anyone?" than meets the eye. It's our job to open their eyes to all the possible consequences—short-range and long-range, for themselves and their partners—of premarital sexual involvement.

Finally, there's another very important moral dimension of any sexual relationship, and that's mutual respect and consent. Says one father:

> "I tell my kids that sex is an adult act, and any time it's not part of an adult relationship, it's wrong. And if two adults are thinking of becoming sexually involved, they need to ask themselves two questions: Am I respecting the other person, or am I acting self-ishly? And is this a completely free decision, or is either person feeling pressure to go along?"

4. **You have the right to say no.** A Boston study found that in a group of pregnant teenagers, many began sexual relations because they were tired of being teased by peers about still being virgins.[13] College men these days report a new campus phenomenon: girls ask them if they're impotent or gay if they don't try to get them into bed after the second date. Kids should know in advance that they may very well face these pressures, either from their peer group or a partner. And they should know that they'll feel better about themselves, not worse, when they exercise their right to say no. If the other person doesn't respect their feelings, well, then he or she is not the person for them.

5. **Losing your virginity is no sign of maturity.** Just the opposite is usually the case with teenagers. It's the kids who are *least* mature who turn to sexual involvement as a security blanket—something that makes them feel needed or grown-up or part of the group. Kids who are developing a mature independence don't need sex to feel like somebody; they already value themselves highly.

6. **Everybody's *not* doing it.** Most teenagers, even those who are independent enough to resist the crowd, are still in the period of their moral development where they worry, "Am I normal? Is there anybody else who's like me?" They still need the reassurance that there's not something wrong with them, and they're not alone, if they remain virgins. So I think it's important to let them know that, in fact, they have plenty of company.

In 1981 the Alan Guttmacher Institute published a report titled *Teen-Age Pregnancy: The Problem That Hasn't Gone Away.* Although the report emphasizes the increase in teen sexual activity and its consequences, the data show that sexual intercourse among high-schoolers is far from a universal phenomenon. Among 15- to 17-year-old males, for example, more than half are *not* sexually active, and among females, two thirds are *not* sexually active. Other studies show that the incidence of sexual relations is significantly lower for college-bound students than it is for the general population of young people (most statistics on teenage sex don't make this kind of breakdown and therefore can create the false impression that all groups of young people are equally sexually active). Moreover, Dr. Laurna Rubinson of the University of Illinois reports that at least among the 18- to 19-year-olds she has studied, college students today are *less* sexually active than their predecessors in the early 1970s. Finally, even within a particular group like "college-bound students," there's great variation in sexual behavior. Everybody in some social circles may indeed be "doing it," but in other social circles almost everybody may be playing it cool (and, in the wake of the herpes epidemic, the percentage choosing to play it cool is likely to grow).

Obviously, widespread sexual activity among immature young people is a very real and serious problem. But the point I want to make here is this: All the talk that makes it sound as if nobody's a virgin appears to be just that—talk. Just as in the old days people were reluctant to admit losing their virginity, today most are reluctant to admit keeping it. But kids should know that there are in fact lots of people like the young woman at the University of North Carolina who said:

"I've been taught to think for myself. I lead a happy, satisfying life without sex. I can handle a deep relationship that does not include going to bed. It's not that I'm saving *myself* for marriage. I'm saving my emotions for marriage."[14]

7. **Sex is not the most important part of a love relationship.** Syracuse University's Sol Gordon asked married couples to rank the 10 most important things in a marriage relationship. "Caring," "a sense of humor," and "communication" came in 1st, 2nd, and 3rd. "Sex" came in 9th, just ahead of "sharing household duties."

Adults know that going to bed isn't the main event in a successful love relationship. Teenagers should know it, too. They should know that real intimacy in a relationship, like real friendship, grows slowly and takes a lot of getting to know the other person. Sex can actually get in the way of that.

When you communicate these or other ideas to kids (obviously not all in one sitting), don't take a hard-sell approach that assumes you're going to get resistance. Kids may be glad to get some clear ways of thinking about sex and some support for resisting peer pressure. If they do argue against your "old fashioned" views, give them some room. Author Elizabeth Tener interviewed Leigh, a woman in her early twenties, who remembered how her mother gave her space to think:

"I was a pretty stubborn kid. I sometimes took the opposite point of view just to be difficult. One day when a conversation about sex was heating up, Mom stopped short. 'Look,' she said, 'things may be different today, but your father and I arrived at our beliefs through a lot of thought and experience. If you decide they're not for you, well, you've got to lead your own life. But don't toss our ideas out without thinking.' I'll never forget what she said. It made me see that rebellion for the sake of rebellion is rather childish."[15]

WHAT SHOULD YOU SAY ABOUT BIRTH CONTROL?

Many parents feel they should talk to their teenagers about birth control. Their reasoning: If kids decide to be sexually active, they should know how to reduce the chances of pregnancy or contracting a sexually transmitted disease.

Many parents, however, sense correctly that talking matter-of-factly to teens about using contraceptives undermines a parent's advocacy of abstinence. It's like saying, "Don't get sexually involved for all the reasons we've discussed, but I'm afraid you will, so here's a way to do it safely."

The birth control issue is also complicated by the fact that different people have different religious convictions about this matter. Some religions hold that artificial birth control separates the procreative and unitive aspects of sexual love and is therefore contrary to God's design. Other religions do not prohibit artificial birth control within marriage. If you have religious convictions about this issue, you'll want to discuss them with your child.

"Why shouldn't we have sex if we have protection?" is a question many teens have—and one that can be answered from a moral perspective regardless of a parent's particular religious beliefs. Using contraceptives does not make sex outside a committed relationship morally responsible. That's because the girl can still get pregnant—condoms have a 10% failure rate in preventing pregnancy—and the protection condoms provide against AIDS may be considerably lower. Moreover, condoms do nothing whatsoever to make sex emotionally safe. People can still get hurt in deep and lasting ways. Kids need to know that.

Make sure that your kids also know that, regardless of your feelings about sex, you want them to come to you, *no matter what happens.* One mother said to her daughter, "No matter what you do, no matter how terrible you might think it is, I want you to feel that you can come and talk to me about it." And to make her point she added, "Even if you were to kill somebody."

And when kids do get in trouble, we need to be there for them. Peggy, a woman in her early thirties, remembers how her mother was there for her:

> "Once in high school I thought I was pregnant. My mother discovered my dilemma when she overheard me talking to a friend on the phone.
> "Her immediate reaction was to take me for a pregnancy test. On the way, she discussed alternatives to going away to college if I was pregnant. I could go to one closer to home, for example. At

work that afternoon I received a vase of flowers. The card said simply, 'I love you. Mother.'

"Though I knew she was terribly disappointed, not once did she say any words of judgment. Her conversation was both practical and sympathetic.

"I will never forget this. I want to try to be as understanding, loving, and forgiving with my own children."

WHAT ABOUT LIVING TOGETHER?

Estimates vary, but surveys generally indicate that about 1 in 5 young people today will at some time live with a member of the opposite sex without being married.

People decide to live together for different reasons. Some prefer an "emotional commitment" to the legal commitment of marriage; some are turned off to marriage because of the high divorce rate; others see living together as a kind of a "trial marriage."

You may feel that living together is a sensible thing for young people to do in this day and age, as long as they're both mature and they genuinely love each other. However, if your son or daughter is thinking about entering into this kind of relationship and you *don't* approve, be honest about your feelings, but in a way that respects your child's right to lead his or her own life. You could say something like this:

"You know how I feel about marriage, but you're obviously old enough to make your own decisions about these things. All I can ask of you at this stage of your life—and I do it out of love—is that you think very carefully about what you're doing and that you go into it with your eyes open.

"It's helpful to know, I think, that people who live together usually don't end up staying together. Studies show that 2 out of 3 couples split up. And those who do get married are just as likely to get divorced as those who don't live together. So it's not really a trial marriage that guarantees you won't make a mistake. People who live together and then get married will tell you that, psychologically, it's very different to be married. It's a commitment.

"Living together doesn't involve that kind of commitment, of course; either person is free to leave. And while that freedom may seem like a good thing before you're in the relationship, it can actually be quite a burden once you're in it. People who live together have two questions hanging over their heads: Will the other person stay or leave? Do *I* want to stay in the relationship? It's a subtle but very real pressure.[16]

"So ask yourself, 'What do I really expect to gain by living together? Do I want to be intimate without having the security of a lasting relationship? Am I willing to risk getting hurt?'

"Whatever decision you make, I don't want it to come between us. You know that I'll love you and wish the best for you no matter what. And if you go ahead and it doesn't work out, I'll never say, 'I told you so.'"

What if your unmarried 20-year-old son wants to sleep with his girl friend in your house and you don't approve? Some people feel hypocritical if they prohibit in the home what they know is going on outside the home anyway. I think just the opposite is true: it's hypocritical if you feel one way (you disapprove) and act another (you pretend you don't). If you don't approve of premarital sexual relations, you can say, matter-of-factly,

"Look, what you do outside the house is your business. But you know I don't approve of sex before marriage, so I can't be comfortable with that in my own house. So if you wish to have Shari stay overnight, it'll have to be in separate rooms. If that feels hypocritical to you, then maybe you'd rather not have her stay over. I'll leave that up to you."

With matters like this, as with other problems in parent-child relations, there are moral issues—rights and obligations—for everybody to be aware of. You have an obligation to respect your child's autonomy as a young adult, but a right to expect respect for your own feelings. Your child has a right to control his own life, but an obligation to do that without infringing on you.

MASTURBATION

Said a mother of a six-year-old: "I'm not sure how I should respond to my son's touching himself. I'd rather he didn't develop a habit of doing this, but I don't want to give him negative feelings about his sexuality."

Masturbation or any kind of genital self-stimulation is something many parents aren't comfortable dealing with. Some parents remember being told as children that masturbating would make you blind or crazy, and they wouldn't consider using that kind of fear or guilt approach with their own child. But at the same time they feel intuitively that in this area of sexuality, as in others, some kinds of limits are desirable.

Here are some general guidelines:

During infancy and toddlerhood, most children engage in some genital self-stimulation. This is normal curiosity, part of exploring their bodies. To keep self-stimulation from becoming a compulsive habit, you can casually divert your child to another activity. During the preschool years, most parents teach children that it's not polite to touch themselves when other people are around (it's embarrassing).

Beyond that, how a parent handles masturbation depends a lot on personal values. Sexual self-stimulation during childhood and the teens is certainly common behavior, not something a parent should react to with alarm or disgust. But even while understanding that, many parents want to gently encourage their child to resist this temptation. The reason may be religious—the belief that sex is meant by God to be relational, an expression of love between two persons. From this perspective, as one father explained to his thirteen-year-old son, "The problem with masturbation is that it's sex with yourself."

There are also psychological considerations: (1) Once masturbation becomes a habit, it's hard to stop. That habit may lessen a child's feelings of self-control and self-respect. (2) Some kids use masturbation as a way to escape emotions of anxiety and depression, and end up feeling worse because the problem is still there. (3) If kids regularly indulge in *self-stimulation*, they aren't developing the sexual self-control that they'll need when they begin heterosexual relationships.

PORNOGRAPHY

It's no secret that teenage boys like to look at pictures of naked women. That's normal. (Most girls do not show a reciprocal interest.)

At the same time, however, I don't agree with the idea that this sort of thing is a "healthy outlet" for sexual curiosity which parents should cheerfully ignore. In the first place, at least for a teenage boy, erotic photographs or literature can greatly stimulate sexual thoughts or desires at the very time when those are hardest to control. If kids are going to exercise self-control, they don't need to do anything to stoke the fires.

Second, magazines like *Playboy* and *Penthouse* teach boys that women are sex objects, not persons, and are to be packaged and marketed for the pleasure of men. That's the same attitude that underlies prostitution. It's also an attitude that explains in part why a lot of men aren't terribly upset by women being raped or beaten. So, if we want our sons to respect women, we should make very clear our disapproval of anything that exploits them. And both sons and daughters should learn that sex in general should never be exploited, never be used to demean the dignity of any person. Sex should enhance our humanity, not diminish it.

Some sex magazines are worse than exploitative; they're just plain sick. One father found, on his 14-year-old son's desk, a small, slick magazine with "true story" articles glorifying everything from group sex to incest. Tim said he got it from a friend. Tim's father said, calmly but seriously:

> "Tim, I know how tempting it can be to read this stuff. I read some of it when I was young, and it's very powerful. It gets in your head, in your bloodstream, almost like a poison. And this is much worse than anything I ever read. It's sick, really. It completely separates sex from love. It's exciting when you first read it, but when you're done you have a crummy feeling and sex seems like something dirty and subhuman rather than something beautiful and good, which it's meant to be. So believe me, you'll feel better about yourself and better about sex if you stay away from stuff like this."

Whatever aspect of sex we're talking to kids about, the basic themes are the same: It's natural and it's good, but it has a place and a purpose. It's an area of their lives where they should seek conscientiously to live out the same values that govern the rest of their lives. And it's an area we need to talk with our children about—not once, but many times as they experience new stages in this dimension of their growth toward personal and moral maturity.

CHAPTER 18

DRUGS AND DRINKING

There's good news about drug use among teenagers: it seems to be declining. And according to a recent study by the National Institute on Drug Abuse (NIDA), the proportion of high school seniors who think their close friends do *not* approve of smoking marijuana has risen to 72 percent.

But there's bad news, too.

- America's teenagers "still show the highest level of drug use of young people anywhere in the industrialized world," according to the NIDA.
- A recent book estimates that a large majority of kids over 10 try drugs, primarily marijuana.
- Pot is more potent than ever before. NIDA says that marijuana samples confiscated by police 5 years ago rarely exceeded 1 percent THC (the primary psychoactive ingredient in pot). Samples from today's drug market show THC levels as high as 5 and 6 percent.
- Contrary to previous beliefs, new evidence from NIDA shows that regular marijuana use *does* often lead to hard drugs such as cocaine or heroin, and that heavy pot smoking has a "significant relationship" with crime.
- Contrary to earlier beliefs, even light-to-moderate marijuana use may be dangerous to health.

Item: One joint of marijuana inflames the lungs as much as an entire pack of cigarettes.

Item: In July 1978, 50 researchers from 14 countries gathered at the International Symposium on Marijuana in Reims, France, to present new findings that marijuana is harmful to the reproductive organs, the lungs, cellular metabolism, and the brain.

Item: In July 1981, the American Medical Association issued a new statement about marijuana:

> There is now no doubt that marijuana is a dangerous drug. . . . Target organ for marijuana is the brain. . . . Acute marijuana intoxication impairs learning, memory, and general intellectual performance. Even at moderate levels of use, driving skills are impaired. . . . Chronic use of marijuana may be associated with disruption of the menstrual cycle and at least temporary infertility. . . . Regular use may seriously interfere with psychological functioning, personality development, and emotional growth, especially in childhood and adolescence. Psychological damage may be permanent. . . . Even moderate use is associated with psychoses, panic states, and with adolescent personality disorders.

Marijuana's greatest threat is to the brain and reproductive organs.

Investigator Peggy Mann tells the story of "Steven," a teenager who came in 1976 to Dr. Robert C. Gilkeson of Cleveland, a psychiatrist and marijuana researcher. Steven complained of poor grades—he had been a good student—and of trouble concentrating and remembering things. He said: "Everything I used to like has become a drag. Even chicks. I feel bummed out all the time."

Dr. Gilkeson discovered reversed *d*s and *b*s in Steven's handwriting, so he recommended an electroencephalogram (EEG)—a brain-wave test. The results: Steven's brain waves were "markedly immature," typical of those of a 6- to 8-year-old.

Steven admitted to being a chronic (near-daily) pot smoker. The psychiatrist advised him to give it up for two months. He agreed to do so.

In two months his EEG still wasn't normal; but, said Dr. Gilkeson, there was real improvement in Steven's grades, mood, memory, humor, and speech patterns. Encouraged, Steven stayed off pot for another two months—and his EEG returned to normal.

Steven's cure spurred Dr. Gilkeson to give EEG's to 69 other teenagers who had smoked pot at least twice a week for the previous two months (but not for 48 hours preceding the test). The results: All 69 EEG's, like Steven's, were markedly immature and revealed diffuse brain impairment.[1]

Teenagers told of studies like these might dismiss them as "scare tactics" unless they understand how marijuana works in the body. Marijuana contains 61 cannabinoids—substances found exclusively in the cannabis plant. The main psychoactive (mind-altering) cannabinoid is delta-9-tetrahydrocannabinol (THC). THC, like other cannabinoids, is soluble in fat.

Alcohol, which is dangerous for other reasons, is soluble in water, so the body gets rid of it through urine and sweat in a matter of hours. But THC, being fat-soluble, goes straight for the body organs, like the brain and the testes and ovaries, that are high in fatty tissue. It enters the cells of these organs—and stays there for an astonishingly long time. Radioactive tracing shows that it takes up to a week for just half the THC in a single joint to clear from the body. The rest of the THC from that one joint may still be present weeks later.

What's the THC doing while it sits there in the brain cells?

Brain work on rhesus monkeys offers a clue. When the monkeys were exposed to enough marijuana smoke (a quarter of a joint) to produce the THC blood level that a human gets from one joint, their brain cells showed striking changes. The "cleft" (opening) between neurons got wider and started to fill in with abnormal deposits of opaque material. Said Dr. Robert Heath, the Tulane Medical School professor of neurology who did the research: "This condition may cause a slowing down or interruption in the movement of brain messages."[2] Small wonder that pot smokers seem "spacey"—or that University of British Columbia tests show a 42 percent decline in driving skills after one marijuana cigarette and a 63 percent decline after two.

Research on both animal and human males finds that THC intake is associated with lowered sperm count and a greater number of abnormally shaped sperm. In 1974 Dr. Gabriel Nahas of the Columbia University College of Physicians and Surgeons discovered that THC inhibits formation of DNA, the genetic material that tells the body's cells how to grow. DNA damage can mean abnormal offspring. Says Dr. Nahas, whose findings have been replicated in other countries: "Today's pot smoker may not only be damaging his own mind and body, but may be playing genetic roulette and casting a shadow across children and grand-children yet unborn."[3]

DRUGS AND MORAL DEVELOPMENT

What's the connection between drugs and moral development?

Poisoning your body, first of all, violates self-respect. You're abusing yourself when you use harmful drugs.

Second, drugs cost money—more than most kids have. That means they steal or start pushing drugs themselves to get it. Said one boy who had been deep into drugs by 9th grade: "Lying, cheating, and stealing became part of my life-style."

And kids who are heavily into drugs, just like kids who are heavily involved with sex, are less likely to be involved in health-ful activities (sports, clubs, a job, social commitments) that might stimulate their personal and moral growth. For drug-dependent kids, getting high becomes what they live for.

WHAT CAN PARENTS DO ABOUT KIDS AND DRUGS?

Is there anything we can do as parents about the menace of drugs in our children's lives?

1. Obviously, it helps to be straight ourselves. Our credibility regarding the evils of drugs won't be too great if we're using them. But even if you use drugs yourself, don't let that be a reason to allow or ignore drug use by your child. Teenagers, who are morally less mature than adults and under a lot more social pressure, are far less able to handle drugs in their lives.

2. Make sure kids know about drugs and what they do. If you think you'll get a defensive reaction, you can head it off by saying, "I know a lot of kids are turned off by adults trying to scare them away from drugs with horrible stories and statistics. The fact is, though, there's some pretty impressive evidence that anybody who's looking out for his own welfare ought to know about."

Kids should know what marijuana is and does. They should know that PCP ("angel dust") upsets the mind's ability to interpret sensory input and may also bring out violent tendencies; it has caused people to drown in shallow water (because they can't tell which way is up) and to kill others or themselves. They should know that cocaine snorted into the nose produces extreme contraction of the blood vessels supplying blood to the nose; this eventually destroys nose tissue and often produces a hole in the nasal septum—the cartilage which divides the nose into right and left sides. In high or repeated doses, cocaine has also caused convulsions and death. Other kinds of "speed" (drugs which are psychic energizers), like Benzedrine and Dexedrine, can cause a fatal drug depression. Sniffing glue (or any other solvent), popular among some elementary-schoolers, can produce toxic effects ranging from dizziness to very serious disorders of the brain, liver, kidneys, bones, nervous system, and heart. Heart irregularities from glue-sniffing are believed to have been responsible for at least 110 sudden deaths of otherwise healthy teenagers on the West Coast in the 1960s.[4]

The worst effects of drugs don't always happen, of course. But there's always a risk. And there's a hidden risk that many kids don't know about: With any drug, you can never be sure what you're getting. In a roundtable drug discussion among teenagers, one girl said, "I don't see anything wrong with smoking pot, like once a week or every other week. I've done that, but I would never get into hard stuff." A boy responded: "I think you're fooling yourself if you think that casual drug use is okay. For one thing, you don't know what you're getting. Pot can be dusted—laced with PCP. You can go insane as a result of that stuff. It happened to my brother. He got some pot that was dusted—and he sat watching fish for two days. He never touched anything again."

Kids may learn all this in health class at school. Find out. Even if they do, it's still important for you to discuss it with them.

With drugs, as with sex, you may also find it helpful to get a book on the subject that's written for kids. Ask your librarian, pediatrician, or school counselor to recommend one.

3. I think it's very important to help kids *anticipate* the situation where somebody comes up to them on the playground or

puts pressure on them at a party to try drugs. I've pointed out before that preteens and teens at Stage 3 of moral development, when they want so much to conform and to be accepted, need to be prepared to resist the line, "Everybody's doing it." If kids think ahead and actually *decide* ahead of time that they're going to say "No, thanks" or "Bug off," it'll be easier to do when the real situation comes along.

4. Remember that self-esteem is the backbone of an independent personality. When you help kids feel good about themselves, you help them stand up to peer pressure to get into drugs.

5. Keep kids involved in family life, and keep up communication. When you're in close touch with kids, it's harder for them to get into drugs—and easier for you to spot it if it starts.

6. Encourage kids' involvement in activities that give them goals and a sense of purpose. Kids with little to do are easier targets for drug dealers than kids whose lives are full and rewarding. Said one young woman: "Once you get a sense of purpose about life, you can't afford to take your mind out of circulation."[5]

7. Be alert for signs that your child may be using drugs. If you detect a definite, puzzling change in your child's behavior—unusual irritability, surprising hostility and disrespect toward you, complete withdrawal and avoidance of conversation with the family, indifference and lethargy, dropping old friends for ones you don't know anything about, clipped phone conversations—anything that doesn't seem quite "right" for your child, drugs may be the reason. Some changes in the teens, of course, are developmentally caused and normal, but knowledge of your child's personality will help you distinguish these from drug-induced changes.

What should you do if you suspect your child is using drugs?

1. Try talking first. Be direct:

"You know, you've been acting strange lately. Not like your normal self. [Give some examples.] I hope you'll give me an honest answer, and I promise I will not be angry: Are you using drugs?"[6]

If your child admits to using drugs, a good, honest talk—where you draw out your child's feelings as well as sharing your own—might set your youngster on a different course.

2. Be prepared for talking to fail.

A reasonable, talk-it-out approach may not work for any of several reasons.

Kids often lie and say they're not on drugs when they are. A mother of two boys, both of whom started on pot in elementary school, said: "The kids for the longest time wouldn't admit what they were doing. It wasn't until later, in therapy, that we learned that denial is part of the problem, a classic symptom."

Even after kids admit what they're doing, the drugs may cloud their mind to the point where you can't reach them. Said a father: "Communicating with Eric when he'd been smoking pot was impossible. He just wasn't *there*. When he was off marijuana, there was a day-and-night difference. He'd be able to think clearly and *respond* to what you were saying."

Even if you can get through to kids, they may be too dependent on the drug, psychologically or physically, to stop.

3. Get support for dealing with your own feelings and help in dealing with your child's problem.

When you know your kids are on drugs, and you can't get them to stop, the hardest thing to deal with may be your own feelings. Says the mother of the two boys who started in grade school:

"The feeling of helplessness was one of the hardest parts. And anger. I was so *angry* with them for doing this to themselves. Couldn't they find life interesting enough without depending on drugs? Why did they have to do this?"

Faced with feelings of frustration, rage, and fragility, parents desperately need support themselves. Some support they can get from each other, and this is a crucial time for parents—whether they're living together or divorced—to pull together. But it also helps greatly to go outside the family for help, both for emotional support and for expert guidance in dealing with their youngster's problem. If your child is on drugs, ask your school's guidance counselor, your pediatrician, or your church where you can go for competent assistance. In some communities there are established drug-treatment programs; in most, there are psychologists or psychiatrists experienced in treating such problems. Try to get professional help if you possibly can.

It's important to recognize that kids aren't necessarily going to happily accept your offer of help. On the contrary, they may fight you tooth and nail. If they're deep in the grip of drugs, they may see you as the enemy, standing between them and their high. So they may need you to take charge and to tell them:

> "You're not able to help yourself in this situation, so we're going to have to help you. We are going to do everything in our power to stop you from using drugs, no matter how hard it is for you or us. We're doing this because we love you. You simply must stop using drugs, completely."

This is the approach advocated by David Toma, the ex-detective whose celebrated undercover work resulted in two television series, who saw scores of young lives wrecked by drug addiction, and who now lectures on drugs to students and parents all over the country. In his recent book, *Toma Tells It Straight—With Love* (Books In Focus, Inc. 1981), he recommends take-charge steps such as telling your child that: you're prepared to contact the parents of his friends and tell them that your son or daughter is on drugs and you intend to stop it; you're prepared to say the same thing to his teachers and school principal and to ask for their help—such as notifying you when he's absent from class or school; you will find out who the pushers are and will notify the police and school administration; until you're convinced he's off drugs, he won't be allowed to drive a car or have any money that can't be accounted for; you must know where he is, day and night, and whom he's with; you plan to inspect his room periodically to make sure there are no drugs in your home.[7]

I wouldn't launch into such an approach without professional guidance, however. For one thing, a teenager's drug problem may be a symptom of a deeper problem (anxiety, depression, feelings of inadequacy) that can be diagnosed and helped only by sensitive counseling.

Moreover, if your emotional reserves are already depleted, you may simply not be up to the demands of constantly monitoring your child's behavior. An alternative route is to find a recommended live-in drug-treatment program for your youngster. Andy is a boy who, by the time he was a freshman, was taking any drug he could get his hands on. Having tried everything else, his parents found out about Straight, Inc., a rehabilitation program in St. Petersburg. They woke Andy up one morning, took him to Straight, and gave him a choice: he'd sign into the program himself, or they'd take out a court order that would force him into the program. Andy signed in, and 11 months later he emerged feeling "very lucky" that "I had parents who cared enough to save me."

No family is immune to the threat of drugs. We can't innoculate kids against the insecurities and pressures of growing up, and it's exactly those insecurities and pressures that make them vulnerable to somebody's "Hey, come on—try this!"

Recently there was a letter to our local paper from a teenage boy, thanking the New York Prison Ministry for getting him out of jail, out of a life of drugs, and into the national "Teen Challenge Program." He wrote:

> "I started using drugs at the age of 12, and from then on drugs became as common to me as breathing. I started with marijuana and regressed on to the chemical drugs such as barbiturates, LSD, cocaine, methamphetamine, and even heroin a few times. I did all of this in the quiet little town of Cortland.
>
> "I did not get abused as a child or have alcoholic parents, as you may assume. I came from a loving family, with good parents and a good environment. My family was a middle-class, respectable family, yet I still went the wrong way. My parents tried to raise me well and taught me good moral principles. With all of the opportunities that I could have taken advantage of, I still became a drug-dealer, a disgrace to my family and the community."[8]

So no matter what you do, kids may still go wrong, and it isn't your fault. But never give up. The boy who wrote this letter did drugs for six years and at age 18, in jail for the second time, faced a possible 2- to 5-year sentence for three felonies. It was his parents who got the prison ministry to intervene and turn his life around.

For information about programs for the treatment and rehabilitation of drug abusers, call your church, school, or local mental health agency.

KIDS AND DRINKING

A friend of mine, who moved to a small, middle-American town of 5,000 people, was flabbergasted by the number of invitations his 16-year-old daughter got to parties where there was drinking. "If we let her," he said, "Laura could go to a party *every* weekend where liquor is served."

Kids get most drugs surreptitiously from their friends or dealers. But there's one drug they all too often get handed to them by us: alcohol.

Listen to these teenagers discussing the role we adults play in encouraging young people to drink:

Stan: I stopped smoking pot a couple of years ago, but now that I'm 17 there's a pressure to drink, and it comes from adults more than other kids. My father will say, "How about a beer?" or "How about a glass of wine?"

Jackie: I agree that there's a subtle pressure from adults. You go to parties, or you see people at the parties your parents have, and the adults are sloshed. I think the whole society encourages people to drink.

Cara: But I think there's peer pressure, too. I went to my first party since we moved here the other night. All the kids were drinking. Somebody asked me if I wanted a drink. I really wondered, do I want to do this? Maybe I should. Everybody else was doing it.

Doug: Sure, there's peer pressure, but who put all that booze out in the first place? Your friend's parents, right?

Art: Yeah, and what do you do when you're in the city and you have no money, and a friend of your mother picks you up and she's got a buzz on? You don't want to say anything to hurt her feelings.

Says a mother of a 16-year-old boy:

"We're just waiting for the night when a car of kids are going to wrap themselves around a tree. It seems inevitable, there's so much drinking. Parents will have a party for their child and put out a couple of kegs. I just don't understand it."

Many of today's parents, says a former president of the New York Council on Alcoholism, don't worry about the example they set and don't worry about their kids drinking because they're relieved they're not on drugs.

But alcohol *is* a drug, and it's raising havoc with the lives of young people:

- According to the National Institute on Alcohol Abuse and Alcoholism, over 3 million teenagers between the ages of 14 and 17 have a serious drinking problem.
- A third of our high school students get drunk at least once a month.
- Arrests of teenagers for drunken driving have tripled in the last two decades.
- Four of every 10 people killed in drunken driving accidents now are teenagers.

What can we do about kids and drinking?

Take a very tough line: No drinking until you're out of high school.

No drinking in the home. No drinking at parties. No drinking, period.

A mother told me the following story. Her daughter Betsy, a 17-year-old high-school senior, went to a party after a football game and came home, driving a carload of friends, drunk.

"This was the first time anything like this had happened," the mother said. "I was so upset I couldn't talk to her."

Later, when she calmed down, the mother sat down with her daughter and asked her this question: "Betsy, what would you do if you were the parent in this situation?"

Betsy said, "I don't know what I'd do."

The mother persisted: "I really want to know what you think is fair. You know that I'm very upset about what you did, but I intend to make a decision that's fair, and I want to know your feelings."

Betsy replied: "Well, if I were the parent, I probably wouldn't let my daughter go to any of those parties, because that's [drinking] what always goes on there."

So that was the decision—no more parties for the rest of Betsy's senior year. She accepted that without protest.

I told this story to a friend and he said, "But how will she learn to drink responsibly around other people? You have to learn that."

"True," I said, "but the interesting thing was that the daughter didn't fight it. She accepted the no-parties decision quite readily."

"Hmmm," my friend said, "she probably didn't *want* to go to the parties anyway—and now she had the perfect excuse."

"Right," I said. "Now she could say, 'My parents are hopelessly straight—I can't go.' It takes the heat off her."

What Betsy really wanted—and what I think a lot of teenagers want in many cases—is not freedom, but *protection*. Protection from the pressure, which they feel so acutely at this stage of their moral development, to do things they really don't want to do. So when we make tough rules, even if kids put up a show of protest, we may really be allies in their cause.

But what about my friend's objection that kids need to learn to "drink responsibly"?

They're not going to do that at a party. Teenagers at a party are under pressure not only to drink, but to drink to excess.

But what if you supervise the party?

You're still encouraging kids to drink at an age when their developmental capacities are already being taxed to the limit. They don't need alcohol on top of everything else. They shouldn't be drinking when they're trying to develop the courage and will power to stand up to peer pressure. They shouldn't be drinking when they're learning to drive. And they shouldn't be drinking when they're learning to cope with all the day-to-day stresses that growing up involves. Many teenage alcoholics, just like their adult counterparts, got hooked on drink when they discovered that their anxieties were soluble in alcohol. "When I drank, I lost my fears," says one boy. "I could talk to people." Says a girl: "I didn't feel comfortable with myself when I wasn't drinking."[9]

Will kids accept a ban on drinking?

Obviously, we can't control their actions in this area (when they're outside the home) any more than we can control their sexual behavior when they're on a date. And we can be pretty sure that most kids are going to have a drink or two along the way, as a rite of passage from adolescence to adulthood. But I think we can—and should—use our influence to *try* to forestall drinking as a regular activity until kids are well on their way to maturity. We can say something like this:

> "We'd like you to wait until you're out of high school before you start drinking. You've got enough to handle right now without adding alcohol. These are critical years, when you're laying the foundation for your future and when it's important to be at your best. And if you get into drinking, you'll have to face the pressure to have another drink, and another. So leave drinking until later, when you'll be able to enjoy it in moderation."

The father I quoted earlier as objecting to all the drinking parties his 16-year-old daughter was being invited to agreed to let Laura have a party of her own, on one condition—that it be dry. "Oh, *Dad*!" she said. "Nobody will come, and even if they do, they won't have a good time." The father held to his terms. Finally, Laura agreed. When the party was over, a surprised daughter said to her father: "I couldn't believe it. It was great! People really *talked* to each other. I want to have all my parties dry."

As a further incentive to postponing young people's drinking, both parents and kids might reflect on a well-known fact: drinking can dissolve moral inhibitions and lead kids to do things they'd never do sober. Many a teenage pregnancy can be blamed on the bottle. And coupled with drugs (in addition to being potentially lethal), alcohol is even more capable of obliterating conscience and inducing kids to perform actions that are completely out of character. Here's a teenager who learned that the hard way:

Dear Ann Landers:

My mother would die if she knew about this. My father would kill me. The priest is out of the question. I've cried my eyes out every night since Jan. 1. Here's the whole ugly story and I need your help.

Four couples, all good friends 17 and 18 (from the same high school), decided to spend New Year's Eve together. One of the guys had the house to himself. His folks were out of town. I was cleared at home to stay overnight with my girl friend.

The music on the stereo was terrific, great dancing, neat refreshments, plenty of laughs. Someone brought pot. There was a lot of smoking. Then came the booze. That's when everything started to go haywire. We started with kissing games.

By midnight we were all bombed. One of the girls suggested strip poker. Why not? More pot. More booze. Pretty soon we were all practically naked. Then one of the guys suggested "round-robin."

We coupled off, went into separate bedrooms, and set the alarm clock in the hall for one hour. When the alarm went off, we switched partners for another hour. After four hours we were back with our original partners. By 7 A.M. the party ended, but it wasn't the end for me.

I have been miserable and depressed ever since. Crummy, immoral behavior is against everything I believe in. I can't look at any of the guys I was with. One is a super person, and he hasn't spoken to me since that night. I don't know if he is as ashamed as I am, or if he thinks I'm a tramp.

Will I ever live that night down? Has it ruined my life forever? I am only 17.

No Swinger in Texas

This young lady's life obviously isn't ruined forever, but it will take a long time for the wound in her self-image to heal. Had she thought ahead of time about the dangers of drinking and drugs, she might have avoided this sorry episode. Part of the responsibility for what happened, of course, goes to the parents who left their teenage son with the house on New Year's Eve.

What if Kids Resist a No-Drinking Policy?

What if you try to establish a no-drinking policy, but your child fights you all the way? Says the mother of a 16-year-old:

"I have trouble getting to first base with my son about drinking. We don't want him to drink at all. I've told him I worry about what could happen if there's too much drinking. He says, 'Okay, I know you're worried I'll have too much, and I did once. But that was when I was younger. I'm more mature now, and I can handle it.' He says times have changed, I'm out of it. You begin to wonder, 'Am I?'"

First, I think we need to be clear in our own minds that there's nothing wrong with *us* if we object to kids' drinking; the problem is with a culture that encourages young people to drink. If we're confident that we're acting in our children's best interest by saying no to drinking, we have a better chance of winning their compliance. But if your child still resists, and you don't want to lay down a law you *know* your child is going to break, you could say:

> "You know how I feel about drinking at your age. I can't give you my approval for it because I don't think it's in your best interest, for all the reasons I've explained.
>
> "Still, I recognize that you're at an age where I can't stop you from doing something you're determined to do. So I'm not going to say, 'I forbid you to drink.' I sincerely do hope that you'll decide not to drink right now. But if you do drink, I expect you to do it with great care and responsibility. I hope you'll never drink if you're going to be driving, and that you'll never get into a car with a driver who's been drinking. If you can't get a ride with someone who's sober, call me and I'll come and get you."

If your child is doing some drinking, I think the critical thing is to keep this subject on the agenda. Keep talking about it; keep in touch with what's going on. If you show your concern in this way, chances are good that you'll be an influence on the side of restraint even if you can't get your youngster to forgo drinking entirely. But I recommend that you try first to get your child to go along with a policy of no drinking at all until after high school.

What else can we do to combat the problem of teenage drinking?

The same ideas that applied to preventing and dealing with drug use apply to alcohol, too. Don't abuse alcohol yourself; educate kids about the dangers of drink; help them anticipate what they're going to say when they're offered a drink; try to help them stay involved in the family, involved in life, and feeling good about themselves; and keep an eye on who their friends are. If you think they're into drinking, sit down and calmly talk about it. One father describes an approach that worked for him:

> "When our son was 16, he came home from a party drunk. I taped the teary, maudlin, incoherent monologue he recited in my presence that night and played it back for him (privately, of course) the next afternoon. He was ashamed and appalled. Had

he not heard it himself, he never would have believed how he sounded.

"Today he is a healthy, well-adjusted 24-year-old man who takes an occasional drink—but never to excess."[10]

If you have drinking problems yourself, or some other adult in your family does, discuss it frankly with your child. That will reduce, not increase, the chances of his going down the same path.

If you determine that your youngster is hooked on alcohol, get help immediately. Alcoholics Anonymous is active in nearly every community, and in many communities so is Al-Anon (for people whose lives are deeply affected by a problem drinker); check your phone book. Ask them about their programs and where you can go for professional counseling. In some communities there are also self-help support groups that bring together parents of kids who are in trouble with drinking, drugs, or both.

Drinking, like drugs, very often lands kids in trouble with the law. Shocked parents find themselves going down to the station to pick up their son or daughter, or having the police show up at their front door with a warrant for the arrest of their child. Faced with such a situation, a parent would do well to call a lawyer. That's a concrete, positive step that helps to keep emotions under control and find out how best to proceed.

Talk with your child only after the inner weather has calmed down. Try to get the facts of what happened without landing on your youngster like a ton of bricks. He or she will almost certainly know how you feel without your saying a word. Once you've found out what happened, take a forward-looking, problem-solving approach: Where do we go from here? What can we do to avoid this in the future?

If your teenager *continues* to break the law—or to violate your rights through any kind of abusive behavior (some kids, sad to say, even physically abuse their parents), get tough fast. Don't let it snowball. Let kids know that you love them, try to keep two-way communication going (get their point of view), but be very clear that you will not tolerate abusive or illegal behavior. Try to get your child to go with you for counseling. Use the fairness approach to make a hard-nosed behavior contract that spells out, with clear consequences for violation, the behaviors you find unacceptable while your child is living under your roof. Kids should get the message, "If you want to be part of a family, you have to behave like a member of a family. Home is not a no-strings-attached proposition."

In extreme cases, when kids are too far into drugs or drinking to respond to any parental efforts, parents have turned to the police and the courts for help in dealing with their out-of-control child. But I'd urge you to get professional guidance before taking drastic steps and, whatever happens, to do everything you can to keep the channels open between you and your child.

All of us want our children to make something good of their lives. We want them to be in control of their lives and to realize their promise. We know that drugs, drinking, and premature sex can rob them of that control and blight that promise.

In the recent past, many parents have felt helpless in the face of these and other threats to their children's personal and moral development. But a growing number, I think, are gaining the confidence that they can fight back. They are coming to realize that we can be, while our children are with us, the most important stabilizing influence in their lives. We can have an impact on their moral values, and we can influence their developing moral judgment and behavior.

That doesn't mean kids will turn out to be exactly like us (they won't), or that they'll never make mistakes (they will). But no matter how far they go astray, they'll be better for our efforts; they'll have basic values, and a view of the dignity of people and the worth of life, that they can come home to. We should, therefore, give them all that we can—our love, our discipline, our forthright moral teaching—as they struggle to grow into capable, happy, and upright human beings.

APPENDIX A:
THE RESEARCH BEHIND THE STAGES

The idea that morality develops through stages is very old. In ancient Greece, the philosopher Plato argued that citizens were at different "levels" of understanding "the good." Moral education, Plato said, is a process of leading people upward to higher levels of moral understanding.

Not until the twentieth century, however, did psychologists begin to actually study how moral understanding develops in children and adolescents. Switzerland's Jean Piaget, now ranked with Freud as one of the giants of psychology, broke the first ground in the 1920s with his studies of 5- to 12-year-old children. Piaget's genius was to ask children questions that drew out their ideas about right and wrong. He watched them playing marbles and asked them, "Where do the rules of the game come from?" "Can they ever be changed?" "What makes a rule fair?" He told children fictional stories about things that boys and girls did and asked them questions like, "What is a lie?" "Why is it wrong to cheat?" "Is it ever right to disobey?" "How should parents punish naughty children?"

Piaget reported his pioneering research in 1932 in a book that is still read today: *The Moral Judgment of the Child.* There he described three overlapping phases or stages in the development of a child's moral thinking. The first stage he called a "morality of constraint," in which children regard rules as unquestionable, unchanging absolutes handed down by adult authority. The second stage he called a "morality of cooperation," in which children see morality as a matter of strict fairness among equals. In the third stage, Piaget found, fairness was softened by "equity" (an ability to consider extenuating circumstances) and "ideal reciprocity" (an understanding of the Golden Rule).

Some of Piaget's findings turned out to be descriptive of Swiss children rather than all children, but the major features of his three stages have stood the test of time. Dozens of studies, including my own studies of children's judgments of responsibility, have been carried out by researchers on several continents (Africa, Asia, Europe, North America) and have reproduced Piaget's basic findings.[1]

THE WORK OF LAWRENCE KOHLBERG

As a doctoral student at the University of Chicago in the 1950s, Lawrence Kohlberg (now at Harvard) undertook the first major extension of Piaget's work. Kohlberg used a new tool, the "moral dilemma," to probe moral reasoning. For example:

> In Europe, a woman was near death from a special kind of cancer. There was one drug that the doctors thought might save her. It was a form of radium that a druggist in the same town had recently discovered. The drug was expensive to make, but the druggist was charging ten times what the drug cost him to make. He paid $200 for the radium and charged $2,000 for a small dose of the drug. The sick woman's husband, Heinz, went to everyone he knew to borrow the money, but he could get together only about $1,000, which was half of what it cost. He told the druggist that his wife was dying and asked him to sell it cheaper or let him pay later. But the druggist said, "No, I discovered the drug, and I'm going to make money from it." Heinz got desperate and broke into the man's store to steal the drug for his wife.

> Should Heinz have done that? Was it right or wrong? Why?

As Kohlberg interviewed his subjects about dilemmas like these, he was less concerned with what the person thought was right than with *why* he thought it was right. Kohlberg's interviews showed that two subjects could offer the same solution—such as, "Heinz should steal the drug"—but be reasoning at different stages. One teenager, for example, might justify stealing with a selfish, Stage 2 reason: "If his wife dies, who will cook his meals and wash his clothes?" Another youngster might show a Stage 3 concern about social disapproval: "What will people think of Heinz if he lets his wife die?" It was a child's underlying moral reasoning that revealed the "structure" of his world view—his stage.

Kohlberg began his program of research with some 50 boys who at the time were 10, 13, and 16 years of age. Like a dogged detective, he stayed on the trail of these same individuals for 20 years—confronting them at 3-year intervals with the same moral dilemmas to see if and how their reasoning had changed. On the basis of this "longitudinal" research, rare in psychology, Kohlberg confirmed and elaborated Piaget's three childhood moral stages and added a description of stages of moral reasoning in adolescence and adulthood.

At the completion of this 20-year study in the late 1970s, Kohlberg and his colleagues reported these findings:[2]

- Fifty-six of the 58 subjects showed upward stage movement (one stayed the same, and one fluctuated);
- Only four subjects showed a downward shift (to a lower stage) between any two testings;
- No subject skipped any stages;
- Stage development was slow; changes over the 3-year testing interval were usually less than a whole stage;
- Stage 4 was the typical end point; only 8 subjects in the sample—14 percent—showed evidence of Stage 5 thinking;
- No subject attained Kohlberg's "Stage 6," a more philosophically elaborate version of Stage 5 that Kohlberg now regards as a "theoretical construction suggested by the writings of figures like Martin Luther King" rather than as a proven psychological stage.[3] (Consequently, Stage 6 no longer appears in the scoring manual that Kohlberg and his colleagues use in their research.)

Dr. James Rest, a respected developmental psychologist at the University of Minnesota, has analyzed several different moral reasoning investigations that have followed the same subjects over time, including studies carried out by researchers other than Kohlberg. Rest concludes: "In general, subjects show significant change in the direction postulated by [Kohlberg's] stage theory."[4] Among the specific findings Rest reports is one pointing to the importance of education: after adults finish formal schooling, they tend to "plateau," staying at the same stage of moral reasoning.

Kohlberg, however, reports evidence that adults, like children, are able to comprehend moral reasoning at one and occasionally two stages higher than their own stage. Even though they can't actively produce this higher-stage reasoning themselves, they can understand it when they hear it—and they actually rank it as better reasoning than their own. "This fact," Kohlberg points out, "is basic to moral leadership in our society."[5] The moral reasoning of a particular public figure may be higher than that of most people, but many people can nevertheless understand it and respond positively to it.

IS KOHLBERG'S SYSTEM BIASED AGAINST FEMALES?

Recently, some writers have criticized Kohlberg for including only males in his original sample (an unfortunately common research practice at the time he began his testing) and have charged that his scoring system is biased against women. However, Professor Rest, in a comprehensive review, reports that the Kohlberg system has produced "a mix of studies, some with men ahead of women, some the opposite, and some with no difference." A review of studies using the "Defining Issues Test" (Rest's paper-and-pencil adaptation of Kohlberg's interview) finds that "over 90 percent show no sex difference. The evidence at hand hardly supports the view that the six-stage model is biased against women. When sex differences occur, they are likely due to differences in educational opportunity, suggesting a bias in the social system, not in the stage scheme."[6]

One advocate of the view that there are sex differences in moral development is Harvard professor Carol Gilligan. An associate of Kohlberg, Gilligan says that Kohlberg defines the highest level of moral reasoning as being concerned with working out just solutions in situations where people's rights conflict ("How can I exercise my rights without interfering with yours?"). That's how *men* tend to look at morality, Gilligan says. Women, by contrast, focus less on rights and more on responsibilities ("How can we all help each other and make it a better world to live in?"). In her recent book, *In a Different Voice,*[7] Gilligan argues that women give special emphasis to themes of responsibility and caring and that women's thinking has not been fully and fairly represented by male theorists of human development.

Full human development, Gilligan maintains, must include both an "ethic of responsibility" (asserting our obligation to care for each other) and an "ethic of justice" (asserting our individual rights or liberties). My own view is that rights and responsibilities are opposite sides of the same coin, and that Kohlberg's concept of "justice" has from the start included responsibility for the "welfare of others." Indeed, you can't be a just person without having some sense of positive responsibility for other people's well-being (the same sort of concern you'd want them to have for you). Each of Kohlberg's stages, in fact, widens a person's sphere of responsibility (at Stage 2, I feel obligated only to look out for myself; at Stage 3, I feel I should care about people I know personally; at Stage 4, I feel an obligation to contribute to my social system, and so on).

Recently, Dr. Mary Brabeck, professor of educational psychology at Boston College, reviewed a variety of studies of moral functioning; she found, like Rest, no evidence of sex bias in Kohlberg's method of measuring moral reasoning and no consistent evidence of sex differences in any other area of moral orientation or behavior.[8] One exception: females have stronger emotional reactions to others' feelings than do males. More research is needed to settle the question of what, if any, differences exist in the moral tendencies of men and women. In the meantime, parents and teachers should strive to help children of both sexes develop an ethic of caring as well as an ethic of fairness, a concern for responsibility as well as a concern for rights.

ARE THE STAGES UNIVERSAL?

Do the stages of moral reasoning describe just Americans, or are they found the world over? Kohlberg and his colleagues have done research in many different countries; among them are the United States, Great Britain, Israel, Mexico, Turkey, Malaysia, and Taiwan. They report that in all cultures studied, people go through the stages in the same order, though there are cultural differences in how fast and how far people develop through the stage sequence. In 1975 Kohlberg and Donald Elfenbein reported that "although no reasoning above Stage 3 or Stage 4 occurs in some of the primitive cultures studied, some Stage 5 thinking occurs in all complex societies with a literate urban component."[9]

Other scholars,[10] however, argue that the evidence is not sufficient to show that all the stages are universal, and this issue continues to be the subject of lively debate.

THE WORK OF OTHER STAGE PSYCHOLOGISTS

While not all psychologists subscribe to a stage approach (see the book I edited for alternative theoretical approaches[11]), the evidence continues to accumulate that growing up morally is a process of going through phases or stages. Clark University psychologist William Damon, for example, did intensive research in the 1970s on the social-moral reasoning of 4- to 10-year-old children and found three "levels" (each with two substages) that both confirm and refine the findings of Piaget and Kohlberg.[12] Damon's work, along with the research of Harvard's Robert Selman on the development of children's perspective-taking ability,[13] also provides the basis of Stage 0 in early childhood, an important addition to the Piaget-Kohlberg scheme.

Washington University psychologist Jane Loevinger[14] and Harvard's Robert Kegan[15] have mapped stages of "ego development" in children, adolescents, and adults. They find, in the changes that occur in people's understanding of themselves and their relationship to the world, a moral progression very much like Kohlberg's. Emory University Professor James Fowler, studying subjects ages 4 to 80, has gone beyond ego to describe stages in the development of "faith": the way people reason about ultimate questions like the meaning of life.[16] Fowler, too, finds in his data a moral progression very much like Kohlberg's. In Chapter 11, on Stage 5, I cited work by Robert Peck and Robert Havighurst that defined a succession of "character types."[17] Even though Peck and Havighurst formulated their scheme in the 1940s, more than a decade before Kohlberg's work, their character types bear a general resemblance to his stages of moral reasoning.

When you step back from the Kohlberg canvas to consider its broad strokes, it's not surprising that other researchers and theorists—even, ironically, some of Kohlberg's critics[18]—have painted a similar picture of moral growth. Kohlberg calls his first two stages (and you can add Stage 0 to this group) "preconventional," his middle stages, 3 and 4, "conventional," and his highest documented stage, 5, "postconventional." In other words, the developing person begins by being largely "premoral": self-centered, following rules only when it's in his interest to do so. In the shift to conventional morality, the person "joins the group," wants to be a "good person" in the conventional, conformist sense of trying to meet the expectations of others—either interpersonal others like family or friends (Stage 3) or impersonal others like one's community, institutions, or nation (Stage 4). In the shift to postconventional, principled morality, the individual is no longer completely identified with or locked into the prevailing conventions—the roles, rules, and regulations—of his social system. Now he can mentally stand outside his system, evaluate it, change it if necessary, operating from an independent, principled moral perspective. Is the system just? Does it fully protect human rights? Does it adequately promote the general welfare?

This broad sweep of moral development—from self-centeredness to conformity to independent, principled morality—is the core of Kohlberg's scheme. And it's the pattern that keeps cropping up, in one or another form, in the work of other people who have studied how we grow toward moral maturity.

APPENDIX B:
HOW TO DRAW OUT YOUR CHILD'S MORAL REASONING

Sometimes kids wear their moral stage like a badge; we don't have to do anything to discover it. But lots of times we don't know what they're thinking about moral issues unless we draw them out. Here are a few suggestions for how to get your youngster talking and some moral dilemmas that are usually successful in getting children or teenagers to reveal something about how they reason morally.

1. Choose a comfortable time for talking—riding in the car, doing dishes, taking a walk. Use a casual sort of lead-in, whatever is appropriate to the material you're presenting. For example, "I heard this story, and I'm curious to know what you think about it. . . ." or "I read about this controversy in the paper, and I wondered what your opinion would be. . . ."

2. With young kids—7 and under—I find it helps to make the dilemma concrete by using pictures or props. For example, in the story that follows about Kenny's dilemma (what should he do with a wallet he finds?), you can use a real wallet and money.

3. With young children, after you tell them the story, ask them to repeat it to make sure they've got the facts straight.

4. Ask kids for their judgment about what the story character should do ("So, what do you think Kenny should do?"), then bounce back what they say to let them know you understand and are interested in their answer ("So, you think Kenny should . . ."). Paraphrasing also "softens" your follow-up questioning so it doesn't seem like an interrogation.

5. Draw out your child's reasoning, *including the reasons behind the reasons*. This is usually necessary to uncover a child's stage. For example, if you ask, "Why should Kenny return the wallet?" and kids say, "Because it would be stealing to keep it,"

you know that they think stealing is wrong but you don't know *why* they think it's wrong. To get at your child's stage or stages of moral reasoning, you'd have to ask another question: "Why would it be wrong to steal the wallet?" If your child said, "Because he might get in trouble," you'd be able then to classify his reasoning into a stage—in this case, Stage 1.

6. "Test the limits" of your child's reasoning. That is, see if your youngster can come up with a better reason than the one first given. Ask, for example, "What other reasons can you think of why Kenny shouldn't steal the money?" or "What's the *best* reason you can think of?"

7. Respond to your child's reasoning in a respectful way. In addition to paraphrasing, you might say something like, "Hmmm, those are interesting thoughts." Remember, if we want kids to tell us what they think, we should listen respectfully when they do.

8. After you've drawn out your child's reasoning about the dilemma, feel free to share your own thoughts about it. You might say, "Would you like to hear what I think Kenny should do?" Kids will usually want to know what you think. (But be sure to get their reasoning first.)

9. If your child doesn't "get into" the dilemma on your first try, don't push it. It's better to come back to it later. One mother reports that her 10-year-old daughter gave Stage 1 responses in a half-interested way when the mother first presented a dilemma; a day later her daughter, more attentive, showed Stage 3 reasoning about the same dilemma.

If you aren't used to having "moral conversations" like these, they may seem a little awkward at first. But after a while, they'll come naturally, and you and your youngster could easily come to enjoy them.

Don't be surprised or discouraged if at first you can't figure out what stage or stages your child is using. For one thing, kids say a lot of things that don't fit into a stage. For another, it takes a lot of practice to get good at asking the follow-up questions that dig beneath surface opinions and get at underlying moral reasoning.

Keep in mind, too, that dilemmas and questions like the following are only one way to learn about your child's moral reasoning. You can learn a lot just by being a good listener and by discussing real-life moral problems when they come up.

That said, here are two fictional moral dilemmas you can use to try to draw out your child's moral reasoning. The first is appropriate for children, the second for teenagers.

KENNY'S DILEMMA
(For Children)

Kenny is walking to the store. It's his mother's birthday on Saturday. He's feeling bad because he hasn't been able to save up enough money to get her the present he'd like to give her. Then, on the sidewalk, he finds a wallet with $10 in it—just what he needs to buy the present! But there's an identification card in the wallet telling the name and address of the owner.*

QUESTIONS

1. What should Kenny do? Why?
2. What would be a good reason for Kenny to return the wallet? Can you think of any other reasons?
3. Would it be stealing to keep the money? Why is it wrong to steal?
4. What if the owner of the wallet were rich and greedy and wouldn't even give Kenny a reward for returning it—should he return the wallet then?

*Adapted from D. Adams, "Building Moral Dilemma Activities," *Learning* magazine, March 1977.

In the same conversation, your child may reveal several different stages of reasoning. That's what happened with 8-year-old Amy. Her teacher read her the story about Kenny and the $10 he found in the lost wallet.

Teacher: What do you think Kenny should do?
　　Amy: Kenny should return the money.

Teacher: Why do you think that would be the best thing to do?

Amy: If anyone found out that he kept the money, he would get in trouble. His mother would punish him for lying. Anyway, keeping money that didn't belong to him would be like stealing. Someone might tell the police.

Amy's reasoning here is obviously Stage 1. Fear of punishment is the basis for deciding what's right to do. Later, however, Amy showed a different stage of reasoning:

Teacher: Are there any other reasons why Kenny should return the money?

Amy: If Kenny returned the money, he could tell his mother what happened. She would be glad he'd been honest. That would be birthday present enough.

Teacher: Is it always easy to be honest?

Amy: No, it's *not* always easy, because sometimes telling the truth can get you into trouble, like if you did something wrong. But at least everybody trusts you if you tell the truth. Being honest is best.

Teacher: Should Kenny return the wallet even if he won't get a reward?

Amy: Yes. It would be doing a good deed. That would make Kenny feel better. He wouldn't have a guilty conscience either.

"These reasons," Amy's teacher accurately summarized, "all seem to fit Stage 3 reasoning, which centers on earning social approval by being a good person and meeting the expectations of others."

But when her teacher gave the story a new twist, Amy slipped into Stage 2 reasoning:

Teacher: What if the owner of the wallet were a rich and greedy man who would not reward Kenny's honesty?

Amy: A greedy man keeps things for himself. He never gives to others. Kenny should keep the wallet and let the man see what it feels like not to have everything he wants.

Through her questioning, Amy's teacher drew out the full range of Amy's moral reasoning. She learned that Stage 1 was

SHARON'S DILEMMA
(For Teenagers)

Sharon and her best friend, Jill, walked into a department store to shop. As they browsed, Jill saw a blouse she really liked and told Sharon she wanted to try the blouse on. While Jill went to the dressing room, Sharon continued to shop.

Soon Jill came out of the dressing room wearing her coat. She caught Sharon's attention with her eyes and glanced down at the blouse under her coat. Without a word, Jill turned and walked out of the store.

Moments later the store security officer, a salesclerk, and the store manager approached Sharon. "That's her—that's one of the girls! Check her bags!" blurted the clerk. The security officer pointed to a sign over the door saying that the store reserved the right to inspect bags and packages. Sharon gave him her bag. "No blouse in here," he told the manager. "Then I know the other girl has it," the clerk said. "I saw them just as plain as anything. They were together on this."

The security officer then asked the manager if he wanted to follow through on the case. "Absolutely," he insisted. "Shoplifting is getting to be a major expense in running a store like this. I can't let shoplifters off the hook and expect to run a successful business."

The security officer turned to Sharon. "What's the name of the girl you were with?" he asked. Sharon looked up at him silently. "Come on now, come clean," said the security officer. "If you don't tell us, you can be charged with the crime or with aiding the person who committed the crime."*

QUESTIONS

1. Should Sharon tell Jill's name to the security officer? Why or why not?

2. Would it make any difference if Jill had recently done a big favor for Sharon?

3. Would it make a difference if they were not good friends?

4. What factors should Sharon consider in making her decision?

5. Is shoplifting wrong? Why? What's the most important reason why it's wrong?

*Developed by Dr. Edwin Fenton for *Teacher Training in Values Education: A Workshop* (Guidance Associates, New York: 1975).

still part of Amy's thinking, but that she was capable of going as high as Stage 3. Knowing the upper limits of kids' reasoning enables you to capitalize on their highest capacity—in Amy's case, to appeal to her desire to do good deeds and to maintain trust by being truthful and honest.

The following are examples of different-stage responses to Sharon's dilemma (facing page). (Again, note that the same stage of reasoning can underlie different judgments about whether Sharon should tell.)

Stage 1: "If she doesn't tell, she's going to be in big trouble herself. She should do what the security officer says."

"If she tells, she's going to be in hot water with her friend. Jill might beat her up or something."

Stage 2: "Most stores rip off people by the prices they charge. So what's the big deal if you steal from them?"

"Why should she have to take the rap for Jill? Jill looked out for herself, didn't she? Sharon should do the same."

"It depends on whether she owes Jill anything—or whether she'd want Jill to cover for her sometime."

Stage 3: "What kind of a friend would turn in her best friend? She'll really feel terrible if she tells. And everybody will think she's a fink."

"You should help a friend no matter what. Even if you have to lie."

"It's really tough to decide. If she tells, she lets down a friend, and she's going to feel rotten about that. If she doesn't tell, she's an accomplice to a crime, and what's that going to do to her reputation?"

Stage 4: "Sharon should tell, even though it would be very hard to do. Friendship is important, but it's just not fair for people to go around stealing. If you don't obey laws, society will fall apart."

"Jill should have to suffer the consequences for what she did. Besides, if she gets caught now, maybe she'll learn a lesson and grow up to be a responsible person instead of a lawbreaker."

Stage 5: "Even if everybody didn't go around shoplifting, it'd still be wrong. It'd be wrong even if there were only one thief and one victim. Shoplifting violates the store owner's rights as a person, and that's the reason for the law in the first place—to protect the rights of all of us."

"Sharon should think of the rights of the store owner, as well as the rights of other people who are the victims of shoplifting. Other consumers, including poor people, have to pay higher prices because of shoplifting. If Sharon covers up for Jill, she's actively contributing to disrespect for people's rights."

APPENDIX C:
"DEAR ABBY" FOR DINNER

If you put letters to Dear Abby or Ann Landers on the dinner menu at your house, you'll have to be selective; not all the letters they get are family fare. But many are—and give parents and children a chance to talk together about how to solve real-life moral problems.

How can a 5-year-old girl help a classmate she likes but who is disliked by all the other children because he wears dirty clothes and "smells"? What should an 11-year-old girl do about a 13-year-old brother who taunts and hits her? Should a 12-year-old boy be punished or commended for calling the police to report that his next-door neighbors have marijuana growing in their garden? Should an 11-year-old girl be allowed to remain friends with a girl who talks about her mother's sexual escapades? Do parents have the right to forbid their teenager to listen to rock music? What should a 14-year-old girl do if she believes her father is being unfaithful to her mother? What should a 19-year-old girl do if she's pregnant but feels she can't tell her parents because "it would kill them"?

Besides stimulating moral reasoning, these letters, sensitively discussed, can expand kids' awareness of the many kinds of problems people have and help them become a little more understanding and sympathetic toward others. Here are a few guidelines that can help you get the most out of discussing advice-column dilemmas with your family:

1. Read the letter aloud—or let one of your children read it—but not the advice. Later, after discussion, it can be fun to compare the opinions around the table with the advice that's in the paper. But don't let kids rush the discussion to find out what "the right answer is." Make the point that people who write advice columns aren't infallible and that you're not trying to guess their advice but to develop thoughtful answers of your own.

2. Try to draw out everybody's opinion, and the reasoning behind their opinion ("Why do you think that?"). Add your opinion, too, but don't dominate the discussion.

3. Ask an occasional question to stimulate discussion and stretch kids' moral reasoning. Let me illustrate the different kinds of questions you can ask by taking as a case in point a letter that sparked a lively conversation one night when my parents were having dinner with us.

> DEAR ABBY: Shortly before our 16-year-old daughter was to receive her driver's license, I made the statement that if she were involved in an accident that was her fault, or was arrested for a traffic violation, I would take her license away for one year. Everyone in the family heard me make this statement.
>
> Last week my daughter was driving and my wife was with her. My daughter was trying to look at a road map as she drove.
>
> Her mother told her to stop the car if she was going to look at the map, but she didn't stop—until she hit a highway post about five seconds later.
>
> Now my wife feels that the one-year penalty was too strict to begin with. I believe it will not only teach the girl a lesson, but will serve as an example to the younger children. If you say the one-year penalty is too harsh, I may reconsider.
>
> Pop

Opening Questions

- What advice do you think Abby should give this father?
- Do you think his original punishment was too strict?

Why Questions

- Why do you think that?
- Why was the daughter's behavior (reading the map while driving) wrong?

Interaction-Encouraging Questions

- What do you think of your mother's idea?
- Who agrees or disagrees with what _____ said?

Perspective-Taking Questions

- What is the problem from the father's point of view?

- How would you feel if you were in the daughter's shoes?
- What advice would you give the father if you were a judge who deals with traffic accidents caused by careless or reckless teenage driving?

Alternatives and Consequences Questions

- What alternatives does the father have?
- What are the likely good and bad consequences of the different alternatives?
- All things considered, what's the best alternative?

Fairness Questions

- What's the fairest solution to this dilemma?
- Is it fair from everybody's point of view?

What-If Questions

- What if the daughter had injured a passenger or pedestrian through her careless driving? (Should that make a difference in the father's decision?)
- What if the daughter had *agreed* to the no-license-for-a-year punishment ahead of time?

Devil's Advocate Questions (Ones that obviously don't reflect your own thinking but that provoke discussion)

- Suppose somebody said, "Why is the father making such a big deal out of a little accident? Plenty of kids drive a lot worse than that." What would you say to that?

What's-the-Principle Questions

- What principle should the father use to guide his decision ("Stick to your word"? "Temper justice with mercy"? "Be big enough to change your mind"?)
- Should parents always stick to what they say will be a punishment? Why or why not?

Don't "overmanage" the discussion with too many questions; use them sparingly when you think they'll help. (In any given discussion, you'll have an opportunity to use only a few of the questions listed above.)

APPENDIX D:
BOOKS FOR KIDS THAT FOSTER MORAL VALUES

There are so many good books for kids that it's hard to keep up with them. The list that follows focuses just on books that have a moral theme or value dimension, and it certainly doesn't include all of those. I have not included books of poetry for children, for example, or nonfiction books about nature or animals, although those are good sources of values. (Our younger son's love of whales began with books on the sea.)

Most of what follows is fiction, ranging from short picture books for young children to full-length novels for older children and the whole family. Many can be read by kids themselves, while others need to be read to children, especially younger ones. Some teach a moral lesson quite directly, most more subtly. I think it's helpful to discuss the moral issues in a story now and then and make connections with a child's own experience, but be careful not to turn story hour into lecture time. A good story will do its own work in a child's moral imagination.

You can learn about some of the good new books for children by asking your local librarian for the winners and runners-up for the annual Caldecott Medal (best picture book) and the Newbery Medal (best work of children's literature). There are many, many good books that don't win awards, however, so ask your librarian for other recommendations, too.

Even if kids don't become passionate readers as children (some may bloom later as adult readers), it's important to introduce them to the world of literature and to make books part of the life you share. So read with kids at bedtime, give them a reading period in bed when you can't read together, spend time together browsing in the children's room of your library, give them at least as many books as you do toys, read some books aloud as a family, and talk about books you're reading. Sharing good books with kids is one of the pleasures of parenthood—and one of the truly enjoyable ways of raising good children.

Here are my recommendations:

1. A good book of nursery tales (stories that teach a simple moral, like *The Three Little Pigs* and *The Little Red Hen*) and a good book of fairy tales (stories that depict goodness and wickedness in a world of enchantment, like *Snow White, Cinderella,* and *Pinocchio*). These childhood classics can also be purchased as individual books.

2. *Aesop's Fables.* Timeless tales that still teach much wisdom to all ages. I recommend the Columbia record and accompanying 96-page illustrated book with stories adapted by Louis Untermeyer.

3. Andrew Andry and Suzanne Kratka, *Hi, New Baby;* 2 to 6. Facts about new babies and what older brothers or sisters can do to help themselves, their baby siblings, and their families.

4. Andrew Andry and Steven Schepp, *How Babies Are Made;* 4 to 10. A Time-Life book that goes from flowers and animals to human reproduction. A tasteful and gentle treatment; text and illustrations are simple yet accurate.

5. Richard Adams, *Watership Down;* appeal for all ages, but you'll have to read it to kids. Starts a little slow, then sweeps you into an unforgettable tale of rabbits (who think and talk in their own language) and their dangerous search for a new home; themes of loyalty, bravery, and good versus evil.

6. Louisa May Alcott, *Little Women;* all ages. An enduring classic depicting four sisters, each very much an individual, in a loving family; emphasizes the responsibility of every person to respect and care about others. Less known but also rich in good values: *Little Men.*

7. William Armstrong, *Sounder* (Newbery Medal Winner); 9 and up/family. Deeply moving story of a black sharecropper family that endures poverty and injustice but never loses dignity, love, or hope.

8. L. Frank Baum, *The Wizard of Oz;* all ages. A moral fantasy recounting Dorothy's adventures with Scarecrow, Tinman, and Cowardly Lion.

9. Terry Berger, *Black Fairy Tales;* 7 to 11. Dramatic African fairy tales in which evil is punished and happiness comes to those who deserve it.

10. Bible stories. Some recommendations:

    Marguerite de Angeli, *The Old Testament* (Selections from the Old Testament, illustrated by an award-winning author-artist)

    Kenneth Taylor, *The Bible in Pictures for Little Eyes* (Old and New Testament; 184 pictures; popular with young children)

    Richard and Frances Hook, *Jesus, The Friend of Children* (50 brief stories of Jesus's life, each with a full-color picture)

Catherine Marshall's Story Bible (stories adapted from the Old and New Testament, stunningly illustrated with art work by children from around the world)

The Living Story of Jesus (actual passages from *The Living Bible*).

11. Claire Huchet Bishop, *All Alone;* 6 to 9. Suspenseful and inspiring story of how two 10-year-old boys lead their French village to discover that "there's a better way of life than each man for himself."

12. _____, *Twenty and Ten;* 6 to 9. A French nun and school-children hide Jewish children from the Nazis; a tale of courage, sacrifice, and love. Other books by this French author with strong moral themes include *Pancakes—Paris, A Present for Petros,* and *Toto's Triumph.*

13. _____, *Yeshu, Called Jesus;* 8 and up. Drawing on information made available by Jewish and Christian scholars, this book vividly recreates the childhood of Jesus: his country surroundings, his family life, his work and play, and his religious education.

14. Raphael Brown, *Fifty Animal Stories of Saint Francis;* all ages. Fifty stories, transcribed from the early Franciscan chronicles, of the saint who called all God's creatures his "brothers and sisters" and of how the animals loved and obeyed him in return.

15. John Bunyan, *Pilgrim's Progress;* 7 and up. Several children's versions of this classic are available, such as the one illustrated by Caldecott award-winning artist Robert Lawson, but some parents may prefer to expose their children to the language and charm of the original. Written by a country pastor in seventeenth-century England, this Christian allegory sold 100,000 copies in the first 10 years after it was published. Still a valuable source of moral lessons about the importance of choices and the dangers of shortcuts.

16. Lucy Boston, *A Stranger at Green Knowe;* family. The beautiful story of a gorilla named Hanno and a boy named Ping; one of a series of Green Knowe books.

17. Pearl S. Buck, *The Beech Tree;* 7 to 11. A girl's love and understanding for her old grandfather.

18. _____, *The Big Wave;* 7 to 11. The family and fishing village of a Japanese boy are swept away by a giant tidal wave; a story of rare depth and beauty that shows how goodness can come from tragedy and how life is stronger than death.

19. Frances Hodgson Burnett; *The Secret Garden;* 9 and up. Features a heroine who gradually becomes assertive and independent, a boy who is spoiled at first, and another boy who is kind and wise beyond his years. An unusual book about the transforming power of love.

20. Christian Heroes series by Winston Press; 5 to 10. Individual, illustrated books depicting Christian heroes down through the ages (St. Francis, Joan of Arc, Harriet Tubman, Pope John XXIII, Johann Sebastian Bach, Clara Barton, St. Patrick, and others).

21. Miriam Chaikin, *Light Another Candle;* 8 to 12. The story and meaning of Hanakkah compellingly told against a background of high points in Jewish history. By the same author: *The Seventh Day: The Story of the Jewish Sabbath.*

22. Beverly Cleary, *Ramona the Brave;* 8 to 11. The parents and older sister of a 6-year-old girl persuade her that she is very much loved. In *Ramona and Her Father,* 7-year-old Ramona tries to help her family after her father loses his job. Two of many wholesome books by Beverly Cleary.

23. Vera and Bill Cleaver, *Where the Lillies Bloom;* 9 and up. A 14-year-old girl's valiant effort to mother her brothers and sisters after the death of their parents; set in the Smokies.

24. Thomas Crowell, *A Book of Hugs;* 2 to 5. A warm and whimsical tribute to hugs of all kinds.

25. Ingri and Edgar d'Aulaire, *Abraham Lincoln;* 6 to 10. A clearly told, handsomely illustrated version of Lincoln's life that captures the greatness and goodness of his character.

26. *D'Aulaires' Trolls;* childhood. Delightfully illustrated stories about all kinds of terrible trolls.

27. *D'Aulaires' Book of Greek Myths;* 5 and up. The heroic deeds and petty squabbles of the Greek gods and goddesses, illustrated by two award-winning artists. Children who enjoy this will also like Ingri d'Aulaires' *Norse Gods and Giants* and Virginia Haviland's *North American Legends.*

28. Wendy and Harry Devlin, *Cranberry Thanksgiving;* 3 to 9. Moral: Don't judge a book by its cover (or a person either). Wonderful art.

29. Charles Dickens, *A Christmas Carol.* The ageless tale of how miser Scrooge sees the light.

30. James Dobson, *Preparing for Adolescence;* preteens and teens. Dr. Dobson writes from a Christian perspective, but most of what he has to say—on subjects ranging from peer pressure to physical changes to self-esteem—will be relevant to kids regardless of their religious beliefs. An excellent source of psychological insights and sound values.

31. Joan Fassler, *Howie Helps Himself;* 3 to 8. Warm story of a boy in a wheelchair who discovers that it's how you feel about yourself that really counts. One of a series of books by this author on psychological themes.

32. Florence Fitch, *A Book About God;* 3 to 6. Develops through pictures and text the theme that we know God's love through all things beautiful.

33. Paula Fox, *The Slave Dancer* (Newbery Medal Winner); 11 and up/ family. Story of a boy kidnapped in 1840 and forced to work on a slave ship; a harrowing portrait of the evils of slavery, as seen through the eyes of the boy.

34. Anne Frank, *Diary of a Young Girl;* teens/family. The moving diary of a 13-year-old Jewish girl who spent two years with her family hiding from the Nazis before she was captured and killed.

35. Richard A. Gardner, *The Boys and Girls Book About Divorce;* 5 and up. Dr. Gardner is a child psychiatrist who has worked extensively with children of divorce; he wrote this book, he says, to help such children deal with their feelings and get along better with their parents. Published in 1970, the book doesn't describe the case where children live with their father or live equally with both parents, but otherwise it's a comprehensive, sensitive treatment of the situations and problems that children in divorced families may encounter. If you're a divorced or divorcing parent, I'd strongly encourage you to read this book, give it to your children to read (or read it to them if they can't read), and discuss the ideas in the book together.

36. _____, *Dr. Gardner's Fairy Tales for Today's Children;* 6 and up. These contemporary twists on four traditional tales present realistic approaches to solving life's problems.

37. Howard R. Garis, *Uncle Wiggily and His Friends;* 2 to 8. Tales of kindness.

38. Ravina Gelfand and Letha Patterson, *They Wouldn't Quit;* 5 and up. True stories of 14 successful people who overcame handicaps through persistent effort and belief in themselves.

39. Jean George, *Julie of the Wolves* (Newbery Medal Winner); 11 and up/family. A brave Eskimo girl makes her way alone across the North Slope of Alaska.

40. Fred Gipson, *Old Yeller;* 8 and up. A very touching story of a boy's love for his brave and faithful dog, and his learning about the pain of life.

41. Kenneth Grahame, *The Wind in the Willows;* 4 to 8. The endearing adventures of Toad, Mole, Otter, and friends; themes of loyalty and kindness.

42. Russell and Lillian Hoban, *Emmet Otter's Jug-Band Christmas*; 3 to 9. How happiness comes from thinking of others.

43. Irene Hunt, *Across Five Aprils* (Newbery Honor Book); teens/family. Civil War story of one family's struggle.

44. Wil Huygen and Rien Poortvliet, *Gnomes;* all ages. Truly delightful "facts" and stories about these legendary elflike creatures and their resourceful, brave, and kindly ways. Magnificent illustrations.

45. Spencer and Ann Donegan Johnson, *Values Tales;* 4 to 9. A series of 27 colorfully illustrated books, each dealing with a particular value as exemplified by the life of a famous person. The entire collection is expensive (about $180), so you may want to ask your library to order some or all of the series. Sample Titles:
The Value of Determination: The Story of Helen Keller

The Value of Truthfulness and Trust: The Story of Cochise
The Value of Caring: The Story of Eleanor Roosevelt
The Value of Courage: The Story of Jackie Robinson.

46. Eric Kelly, *The Trumpeter of Krakow* (Newbery Medal Winner); 11 and up/family. Fifteen-year-old Joseph Charnetski and his family risk their lives to keep the Great Tarnov Crystal from the hands of an evil Tartar chieftain. Set in fifteenth-century Poland, where the legendary broken trumpet song still sounds today.

47. Charles and Mary Lamb, *Tales from Shakespeare;* 6 and up. Twenty plays by Shakespeare, simply retold as stories for children.

48. Madeleine L'Engle, *A Wrinkle in Time* (Newbery Medal Winner); *The Wind in the Door;* and *A Swiftly Tilting Planet;* family. A unique blend of science fiction and spiritual values, this trilogy pits the extraordinary Murry children and the power of love against the dark forces of the universe. These highly imaginative novels offer special rewards.

49. _____, *Meet the Austins;* 8 and up/family. About a loyal and happy family, full of laughter and love, who take in a demanding 10-year-old girl who tries to capitalize on the fact that she is an orphan. Patiently, they teach her to relate to others in a less selfish way. First in a series about the Austin family.

50. _____, *A Ring of Endless Light* (Newbery Honor Book); teens/family. Sixteen-year-old Vicky Austin struggles with the knowledge that her beloved grandfather has leukemia.

51. C. S. Lewis, *The Chronicles of Narnia;* all ages. A series of seven fantasies (available as a paperback set in most bookstores) recounting the visits of four English children to the marvelous world of Narnia and their battles there against the forces of wickedness. Can be read as religious allegory or just enjoyed as adventure; wonderful for reading aloud. Don't miss these.

52. Athena Lord, *A Spirit to Ride the Whirlwind;* teens/family. Award-winning story of the moral awakening and courage of a 12-year-old girl.

53. T. C. McLuhan (Editor), *Touch the Earth: A Self-Portrait of Indian Existence;* family. Selections from the speeches and writings of Native Americans between the sixteenth and twentieth centuries. These beautiful passages, read aloud to children, communicate the deep reverence for the environment that was felt by Native Americans, their sense of oneness with nature and the Great Spirit, and their confusion, anger, and despair when the white men killed their herds and violated their sacred lands.

54. Scott O'Dell, *Island of the Blue Dolphins* (Newbery Medal Winner);10 and up. The courageous struggle for survival of a young Native American girl, alone on her home island after her tribe has left and her brother has been killed by wild dogs.

55. Katherine Paterson, *Bridge to Terabithia* and *Jacob Have I Loved* (both Newbery Medal Winners); 10 and up. In the first, an independent and unconventional girl opens up the world of imagination and learning to a 10-year-old boy. In the second, a girl struggles to emerge from the shadow of her "perfect" twin sister.

56. Trina Paul, *Hope for the Flowers;* children/family. A story of hope.

57. Robert Newton Peck, *A Day No Pigs Would Die;* family. Says *How to Grow a Young Reader* about this book: "A bloody and tender book about a 13-year-old Shaker boy whose simple, poverty-striken father works himself to death as a hog butcher . . . powerful lessons in courage, virtue, and love. Should be read aloud only by those who are not ashamed to cry."

58. Bill Peet, *The Wump World;* 2 to 8. Pollutians (from the planet Pollutus) land on the lovely Wump World and nearly destroy it. Our kids asked to have this read again and again.

59. Chaim Potok, *The Chosen;* teens/family. A powerful story of how hatred between two Jewish boys turns to deep friendship and how a father struggles to respect his son's independence, yet teach him what it means to have a soul. A great book.

60. Beatrix Potter, *The Tale of Peter Rabbit;* 2 to 5. Peter disobeys his mother and goes right into Mr. McGregor's garden.

61. *Norman Rockwell's Christmas Book: Carols and Stories, Poems, Recollections;* family. An excellent collection of both secular and religious Christmas literature.

62. *Richard Scarry's Please and Thank You Book;* 3 to 5. Good for teaching manners, sharing, and general consideration of others.

63. Maurice Sendak, *Where the Wild Things Are* (Caldecott Medal winner); 3 to 7. Temper and forgiveness; superb illustrations.

64. Dr. Seuss stories, especially *The Grinch* (love conquers greed), *The Lorax* (who speaks for the trees), *The Sneetches* (the stupidity of prejudice), *Horton Hatches the Egg* (keeping a promise), and *Horton Hears a Who* (a person's a person, no matter how small).

65. Dr. Seuss and Roy McKie, *My Book About Me;* preschool. For developing self-esteem.

66. Anna Sewell, *Black Beauty;* 11 and up/family. Written to inspire kindness to animals; told from the viewpoint of the horse.

67. Elizabeth Speare, *The Bronze Bow* (Newbery Medal Winner); teens/family. Eighteen-year-old Daniel Bar Jamin lived for one thing—to avenge the death of his parents and drive the Roman legions from Israel. But he is thrown into confusion by a rabbi named Jesus teaching a strange and different message. We read this aloud as a family; it's one of my all-time favorites.

68. _____, *The Witch of Blackbird Pond* (Newbery Medal Winner); teens/family. Another favorite. Set in a stern Puritan commu-

nity in Connecticut Colony, this uplifting book combines adolescent romance, the triumph of love and compassion over suspicion and intolerance, and a feisty, irresistible heroine.

69. Marlo Thomas *et al.*, *Free to Be You and Me;* all ages. Stories, poems, and songs about girls' and boys' potential to be what they want to be. I'd also recommend the record by the same title.

70. Mark Twain, *The Adventures of Tom Sawyer* and *The Adventures of Huckleberry Finn;* 7 and up. High adventure and struggles of conscience; good bedtime fun.

71. E. B. White, *Charlotte's Web* (Newbery Honor Book); family. A humorous but touching story of a spider named Charlotte who saves the life of a fat little pig. A treasured classic.

72. Laura Ingalls Wilder, *Little House* series; 7 and up/family. The basis of the popular television show, these eight books tell the story of Laura Ingalls Wilder's life. Makes early America come to life for a child and shows how a family's love for each other can see them through the hardest of times. Try these books at bedtime.

73. Brian Wildsmith's *Mother Goose* (or any other good collection of Mother Goose nursery rhymes). A great introduction to the world of books; you can start reading these rhymes to children even before they're a year old.

74. Margery Williams, *The Velveteen Rabbit;* 5 to 9. How love makes us real.

75. Maia Wojciechowska, *Shadow of a Bull* (Newbery Medal Winner); 10 and up. Manolo Olivar's late father was the greatest bullfighter in all Spain, but Manolo does not wish to follow in his footsteps. A boy's quest for self-respect and independence.

76. Taro Yashima, *Crow Boy;* 5 to 8. How a Japanese boy gradually overcomes ridicule by his classmates; teaches the lesson that everyone has a talent.

77. Jane Yolen, *The Emperor and the Kite;* 4 to 7. How an emperor, rescued by his smallest daughter from evil men, learns that size is not the measure of courage or love.

78. Charlotte Zolotow's books for young children (3 to 8). Among them: *Do You Know What I'll Do?* (a sister's kindness to her little brother); *It's Not Fair* (good for discussions of fairness); *The Quarreling Book* (how we pass on our bad and good moods); and *William's Doll* (helps boys feel good about nurturing).

The following sources have been helpful to my wife and me in finding many of the books I've recommended: *How to Grow a Young Reader* by John and Kay Lindskoog; *Children's Literature: An Issues Approach* by Masha Kabakow Rudman; *In the Beginning There Were the Parents* by Dolores Curran; *Adventur-*

ing with Books by Mary Lou White (editor); *How to Father* by Fitzhugh Dodson; and Barbara Lamb Coger, the children's librarian of the Cortland Public Library.

Thanks also to Jake Schuhle, librarian at the State University of New York at Cortland, and Catherine Stetson, an avid young reader, for their comments and suggestions concerning the above bibliography.

NOTES

Chapter 1

1. James Garbarino and Urie Bronfenbrenner, "The Socialization of Moral Judgment and Behavior in Cross-Cultural Perspective," in Thomas Lickona (Editor), *Moral Development and Behavior: Theory, Research, and Social Issues* (Holt, Rinehart, & Winston, New York: 1976).

2. K. Montor, "Cheating in High School," *School and Society,* Vol. 99, 1971. For a survey of cheating among 1,600 students in 22 high schools, see F. Schab, "Cheating in High School," *Journal of Youth and Adolescence,* Vol. 1, 1972.

3. Roger V. Burton, "Honesty and Dishonesty," in T. Lickona, *Moral Development and Behavior.*

4. Arthur Levine, *When Dreams and Heroes Died: A Portrait of Today's College Student,* A Report for the Carnegie Council on Policy Studies in Higher Education (Jossey-Bass Publishers, San Francisco: 1981).

5. Carol Stocker, "Teenage Pregnancies," *Boston Globe,* August 5, 1979.

6. K. Montor, "Cheating in High School."

7. Arthur Levine, *When Dreams and Heroes Died.*

8. Adapted from Ann Landers, "Say No to Your Children," *Family Circle,* June 1968.

9. For research on the positive effects of moral discussion, see, for example, James S. Leming, "Curriculum Effectiveness in Moral Values Education: A Review of Research," *Journal of Moral Education,* Vol. 10 (3), 1981.

Chapter 2

1. Reported in Urie Bronfenbrenner, *The Ecology of Human Development: Experiments by Nature and Design* (Harvard University Press, Cambridge, Mass.: 1979).

2. William Goldfarb, "Psychological Privation in Infancy and Subsequent Adjustment," *American Journal of Orthopsychiatry,* Vol. 15, 1945.

3. William and Joan McCord, *Psychopathy and Delinquency* (Grune & Stratton, New York: 1956).

4. Adapted from Eleanor E. Maccoby, *Social Development: Psychological Growth and the Parent-Child Relationship* (Harcourt Brace Jovanovich, Inc., New York: 1980).

5. Mary S. Ainsworth and S. M. Bell, "Some Contemporary Patterns of Mother-Infant Interaction in the Feeding Situation," in A. Ambrose (Editor), *Stimulation in Early Infancy* (Academic Press, New York: 1969).

6. E. Waters, J. Wippman, and L. A. Sroufe, "Attachment, Positive Affect, and Competence in the Peer Group," *Child Development,* Vol. 50, 1979.

7. William McCord, *The Psychopath: An Essay on the Criminal Mind* (Van Nostrand, Princeton, New Jersey: 1964).

Chapter 4

1. Fern Chamberlain, *Handbook for Coping with the Terrible Twos*, unpublished Master's project, SUNY, Cortland: 1983.

2. Lucie W. Barber, *When a Story Would Help: An Approach to Creative Parenting* (Abbey Press, St. Meinrad, Indiana: 1981).

3. Credit for this advice goes to one of the pioneers in child development research and childrearing guidance, Dr. Arnold Gesell.

Chapter 5

1. Arnold Gesell, *The First Five Years of Life* (Harper & Row, New York: 1940).

2. Robert G. Kegan, "There the Dance Is: Religious Dimensions of a Developmental Framework," in *Toward Moral and Religious Maturity* (Silver Burdett Co., Morristown, NJ: 1980).

3. I owe the felicitous phrasing of this point to Phyllis McGinley's wise and witty book, *Sixpence in Her Shoe* (Dell Publishing Co., New York: 1965).

Chapter 6

1. Robert L. Selman, "Social-Cognitive Understanding: A Guide to Educational and Clinical Practice," in Lickona (Editor), *Moral Development and Behavior*.

2. This example is taken from the fine book, *Parents Ask* by Frances L. Ilg and Louise Bates Ames (Harper & Row, New York: 1962).

3. I am indebted for this discussion of the value of games for children's moral development to Constance Kamii and Rheta DeVries, authors of *Group Games in Early Education: Implications of Piaget's Theory* (National Association for the Education of Young Children, Washington, DC: 1980).

4. Lois B. Murphy, *Social Behavior and Child Personality* (Columbia University Press, New York: 1937).

5. For a discussion of how children's position in the family influences the social role they choose to play, see Chapter 2 of the helpful book, *Children: The Challenge* by Rudolph Dreikurs (Hawthorn Books, Inc., New York: 1964).

Chapter 7

1. Adapted from William Damon, *The Social World of the Child* (Jossey-Bass Publishers, San Francisco: 1977).

2. Thanks for this point to a story in *Today's Child*, superbly edited for many years by an esteemed colleague, Virginia North Edwards, and long a source of valuable information on children's learning and development.

Chapter 8

1. Unfortunately, there are not many nuts-and-bolts descriptions of how to foster moral development in classrooms and schools. For elementary school teachers, I'd suggest a chapter I wrote, "Beyond Justice: A Curriculum for Cooperation," for the book *Development of Moral Reasoning*, edited by Don Cochrane and Michael Manley-Casimir (Praeger, 1980). For persons working at the junior-high and high-school level, I'd recommend the readable and inexpensive paperback, *Models*

of *Moral Education,* by Richard H. Hersh, John P. Miller, and Glen D. Fielding (Longman, Inc., New York: 1980). For up-to-date coverage of moral education programs in schools and new books and resource materials in this field, I recommend the quarterly periodical, *Moral Education Forum* (Lisa Kuhmerker, Editor; 221 East 72nd Street; New York, NY 10021: $14 a year) and the fine monthly publication, *Ethics in Education* (Donald Craig, Editor; Box 580, Lunenburg, Nova Scotia, Canada B0J 2C0: $15 a year).

2. Thanks for this idea to Dr. Henri Parens, Director of the Early Childhood Development Program at the Eastern Pennsylvania Psychiatric Institute-Medical College.

Chapter 9

1. The point that parents and teachers should respect children's need to trust in adult authority is well made by Professor Louis Chandler of the University of Pittsburgh's School of Education in his article, "What Teachers Can Do About Childhood Stress," *Phi Delta Kappan,* December 1981.

2. Christiaan Barnard, "Selections from *One Life,*" in Joel L. Milgram and Dorothy J. Sciarra (Editors), *Childhood Revisited* (Macmillan Publishing Co., New York: 1974).

3. Stanley Coopersmith, *The Antecedents of Self-Esteem* (W. H. Freeman, San Francisco: 1967).

4. If you want to sensitize teenagers to the destructive effects of put-downs, have them read the chapter on "The Secret of Self-Esteem" in Dr. James Dobson's *Preparing for Adolescence.*

5. Cited in Ervin Staub, *Positive Social Behavior and Morality, Vol. 2* (Academic Press, New York: 1979).

Chapter 10

1. Adapted from Anne Colby *et al.,* "Secondary School Moral Discussion Programs Led by Social Studies Teachers," *Journal of Moral Education,* Vol. 6, January 1977.

2. Anne Colby and Lawrence Kohlberg, *The Measurement of Moral Judgment* (Cambridge University Press, New York: in press).

3. Ibid.

4. Thomas and Muriel Ladenburg and Peter Scharf, *Moral Education: A Classroom Workbook* (Responsible Action, Davis, CA: 1978).

5. Ibid.

6. Thanks for this point to Fitzhugh Dodson, author of *How to Father* (Castle Books, 1974).

7. Eleanor Roosevelt, "Selections from *The Autobiography of Eleanor Roosevelt,*" in Milgram and Sciarra, *Childhood Revisited.*

Chapter 11

1. Stanley Milgram, *Obedience to Authority* (Harper & Row, New York: 1974).

2. Stanley Milgram, "Behavioral Study of Obedience," *Journal of Abnormal and Social Psychology,* Vol. 67, 1963.

3. Peter Scharf, *Moral Education* (Responsible Action, Davis, CA: 1978).

4. Ibid.

5. Daniel Candee, "The Moral Psychology of Watergate," *Journal of Social*

Issues, Vol. 31, 1975.

6. Egil Kroh, "Statement," *New York Times,* January 25, 1974.

7. Colby and Kohlberg, *The Measurement of Moral Judgment.*

8. Ervin Staub, *Positive Social Behavior and Morality, Vol. 2* (Academic Press, New York: 1979).

9. Robert F. Peck and Robert J. Havighurst, *The Psychology of Character Development* (John Wiley & Sons, Inc., New York: 1960).

10. Ibid.

11. Ibid.

12. David L. Rosenhan, "Some Origins of Concern for Others," in Paul Mussen, Jonas Langer, and M. Corington (Editors), *Trends and Issues in Developmental Psychology* (Holt, Rinehart, & Winston, New York: 1969).

13. Robert Bolt, *A Man for All Seasons* (Random House, New York: 1960).

14. David Mark Mantell, "Doves vs. Hawks: Guess Who Had the Authoritarian Parents?" *Psychology Today,* September 1974.

15. Lawrence Kohlberg, *Collected Papers on Moral Development and Moral Education* (Harvard University Center for Moral Education, Cambridge, MA: 1973).

16. Ibid.

17. Clive Beck, "Comments on 'Stages of Moral Development,'" in Clive Beck and Edmund Sullivan (Editors), *Moral Education* (University of Toronto Press, Toronto: 1970).

Chapter 12

1. Torey L. Hayden, "Conversations Kids Crave," *Families,* June 1982.

2. Ibid.

3. For a good source of family communication games, I recommend the book *Helping Your Child Learn Right From Wrong* by Sidney Simon and Sally Wendkos Olds (Simon & Schuster, New York: 1976).

4. Rhea Zakich, quoted in newspaper article reprint (The Ungame Co., Anaheim, CA: 1975).

5. Brian Walton, quoted by Kevin Hyland, "What Happened to the Family Dinner?" *Syracuse Herald American,* June 7, 1981.

6. Adapted from a Sidney Simon workshop, Cornell University, December 1980.

7. Thanks for this point to Letty Cottin Pogrebin, who has an excellent discussion of the value of dinnertime conversation in her book *Family Politics* (McGraw-Hill, New York: forthcoming).

8. Many parents have also benefited by taking the 8-week evening course offered by Parent Effectiveness Training (P.E.T.). You may not agree 100% with the P.E.T. philosophy; I personally think that parental authority plays a more important role in raising good children than P.E.T. assigns it. But P.E.T. workshops can help you learn and practice communication skills that are helpful in all family relationships. To find out where your nearest P.E.T. class is, write to P.E.T. Information, 531 Stevens Avenue, Solana Beach, CA 92075.

Another course that many parents have found helpful is STEP (Systematic Training in Effective Parenting). The materials and leader's handbook for this course were developed by Dr. Don Dinkmeyer and are published by American Guidance Service, Inc., Circle Pines, Minnesota (55014). In many counties, STEP is offered by Cooperative Extension, which provides a trained facilitator for the course (a key factor in its success). Some school systems that have a skilled facilitator available have written for the STEP materials and offered the course on their own.

9. John Holt, "Free the Children—They Need Room to Grow," in R. E. Schell (Editor), *Readings in Developmental Psychology Today* (Random House, New York: 1977).

Chapter 15

1. James R. Jeffreys, quoted by Joseph Whitaker, "Against All Odds . . . ," *Poughkeepsie Journal*, November 16, 1977.

2. Jenkin Lloyd Jones, "Teach Your Child to 'Love the Storm,'" *Los Angeles Times Syndicate*, 1962.

3. Thomas D. Murray, *A Child to Change Your Life* (Mary Yost Associates, 1976).

4. Ardis Whitman, "Five Enduring Values for Your Child," *Reader's Digest*, June 1981.

5. "What's Happening to the American Family?" *Better Homes and Gardens*, September 1978.

6. Adapted from Dolores Curran, *In the Beginning There Were the Parents* (Winston Press, Minneapolis: 1978).

7. C. S. Lewis, *Mere Christianity* (The Macmillan Co., New York: 1960).

8. Whitman, "Five Enduring Values for Your Child."

9. Paul Chance, Trudy Schlachter, and Leslie Elliott, "The Roots of Success," *Family Circle*, April 24, 1978.

10. Daniel C. Maguire, "A 'New' View of Sin: Our Growing Awareness of Social Evil," *Catholic Update*, August 1981.

11. Cleveland Amory, "Good Guys, Bad Guys," *Parade Magazine*, March 20, 1983.

12. Ibid.

13. Curran, *In the Beginning There Were the Parents*.

14. Ibid.

15. Perry London, "The Rescuers," in Jacqueline R. Macaulay and Leonard Berkowitz (Editors), *Altruism and Helping Behavior* (Academic Press, New York: 1970).

16. Ibid.

17. Ibid.

Chapter 16

1. My thanks to Dr. Michael Rothenberg, who used these lines from Whitman as a backdrop for an excellent article on television violence in *JAMA*, December 8, 1975. I am indebted for the title of this chapter, "Television as a Moral Teacher," to Dr. Robert M. Liebert, whose book *The Early Window* (with John M. Neale and Emily S. Davidson) is still a superb analysis of the effects of television on children.

2. Lynda Hirsch, "Joe Rescues Leora from a Strangling by Curt: Last Week on the Soaps," *Poughkeepsie Journal*, March 22, 1981.

3. Ibid.

4. "Why We Are and Why You Should Be Concerned About Your Youngster's Viewing Habits," *Television and Movie Facts for Parents* (a newsletter that is unfortunately no longer published), Spring 1979.

5. Tony Schwartz, "Do the Networks Need Violence?" *New York Times*, May 23, 1982.

6. R. S. Drabman and M. H. Thomas, "Does media violence increase children's toleration of real-life aggression?", *Developmental Psychology*, Vol. 10, 1974.

7. V. B. Cline, *et al.*, "The desensitization of children to television violence," *Proceedings of the American Psychological Association*, Vol. 80, 1972.

8. Harry F. Waters, "What TV Does to Kids," *Newsweek*, February 21, 1977.

9. Marie Winn, *The Plug-In Drug* (Bantam Books, New York: 1977). This is an inexpensive paperback that I would highly recommend to all parents.

10. Urie Bronfenbrenner, "Developmental Research and Public Policy," in J. Romanyshyn (Editor), *Social Science and Social Welfare* (Council on Social Work Education, New York: 1974).

11. Cited in Dorothy C. Singer, "How Much Television is Too Much?" *Panorama Magazine*, May 1980.

12. Edward B. Fiske, "Schools vs. Television," *Parents' Magazine*, January 1980.

13. Thanks for the list-on-the-refrigerator idea to Joan Anderson Wilkins, author of "Why Is This Child Always Watching?", *Health*, September 1981.

Chapter 17

1. Francine Klagsbrun, "Teaching Your Children About Sex," *Family Circle*, July 1, 1981.

2. From a letter to Ann Landers, July 16, 1981.

3. David Gelman *et al.*, "The Games Teenagers Play," *Newsweek*, September 1, 1980.

4. Credit for this analysis of Kinsey's impact goes to Robert Hogan and David Schroeder, authors of "The Joy of Sex for Children and Other Modern Fables," in Edward A. Wynne (Editor), *Character Policy: An Emerging Issue* (University Press of America, Washington, DC: 1982).

5. Credit for this apt phrase goes to Daniel Maguire's excellent book, *The Moral Choice* (Winston Press, Minneapolis: 1979).

6. David Gelman, *et al.*, "The Games Teenagers Play."

7. Elizabeth Tener, "How to Talk to Your Teenagers About Sex," *Woman's Day*, September, 1979.

8. Howard R. and Martha E. Lewis, *The Parent's Guide to Teenage Sex and Pregnancy* (St. Martin's Press, New York: 1980).

9. James Dobson, *Preparing for Adolescence* (Bantam Books, New York: 1980).

10. Gelman, *et al.*, "The Games Teenagers Play."

11. Ibid.

12. Howard and Martha Lewis, *The Parent's Guide to Teenage Sex and Pregnancy*.

13. Ibid.

14. Kenneth and Betty Woodward, "Why Young People Are Turning Away From Casual Sex," *McCall's*, April 1974.

15. Tener, "How to Talk to Your Teenagers About Sex."

16. Thanks for this point to Marcia Lasswell, quoted by Norman M. Lobsenz, "When a Roommate Is More Than a Friend," *Families*, February 1982.

Chapter 18

1. Peggy Mann, "Marijuana Alert: Brain and Sex Damage," in *Raising Kids* (Berkley Books, New York: 1981).

2. Ibid.

3. Ibid.

4. Cited in Leonard H. Gross (Editor), *The Parent's Guide to Teenagers* (Macmillan Publishing Co., New York: 1981).

5. Norman Lobsenz, "Why Young People Are Giving Up Drugs," *McCall's*, September 1974.

6. Adapted from Fitzhugh Dodson, *How to Father* (The New American Library, Inc., New York: 1974).

7. David Toma and Irving N. Levey, *Toma Tells It Straight—With Love* (Books in Focus, Inc., New York: 1981).

8. Scott M. Jackson, Letter to the Editor, *Cortland Standard*, April 1, 1982.

9. James Lincoln Collier, "New Driving Menace: Teenage Drinking," in *Raising Kids* (Berkley Books, New York: 1981).

10. Letter to "Dear Abby," Universal Press Syndicate, 1980.

Appendix A

1. See my chapter, "Research on Piaget's Theory of Moral Development," in Thomas Lickona (Editor), *Moral Development and Behavior* (Holt, Rinehart, & Winston, New York: 1976).

2. Lawrence Kohlberg, "The Meaning and Measurement of Moral Development," Clark Lectures, Clark University, 1979. For further information on Kohlberg's longitudinal study, see his forthcoming book, *Essays on Moral Development, Volume 2: The Psychology of Moral Development* (Harper & Row, San Francisco).

3. Lawrence Kohlberg, "Revisions in the Theory and Practice of Moral Development," in William Damon (Editor), *New Directions for Child Development: Moral Development* (Jossey-Bass, Inc., San Francisco: 1978). For Kohlberg's earlier writings on Stage 6, see his book, *Essays on Moral Development, Volume 1: The Philosophy of Moral Development* (Harper & Row, San Francisco: 1981).

4. James R. Rest, "Morality," in John Flavell and E. Markman (Editors), *Carmichael's Manual of Child Psychology, 4th Edition* (John Wiley & Sons, Inc., New York: forthcoming).

5. Lawrence Kohlberg, *The Philosophy of Moral Development*.

6. Rest, "Morality."

7. Carol Gilligan, *In a Different Voice* (Harvard University Press, Cambridge: 1982).

8. Mary Brabeck, "Moral Orientation: Alternative Perspectives," in *Psychological Foundations of Moral Education* (Council for Studies in Values and Philosophy, Washington, D.C.: forthcoming).

9. Lawrence Kohlberg and Donald Elfenbein, "The Development of Moral Judgments Concerning Capital Punishment," *The American Journal of Orthopsychiatry*, Vol. 45, 1975. For a fuller presentation of Kohlberg's cross-cultural research, see his chapter, "Stage and Sequence," in D. A. Goslin (Editor), *Handbook of Socialization* (Rand McNally Publishers, Chicago: 1969) and his forthcoming book, *The Psychology of Moral Development*.

10. See, for example, the chapter by Carolyn P. Edwards, "The comparative study of the development of moral judgment and reasoning," in R. L. Munroe *et al*. (Editors), *Handbook of Cross-Cultural Human Development* (Garland Publishing Co., New York: 1980).

11. Lickona, *Moral Development and Behavior*.

12. William Damon, *The Social World of the Child* (Jossey-Bass, Inc., San Francisco: 1977).

13. Robert L. Selman, *The Growth of Interpersonal Understanding* (Academic Press, New York: 1980).

14. Jane Loevinger and Ruth Wessler, *Measuring Ego Development* (Jossey-Bass, Inc., San Francisco: 1970).

15. Robert Kegan, *The Evolving Self* (Harvard University Press, Cambridge: 1982).

16. James W. Fowler, *Stages of Faith: The Psychology of Human Development and the Quest for Meaning* (Harper & Row, San Francisco: 1981).

17. Robert F. Peck and Robert J. Havighurst, *The Psychology of Character Development* (John Wiley & Sons, Inc., New York: 1960).

18. For the most common criticisms of Kohlberg's theory and a reply by Kohlberg and Charles Levine, see Kohlberg's forthcoming book, *The Psychology of Moral Development*.

INDEX

ABOUT THE AUTHOR

DR. THOMAS LICKONA, a developmental psychologist and educator, is an internationally respected authority on moral development. He is Professor of Education at the State University of New York at Cortland, where he has done national-award-winning work in teacher education. A past president of the Association for Moral Education, he has also held teaching appointments at Harvard and Boston Universities and is a frequent speaker at conferences and workshops for parents, public school teachers, religious educators, and other groups concerned about the moral development of young people.

Dr. Lickona's twenty years of work in parent and teacher education include experience as a family counselor and as a consultant to schools across the country. He holds a Ph.D. in psychology from the State University of New York at Albany, and has done research on the growth of children's moral understanding. His book, *Moral Development and Behavior*, is widely used in graduate study. Dr. Lickona lives in Cortland, New York, with his wife and two sons.